Using Tasks in Second Language Teaching

SECOND LANGUAGE ACQUISITION

Series Editors: **Professor David Singleton,** *University of Pannonia,* *Hungary* and Fellow Emeritus, *Trinity College, Dublin, Ireland* and **Associate Professor Simone E. Pfenninger,** *University of Salzburg, Austria*

This series brings together titles dealing with a variety of aspects of language acquisition and processing in situations where a language or languages other than the native language is involved. Second language is thus interpreted in its broadest possible sense. The volumes included in the series all offer in their different ways, on the one hand, exposition and discussion of empirical findings and, on the other, some degree of theoretical reflection. In this latter connection, no particular theoretical stance is privileged in the series; nor is any relevant perspective – sociolinguistic, psycholinguistic, neurolinguistic, etc. – deemed out of place. The intended readership of the series includes final-year undergraduates working on second language acquisition projects, postgraduate students involved in second language acquisition research and researchers, teachers and policymakers in general whose interests include a second language acquisition component.

All books in this series are externally peer-reviewed.

Full details of all the books in this series and of all our other publications can be found on http://www.multilingual-matters.com, or by writing to Multilingual Matters, St Nicholas House, 31-34 High Street, Bristol BS1 2AW, UK.

SECOND LANGUAGE ACQUISITION: 143

Using Tasks in Second Language Teaching

Practice in Diverse Contexts

Edited by
Craig Lambert and Rhonda Oliver

MULTILINGUAL MATTERS
Bristol • Blue Ridge Summit

DOI https://doi.org/10.21832/LAMBER9448
Library of Congress Cataloging in Publication Data
A catalog record for this book is available from the Library of Congress.
Names: Lambert, Craig (Craig P.), editor. | Oliver, Rhonda, editor.
Title: Using Tasks in Second Language Teaching: Practice in Diverse
  Contexts/Craig Lambert, Rhonda Oliver.
Description: Blue Ridge Summit: Multilingual Matters, 2020. | Series:
  Second Language Acquisition: 143 | Includes bibliographical references
  and index. | Summary: 'This book examines the use of tasks in second
  language instruction in a variety of international contexts, and
  addresses the need for a better understanding of how tasks are used in
  teaching and program-level decision-making. The chapters consider the
  benefits and challenges that teachers, program designers and researchers
  face in using tasks' – Provided by publisher.
Identifiers: LCCN 2020012139 (print) | LCCN 2020012140 (ebook) | ISBN
  9781788929431 (paperback) | ISBN 9781788929448 (hardback) | ISBN
  9781788929455 (pdf) | ISBN 9781788929462 (epub) | ISBN 9781788929479
  (kindle edition)
Subjects: LCSH: Second language acquisition | Language and languages – Study
  and teaching.
Classification: LCC P118.2 .U836 2020 (print) | LCC P118.2 (ebook) | DDC
  418.0071 – dc23
LC record available at https://lccn.loc.gov/2020012139
LC ebook record available at https://lccn.loc.gov/2020012140

British Library Cataloguing in Publication Data
A catalogue entry for this book is available from the British Library.

ISBN-13: 978-1-78892-944-8 (hbk)
ISBN-13: 978-1-78892-943-1 (pbk)

Multilingual Matters
UK: St Nicholas House, 31-34 High Street, Bristol BS1 2AW, UK.
USA: NBN, Blue Ridge Summit, PA, USA.

Website: www.multilingual-matters.com
Twitter: Multi_Ling_Mat
Facebook: https://www.facebook.com/multilingualmatters
Blog: www.channelviewpublications.wordpress.com

The policy of Multilingual Matters/Channel View Publications is to use papers that are natural, renewable and recyclable products, made from wood grown in sustainable forests. In the manufacturing process of our books, and to further support our policy, preference is given to printers that have FSC and PEFC Chain of Custody certification. The FSC and/or PEFC logos will appear on those books where full certification has been granted to the printer concerned.

Typeset by Riverside Publishing Solutions.

Contents

Contributors

Mohammad Javad Ahmadian is Lecturer in TESOL and programme director for the MA TESOL Programme in the School of Education at University of Leeds. He is interested in Instructed SLA and Task-Based Language Teaching. His publications have appeared in *TESOL Quarterly, System, Language Teaching Research, ELT Journal, International Journal of Applied Linguistics* and *Language Learning Journal*. He is currently co-editing (with Professor Mike Long) *The Cambridge Handbook of Task-Based Language Teaching.*

Scott Aubrey is an Assistant Professor in the Department of Curriculum and Instruction, Faculty of Education, at the Chinese University of Hong Kong where he teaches ELT methodology courses to BA/BEd and MA students. He is currently the Deputy Coordinator of the BA (English) and BEd (English Language Education) joint degree programme at CUHK. His research interests include L2 motivation, task-based language teaching and L2 writing instruction. His publications have appeared in such journals as TESOL Quarterly, Modern Language Journal, Language Teaching Research and RELC Journal.

Tatiana Bogachenko is a linguist, educator and researcher. Her research interests include second and foreign language teaching, TBLT, educational change, equity in education and comparative education. The overarching goal of her research is to promote positive educational practices and experience exchange, and to facilitate provision of better opportunities for underprivileged and challenged communities around the world. Her research has been published in national and international journals and edited volumes and presented at various conferences in Australia and internationally.

Trang Le Diem Bui is a Senior Lecturer in the Faculty of Foreign Languages at An Giang University, Vietnam National University, Ho Chi Minh City. She has a PhD in Applied Linguistics from Victoria University of Wellington, New Zealand and over 15 years of teaching experience, specializing in training pre-service and in-service EFL teachers. Her professional interests include language teacher education, task-based language teaching (TBLT) and content and language integrated learning (CLIL).

Hyejin Cho is currently a PhD student at Georgia State University. Her areas of research interest include task-based language teaching (TBLT), second language writing and digital multimodal literacies.

Rod Ellis is currently a Research Professor in the School of Education, Curtin University in Perth Australia. He is also a visiting professor at Shanghai International Studies University and an Emeritus Distinguished Professor of the University of Auckland. He has recently been elected as a fellow of the Royal Society of New Zealand. He has written extensively on second language acquisition and task-based language teaching. His most recent book is *Reflections on Task-Based Language Teaching* (2018) published by Multilingual Matters. He is currently completing research funded by the Australian Research Council investigating second language learners' pragmatic knowledge of English.

Priscila Fabiane Farias is a Professor of Teacher Professional Development at the Teaching Methodologies Department in the Federal University of Santa Catarina (UFSC), in Brazil. Her main research interests include Task Based Language Teaching, Critical Pedagogy and Foreign Language Teacher Professional Development. She holds a master's degree and a PhD in language studies and her most recent publications focus on the use of tasks as pedagogical tools for English as a Foreign Language learning and critical awareness development.

Raquel Carolina Souza Ferraz D'Ely is a Professor of English as a Foreign Language at the Foreign Languages Department in the Federal University of Santa Catarina (UFSC), in Brazil. Her main research interests include Task Based Language Teaching, Oral Production of EFL and Foreign Language Teacher Professional Development. She holds a master's degree and a PhD in language studies and her most recent publications focus on the use of tasks for collaborative strategic planning in oral L2 development and on strategic planning and repetition as metacognitive processes in task performance.

María del Pilar García Mayo is Full Professor of English Language and Linguistics at the University of the Basque Country (Spain) and director of the Language and Speech research group (http://www.laslab.org). She has published widely on the L2/L3 acquisition of English morphosyntax and the study of conversational interaction in EFL. She has been an invited speaker to universities in Asia, Europe and North America and is an Honorary Consultant for the Shanghai Center for Research in English Language Education. Prof. García Mayo is the director of the

MA program Language Acquisition in Multilingual Settings, the editor of Language Teaching Research and belongs to the editorial board of numerous journals, among others Language Teaching for Young Learners.

Marta González-Lloret is a Professor of Spanish Applied Linguistics at the University of Hawai`i. Her main areas of interest are the intersections of technology and TBLT (Task-based Language Teaching) and technology and L2 pragmatics. Her most recent books are *A Practical Guide to Integrating Technology into Task-based Language Teaching* (Georgetown University Press, 2016), and a 2018 edited volume in Spanish (with Dr Marga Vinagre) on technology-mediated communications (Equinox). She is the editor of the book series Pragmatics & Language Learning (NFLRC) and co-editor of *System* journal (Elsevier).

Justin Harris is an Associate Professor at Kindai University in Japan. He has been teaching English in Japan for more than 20 years in various teaching contexts. His research interests include TBLT, student motivation, and English as a lingua franca. He is co-founder and coordinator of the JALT (Japan Association for Language Teaching) Special Interest Group on TBLT and co-organizes the biennial TBLT in Asia conference. He is co-author of the *On Task* series of textbooks for English language learners which follow a TBLT approach.

Kyoko Kobayashi Hillman is a PhD candidate in the Second Language Acquisition program at the University of Maryland and is a lecturer in the Department of Asian Studies at the University of British Columbia. Her research interests include needs analysis and input elaboration in TBLT (Task-Based Language Teaching), incidental vocabulary learning in instructed second language acquisition and second language research methodology, such as reaction times in psycholinguistic experiments. Her co-authored articles appeared in *The Cambridge Handbook of Language Learning* (2019, with Michael H. Long & Jiyong Lee) and in *Applied Linguistics Review* (2017, with Steven J. Ross & Gabriele Kasper).

Ainara Imaz Agirre teaches in Infant and Primary Education at the Mondragon Unibertsitatea. After graduating in English Philology at the University of the Basque Country, Dr Imaz Agirre received her PhD in 2015 within the program 'Language Acquisition in Multilingual Settings' with a dissertation entitled *The acquisition of gender agreement in L3 English by Basque/Spanish bilinguals* supervised by Prof. María del Pilar García Mayo and was awarded the Outstanding Thesis Award for the Academic Year 2015/2016.

Curtis Kelly is a Professor at Kansai University in Osaka and a Teaching Fellow in the Harvard course *The Neuroscience of Learning*. He writes materials for '3L' students with Low ability, Low confidence and Low motivation, including *Active Skills for Communication* (Cengage), *Writing from Within* (Cambridge) and *Significant Scribbles* (Longman). He is one of the founders of the JALT BRAIN SIG and producer of the *MindBrainEd Think Tanks,* a magazine that connects brain sciences to language teaching.

YouJin Kim is an Associate Professor in the Department of Applied Linguistics and ESL at Georgia State University and Korea Advanced Institute of Science and Technology. She specializes in second language acquisition, task-based language teaching and classroom-based research. She is a co-editor *of Task-Based Approaches to Teaching and Assessing Pragmatics* (2018), and a co-author of *Pedagogical Grammar* (2014). Her work can be found in major applied linguistics journals such as *TESOL Quarterly, Language Learning, Studies in Second Language Acquisition* and *Modern Language Journal.*

Craig Lambert is Associate Professor of Applied Linguistics in the School of Education at Curtin University. His research has appeared in *Studies in Second Language Acquisition, Applied Linguistics, Modern Language Journal, TESOL Quarterly* and *Language Teaching Research.* His recent books include *Task-Based Language Teaching: Theory and Practice* (with R. Ellis *et al.,* Cambridge, 2020) and *Referent Similarity and Nominal Syntax in Task-Based Language Teaching* (Springer, 2019). He guest edited a special issue of *Language Teaching Research* on *Affective Factors in Second Language Task Design and Performance* (2017) and received the *Journal Article of the Year* award from the Faculty of Humanities at Curtin University in 2018.

Paul Leeming is an Associate Professor at Kindai University in Japan, and an adjunct professor at Temple University, where he teaches courses in SLA. He has taught at various levels of education in Japan for more than 20 years. His main research interests are TBLT, groups in language learning and motivation. He is also heavily involved in the JALT (Japan Association for Language Teaching) Task-Based Language Teaching Special Interest Group which organizes the biennial TBLT in Asia conference. He is also co-author of *On Task,* a textbook series following a TBLT approach.

Michael H. Long is Professor of SLA at the University of Maryland. Author of over 100 journal articles and book chapters, recent publications include *The Handbook of Second Language Acquisition* (Blackwell, 2003), *Second Language Needs Analysis* (CUP, 2005), *Problems in SLA* (Erlbaum, 2007), *The Handbook of Language Teaching* (Wiley-Blackwell, 2009), *Sensitive Periods, Language Aptitude, and Ultimate*

L2 Attainment (Benjamins, 2013) and *Second Language Acquisition and Task-Based Language Teaching* (Wiley-Blackwell, 2015). In 2009, he was awarded a doctorate honoris causa by Stockholm University for his contributions to the field of SLA. In 2017, he received a lifetime achievement award from the International Association for Task-Based Language Teaching.

Abbas Mansouri is a PhD candidate in TEFL at Allameh Tabataba'i Universtiy in Iran. He has been teaching English as a Foreign Language for 10 years. He is interested in Task-Based Language Teaching, Instructed SLA and Second Language Teacher Education.

Jonathan Newton is an Associate Professor and Programme Director for the MA in TESOL at the School of Linguistics and Applied Language Studies (LALS), Victoria University of Wellington, New Zealand. He has published more than 60 book chapters and articles on teaching English as a second/foreign language. His scholarship spans task-based language teaching (TBLT), teaching listening and speaking, teaching vocabulary and teaching for intercultural competence. He has co-authored three books: *Teaching ESL/EFL Listening and Speaking* (2009), *Workplace Talk in Action: An ESOL Resource* (2010) and *Teaching English to Second Language Learners in Academic Contexts* (2018).

Lindy Norris is an Honorary Research Fellow in the School of Education at Murdoch University in Western Australia. While her principal focus is within the area of languages and literacy education, her research and professional activities have encompassed many additional dimensions including the professional development of educators, curriculum design, and program evaluation and change management. Her research interests have encompassed many dimensions of languages education policy and practice. She is currently involved in research projects and doctoral supervision in areas associated with interculturality and the development of academic discourse socialization, second language socialization and language use, and language teaching and learning in a variety of contexts including the design and use of tasks.

Rhonda Oliver is a Professor and Head of the School of Education at Curtin University, Perth, Australia. She is widely published in the area of second language acquisition with nearly 5000 citations to her publications. Internationally she is best known for her work in relation to child language learners. As well as work within the interactionist paradigm, she has also conducted numerous studies on language learners in schools and universities. She has also undertaken work in the area of Aboriginal education, particularly for those students who have Standard Australia English as their second language or dialect.

Haoshan (Sally) Ren is a PhD student in the Department of Applied Linguistics and ESL at Georgia State University. Her research interests include corpus linguistics, language assessment, sociolinguistics, and second language acquisition. She is active in initiating and participating in interdisciplinary and cross-institutional collaborations.

Masatoshi Sato (PhD: McGill University) is Professor in the Department of English at Universidad Andrés Bello, Chile. His research interests include peer interaction, corrective feedback, learner psychology, professional development, and research-pedagogy link. In addition to his publications in international journals, he recently co-edited books from John Benjamins (2016, with Susan Ballinger: *Peer Interaction and Second Language Learning*), Routledge (2017, with Shawn Loewen: *The Routledge Handbook of Instructed Second Language Acquisition*) and Routledge (2019, with Shawn Loewen: *Evidence-Based Second Language Pedagogy*). His co-authored textbook with Shawn Loewen (*A Practical Guide to Second Language Acquisition*) from Cambridge University Press will appear in 2021. He is the recipient of the 2014 ACTFL/MLJ Paul Pimsleur Award.

Maria-Elena Solares-Altamirano works for the Department of Applied Linguistics at Escuela Nacional de Lenguas, Lingüística y Traducción, Universidad Nacional Autónoma de México. She holds a PhD in Applied Linguistics from Lancaster University and a Master's Degree in TESOL from University College London, Institute of Education. Her publications include Promoting teacher professional development through online task-based instruction (2010, *International Journal of Virtual and Personal Learning Environments*), Textbooks, Tasks and Technology: An Action Research Study in a Textbook-bound EFL Context (2014, John Benjamins Publishing), Transcribing and analysing spoken data looking beyond the implicit in TV interviews (2013, *Signos Lingüísticos*). Her research interests include task-based language teaching, instructed second language acquisition, written corrective feedback, noticing and cognitive processes in L2 learning, teacher development and online education.

1 Introduction: Tasks in Context

Craig Lambert and Rhonda Oliver

In the last 40 years, the use of 'tasks', at least to some degree, has permeated second language (L2) instruction in many diverse contexts around the world. In organizing the present volume, we have not imposed a specific set of pedagogic practices associated with the use of tasks in L2 instruction, but rather we have attempted to capture this diversity by investigating issues, approaches and observations on how tasks are actually used both in teaching and research. In line with this, we have applied only a minimal definition of 'task', namely: a meaning-focused pedagogic tool that requires learners to employ their own resources to fill gaps in knowledge and arrive at communicative outcomes (Ellis *et al.*, 2020). However, we acknowledge that, in many contexts, this definition may not be sufficient, particularly in countries where the target language is spoken outside of the classroom and learners have a clear need for it. In such contexts, an essential dimension of tasks is a clear real-world connection associated directly with the learners' needs (Long, 2015). In other contexts, however, such as in countries where the target language is not used outside of the classroom, learners may not have a clear need for the target language. In these contexts, tasks are often selected based on their inherent interest and enjoyability for learners (Ellis *et al.*, 2020; Chapter 4, this volume). Furthermore, in some research contexts, tasks may be selected based solely on their communicative demands without consideration of real-world connections or interest (Yule, 1997).

For these reasons, what counts as 'context' can be quite different throughout this volume. Generally, however, the focus shifts from considerations for implementing tasks to specific uses of tasks in both teaching and research in different international contexts. Most of the chapters are descriptive in nature, and the authors clearly point out that their observations are limited to the specific contexts in which they work. In this way, different parts of the book will appeal to different readers. Many chapters reach out to pre-service and in-service teachers because of their content. This is particularly true of the initial chapters, which provide concrete advice about practical issues to address when using tasks in different contexts. Subsequent chapters then describe actual practices that have been used in various regions of the world, with different learners and through different media. Later chapters in the book may be of more interest to second language acquisition (SLA) researchers and students in MA courses in that they provide observations from different regional contexts on the effects of implementing tasks in different ways on L2 performance and acquisition.

In these ways, the book has three primary goals, addressed in the three parts of the book, so that a broad audience of readers can draw on different elements of the book according to their needs.

- *Part 1 clarifies key issues when using tasks for L2 instruction.*
- *Part 2 describes approaches practitioners have adopted when using tasks in challenging international educational contexts.*
- *Part 3 consists of studies which investigate the relationship between tasks and performance in a range of international contexts.*

Before moving on to a summary of each of the three parts, the following provides some general background to contextualize the chapters.

Tasks in Second Language Teaching

In the 1980s, the importance of tasks in L2 instruction was recognized in several seminal publications such as those by Brown and colleagues (Brown & Yule, 1983; Brown *et al.*, 1984; Yule, 1997), Breen (1984), Long (1985), Prabhu (1987) and Nunan (1989). For nearly two decades following these initial pedagogic proposals, the L2 literature on tasks became progressively more focused on establishing an empirical basis for using tasks as the primary organizational element in L2 instruction and establishing accountable learning outcomes associated with such an approach (e.g. Skehan, 1996; Robinson, 2001). Although research findings are variable, the attention that tasks have received has resulted in uptake by decision-making bodies around the world. For example, the use of tasks is being encouraged or formally mandated in curriculum statements in countries where English is taught as a foreign language (Butler, 2011). Such mandates reopen the practical concerns that motivated early proposals for tasks nearly four decades ago. Teachers are now under pressure to develop feasible ways of incorporating tasks into current L2 instruction practices, including instruction in contexts where structural syllabuses and intentional learning are the norm, standardized discrete-point tests are mandated and learners have little need for the target language outside of the classroom (Adams & Newton, 2009; Carless, 2004).

Prabhu's (1987) Communicational Language Teaching Project (more commonly known as the Bangalore Project) was the first documented case of tasks being used systematically in the planning, implementation and evaluation of an L2 curriculum in a specific educational context. Conducted between 1979 and 1982, the project is remarkable in that it involved using tasks in what is still today considered to be a very challenging context – namely, general English classes in public secondary schools in India where a teacher fronted, structural syllabus and discrete-point assessments governed expectations about L2 teaching and learning. Instruction in the Bangalore Project was organized around general topics thought to be familiar to learners with a range of tasks, selected for their anticipated interest for learners, loosely sequenced based on their procedural demands. These task sequences were suggested as a means of helping teachers in the program address each topic successfully with their learners. Prabhu's approach to using tasks represented an expedient solution within his educational context, and in spite of nearly forty years of empirical work on the role of tasks in L2 performance and acquisition, the challenge facing teachers and course administrators in using tasks in many foreign language (FL) contexts around the world remains much the same as it was for Prabhu in the late 1970s. Practitioners are typically faced with finding solutions which balance institutional requirements, available resources, and learners' dispositions with their own professional skill sets.

In rationalizing his approach, Prabhu (1987) makes an important distinction between two functions of the L2 syllabus in language instruction that is critical to understanding approaches when using tasks in diverse contexts. Specifically, he distinguishes between the L2 syllabus as an operational construct and then as an illuminative construct (see Ellis *et al.*, 2020: chap 7). In brief, a syllabus which aims to function as an 'operational' construct only specifies what is to be taught and provides general resources for teaching it. Decisions on how to implement tasks with specific groups of learners is left to teachers to negotiate *in situ* based on their experience with what works in their context and with their learners (Ellis, 2003; Skehan, 1996, 2016). Such a syllabus is low in structure, and the teacher plays a critical role by making the adjustments necessary to reach task outcomes based on individual learners' needs, dispositions and contextual constraints. An 'illuminative' approach, on the other hand, aims at accountability for what will be *taught* as well as what will be *learned* as a result (e.g. Long, 2015; Robinson, 2011). In such an approach, tasks are carefully designed and sequenced to connect task performance with specific learning processes and criterion-referenced outcomes for *all* learners, regardless of context or individual differences. A syllabus which aims to function as an illuminative construct in L2 instruction will be highly structured (see Lambert & Robinson (2014) for an example), and the role of teachers' intuition and *in situ* decision making on how to adapt the syllabus in different classes is greatly reduced: teachers implement task sequences as prescribed and provide feedback regarding necessary adjustments in learners' performances. An illuminative syllabus is certainly a worthy ideal, particularly in contexts where learners have specific language needs in common and accountability in training learners in meeting these needs is the priority. However, a sound empirical basis for such a syllabus is currently lacking (Long, 2015). In most contexts internationally, using tasks within an operational syllabus is the most practical option for teachers, and a case can be also made for the theoretical advantages of this approach (Ellis *et al.*, 2020).

Although the distinction between illuminative and operational syllabuses is one key to understanding diversity in the use of tasks in L2 instruction in different contexts, it is also important to understand that there are different theories of learning that inform the use of tasks. Cognitive-interactionist theories of SLA have provided the primary rationale for the use of task in L2 instruction, namely that tasks should be the primary element for planning, implementing and evaluating such instruction (Ellis *et al.*, 2020; Long, 2015; Robinson, 2011). These approaches are commonly referred to as task-*based* language teaching (TBLT) as tasks provide the central focus at all stages of L2 instruction. Task-based syllabuses can be either illuminative (Long, 2015; Robinson, 2010) or operational (Ellis, 2003; Skehan, 1996, 2016), and instructional frameworks have been proposed based on both approaches in the form of the simplify, stabilize, automatize, restructure, complexify (SSARC) and the pre-task, task, post-task (PTP) frameworks discussed in Chapter 2 (present volume). Regardless of whether tasks function illuminatively or operationally, however, the focus in TBLT is on acquiring language incidentally through task performance rather than intentionally in preparation for doing such tasks. Fundamental to tasks is that they provide learners with a communicative need for using language and the opportunity for negotiation of understanding based on their own L2 resources. In so doing, learners notice and fill gaps in their linguistic resources and develop the interactive competence necessary to complete tasks and communicate effectively in the target language. Tasks are also argued to motivate learners either through their connections to learners' real-world needs (Long, 2015; Chapter 8, this volume) or through the interest that they have for learners (Ellis *et al.*, 2020; Chapter 4, this volume).

An alternative rationale for the use of tasks in L2 instruction is provided by Skill Acquisition Theory (SAT) (DeKeyser, 2007). This rationale also provides an understanding of how tasks can be used in many contexts internationally. SAT is based on well-established findings in cognitive psychology, particularly Anderson's Adaptive Control of Thought-Rational (ACT-R) Model of the acquisition of relatively *simple, discrete* skills (Anderson, 1982, 1993; Anderson *et al.*, 2004). According to SAT, tasks are a necessary tool in L2 instruction, particularly in the final stages of acquisition of specific forms when learners need to fully automatize language knowledge after they have intentionally learned specific rules and proceduralized this knowledge through focused practice. Instructional frameworks for using tasks in this way are also available. The most common of these is the present, practice, produce (PPP) framework, which is also discussed in Chapter 2 of the present volume (see Ellis (2018: chap 10) for other options). In contrast to TBLT, where tasks are the basis for organizing instruction, this approach to using tasks is commonly referred to as task-*supported* language teaching (TSLT). An understanding of TBLT and TSLT practices is important for those interested how tasks may be used in diverse contexts internationally. Furthermore, and as argued by some of the authors in this volume, use of tasks in a PPP framework may help teachers transition to the use of TBLT in their teaching (see Chapters 7 & 10, this volume).

Finally, it is important to recognize that simply performing tasks may not be sufficient for learners to reach their proficiency goals in an L2. Although some aspects of L2 proficiency are necessary for successfully completing tasks and may be acquired incidentally in conjunction with their performance (e.g. fluency in using frequent lexis and common forms), it has been suggested that other aspects of L2 proficiency may be more difficult to acquire through task performance alone (e.g. accuracy in using non-salient or redundant forms and infrequent lexis). For this reason, pedagogic interventions also may be necessary for using tasks effectively in L2 instruction. Interventions commonly discussed in the literature are communicative focus on form (Long, 1991), planning time and task repetition (Skehan *et al.*, 2012) and the provision of task-relevant input (Ellis, 2018: chap. 3; Long, 2016). The present volume expands the discussion of such interventions.

The Organization of the Book

The book consists of three parts. The first is made up of position papers which clarify key issues facing practitioners when using tasks. These issues involve the choice of an appropriate instructional framework, using tasks with low-proficiency learners, designing tasks to motivate general-purpose learners, using technology-mediated tasks, contextual challenges when using tasks and teacher preparation. The second part of the book then contains data-based studies relating to program-level planning issues. Examples of how tasks have been used by teachers and program designers in rural Australia, Ukraine, Brazil and Mexico are included. Finally, the third part of the book consists of studies on the effects of different approaches to task implementation in contexts including Japan, Iran, Chile, Spain and the United States.

Part 1 – Issues in Using Tasks

Teachers and program planners adopt different frameworks when planning lessons either tacitly or explicitly. In Chapter 2, Craig Lambert discusses three theoretically-motivated lesson-planning frameworks as a basis for making informed decisions between them. The rationale for each framework is discussed and potential pros and cons are outlined. An example of how each has been realized in practice and references to sample materials are provided.

A common misconception about the use of tasks is that they cannot be used with low-proficiency learners because they require learners to use the target language in pairs and small groups. In Chapter 3, Jonathan Newton and Trang Le Diem Bui address this misconception by providing guidelines for using tasks with low-proficiency learners which they illustrate with an account of how task-based teaching was successfully carried out with young, beginning-level learners in Vietnamese primary schools.

A typical situation facing teachers with young learners and in general-purpose programs in schools and universities in countries where the target language is not used outside of the classroom is that learners have no clear need for the target language and in some cases have limited motivation to use the language interactively to complete pedagogic tasks which simulate the real-world tasks that they may need to complete (see Ellis *et al.*, 2020: chap. 7; Lambert, 2010, for discussions). In Chapter 4, Curtis Kelly outlines a set of principles that he has found effective in designing tasks for textbooks aimed at such learners in East-Asia. Examples of these materials are provided.

A key aspect of L2 pedagogy for teachers in the 21st century is developing tasks to connect L2 learners in online environments. In Chapter 5, Marta González-Lloret discusses key considerations in integrating technology-mediated tasks into the L2 curriculum. References and online resources are provided for practitioners interested in using technology-mediated tasks in their own contexts.

Using tasks can be problematic in contexts where time constraints and accountability requirements may work against L2 teachers' attempts to experiment with tasks in their teaching. In Chapter 6, Lindy Norris discusses the case of how teachers in Australia are faced with negotiating institutional and educational values in order to discover manageable, contexts-specific solutions to using tasks. The chapter might serve as an example for teachers who face similar constraints in other contexts.

Finally, in Chapter 7, Rod Ellis discusses the background that teachers need to effectively negotiate the use of tasks in their own contexts. Ellis argues that teachers need to be prepared to challenge current curricula, pedagogic practices and the methods of assessment. They also need strategies for modifying task-based instruction for specific contexts. Ellis provides a list of factors for successful teacher preparation and illustrates these factors with an example of a teacher preparation course.

Part 2 – Approaches to Using Tasks

Part 2 begins in Japan. In Chapter 8, Kyoko Hillman and Mike Long discuss how they analyzed the Japanese language needs of US foreign service officials. They focus on how to create samples of language for a critical pedagogic task identified in their needs analysis.

The context then changes to rural Australia. In Chapter 9, Rhonda Oliver discusses how tasks derived from an analysis of Aboriginal learners' needs were used in a vocational training program. Oliver summarizes pedagogic tasks from the program to illustrate how each of the identified needs were addressed. The examples illustrate how tasks were incorporated into instruction to develop contextually relevant tasks for learners that facilitate their successful transition into life beyond the classroom.

In Chapter 10, Tatiana Bogachenko and Rhonda Oliver then provide a situational analysis of three instructional contexts in Ukraine. They identify task-like elements in current teaching practices and the contextual constraints that make the use of task-based instruction challenging. They discuss how teachers in Ukraine might move toward task-based teaching.

Chapter 11 then provides an example of how teachers attempted to put a form of TBLT into practice with a group of 7th grade EFL students at a public school in Brazil. Priscila Fabiane Farias and Raquel Carolina Souza Ferraz D'Ely report on their attempt to conduct a needs analysis, select tasks and implement a program based on a PTP framework.

Finally, in Chapter 12, Maria-Elena Solares-Altamirano provides an account of the implementation of an online TBLT teacher training course in Mexico. Problems that were encountered and suggestions for planning online courses in similar contexts are discussed.

Part 3 – Research on Using Tasks

In Chapter 13, Masatoshi Sato investigates how providing high school English learners in Chile with explicit instruction in collaborative strategies improved their subsequent task performance in terms of more frequent use of these strategies (appeals for help, clarification requests, comprehension checks) and more comprehensible language. Sato's study demonstrates how such support may be beneficial in some contexts.

In Chapter 14, Mohammad Ahmadian and Abbas Mansouri then discuss how allowing English learners in Iran to use their L1 during a pre-task planning phase of their lessons had a positive impact on their subsequent engagement in task performance. They point out that this went against the general policy, in this education context, of encouraging learners to use only English in the classroom. Their study points to the importance of teachers' *in situ* decision making in implementing tasks. Teachers have critical insights into optimizing L2 performance with different learners and in different contexts.

The context then changes from Iran to the United States, where YouJin Kim, Hyejin Cho and Haoshan Ren consider the option of encouraging beginning-level learners of Korean as a Foreign Language to use their common L1 (Chinese) in their Korean language classes. However, the authors found that such 'translanguaging' during task-based discussions had no clear impact on the quality of learners' subsequent L2 writing. The study points to the importance of context. Teachers should not adopt pedagogic practices advocated in the L2 literature uncritically. What works in some contexts may not work in others.

In Chapter 16, Scott Aubrey then considers two options for implementing tasks with EFL learners in a Japanese university. Aubrey found that in his instructional context pairing learners from different cultural backgrounds resulted in more accurately resolved language-related episodes and more awareness of language used than pairing learners of similar cultural backgrounds. Furthermore, requiring his learners to engage in goal tracking by making written notes on their oral task performances and subsequently completing self-reported learning charts also raised their attention to the language that they used on tasks.

Also relating to the formation of groups in implementing tasks, Chapter 17 investigates agency in choosing interlocutors with young EFL learners in Spain. Ainara Imaz Agirre and María del Pilar García Mayo compare the performance of pairs that were assigned based on their proficiency level, pairs that were assigned by the teacher, and pairs that were chosen by the learners themselves. They found that learners who were paired based on proficiency level produced the most turns when performing tasks.

Finally, an issue facing teachers in some instructional contexts may be the need to reconcile what learners do on tasks with coverage of mandated structural syllabus content. In Chapter 18, Justin Harris and Paul Leeming investigate the extent to which tasks had predictable relationships with target English structures and lexis. They found that the more open tasks were in terms of the number of possible solutions, the harder it was for the teachers who were working in their program to predict the language forms their learners would use in completing the tasks. The authors are optimistic that some tasks may naturally be structure-trapping and, like Ellis (Chapter 7) and Bogachenko and Oliver (Chapter 10), they argue that a piloted task bank that teachers can share might be beneficial in their program.

Conclusion

The pressure on teachers to use tasks is increasing in many countries, while support for teachers in meeting these demands is typically in short supply. In spite of laudable theoretical advances on the role of tasks in L2 instruction, teachers and course designers are still faced with the situation of finding expedient solutions for how to incorporate tasks effectively given the expectations and constraints of the contexts in which they work. Insights are needed into the issues and constraints involved in using tasks in context, how these constraints are being overcome, and the skills required by teachers to negotiate effective context-based solutions. The present volume represents an initial attempt to addresses this gap in the task literature by outlining key issues involved in the successful use of tasks by researchers and practitioners, providing examples of how tasks have been used in little researched contexts, and considering how pedagogic interventions in using tasks might impact L2 performance and acquisition in specific contexts. The volume highlights issues associated with teacher readiness for using tasks and provides some insights into what is involved in successfully using tasks in challenging contexts.

References

Adams, R. and Newton, J. (2009) TBLT in Asia: Constraints and opportunities. *Asian Journal of English Language Teaching* 19, 1–17.

Anderson, J.R. (1982) Acquisition of cognitive skill. *Psychological Review* 89, 369–406.

Anderson, J.R. (1993) *Rules of the Mind*. Hillsdale, NJ: Lawerence Erlbaum Associates.

Anderson, J.R., Bothell, D., Byrne, M.D., Douglass, S. Lebiere, C. and Qin, Y. (2004) An integrated theory of mind. *Psychological Review* 111, 1036–1060.

Breen, M. (1984) Process syllabus for the language classroom. In C.J. Brumfit (ed.) *General English Syllabus Design ELT Document* (pp. 47–60). Oxford: Pergamon Press.

Brown, G. and Yule, G. (1983) *Teaching the Spoken Language*. Cambridge: Cambridge University Press.

Andersen, A., Brown, G., Shilcock, R. and Yule, G. (1984) *Teaching Talk: Strategies for Production and Assessment*. Cambridge: Cambridge University Press.

Butler, Y. (2011) The implementation of communicative and task-based teaching in the Asia-Pacific region. *Annual Review of Applied Linguistics* 31, 36–57.

Carless, D. (2004) Issues in teachers' reinterpretation of a task-based innovation in primary schools. *TESOL Quarterly* 38, 639–662.

DeKeyser, R. (2007) Skill acquisition theory. In B. VanPatten and J. Williams (eds) *Theories of Second Language Acquisition: An Introduction* (pp. 94–112). New York: Routledge.

Ellis, R. (2003) *Task-Based Language Learning and Teaching*. Oxford: Oxford University Press.

Ellis, R. (2018) *Reflections on Task-Based Language Teaching*. Bristol: Multilingual Matters.

Ellis, R., Skehan, P., Li, S., Shintani, N. and Lambert, C. (2020) *Task-Based Language Teaching: Theory and Practice*. Cambridge: Cambridge University Press.

Lambert, C. (2010) Task-based needs analysis: Putting principles into practice. *Language Teaching Research* 14, 99–112.

Lambert, C. and Robinson, P. (2014) Learning to perform narrative task: A semester long study of task sequencing effects. In M. Baralt, R. Gilabert and P. Robinson (eds) *Task Sequencing and Instructed Second Language Learning* (pp. 207–230). London: Bloomsbury.

Long, M. (1985) A role for instruction in second language acquisition: Task-based language teaching. In K. Hyltenstam and M. Pienemann (eds) *Modelling and Assessing Second Language Acquisition* (pp. 77–99). Clevedon: Multilingual Matters.

Long, M. (1991) Focus on form: A design feature in language teaching methodology. In K.D. Bot, R. Ginsberg and C. Kramsch (eds) *Foreign Language Research in Cross-Cultural Perspective* (pp. 39–52). Amsterdam: John Benjamins.

Long, M. (2015) *Second Language Acquisition and Task-Based Language Teaching.* Malden, MA: Wiley Blackwell.

Long, M.H. (2016) In defence of tasks and TBLT: Nonissues and real issues. *Annual Review of Applied Linguistics* 36, 5–33.

Nunan, D. (1989) *Designing Tasks for the Communicative Classroom.* Cambridge: Cambridge University Press.

Prabhu, N.S. (1987) *Second Language Pedagogy.* Oxford: Oxford University Press.

Robinson, P. (2001) *Cognition and Second Language Instruction.* Cambridge: Cambridge University Press.

Robinson, P. (2010) Situating and distributing cognition across task demands: The SSARC model of pedagogic task sequencing. In M. Putz and L. Sicola (eds) *Inside the Learner's Mind: Cognitive Processing in Second Language Acquisition* (pp. 243–268). Amsterdam: John Benjamins.

Robinson, P. (2011) Task-based language learning: A review of the issues. *Language Learning* 61 (Suppl. 1), 1–36.

Skehan, P. (1996) A framework for the implementation of task-based learning. *Applied Linguistics* 17, 38–62.

Skehan, P. (2016) Tasks versus conditions: two perspectives on task research and their implications for pedagogy. *Annual Review of Applied Linguistics* 36, 34–49.

Skehan, P., Xiaoyue, B., Qian, L. and Wang, Z. (2012) The task is not enough: Processing approaches to task-based performance. *Language Teaching Research* 16, 170–187.

Yule, G. (1997) *Referential Communication Tasks.* Mahwah, NJ: Lawrence Erlbaum.

Part 1: Issues in Using Tasks

2 Frameworks for Using Tasks in Second Language Instruction

Craig Lambert

Language teaching is a complex process that must be addressed systematically. In order to do so, teachers typically adopt or develop their own frameworks for instructional planning. This is either done implicitly through practice or explicitly through informed decision making regarding available options. There is currently no commonly agreed framework for using tasks in second language (L2) instruction that is suitable across all educational contexts. This chapter thus outlines some common frameworks proposed in the literature as a basis for informed decision making regarding a framework suited to context. Three frameworks are outlined, the underlying rationales for each are provided and potential pros and cons of each are discussed. In addition to two frameworks for task-based instruction, a framework for task-supported instruction is also provided as task-supported approaches might be the only viable option for teachers in many contexts to begin experimenting with the use of tasks in their programs. Examples of how each framework has been applied in creating lessons are presented and illustrated with teaching materials.

Introduction

Effective language teaching is a complex process that typically requires teachers to interact dynamically in planning, implementing and evaluating instruction that effectively addresses their learners' needs. In doing so, teachers find ways to effectively reach learning objectives in relationship to situational constraints (e.g. mandated teaching materials and tests, available contact time, seating arrangements, administrative expectations, etc.). Effective teachers typically make in situ micro-adjustments based on all these factors to optimize learning in their classrooms. This is a complex process that requires experience and that must be approached systematically. To develop systematicity in their instruction, teachers typically develop instructional frameworks that work for them. In many cases, this is an implicit process that develops through practice. However, a sound knowledge of available options might save novice teachers time and effort while increasing their efficacy in reaching instructional objectives. This chapter considers three different frameworks for using tasks in L2 instruction, pointing out some potential strengths and limitations of each as a basis for informed decision making on how best to use tasks within a given instructional context.

As tasks might be used within task-*based* or task-*supported* approaches to instruction, we will adopt the general definition of 'task' proposed by Ellis (2009). According to Ellis, tasks are pedagogic tools that have four essential characteristics: (1) an overt focus on meaning (what is said rather than how it is said), (2) a gap in information, opinion or inference which necessitates meaning-focused language use, (3) a communicative outcome beyond using language for its own sake and, crucially, (4) learners drawing on the full range of their own linguistic and non-linguistic resources during performance. Ellis uses these four criteria to distinguish *tasks*, as unique L2 instructional tools, from the range of other *exercises* that are used in L2 instruction. When these four criteria are met, tasks might provide a means of addressing a range of L2 instructional objectives, including allowing learners to consolidate and automatize their L2 knowledge, promoting fluency in L2 processing, acquiring new language incidentally during communication and improving learners' engagement and motivation.

The need for tasks in L2 instruction has been widely recognized, and national curricula have begun to explicitly require their use in L2 instructional practices (Butler, 2011; Bogachenko & Oliver, this volume, Solares-Altamirano, this volume). However, many teachers are still unclear about what tasks are and how to use them effectively in their own teaching contexts. This has led to a range of misconceptions, challenges and *faux pas* in initial attempts to incorporate the use of tasks and task-based instruction (Adams & Newton, 2009; Carless, 2009). The present chapter seeks to remedy this situation by providing a basis for practitioners to select effective instructional frameworks for their educational contexts.

Frameworks for Using Tasks in Second Language Instruction

Several proposals have emerged in the SLA literature which support the use of tasks in L2 instruction. In this section, we will consider three instructional frameworks for using tasks in L2 instruction that have an explicit basis in cognitive psychology as it relates to L2 processing and acquisition. The first is the **PPP Framework** (Present, Practice, Produce), which is based on theories of the acquisition of relatively simple, discrete skills (see DeKeyser (2007) for an overview) and involves using tasks within a structural syllabus to automatize the vocabulary, structures and other linguistic information that has been learned explicitly and practiced intensively earlier in lessons. The second framework brings tasks to the centre of lessons rather than using them to support the teaching of linguistic targets. It is based on a theory of limited attentional capacity and involves conceptualizing L2 lesson in terms of a **PTP Framework** (Pre-Task, Task, Post-Task) that focuses on what can be done in lessons prior to, during and after tasks are performed to facilitate balanced development of the fluency, accuracy and complexity in learners' task performances (see Ellis, 2003; Skehan, 1996; Willis, 1996). Finally, in the third framework, L2 instruction is based on initially simple, progressively more complex, sequences of tasks. The **SSARC Framework** (Simplify-Stabilize, Automatize, Restructure-Complexify) is based an action-control theory of attention and memory (see Robinson, 2010, 2011). This third framework provides a basis for sequencing tasks in non-linguistic terms (Long, 2015: 231–234) (based their cognitive demands) and in line with learners developing capacities to complete them.

The PPP Framework (Present, Practice, Produce)

A common framework for using tasks in L2 instruction is simply to add them into an existing syllabus at the end of lessons (as time permits) in order to provide learners with the opportunity to practice the language covered in the lesson in a relatively meaning-focused situation. In a PPP framework, the lesson typically begins with the teacher presenting target language to learners (e.g. key sentence structures and lexical items). Following this, learners typically complete focused and structured exercises in which they gain intensive practice in manipulating the target structure and vocabulary items (e.g. repetition, transformations, substitutions, etc.). This phase might consist of teacher-fronted class work or pair and small group work. Finally, the last stage of the lesson involves learners in completing a 'task', which serves the purpose of allowing them to further automatize the forms that they have learned and practiced within the context of a less-structured, meaning-oriented situation.

Theoretical, empirical and practical rationales for the benefits of a PPP framework have been advanced in the literature. Based on extensive research in the acquisition of relatively simple, discrete skills in cognitive psychology, for example, DeKeyser (2007) argues that adult L2 learners must proceduralize declarative knowledge through focused practice of specific forms and only then can they fully automatize these forms under the operating conditions that are provided by tasks. Ellis (2018:

chap. 10) also argues that explicit instruction of the type provided by a PPP framework can complement the learning that takes place on tasks, particularly at the more advanced stages of proficiency when learners have developed fluency and interactive competence in using basic communicative resources.

What is probably more important for many practitioners, however, is the expediency of using tasks within a PPP instructional framework. Slotting tasks in at the end of existing lessons as time permits allows teachers to use, and perhaps build on, current practices in experimenting with tasks in their teaching (see Bogachenko & Oliver, this volume; Ellis, this volume). Using tasks immediately after explicit instruction and practice of grammar and vocabulary is also expedient in many contexts in that it may increase the likelihood of targeted vocabulary and structures being used more frequently than they might otherwise on the same tasks, thereby providing coverage of the content of a structural syllabus (see Harris & Leeming, this volume) and helping learners' to prepare for discrete-point tests of their ability to manipulate these items. In fact, PPP is probably the preferred framework for using tasks in many contexts (Adams & Newton, 2009; Bogachenko & Oliver, this volume; Carless, 2002, 2009; Jeon & Hahn, 2006; Harris & Leeming, this volume; Solares-Altamirano, this volume).

A primary problem with a PPP Framework, however, is that learners might interpret tasks as simply another practice exercise for manipulating targeted forms. The approach thus runs the risk of compromising the integrity of the tasks as L2 learning tools. It will be remembered that two of the defining criteria of tasks proposed by Ellis (2009) are that: (1) learners are focused on the meaning of what they are saying rather than on the forms that they are using to say it, and (2) learners are drawing on the full range of their own linguistic and non-linguistic resources in completing tasks rather than being pre-disposed to the use of specific forms. The fact that an exercise is task-*like* in having an information gap and resulting in a communicative outcome is not enough. It might be argued that when learners are completing tasks within a PPP framework, they are not always focused on meaning (what they are saying) rather on using targeted forms (how they are saying it). Furthermore, when learners use pre-set language to complete a task, they may not be developing their own linguistic strategies for addressing task demands, and such strategic competence is important in their becoming effective users of a language (Lambert, 2018).

PTP Framework (Pre-Task, Task, Post-Task)

Skehan (1996, 2009) proposes a framework for implementing tasks which conceptualizes L2 lessons in terms of pre-task, during-task and post-task phases, and he discusses activities during each of these phases aimed at facilitating balanced language use on tasks in terms of fluency, complexity and accuracy. Willis (1996) proposes a related framework based on these same stages, and Ellis (2003: chap. 8) also adopts this framework for using tasks in L2 instruction. Furthermore, variations on the pre-task, during-task and post-task framework have been adopted in several textbooks which use a task as the focal point of each lesson (e.g. Benevides & Velvona, 2008; Cutrone & Beh, 2014; Harris & Leeming, 2018; Kelly & Kelly, 1991; Lambert & Hailes, 2002). Although this chapter will focus on Skehan's perspective on the framework, the reader might refer to these other publications for additional perspectives on activities that can be used in each of the three phases of the framework.

The psycholinguistic rationale that Skehan provides for the PTP Framework is based on the notion of limited attention (see Skehan (2014) for a recent discussion of his Limited Attention Capacity Hypothesis). Skehan argues that L2 learners typically do not have the attentional capacity to deal with the demands of real-time communication while also paying attention to the use of novel L2 forms. As a result, when learners are completing demanding communication tasks, there is a risk that they will become over-reliant on chunks of language to which they have easy access and forego experimentation with new and partially mastered forms. This could ultimately result in a slow-down in their progress in the language with fluency dominating at the expense of ongoing development. In contrast, if learners' attention is consistently focused on incorporating novel language into their task performances, they will not have the opportunity to develop automated access to these new L2 resources as required for fluent real-time communication. This could ultimately result in learners with knowledge of a language that they cannot act on in real-time communication.

Skehan (1996, 2009) proposes his version of the PTP Framework as a way of alternating learners' attentional resources between meaning and form so that fluency does not dominate at the expense of complexity, on the one hand, and so that complexity does dominate at the expense of fluency, on the other. In the former case, learners become fluent in using simple, imperfect language. In the latter case, they have language knowledge that they cannot use in real time communication. Hence this framework is used to promote learners' capacity for 'dual-mode processing' in which they develop the capacity for both rule-based processing and exemplar-based processing while completing tasks. Rule-based processing involves experimentation with novel and more syntactically complex language with a slower rate of speech and more reformulations, hesitations, and redundancies. Exemplar-based processing, on the other hand, is characterized by fluent production of known forms and the avoidance of new and partially mastered ones.

In terms of activities, the **pre-task phase** of a lesson, according to Skehan, should function to ease the processing load of tasks in order to allow learners to pay more attention to the language that they use in completing them. These activities should also help draw learners' attention to novel forms that they can incorporate into their task performance by activating and making salient new and partially mastered language. Skehan proposes three types of pre-task activities. The first familiarizes learners with the schema required for the task by observing similar tasks being completed by proficient speakers of the language. Such **input-based tasks** could be provided in the form of videos of performances, audio recordings of performances, written materials or transcriptions (see Ellis, 2018: chap. 3; Hillman & Long, this volume). A second type of pre-task activity is asking learners to complete similar tasks so that they have some experience with task demands before they have to meet them. This rehearsal or **task repetition** might involve repeating the exact same task or a similar parallel task (see Lambert *et al.* (2017a) for a recent review of work on task repetition). Finally, a third type of pre-task activity is to provide learners with pre-task **planning time**. If learners are given time to plan their performances, they have the opportunity to activate new and partially mastered language that they might be able to incorporate to both improve their performance and promote automaticity of these novel forms (see Skehan *et al.*, 2012).

In the **during task phase** of the lesson, Skehan recommends adjustments on the part of the teacher to ensure learners can succeed as well as optimize their performance. One is simply by **orienting learners** to their performance. If accuracy needs to be dealt with, learners can be told not to make any mistakes. Alternatively, if fluency is an issue, a **time constraint** can be imposed on the task so that learners have to speak as quickly as possible. Orienting learners toward the accuracy or fluency of their performance might ease the processing demands of tasks and allow teachers to alternately address instructional objectives that result in dual-mode processing ability.

A second during-task intervention that Skehan mentions is altering the amount of control that learners have over the tasks by allowing them the freedom to **select and organize the content** that they need to encode for the task. For example, requiring learners to narrate a story based on a specific picture strip provides them very little freedom in selecting lexis and grammatical structures and forces them to stretch the L2 resources to make ends meet in communicating the objects and events specified. This can be cognitively demanding. On the other hand, asking learners to create a fictitious story allows them some freedom in selecting and organizing the objects and events in the narrative in line with their current vocabulary knowledge and syntactic abilities (Foster & Skehan, 1996). The latter approach may help learners develop fluency in using known L2 resources, whereas the former might push learners to incorporate new targets, or develop circumlocution skills, once a basic level of fluency in narrating stories based on their existing language has been developed. Alternatively, tasks might be designed to engender a *personal investment* on the part of learners by asking them to discussing stories that (1) really happened to them, (2) they want to share and (3) they think their partner(s) will be genuinely interested in hearing about. This *learner-generated content* might have the additional advantage of increasing learners' engagement in language use (Lambert, 2017; Lambert & Minn, 2007; Lambert *et al.*, 2017b) as well as their use of devices to create pragmatic meanings which are not required when the participants are not personally involved (Lambert & Zhang, 2019; Ellis *et al.*, 2020: chap. 6).

The third and last during-task intervention that Skehan (1996, 2009) discusses involves the provision of *visual support* to learners while completing tasks in the form of pictures, charts, diagrams, lists or other representations of task content. Such support might decrease the amount of material that learners have to keep in mind during task performance. Being able to refer to a map while giving street directions, for example, can greatly reduce processing demands so that learners can focus on rule-based processing and experiment with novel forms. Having the map removed during performance, however, might increase the processing demands of the task and force learners to rely on exemplar-based processing which involves the automatic use of stored chunks of language. In short, Skehan argues that the *in situ* decisions that teachers make in implementing tasks can be critical to optimizing learners' task performances and promoting balanced development of fluency, accuracy and complexity in their L2 use.

Finally, Skehan (1996) argues that activities can also be used during the *post-task phase* of a lesson to direct learners' attention to different aspects of their task performances. In all cases, it is important that learners are aware of these activities before and during their performances as this will direct their attention both in planning and performing the task. One post-task intervention involves letting learners know that they are not just doing the task once, but that they are going to have to repeat it (*task repetition*). There are options available in doing this. Learners can be told that they are going to have to repeat the same task or a parallel version of the task with similar procedures, but different content. They can also be told whether they will repeat it immediately or in a subsequent class. Very importantly, they can be told that they will have to repeat the task with their peers in pairs or small groups, publicly (e.g. in front of class and teacher), or even on a video which will be used for some subsequent purpose. This brings us naturally to a second post-task intervention discussed by Skehan which is requiring learners to *review and analyse* their own performances in some way (e.g. transcribe the performance, identify and correct the errors, etc.). In this way, learners' attention might be focused on avoiding errors in performing tasks as they know that they will not only be recorded, but that they will have to transcribe the recording and correct any errors. Finally, the third and last post-task invention that Skehan mentions is one that will be familiar to most teachers around the world – namely, telling learners to pay attention as there will be *a test*. As teachers know, simply warning students that they should be paying attention to one thing or another as a test is coming tends to wake them up and focus their attention.

In contrast to the PPP Framework, the PTP Framework allows learners to develop their language skills based on their own dispositions and internal syllabuses, rather than assuming that all learners will acquire the same structures in a linear and additive fashion. This is more in line with what is known about the processes of SLA (Ellis *et al.*, 2020; Long, 2015). The PTP Framework also has the practical advantage of providing L2 teachers with a simple and intuitive way to conceptualize what they are learning in a lesson and why they are learning it. It puts teachers' practices in the classroom on a psycholinguistic foundation that potentially accounts for balanced development of fluency and accuracy of new L2 resources. It also provides them with relatively clear and immediate feedback on the impact of different interventions on learners' performance rather than having to wait for the results of discrete-point post-tests later in the term. It might thus provide teachers with the opportunity to engage more interactively as decision makers in their classrooms. In addition to vocabulary and syntax, learning outcomes can be conceptualized in terms of broader aspects of L2 performance such as interactive competence, pragmatic competence, comprehensibility and learner engagement.

However, the PTP Framework is not without limitations in the way that it has been put into practice. Although tasks are the central focus of each lesson rather than providing supplementary practice as in a PPP framework, instruction based on the PTP framework has tended to result in learners' spending a considerable amount of contact time doing things other than tasks, and, in many cases, these pre-tasks and post-tasks exercises are very similar to the exercises that might be used in PPP (e.g. Cutrone & Beh, 2014; Farias & D'Ely, this volume; Harris & Leeming, 2018; Solares-Altamirano, this volume). The fact that the framework accommodates slotting traditional language-focused materials into lessons makes it a very expedient solution to using tasks in many contexts, but frequently opens the resulting instruction to the same criticisms that were made of instruction based on a PPP framework in the previous section.

The SSARC Framework (Simplify, Stabilize, Automatize, Restructure, Complexify)

The third framework to be discussed potentially addresses the short-comings of the PTP framework pointed out in the previous section by providing a basis for planning language lessons as *sequences* of tasks that move from simple to complex in line with learners' developing capacities to complete them. Robinson's (2010) SSARC framework also connects tasks to the psycholinguistic processes of acquiring new language and automatizing it for use in real-time communication. However, Robinson advocates doing this through *task sequencing*. In contrast to Skehan's (1996, 2009) framework, there is no pre-task stage or post-task stage in the SSARC framework. In Robinson's approach, the demands of the tasks in each sequence are carefully controlled to ensure that learners' alternately push their L2 resources and automatize these resources as a product of completing tasks.

Robinson advocates sequencing tasks into lessons based on factors that he argues will impact the cognitive demands placed on all learners regardless of individual differences or learning context. To this end, he distinguishes between two types of cognitive task design factors. The first directs learners' attention to specific task content and the language needed to express it. Robinson argues that these **resource-directing** task design factors include the number of elements in the task, the temporal and spatial displacement of these elements, the need to make the reasoning connecting the elements explicit, and the need to make multiple perspectives explicit. By contrast, the second type of task design factor disperses learners' cognitive resources over several aspects of task-essential content, language and the performance context. Robinson argues that these **resource-dispersing** factors include the number of steps in the task, the independence of these steps, the amount of structure governing the task performance, the need to multi-task, and the absence of prior knowledge and time to plan.

The SSARC Framework employs these resource-directing and resource-dispersing task design factors in a three-stage model: (1) Simplify-Stabilize, (2) Automatize and (3) Restructure-Complexify (SSARC). The first of these stages involves simplifying a task in terms of both resource-directing and resource-dispersing demands in order to allow successful performance and to activate learners' current L2 resources. The second stage consists of automatizing these resources through practice on versions of the tasks which gradually increase in terms of resource-dispersing demands. Finally, the third stage consists of increasing resource-directing demands while again initially reducing resource-dispersing demands in order to require learners to analyse and restructure the resources automatized in the previous stage in line with the demands of the more complex versions of the task. This cycle continues until learners can complete un-simplified versions of the task in question. Robinson's framework thus provides a basis for the type of task-based language teaching advocated by Long (2015: 231–234) in which tasks are sequenced in terms of their cognitive rather than their linguistics demands. Learners do not work on activities in preparation for tasks or as a follow-up to tasks. Rather, they learn *through* the completion of progressively more complex versions of tasks.

In many contexts, however, Robinson's SSARC framework may be challenging in that it represents a completely new way of conceptualizing instruction and the role of the teacher in the classroom. The teacher no longer 'teaches' in the traditional sense of helping learners to prepare for tasks, and there is very little opportunity to draw on traditional, language-focused teaching material. Methodological decisions tradition-ally made by the teacher in the classroom (e.g. whether and how much planning, repetition and input is required) are made for all learners at the time that the syllabus and materials for the program are written. The role of the teacher is to implement task sequences as specified, monitor learners' performance and provide reactive feedback to draw their attention to their problems with L2 form. This means that key decisions regarding SLA processes and individual needs are not left to teacher intuition. Robinson (2011) advocates addressing individual needs through an ability analysis of pedagogic tasks and matching learners of different motivational and aptitude profiles with tasks that are suited to them. However, it remains unclear how this matching process can be realized in planning and implementing L2 programs in many contexts, and reconceptualizing the syllabus in the way required by the SSARC Framework may be very challenging for teachers (e.g. Bogachenko & Oliver, this volume; Ellis, this volume).

Applications in Lesson Planning and Materials Design

This section illustrates how the three frameworks discussed in the previous sections have been used in lesson planning and materials design. Examples from published textbooks and course design projects are provided for those who wish to experiment with the respective frameworks.

An Example of the PPP Framework

Kelly and Kelly (1991) provide a conversation course for East-Asian university students organized as a detective school in which learners solve mysteries (see Kelly, this volume). One section of the textbook provides sequences of mystery tasks with an integrated goal-tracking system where learners earn detective points based on solving the mysteries by communicating in the L2. A separate section of the book provides supplementary lessons based on a PPP Framework that teachers can draw on in part or in whole to support their learners' performances on the main task sequences. These PPP lessons were designed to function as a complex pre-task phase but provide an example of how tasks can be used within a PPP Framework.

One such example requires learners to rescue someone from a large building (see Appendix 2.1), and the language that is presented and practiced before the task relates to vocabulary and sentence structures anticipated as being useful for giving indoor directions. The lesson plan is as follows:

(1) *Present vocabulary:* The teacher covers the vocabulary required to identify different rooms within a building (e.g. office, closet, storage room, study, game room, etc.).
(2) *Practice vocabulary:* Learners complete two input-based tasks in which someone describes a house. In the first, they label a floorplan with the names of rooms that they have learned. In the second, they fill in the missing words in a cloze activity.
(3) *Present structures:* Learners are provided with structures that are useful for giving directions indoors. Importantly, they are also provided with phrases exemplifying interactive strategies that they can use on the task (cf. Sato, this volume). In this case, asking to someone to repeat.
(4) *Practice structures:* Learners engage in structured practice of these phrases by describing routes on a simple map with the help of a dialogue.
(5) *Produce:* Learners use the language that they have practiced on a less-structured task. They think of different places on campus and give real directions from their classroom to the place that they choose (e.g. the cafeteria, the library, a bus stop, etc.). Their partner listens and asks for repetition as required to guess the destination.

In this example, learners are presented with and practice specific language through both receptive and productive exercises, and the language targets are presented in two manageable cycles of present and practice before the final produce phase when they bring this language together to complete the task of giving directions within their own university. Appendix 2.1 provides the materials set for this lesson.

An Example of the PTP Framework

In this section, a set of suggested guidelines for implementing a PTP Framework is provided based on a course design project at a Japanese university. An example unit of materials is provided in Appendix 2.2. The project involved writing materials for a two-year oral English course for intermediate-level English majors (TOEIC 450–750, with outliers on either end) at a large public university in Japan. Classes met for 90 minutes each week over four 15-week semesters. It was decided that providing learners with input in the pre-task stage did not optimize uptake during task performances as their attention was not focused enough to notice useful forms. Learners were thus given opportunities to do the tasks using their own L2 resources initially to sensitize them to gaps in their L2 resources before completing input-based versions of the tasks.

Each lesson consisted of six stages, involving two cycles of task performances supported by complementary pre-tasks and post-tasks. These two cycles can be implemented in one or two lessons, depending on learners' proficiency level and whether the lessons are 60 or 90 minutes. The stages are summarized here, and a sample materials set is provided in Appendix 2.2.

(1) **Warm Up:** Learners are introduced to the nature of the tasks and review some task-specific language. Four activities were alternated for this stage based on their relevance to the unit's tasks as well as to provide variety for learners:

   (a) *Matching:* Learners match the beginning and ending of sentences in task-based discourse then listen and check their answers (see Appendix 2.2).

   (b) *Cloze:* Learners guess missing words in task-based discourse then listen and check their answers.

   (c) *Ordering:* Learners order sets of sentences to create task-relevant discourse then listen and check their answers.

   (d) *Labelling:* Learners are given samples of task-based discourse and a set of communicative functions that are relevant to the task (e.g. invite, accept, decline, apologize, provide reason, suggest alternative, close conversation, etc.). They label each sentence or turn with the communicative function it serves.

(2) **Share Your Own Ideas:** Learners activate relevant task-specific background knowledge from long-term memory. This was intended to provide learners with a richer range of ideas to draw on in subsequent task performances. Again, four activities were alternated for this stage:

   (a) *Question boxes:* Questions related to learners' experiences with the task are provided in a grid (see Appendix 2.2). Learners take turns choosing questions and asking them. Their partner answers, elaborates and clarifies any queries. The question is crossed out, and roles are reversed for the next question. The process repeats until all questions are asked and answered.

   (b) *Brainstorming:* Learners work together to prepare ideas, and perhaps useful language, depending on the demands of the subsequent task. In doing so, they share their own ideas, opinions and experiences on the topic.

(c) *Planning time with content focus:* Learners summarize and compare the homework they have prepared. This frequently involves creating versions of the task based on learner-generated content (see Stage 6 below). Depending on the nature of the task, they make group-level decision based on this material.

(d) *Planning time with language focus:* Learners summarize and compare the homework they have prepared. This frequently involves written performances of tasks (see Stage 6 below). They discuss issues related to performance of the task.

(3) *Try It:* Learners perform one or more parallel versions of the task. These initial versions of the task allow them to activate their current L2 resources in line with the demands of the task and become sensitive to any gaps in their knowledge. Teachers can choose how many of these tasks to use depending on the group's proficiency, motivation and abilities. For example, the teacher might decide to have them repeat the same task multiple times with different interlocutors each time or to complete parallel versions of the task with the same interlocutor, depending on the learners' needs in a given group. Teachers are also free to provide pre-task planning time, or not, before each iteration based on group abilities.

(4) *Learn New Ways to Do It:* Learners listen to proficient speakers perform the same tasks that they just completed in Stage 3. Depending on their needs, the teacher can choose to have them listen to each sample only once or several times. If they listen several times, activities are provided which move from processing general meaning to processing details such as in the following sequence:

(a) *Reciprocal task:* On the first listening, learners do whatever they would normally do when completing the task. This might involve filling out a form by noting key facts, identifying the task outcome, or verifying their understanding of the gist of the discourse (see Appendix 2.2).

(b) *Cloze:* Learners guess the missing words in a transcript of a proficient-speaker completing one of the tasks that they have just completed. They then listen to check their answers. Different aspects of the discourse can be targeted based on the nature of the task and the language it generated with proficient speakers (see Appendix 2.2).

(c) *Dictation with oral correction:* Depending on the demands of the task in the unit, an alternative to the cloze is a dictation in which learners hear useful parts of the task performances three times. The first two times, the sentences are provided slowly and clearly with a pause after each phrase to provide time to write. The third time, the passage is read at normal speed to allow learners to confirm what they have written. Learners then check their work orally. They take turns reading their work to a partner who follows on the transcription in the appendix to the book and corrects any mistakes. Learners are forbidden to look at one another's written material while completing this task. They negotiate the corrections orally.

(d) *Form-to-function mapping:* Learners are given a sample of task-based discourse and a set of task-relevant communicative functions (e.g. eliciting opinions, suggesting alternatives, supporting a suggestion, confirming a conclusion, etc.). They label each sentence with the number of the function that it achieves. They then add other ways they might achieve each function based on their own L2 resources. The aim is to develop awareness of what needs to be done to complete the task appropriately and how these things are accomplished by proficient speakers (see Appendix 2.2).

(5) *Try It Again:* Learners perform more parallel versions of the task. Teachers are free to provide their learners with pre-task planning time with or without access to transcriptions for the listening tasks in Stage 4. This allows learners to incorporate what they have learned in the unit according to their own goals and dispositions. Again, teachers are also free to ask learners to repeat the same task with different interlocutors each time or parallel versions of the task with the same interlocutor depending on what they deem beneficial for the group.

(6) *Revision and Personal Investment:* Learners are given two homework assignments. The first is revision. They study the transcripts of the listening tasks in Stage 4, find ways to improve their performances, and produce a written version of one of the tasks that they performed. They are asked to avoid mistakes and incorporate any expressions from the transcripts that they deem useful. The second assignment is to develop a parallel version of the task based on content they had have actually experienced, want to share, and feel their classmates will be interested in or enjoy (see Lambert & Zhang (2019) for examples). These learner-generated content tasks are performed in subsequent lessons.

There are many ways to employ a PTP Framework for using tasks in L2 instruction (see Ellis, 2003: chap. 8; Skehan, 1996; Willis, 1996, Chapters 3–4 present volume, for examples). This section has provided one example of how such a framework was used successfully in the context of an Oral English program for English majors at a Japanese university. Other textbooks aimed at East Asian learners that employ variations on a PTP Framework are Benevides and Velvona (2008) and Harris and Leeming (2018).

An Example of the SSARC Framework

In this section, an example is provided of how the SSARC Framework (Robinson, 2010) was used in planning a course for second-year English majors at a Japanese university (Lambert & Robinson, 2014). The course was implemented over a 15-week semester, and the task sequence that is discussed in this section required two 90-minute lessons towards the end of the course. As these two lessons were at the end of the course, learners had extensive practice with progressively more complex narrative tasks and were moving on to reading and summarizing authentic stories by Japanese and American authors.

In the task sequence that spanned the two lessons, learners completed narratives based on their own L2 resources. In order to *activate and stabilize* these resources, they were provided with planning time in which they read the story for homework and prepared their summaries in writing. In class, they then completed practice activities to *automatize* these resources by completing versions of the tasks which become gradually more demanding by removing planning time and prior knowledge about the stories. Following this, learners completed input-based tasks which directed their attention to ways in which the reasoning and perspectives of the characters in the task could be made explicit. When they summarized the stories again, they were required to *complexify and restructure* their narratives by specifying the reasoning and perspectives of the characters. The task sequence was as follows:

Task 1: Before class, learners **read** one of four stories and **plan** to summarize it by **preparing a written version** of what they will say. No time limit is imposed.

Lesson 1
Task 2: Summarize stories in groups of four. Learners work in pairs within each group to summarize their own story and make notes to re-tell their partner's story. They then take turns summarizing the new story back to their partner without planning time, check each other's understanding and make any corrections. Learners repeat this process with the other two partners in their group so that they: (1) **summarize the story that they planned three times**, and (2) **retell three new stories** without planning. No time limit is imposed on these task performances.

Task 3: **Listen to proficient speakers summarizing the four stories**, and (1) identify whether key statements were made or not, (2) identify events included and not included in each narrative, (3) identify conclusions that were made and not made about each story and (4) identify which of 48 words were used to explain the mental states (remembers, wonders, hopes, anticipates, etc.).

Task 4: Read the transcript of the proficient speaker telling the story that they prepared for homework from Task 3 and **plan what they will do to improve their summary for 10 minutes.** They are told that they will have to repeat the Task 1 sequence above.

Task 5: Repeat *Task 1 sequence* culminating in learners (1) *summarize the story that they planned three times,* and (2) *retell three new stories.* Each time that they change partners and repeat the task, the time limit for performing it is reduced to promote automaticity.

Homework
Task 6: Review transcripts of summaries from class with key elements highlighted. *Read* one of four new stories and *plan* to summarize it based on what was learned in class and the transcripts. These stories are by an American rather than a Japanese writer (less prior knowledge) and longer than the previous stories that they summarized (more elements). Learners are instructed to pick out only the important events in the story, say what characters are thinking and feeling to motivate their actions and provide conclusions regarding what the story means.

Lesson 2
Task 7: Summarize stories in groups of four. Learners work in pairs within each group to summarize their own story and make notes to re-summarize their partner's story. They summarize the new story back to their partner without planning time, and their partner checks their understanding and makes any corrections. Learners repeat this process with the other two partners in their group so that they: (1) *summarize the story that they planned three times,* and (2) *retell three new stories* without planning. No time limit is imposed on these performances.

Task 8: Change groups. Learners choose one of the three stories that they did not plan for homework. They *tell the story three times* to a different partner each time. Learners are instructed to pick out only the important events in the story, say what characters are thinking and feeling to motivate actions, and provided conclusions regarding what the story means. They *repeat the process two more times* with the remaining two unplanned stories. The time they have to perform the three task repetitions is reduced each time.

This task sequence thus moves through language processing cycles which are assumed to have the same effect on the ability to summarize stories for all learners. All learners plan for, perform and repeat input-based and output-based versions of tasks in order to develop and automatize their ability to complete progressively more demanding versions of tasks until they can perform the un-simplified task of narrating a story fluently.

Conclusion

To support the effective use of tasks in L2 instruction in diverse contexts, teachers need to be aware of their options with respect to instructional frameworks and to understand the advantages and disadvantages of each of these options so that they make educated choices based on their learners' needs, proficiency levels, motivations and aptitudes, whilst taking contextual constraints into account. The present chapter has outlined three frameworks for using tasks in L2 instruction and provided guidelines and examples of how they have been used in L2 materials planning. It is hoped that the chapter will provide a basis for more informed practice in using tasks in diverse contexts internationally.

References

Adams, R. and Newton, J. (2009) TBLT in Asia: Constraints and opportunities. *Asian Journal of English Language Teaching* 19, 1–17.

Benevides, M. and Velvona, C. (2008) *Widgets: A Task-Based Course in Practical English.* Hong Kong: Pearson Longman.

Butler, Y. (2011) The implementation of communicative and task-based language teaching in the Asia-Pacific region. *Annual Review of Applied Linguistics* 31, 36–57.

Carless, D. (2002) Implementing task-based learning with young learners. *ELTJ* 56 (4), 389–396.

Carless, D. (2009) Revisiting the TBLT versus P-P-P debate: Voices from Hong Kong. *Asian Journal of English Language Teaching* 19, 44–66.

Cutrone, P. and Beh, S. (2014) *Welcome to Kyushu, Japan: A Task-Based Approach to EFL Learning Using Authentic Dialogues.* Tokyo: Shohakusha.

DeKeyser, R. (2007) Skill acquisition theory. In B. VanPatten and J. Williams (eds) *Theories of Second Language Acquisition: An Introduction* (pp. 94–112). New York: Routledge.

Ellis, R. (2003) *Task-based Language Learning and Teaching.* Oxford: Oxford University Press.

Ellis, R. (2009) Task-based language teaching: Sorting out the misunderstandings. *International Journal of Applied Linguistics* 16, 221–246.

Ellis, R. (2018) *Reflections on Task-based Language Teaching.* Bristol: Multilingual Matters.

Ellis, R., Skehan, P., Li, S., Shintani, N. and Lambert, C. (2020) *Task-Based Language Teaching: Theory and Practice.* Cambridge: Cambridge University Press.

Foster, P. and Skehan, P. (1996) The influence of planning and task type on second language performance. *Studies in Second Language Acquisition* 18, 299–323.

Harris, J. and Leeming, P. (2018) *On Task, Books 1-3.* Tokyo: ABAX ELT Publishers.

Jeon, I. and Hahn, J. (2006) Exploring EFL teachers' perceptions of task-based language teaching: A case study of Korean secondary school classroom practice. *Asian EFL Journal* 8 (1), 123–139.

Kelly, C. and Kelly, E. (1991) *The Snoop Detective School Conversation Book: Information-Gap Mysteries for Classroom Use.* Tokyo: MacMillan Language House.

Lambert, C. (2017) Tasks, affect and second language performance. *Language Teaching Research* 21 (6), 657–664.

Lambert, C. (2018) Tasks vs. Exercises. In *TESOL Encyclopedia of English Language Teaching.* Malden, MA: Wiley/Blackwell. DOI: 10.1002/9781118784235. https://www.academia.edu/9601849/_2018_Tasks_versus_Exercises_The_TESOL_Encyclopedia_of_English_Language_Teaching_18_January_2018_

Lambert, C. and Hailes, A. (2002) *Simulations.* Kitakyushu: The University of Kitakyushu. Full textbook available: https://www.academia.edu/9943328/_2002_Simulations_A_Task-Based_Approach_EFL_Instruction

Lambert, C., Kormos, J. and Minn, D. (2017a) Task repetition and second language speech processing. *Studies in Second Language Acquisition* 39, 167–196.

Lambert, C. and Minn, D. (2007) Personal investment in L2 task design and learning: a case study of two Japanese learners of English. *ELIA: Estudios de Lingüística Inglesa Aplicada* 7, 127–148, https://editorial.us.es/en/elia/numero-7.

Lambert, C., Philp, J. and Nakamura, S. (2017b) Learner-generated content and engagement in L2 task performance. *Language Teaching Research* 21 (6), 665–680.

Lambert, C. and Robinson, P. (2014) Learning to perform narrative task: A semester long study of task sequencing effects. In M. Baralt, R. Gilabert and P. Robinson (eds) *Task Sequencing and Instructed Second Language Learning* (pp. 207–230). London: Bloomsbury.

Lambert, C. and Zhang, G. (2019) Engagement in the use of English and Chinese as second languages: The role of learner-generated content in instructional task design. *Modern Language Journal* 103 (2), 391–411.

Long, M. (2015) *Second Language Acquisition and Task-Based Language Teaching.* Malden, MA: Wiley Blackwell.

Robinson, P. (2010) Situating and distributing cognition across task demands: The SSARC model of pedagogic task sequencing. In M. Putz and L. Sicola (eds) *Cognitive Processing in Second Language Acquisition: Inside the Learner's Mind* (pp. 243–268). Amsterdam: John Benjamins.

Robinson, P. (2011) Second language task complexity, the cognition hypothesis, language learning, and performance. In P. Robinson (ed.) *Second Language Task Complexity: Researching the Cognition Hypothesis of Language Learning and Performance* (pp. 3–37). Amsterdam: John Benjamins.

Skehan, P. (1996) A framework for the implementation of task-based instruction. *Applied Linguistics* 17 (1), 38–62.

Skehan, P. (2009) Modelling second language performance: Integrating complexity, accuracy, fluency and lexis. *Applied Linguistics* 30, 510–532.

Skehan, P. (2014) *Processing Perspectives on Task Performance.* Amsterdam: John Benjamins.

Skehan, P., Xiaoyue, B., Qian, L. and Wang, Z. (2012) The task is not enough: Processing approaches to task-based performance. *Language Teaching Research* 16 (2), 170–187.

Willis, J. (1996) *A Framework for Task-Based Learning.* Essex: Longman.

Appendix 2.1 A Lesson Based on a PPP Framework (from Kelly & Kelly, 1991)

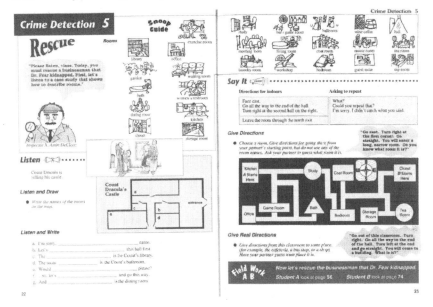

Appendix 2.2 A Lesson Based on a PTP Framework (from Lambert & Hailes, 2002)

UNIT 1: What should be done?

In this unit you will work together to solve problems.

Step 1: Warm up

🖉 1 - Match the beginning and ending of each sentence. Listen and check your answers.

My friend has a problem	one, she can complain; or two, she can move.
She likes her apartment, but	with her accommodation.
I think she's got two options:	her neighbors are really noisy.
My friend lent money to someone who	probably do something soon.
If I were in that situation, I would	mention it to the person.
I might casually	hasn't returned or even mentioned it.
Tom may quit his job to become a painter,	or keep his job?
Should he follow his instincts,	his job and paint in his spare time.
I recommend that he keep	but he is worried about money.

Step 2: Share your own ideas

Work with a partner. Choose any square and read it. Your partner will answer. Cross that square out. Then reverse roles and try again. Continue until all the squares are crossed out.

What advice would you give a friend who gets bad grades?	What advice would you give a friend with noisy neighbors?	What advice would you give a friend who is owed money?
What advice would you give a friend who wants to live abroad but doesn't have her parents' permission?	What advice would you give a friend who wants to change jobs for satisfaction, but would make less money?	What advice would you give a friend whose boss won't let her take time off work to catch up on her studying?

1   Simulations

Step 4: Learn new ways to do the task

Listen to native speakers trying to solve the problems that you just discussed. Decide whether each statement is T (True) or F (False), according to each conversation.

🖉 2 - **Problem 1: Can't get time off work**
1. T F The student should stop working part-time.
2. T F The student should cancel her mobile phone.

🖉 3 - **Problem 2: Can't get her money back**
3. T F It would be best to end the friendship.
4. T F This is a very serious problem.

🖉 4 - **Problem 3: Can't get her parent's permission**
5. T F Getting university credits should be the student's priority.
6. T F America, Britain and Australia are equally suitable.

🖉 5 - With a partner, try to fill in the missing words in the extract from **Problem 2**. Then listen and check your answers.

A: Well, if it were me in _____ situation, I would probably have to _____ something pretty soon, I wouldn't _____ two months anyway.

B: No, no.

A: I would wait for _____ next time I saw that person and _____ it casually – make a joke about _____. I would say, "Could you give _____ three thousand yen because, after all, that's _____ you owe me?"

B: Another option would be just to _____ the same thing. She could ask _____ borrow the same amount of _____ off her friend.

Work in pairs. Discuss each of the expressions below and number them according to the function they are most likely to serve in debating. Then add a phrase of your own for each function.

Doing Things with Language

Common Functions for Solving Problems	My Own Ways
(1) Opening the discussion	(a)
(2) Suggesting a solution	(b)
(3) Suggesting an alternative	(c)
(4) Confirming a conclusion	(d)

Some Language Used when Solving Problems
____ This is a difficult one. I'd like to hear what you think first.
____ So we think he should find a new part-time job.
____ That is a good idea, but it might be better to end the friendship completely.
____ I see what you are getting at, but I feel that she has to accept her parents' opinion.
____ It seems that we agree that she should ask for the money back immediately.
____ I can't help thinking that she should move to a quieter neighborhood.
____ In my opinion he should follow his dream. He should quit work and spend his time painting.
____ Let's see if we can find a solution to this problem. Who's first?

3   Simulations

Step 3: See how well you can do the task

These three letters explain problems. Discuss them and decide what each person should do.

Letter 1: Trouble with Work

Dear Abby,

I'm a nineteen-year-old university student. I have a part-time job to pay my rent and mobile phone bill. It's a very good job, as my wages are higher than those of my friends. The problem is that my boss never lets me have time off. I've worked every weekend for the last six months and my schoolwork is suffering. I have to do something soon.

Worried

Letter 2: Trouble with Friends

Dear Abby,

I went out with friends about two months ago. When it was time to pay, one of my classmates said she had forgotten her wallet. I usually don't lend money, but in this case, I really had no choice. I expected her to pay me back soon, but she hasn't mentioned it. I don't feel comfortable asking for the money, but I feel irritated whenever I meet her. What should I do?

Angry

Letter 3: Trouble with Family

Dear Abby,

Ever since primary school I've dreamed of going abroad, but I always thought it would be too expensive. Recently, I received some information about an affordable study abroad program at my university. It would allow me to earn credits toward my degree while living in a foreign country. I thought my parents would be excited, but they said they were too worried about my safety to let me go. I don't agree, but I don't know what to do.

Disappointed

Simulations   2

Step 5: Try the task again

Here are three more problem letters. Discuss them and decide what each person should do.

Letter 1: Trouble with School

Dear Abby,

First period begins at 9:00 at my university. I've always been conscious of my appearance, and it takes me about two hours to eat and get dressed in the morning. My high school was 20 minutes from home, so I woke up at 6:30 and arrived on time. However, my university is two hours away, so I have to wake up at 4:30. This is making me too tired, and I often feel sick. Recently, I've been turning off my alarm and missing first period. I've always been a good student, but I'm failing three courses this term. What can I do?

Desperate

Letter 2: Trouble at Work

Dear Abby,

I got my part-time job last year. When I started, I was told that I'd get 620 yen an hour for the first year, but 750 yen after that. I'm now in my second year, but my pay is the same. The person who hired me quit, and my manager gets upset easily. I'm afraid to mention the agreement because too many other students are looking for a job like this. However, I really need the extra money. What should I do?

Confused

Letter 3: Trouble with Money

Dear Abby,

I'm having trouble with school. I work every night at my part-time job just to pay for my living expenses. I don't have enough time for studying, and I have no time for relaxation. I'm working very hard, but I'm still doing terribly in school. I'm quite discouraged. My parents are really happy that I'm attending university, but I'm beginning to wonder if it's within our means. I really don't know what to do.

Insecure

Homework: Write a problem letter of your own. Complete the box at the bottom of Page 7.

Simulations   4

3 Low-Proficiency Learners and Task-Based Language Teaching

Jonathan Newton and Trang Le Diem Bui

Introduction

We can only hazard a guess at how many language learners worldwide might be defined as low-proficiency learners (LPLs). But given that the overall number of language learners can be counted not in millions but in billions[1], we can be confident that LPLs make up a substantial proportion of this number. Not surprisingly then, there is no shortage of instructional guidance for teaching LPLs in the general language teaching literature. However, this group, despite its size, has until recently been poorly served in task-based language teaching (TBLT) research and by those who advocate for teaching with tasks. In this chapter we explore this gap while at the same time highlighting a resurgence of interest in research and professional resources focused on TBLT for LPLs.

TBLT has its roots in communicative language teaching (CLT) (Ellis, 2018), an approach in which language learning is seen to occur *through* communicative language use as well as *for* language use. CLT's emphasis on productive use of language, and especially on oral communication has meant that it tends to privilege learners who are sufficiently proficient to communicate in English. As such, it has been criticised for not being suitable for beginners and certainly not for beginners in foreign language contexts who may only experience the target language for two hours or so a week in crowded classrooms and be taught by teachers whose own oral proficiency may not be strong. CLT's failure to clearly articulate a role for the first language (L1) further limits its viability for teaching LPLs in such contexts. TBLT's close association with CLT means that it has inherited these issues and attracted similar criticisms (e.g. Swan (2005), although see Ellis (2009) and Long (2016) for forceful rebuttals). Our purpose in this chapter is not to revisit this debate but to provide and illustrate a principled set of guidelines for teaching LPLs with tasks. We begin the chapter by defining LPLs and discussing TBLT research that has focused on LPLs. We then propose a set of guidelines for using tasks with LPLs, which we illustrate with sample tasks and with an account of how TBLT was used to enhance the teaching of English to young learners in a Vietnamese primary school.

Low Proficiency Learners

Who are LPLs? We see them as falling within the 'A1–A2' level 'Basic User' in the Common European Framework of Reference for Languages (Council of Europe, 2001) as described in Table 3.1.

We present these proficiency descriptors in full because viewing LPLs in these 'can do' terms naturally aligns with the way learning goals are described in TBLT. However, these descriptors tell us little about the learners themselves. This is a non-trivial concern. The characteristics of learners matter, often a great deal, in determining how instructional tasks are used in the language classroom. Consider for example, the contrast between adult LPLs in a Language for Specific or Occupational Purposes (LSP/LOP) program (e.g. Aviation English) compared to young EFL learners at a junior high school in Japan. For the former group, identifying specific target tasks and building a program of tasks designed to lead to successful performance of these target tasks is a well-established task-based approach (Long, 2015). However, for the latter group, the main or only objective of study may be to pass a school exam in which display of language knowledge and skills is the sole measure of success (Sato, 2010). We elaborate on these two illustrative cases in Figure 3.1 where we identify five important contextual factors and learner features which differentiate between different types of LPLs. Needless to say, these factors need to be taken into account in conceptualising and implementing task-based teaching for specific

Table 3.1 A-level descriptors in the Common European Framework of Reference (CEFR) (Council of Europe, 2001: 24)

		Descriptors
Basic user	A2 Waystage	Can understand sentences and frequently used expressions related to areas of most immediate relevance (e.g. very basic personal and family information, shopping, local geography, employment). Can communicate in simple and routine tasks requiring a simple and direct exchange of information on familiar and routine matters. Can describe in simple terms aspects of his/her background, immediate environment and matters in areas of immediate Basic need.
	A1 Breakthrough	Can understand and use familiar everyday expressions and very basic phrases aimed at the satisfaction of needs of a concrete type. Can introduce him/herself and others and can ask and answer questions about personal details such as where he/she lives, people he/she knows and things he/she has. Can interact in a simple way provided the other person talks slowly and clearly and is prepared to help.

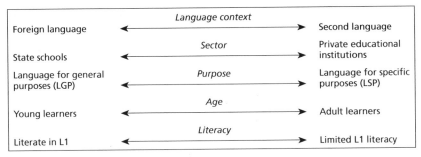

Figure 3.1 Illustrative contexts and characteristics of LPLs

groups of LPLs. But alongside context appropriate pedagogy we take the position in this chapter that it is possible to establish general guidelines for using tasks with LPLs that are broad enough to apply to a wide range of LPLs and that can be reshaped and adapted to work across diverse contexts and types of learners.

Low Proficiency Learners in TBLT research

LPLs are underrepresented in TBLT research and especially in research carried out in the formative years of the field from the 1980s to the 1990s. Much of this early research was carried out in *second* language contexts (in contrast to *foreign* language contexts) involving adolescent or young adult pre-sessional ESL students of intermediate levels of proficiency or above and studying at North American universities or colleges (e.g. Pica, 1988)[2]. In such settings, classroom communication is often exclusively in the second language (L2)[3], not least because learners come from a variety of L1 backgrounds and teachers may not be fluent in their learners' language(s). Thus, early TBLT research on task-based interaction involved either native speaker – non-native speaker (NS-NNS) dyads communicating solely in L2 (e.g. Pica, 1988) or peer–peer interaction between learners who do not share an L1 (e.g. Doughty & Pica, 1986) or who were expressly discouraged from using L1. The theoretical roots of TBLT in Krashen's Input Hypothesis (1985) and Long's Interaction Hypothesis (1996) gave credence (though not necessarily deliberately) to the subtractive view of L1 use that underpinned such practices. It is hardly surprising, therefore, that LPLs who have limited productive language ability would be a dis-preferred participant group for task research which required learners to communicate only in L2.

In contemporary TBLT research, LPLs are still underrepresented. Plonsky and Kim's (2016) meta-analysis of studies involving task-based learner production published between 2006 and 2015, showed that only 27 (32%) of the 85 studies in the corpus involved beginners. Nevertheless, this modest figure suggests growth and promise for the future. Edited volumes such as Shehadeh and Coombe's (2012) collection of papers on TBLT in foreign language contexts and Thomas and Reinders' (2015) collection on TBLT in Asia both also speak to the increasing diversity of contexts in which TBLT is being implemented and researched, with the inevitable consequence that LPLs are becoming more prominent in TBLT research.

Notably, this includes a growing body of research focused on tasks for young learners (Azkarai & Oliver, 2016; Newton & Bui, 2017; Pinter, 2007a, 2007b, 2015, 2017; Shintani, 2016), a trend that in part reflects earlier introduction of English as a second/foreign language in schooling for primary-age learners in recent years (Butler, 2015). A common focus of this research is peer–peer interaction between young learners. Oliver (1998, 2002) was among the first to shed light on interaction and negotiation for meaning (NfM) among children, in this case in an ESL setting in Australia. In her 1998 study, 192 young LPLs were grouped into age- and gender-matched dyads in order to complete a picture description task and an object-placement task. The results indicated that, like adult learners, these young learners negotiated for meaning during interactive tasks although to a lesser degree, and used far fewer comprehension checks but more self- and other-repetitions. Oliver (1998: 379) claimed that although these children were less developed cognitively, socially and linguistically they were 'aware of their conversational responsibility and attempt to work towards mutual understanding'. In her 2002 study, Oliver showed how the proficiency of learner pairs affected the amount of NfM they engaged in, with low-proficiency dyads producing more NfM than higher-proficiency dyads.

Peer-peer interaction was also the focus of Pinter's (2007a) study into the repeat performance of versions of a spot-the-difference task by two 10-year-old beginner learners in a state primary school in Hungary. Although the children were exposed to traditional teaching methods before they undertook the tasks and their level of competence was very low, they were shown to attend carefully to each other's utterances and to assist each other through peer correction during the tasks. Pinter argued that the study provided evidence to support the use of fluency tasks for low proficiency primary school children since such tasks provided them with opportunities for more 'real' communication rather than drilling and pattern practice (Pinter 2007a: 202).

A series of recent studies in Spain continues this tradition of investigating task-based interaction by low proficiency primary school EFL learners (Azkarai & Imaz Agirre, 2016; Azkarai & Oliver, 2016; García Mayo & Imaz Agirre, 2016; García Mayo & Lázaro-Ibarrola, 2015). These studies provide further insights into the way young learners negotiate for meaning, draw on their L1, and provide each other with negative evidence. Task repetition has been a particular focus of this body of research. On repeated tasks learners have been found to collaborate more and use L1 less. When L1 is used, it is mainly to scaffold language production and to manage and expedite the completion of the task.

In the context of EFL classrooms in China, Butler and Zeng (2014) investigated patterns of task-based interaction by 4th and 6th graders. They found that compared to the 4th graders (9–10 years old), the 6th graders (11–12 years old) engaged in more collaborative interactional patterns, more elaborate topic sequences, more dynamic turn-taking patterns and more diverse communicative functions. The lower proficiency and age of the 4th graders appeared to account for their lower quality task interaction.

Also focused on young learners, Shintani (2016) investigated the performance of and learning from input-based tasks (IBTs) by young absolute beginner learners (6 years old) enrolled in a private language school in Japan. A group of 15 children repeated three IBTs over five weeks while a control group just completed pre- and post-tests. Results showed that the children in the IBTs group were able to engage successfully in the tasks and to elaborate on their ideas more and use their L1 less when they repeated the tasks. Overall, the IBT group made significant gains in their receptive and productive vocabulary and grammar knowledge and outperformed the control group.

There has been less research activity addressing tasks for post-childhood LPLs. In a noteworthy action research study, Calvert and Sheen (2015) examined the role of the teacher as task designer and implementer in an adult refugee English program for LPLs. The teacher in the study worked through a cycle of developing, implementing, critically reflecting on and modifying a language learning task. The first unsuccessful experience of teaching with the task gave the teacher valuable insights into designing and implementing tasks for LPLs. The specific problems she identified included underestimating the linguistic demands of the task for LPLs, failing to factor in the implicit unfamiliar cultural schemata built into the task (which involved using checklists), lack of learner familiarity with doing classroom tasks and the need for much more teacher scaffolding to get the task underway. After modifications to address these issues, a second experience of teaching with the task proved successful and led to positive changes in how the teacher viewed task-based teaching. This is a particularly relevant study to this chapter because it highlights the specific challenges involved in using tasks with LPLs

Interestingly, the few recent studies in which beginners are explicitly mentioned in the paper title have involved learners of Chinese as a second language (CSL). For example, Lan et al. (2016) provide evidence of improvements in the oral communicative accuracy and the motivation of young adult beginning CSL learners studying in Taiwan as a consequence of performing information and reasoning gap tasks via Second Life. Learners in the study benefited from peer–peer interaction by imitating their more proficient peers. However, the language forms and items required for the tasks were deliberately taught prior to the task performances, thus approximating a present, practice, produce (PPP) approach. Zhou (2016) describes the introduction of task-based teaching in a CSL college courses for beginners. Here again we see a PPP approach in action since prior to the learners performing the tasks (which included information and opinion gap written and oral production tasks) they engaged in substantial preparatory classroom and individual out-of-class form-focused study and guided, teacher-led practice of situational conversations. These points aside, Zhou (2016: 40) notes that adopting the task-based approach appeared to facilitate the process of the students becoming more autonomous learners.

The Practice of TBLT for LPLs

One of the most salient issue concerning teaching LPLs with tasks involves the choice between a weak form of TBLT represented by the PPP method in which target linguistic features are taught and rehearsed prior to communicative use, and stronger forms of TBLT in which communicative language use is the starting point – what might be considered PPP in reverse. Those who advocate for judicious use of a PPP approach (e.g. Ellis, 2009; Sato, 2010) argue that in certain teaching settings a strong form of TBLT may not be feasible due to factors such as class size, cultural expectations, and curriculum constraints. For these contexts, they argue, PPP offers a viable alternative in which tasks can still feature prominently. Others such as Long (2015) and East (2012) are less convinced. As East concludes in his research on TBLT in foreign language classrooms in New Zealand, 'If [...] TBLT innovation is to be more successful, arguably a more unequivocal message is needed' (2012: 207). In recognition of these different perspectives, the guidelines which follow are applicable to both strong versions of task-based teaching and to using tasks within a PPP framework.

Guidelines for teaching LPLs with tasks

The following guidelines reflect our attempt to tease out from the TBLT literature a set of preliminary principles for using tasks with LPLs. They are not intended to be exhaustive, but they are general enough to apply to the wide range of LPL groups we described earlier in the chapter. We illustrate the guidelines with two sample tasks and with findings from a recent study which addressed the limitations of PPP and, conversely, the affordances for a stronger version of TBLT for primary school EFL learners in Vietnam (Newton & Bui, 2017; Bui, 2019).

(1) Use input-based tasks

Erlam (2016) noted a preference among the foreign language teachers in her study for 'output-prompting tasks' over 'input-providing tasks'. Not surprisingly, this preference led to the teachers designing and using production tasks which turned out to be too linguistically demanding for their LPLs. This in turn lead them to believe that TBLT is not suitable for beginners. Erlam posits that this perception reflects a bias in TBLT research toward output-prompting tasks and towards viewing tasks in ways that privilege language production. Ellis (2009) argues strongly for the value of IBTs as a counter to this perception, a point convincingly demonstrated in Shintani's (2016) research and in Duran and Ramaut's (2006) recommendations for designing tasks for beginners. Such tasks focus primarily on reading and listening for meaning rather than on speaking and writing. IBTs are valuable in their own right, but also as priming tasks (Willis & Willis, 2007) which prepare learners for subsequent production tasks.

(2) Foster co-construction of meaning in teacher–learner(s) and peer–peer task interaction

The benefits of collaborative and dialogic learning are well documented in educational research as well as in applied linguistics research. Communication tasks offer ample opportunities for such interaction, and the research we surveyed earlier in the chapter provides evidence that such affordances are no less of value for LPLs. These benefits include those associated with NfM in the wider SLA literature (Long, 1996) through which learners attend to language issues in their own and each other's utterances (Pinter, 2007a, 2007b). Peer–peer interaction also allows learners opportunities to scaffold each other's language production through co-construction of turns and to convey interest and encouragement to each other. As Foster and Ohta (2005) show, such processes allow learners to engage in richer meaning making than they are capable of alone.

(3) Pair learners in ways which maximise learning opportunities for LPLs

Nguyen and Newton (2019) showed how strategically pairing learners in relation to their relative proficiency (high or low) had significant effects on the extent to which they attended to and successfully resolved language issues during task interaction. While Low-Low pairings engaged in more language related episodes (LREs) they were less successful at resolving these than High–Low pairings, suggesting that the mixed proficiency pairing was more valuable for the lower proficiency learners. There was also evidence from learner reports that higher proficiency learners valued the opportunity to assist their partners (Nguyen, 2013) especially when they understood the value of assisting their less able peers.

(4) Recognise and foster productive roles for L1 use in task performance

The value of L1 use for mediating task performance is widely recognised (Moore, 2013; Seals et al., in press; Storch & Aldosari, 2010; Swain & Lapkin, 2000). A common finding in these studies is that L1 use facilitates task management and deliberations over language (Lasito & Storch, 2013). This is not to say to say that L1 use in TBLT is an unmitigated success. Carless (2008: 336) highlighted the complexity of the issues surrounding L1 use in task-based classrooms in Hong Kong, concluding that 'a balanced and flexible view of MT [mother tongue] use in the task-based classroom' is needed. This balance requires strategic and negotiated roles for L1 use and consideration of how it fits within the different phases of a task-based lesson. For instance, Newton and Nguyen (2019) found that when a speaking lesson involved opportunities for public performance of a task in front of the class after it had been rehearsed, the learners used L1 extensively in the prior task rehearsal, but they did so to *resource* the use of English in the upcoming L2 performance not to replace or avoid it.

(5) Prioritise word and phrase learning

In the natural process of learning a language, words and phrases are learnt first. It follows that lexical learning should be emphasised when using tasks with LPLs. As Willis and Willis (2007: 191–196) argue, the post-task phase is ideally suited to a lexical focus. This might involve getting learners to search a text for and classify phrases that relate to a particular function (e.g. agreeing or disagreeing) or notion (e.g. time, location), or search for a common function word and classify the phrases it occurs in. Willis and Willis also argue that it is the lexical resources needed to perform a task rather than grammar that should be the main focus of priming activities in the pre-task phase.

(6) Recognise the important roles the teacher plays in teaching with tasks

A simplistic and all too widespread perception of the task-based teacher is of someone who is primarily a facilitator of communication. It is perhaps this perception that has led to English language schools in many parts of the world being prepared to employ untrained young native speakers to teach speaking classes, on the assumption that all that is required to teach speaking is native speaker fluency. As is ably illustrated in Shintani (2016) however, teaching LPLs with tasks calls upon the teacher to play a range of roles, including input provider, co-constructor of meaning, leader and organiser of discussion, language knower/adviser, language teacher (Willis & Willis, 2007: 148-151) and nurturer of noticing (Skehan, 2013).

(7) Repeat tasks

Task repetition has received a lot of attention in recent research (Bygate, 2018). Research on task repetition involving young LPLs has shown that repeating tasks with such learners leads to a reduction in L1 use, increased collaboration, and greater attention to peer correction (Azkarai & García Mayo, 2017; García Mayo & Agirre, 2016; Pinter, 2007a, 2007b). Task repetition can involve repeating similar or identical tasks over a series of lessons (Shintani, 2016) or staging repetition within a lesson.

Sample tasks

The following two brief sample tasks illustrate these guidelines.

Sample Task 1. 'Junk we carry around with us' (from Willis & Willis, 2007: 69)

In this task the teacher asks the class to guess what she is carrying in her bag. She then reveals the objects one at a time and talks about them as she does so. Options for extending this task include a memory task in which the objects are covered up and the learners have to recall them, a task in which learners instruct the teacher to put specific objects back in her bag, and a peer interaction task in which learners do the same guessing task in pairs.

This task illustrates the use of an input-based task, a focus on lexical items, learners engaged in communicative language use both with the teacher and with each other, the teacher as input provider, language knower and co-constructor of meaning, and task repetition, with the input task repeated in various forms and then repeated again as a speaking task.

Sample Task 2. 'Party, What party?' (from Meddings & Thornbury, 2009: 24)

The teacher begins the task by saying 'On Saturday I went to a party'. The students work in groups to come up with five questions about the party which they then pass (or email) to the teacher for a response. Questions that contain grammatical or lexical errors are sent back for rewording. When all questions are answered the groups each prepare a short recount of the teacher's party and prepare to present it orally to the class. As the groups listen to each other they note details about the party that they did not know about.

In this task we see a range of types of teacher–learner(s) and peer–peer interaction. Although the *outcome* of the task is intended to be expressed in the target language, learners could be encouraged to move between L1 and L2 in the *process* of doing the task, for example to manage how they do the task and to deliberate over language.

As with Sample Task 1, the teacher plays a range of important roles beyond simply facilitating task-based interaction. Although this task-based lesson does not involve an input-based task as such, meaningful input from the teacher provides core content for learners to draw on in subsequent writing and speaking.

To further illustrate these guidelines we now turn to a more extensive account of task-based teaching for LPLs, in this case low Al-level EFL learners at a Vietnamese primary school.

Innovating with TBLT for low-proficiency EFL learners at Vietnamese primary schools: A case study

I (second author) am a teacher and teacher trainer at a Vietnamese university. In this role I have had first-hand experience with the shortcomings of the PPP approach currently being used in speaking lessons for beginner-level primary school pupils in Vietnam. Such lessons lack of focus on meaningful communication and lead to low levels of learner engagement. To enhance the effectiveness of the speaking lessons, I conducted research to understand how the primary school teachers were delivering the PPP speaking lessons, how they viewed the lessons, and how they and their learners would respond to task-based revisions to these lessons.

In the first phase of the research, seven teachers (three Grade 3 and four Grade 4) were observed teaching one or two speaking lessons followed by stimulated-recall interviews and then, at a later date, by follow-up interviews. The findings showed that while all the teachers acquiesced to the institutional requirement to follow the PPP sequence in the textbook, three commented that the lessons were overly prescriptive and mechanical, making it difficult to attract pupils' interest or enhance their ability to communicate.

In the second phase of the research, we (both authors) redesigned two PPP speaking lessons in the textbook for Grade 4 pupils (nine years old) to reflect principles of TBLT. The redesign drew on Willis's (1996) TBLT framework which involves three-phases: a pre-task phase, a main-task phase and a post-task phase. Here is how one of the lessons was redesigned. For the *pre-task* activity the textbook presentation activity 'Look, listen and repeat' was turned into an input-based listening task in which the learners listen to a recorded dialogue and fill in the blanks in the timetable as they do so. Willis and Willis (2007) describe this as a priming task. This task was designed to address the teachers' dissatisfaction of the mechanical nature of the presentation textbook activity. For the *main task*, the textbook practice activity 'Point and say' was made into an information-gap task. For this task, the learners were paired up and each was given a complete class timetable that their partner needed information from, as well as a second blank timetable for another class for which they needed to get information from their partner. For the *post-task* phase, the bland textbook production activity was made into a public performance of the main task by pairs of learners in front of the class, followed by such language analysis and language practice activities as time allowed. A valuable insight we obtained from this work was that at least on paper we were able to produce a task-based version of a PPP lesson which fitted into the same lesson time and which addressed all the same key language and communicative outcomes of the PPP lesson.

The three Grade 4 teachers (Nam, Nhu and Lan, pseudonyms) who participated in Phase 1 of the study volunteered to implement the two redesigned lessons in their normally scheduled classes. Data were collected from observations and interviews with teachers and their pupils. The results showed that all teachers successfully implemented the two redesigned lessons, although the achieved outcomes of the main task in each lesson varied. All teachers commented that the task-based lessons resulted in greater learner involvement and enhanced opportunities for communicative language use. As one teacher said,

> This approach [TBLT] will help the pupils handle their communication more effectively in real-life situations. Whereas, the PPP approach could merely help them learn the target structural patterns taught to them. (Teacher Lan)

This comment was supported by one of the interviewed pupils in Lan's class:

> I like to exchange information about the timetable with my friend. I tried to help my friend understand using the language I knew. This helps me speak English more naturally.

Among the factors that contributed to the successful implementation of the task-based lessons, three stood out. The first was the role of input-based tasks. As one of the teachers said,

> When the listening activity was delivered in the traditional way [Look, listen and repeat], there was no guarantee that all pupils would listen. Many pupils just listened to the recording with little interest. However, the input-based listening task could attract pupils' attention more effectively [...]. Pupils listened with their book closed, so they concentrated better. I noticed that pupils got more curious and excited. (Teacher Nam)

The pupils held similar views. As one said,

> I like the listening activity because I could understand what I listened to. When I was involved in the listening, I concentrated hard. I could not understand much after the first listening, but then I concentrated harder and could do the task easily.

Pupils across the three classes reported that they picked up language items (i.e. target vocabulary and structures) in the IBTs, which they then incorporated into the main task. As another pupil said,

> As I understood what was talked in the listening task, I learnt some words and structures. Then I used these words [and structures] together with some of the words I knew to make sentences to ask my friend.

The second factor was co-construction which was provided by the teacher and/or the stronger peer to the weaker peer, primarily at the initial stage of the task performance. Often the weaker pupil in each pair relied on the assistance of the teacher or strong peer or both initially to co-construct their utterances and consequently were able to produce these items more independently. Below is an example of an occasion of co-construction.

Extract 1. (Peer co-construction assistance)
1   P2: When ... uhm?
2   P1: When you
3   P2: When you...? When do you have?
4   P1: Môn gì? (What subject?)
5   P2: When you? Nữa quên mất tiêu rồi. (Again I forgot.)
6   P1: do you?
7   P2: When do you have ... Math?
8   P1: Math? ... Monday, Wednesday and Thursday. Hỏi! (Ask!)

Co-construction was particularly noticeable in the initial phase of task performance. However, once a performance was underway it was mainly facilitated by self- and other-correction as shown in Extracts 2 and 3 below.

Extract 2. (Self-correction)
P1: Who ... Who your teacher? ... Who is your English teacher name?

Extract 3. (Other-correction)
1   P1: What subject do you have on Tuesday?
2   P2: It...
3   P1: I
4   P2: I Music
5   P1: I have
6   P2: I have Music and...
7   P1: Music and ...?
8   P2: and IT ... and Vietnamese.

The third factor was use of L1. The pupils in this study used L1 to manage turn-taking and to seek or give assistance on linguistic aspects of the task when they needed to clarify or confirm their understanding.

We see this in Extract 4 when P2 asks for clarification using L1 (Vietnamese) from her peer, P1, regarding how to say the word 'Thứ năm' (Thursday) in English which P1 successfully provides.

Extract 4. (Seeking/giving assistance)
1   **P1:** Bạn học Vietnamese thứ mấy? (When do you have Vietnamese?)
2   **P2:** /vjet.nə miː/ là (is) /ˈtʃuːdeɪ/, /ˈtʃuːdeɪ/. Huh, cái này là …? (this is …?). Thứ năm là gì bạn, thứ năm? (How do I say Thứ năm in English?)
3   **P1:** Thứ năm … thứ năm là (is) … /ˈθɜː deɪ/ … /ˈθɜː deɪ/.

Throughout the task performances, L1 use provided essential support to deal with task demands and to make the tasks more manageable. Overall, the redesign and implementation of the task-based lessons in classrooms provided compelling evidence that in this particular context at least, a stronger form of TBLT was viable for teaching LPLs. From the perspective of both teachers and learners, it led to better learning conditions and learning outcomes.

Conclusions

LPLs in the past have not been particularly well served by TBLT. But as the use of tasks has spread to an increasingly wide range of contexts, greater attention has been paid to LPLs. The growing number of TBLT research studies focused on young LPLs reflects this trend. Notwithstanding these positive trends, factors such as the prevailing association of TBLT with production tasks and the reluctance in many contexts to 'rehabilitate' L1 use in the classroom continue to hamstring uptake of task-based teaching for LPLs. To counter these issues, teachers need more than findings from experimental research if they are to be encouraged to adopt TLBT for teaching LPLs. They need positive models. One source of such models is task-based textbooks for LPLs which offer teachers who have little experience or expertise in TBLT a guide to begin teaching with tasks. Such textbooks are surprisingly hard to find though and those which do purport to be task-based not infrequently adopt a strong grammar focus and a PPP orientation. Two textbooks which we do think provide useful models of TBLT for LPLs are Book 1 of the series 'On-Task' (Harris & Leeming, 2018) and the series of textbooks designed by the Nippon Foundation for use in English classes in Cambodian schools and available as an open educational resources[4]. A second source of models is the growing body of research on tasks in action in real classrooms. Some of the research we reviewed earlier in the chapter is of this kind, as is the study we report on above on the implementation of TBLT in Vietnamese primary schools. Such research tackles the institutional, material and logistical challenges that make teachers reluctant to innovate with tasks and provides teachers with encouragement and strategies to embark on task-based teaching for LPLs.

Notes

(1) https://www.ihlondon.com/news/2014/number-of-english-language-learners-keeps-on-growing/.
(2) There are notable counter examples such as Long and Sato (1983) who focused on teachers interacting with elementary school children.
(3) Research on tasks in immersion or bilingual programs in Canada has long been an exception (e.g. Swain & Lapkin, 1998).
(4) http://oer.moeys.gov.kh/search/label/English.

References

Azkarai, A. and García Mayo, M.P. (2017) Task repetition effects on L1 use in EFL child task-based interaction. *Language Teaching Research* 21 (4), 480–495. doi. org/10.1177%2F1362168816654169.

Azkarai, A. and Imaz Agirre, A.I. (2016) Negotiation of meaning strategies in child EFL mainstream and CLIL. *TESOL Quarterly* 50 (4), 844–870. doi.org/10.1002/tesq.249.

Azkarai. A. and Oliver, R. (2016) Negative feedback on task repetition: ESL vs. EFL settings. *The Language Learning Journal* 1–12. doi.org/10.1080/09571736.2016.1196385.

Bui, T. (2019) The implementation of task-based language teaching in EFL primary school classrooms: A case study in Vietnam. Unpuhlished PhD thesis, Victoria University of Wellington, Wellington.

Butler, Y.G. (2015) English language education among young learners in East Asia: A review of current research (2004–2014). *Language Teaching* 48 (03), 303–342. doi:10.1017/s0261444815000105.

Butler, Y.G. and Zeng, W. (2014) Young foreign language learners' interactions during task-based paired assessments. *Language Assessment Quarterly* 11 (1), 45–75. doi:10.1080/15434303.2013.869814.

Bygate, M. (ed.) (2018) *Learning Language Through Task Repetition*. Philadelphia: John Benjamins.

Calvert, M. and Sheen, Y. (2015) Task-based language learning and teaching: An action-research study. *Language Teaching Research* 19 (2), 226–244. doi: 10.1177/1362168814547037.

Carless, D.R. (2008) Student use of the mother tongue in the task-based classroom. *ELT Journal* 62 (4), 331–338. doi:10.1093/elt/ccm090.

Council of Europe (2001) *Common European Framework of Reference for Languages: Learning, Teaching, Assessment*. Cambridge: Cambridge University Press.

Doughty, C.J. and Pica, T. (1986) Information gap tasks: Do they facilitate SLA? *TESOL Quarterly* 20 (2), 305–325.

Duran, G. and Ramaut, G. (2006) Tasks for absolute beginners and beyond: Developing and sequencing tasks at basic proficiency levels. In K.V.d. Branden (ed.) *Task-Based Language Education: From Theory to Practice* (pp. 47–75). Amsterdam: John Benjamins.

East, M. (2012) *Task-Based Language Teaching from the Teachers' Perspective: Insights From New Zealand*. Amsterdam: John Benjamins.

Ellis, R. (2009) Task based language teaching: Sorting out the misunderstandings. *International Journal of Applied Linguistics* 19 (3), 221–246. doi:DOI: 10.1111/j.1473-4192.2009.00231.x.

Ellis, R. (2018) *Reflections on Task-Based Language Teaching*. Bristol: Multilingual Matters.

Erlam, R. (2016) 'I'm still not sure what a task is': Teachers designing language tasks. *Language Teaching Research* 20 (3), 279–299. doi:10.1177/1362168814566087.

Foster, P. and Ohta, A.S. (2005) Negotiation for meaning and peer assistance in second language classrooms. *Applied Linguistics* 26 (3), 402–430. doi:10.1093/applin/ami014.

García Mayo, M.P. and Agirre, A.I. (2016) Task repetition and its impact on EFL children's negotiation of meaning strategies and pair dynamics: An exploratory study. *The Language Learning Journal* 44 (4), 451–466. doi:10.1080/09571736.2016.1185799.

García Mayo, M.P. and Lázaro-Ibarrola, A. (2015) Do children negotiate for meaning in task-based interaction? Evidence from CLIL and EFL settings. *System* 54, 40–54. doi.org/10.1016/j.system.2014.12.001.

Harris, P. and Leeming, J. (2018) *On Task* (Vol. 1). Korea: Abax.

Krashen, S.D. (1985) *The Input Hypothesis*. New York: Longman.

Lan, Y.-J. Kan, Y.-H. Sung, Y.-T. and Chang, K.-E. (2016) Oral-Performance Language Tasks for CSL Beginners in Second Life. *Language Learning & Technology* 20 (3), 60–79.

Lasito, and Storch, N. (2013) Comparing pair and small group interactions on oral tasks. *RELC Journal* 44 (3), 361–375. doi:10.1177/0033688213500557.

Long, M.H. (1996) The role of linguistic environment in second language acquisition. In W. Ritchie and T. Bhatia (eds) *Handbook of Research on Second Language Acquisition* (pp. 413–468). New York: Academic.

Long, M.H. (2015) *Second Language Acquisition and Task-Based Language Teaching*. West Sussex, England: John Wiley & Sons.

Long, M.H. (2016) In defense of tasks and tblt: Nonissues and real issues. *Annual Review of Applied Linguistics* 36, 5–33. doi:10.1017/S0267190515000057.

Long, M.H. and Sato, C.J. (1983) Classroom foreigner talk discourse: Forms and functions of teachers' questions. In H.W. Seliger and M.H. Long (eds) *Classroom Oriented Research in Second Language Acquisition* (pp. 268–285). Rowley, MA: Newbury House.

Meddings, L. and Thornbury, S. (2009) *Teaching Unplugged: Dogme in English Language Teaching*. Peaslake: Delta Publishing.

Moore, P.J. (2013) An emergent perspective on the use of the first language in the English as a foreign language classroom. *The Modern Language Journal* 97 (1), 239–253. doi:10.1111/j.1540-4781.2013.01429.x.

Newton, J. and Bui, T. (2017) Teaching with tasks in primary school EFL classrooms in Vietnam. In M. Ahmadian and M.P. García Mayo (eds) *Current Trends in Task-Based Language Teaching and Learning* (pp. 259–278). Boston: Mouton de Gruyter.

Newton, J. and Nguyen, B.T.T. (2019) Task repetition and the public performance of speaking tasks in EFL classes at a Vietnamese high school. *Language Teaching for Young Learners* 1 (1), 34–56. doi:10.1075/ltyl.00004.new.

Nguyen, B.T.T. (2013) Tasks in action in Vietnamese EFL high school classrooms: The role of rehearsal and performance in teaching and learning through tasks. Unpublished PhD thesis, Victoria University of Wellington, Wellington.

Nguyen, B.T.T. and Newton, J. (2019) Learner proficiency and EFL learning through task rehearsal and performance. *Language Teaching Research*. doi:10.1177/1362168818819021.

Oliver, R. (1998) Negotiation of meaning in child interactions. *The Modern Language Journal* 82 (3), 372–386.

Oliver, R. (2002) The patterns of negotiation for meaning in child interactions. *The Modern Language Journal* 86 (1), 97–111.

Pica, T. (1988) Interlanguage adjustments as an outcome of NS-NNS negotiated interaction. *Language Learning* 38 (1), 45–73.

Pinter, A. (2007a) Some benefits of peer–peer interaction: 10-year-old children practising with a communication task. *Language Teaching Research* 11 (2), 189–207. doi:10.1177/1362168807074604.

Pinter, A. (2007b) What children say: Benefits of task repetition In K. Van den Branden, K. Van Gorp and M. Verhelst (eds) *Tasks in Action: Task-Based Language Education From a Classroom-Based Perspective* (pp. 131–158). Newcastle: Cambridge Scholars Publishing.

Pinter, A. (2015) Task-based learning with children. In J. Bland (ed.) *Teaching English to Young Learners* (pp. 113–127). London: Bloomsbury.

Pinter, A. (2017) *Teaching Young Language Learners*. Oxford: Oxford University Press.

Plonsky, L. and Kim, Y. (2016) Task-based learner production: A substantive and methodological review. *Annual Review of Applied Linguistics* 36, 73–97. doi:10.1017/S0267190516000015.

Sato, R. (2010) Reconsidering the effectiveness and suitability of PPP and TBLT in the Japanese EFL classroom. *JALT journal* 32 (2), 189–200.

Seals, C.A. Newton, J. Ash, M. and Nguyen, T.B.T. (2020 in press) Translanguaging and TBLT: Cross-overs and challenges. In Z. Tian, L. Aghai, P. Sayer and J. Schissel (eds) *Envisioning TESOL Through a Translanguaging Lens – Global Perspectives*. New York: Springer.

Shehadeh, A. and Coombe, C.A. (2012) *Task-Based Language Teaching in Foreign Language Contexts: Research and Implementation*. Amsterdam: John Benjamins.

Shintani, N. (2016) *Input-Based Tasks in Foreign Language Instruction for Young Learners* (Vol. 9). Amsterdam: John Benjamins.

Skehan, P. (2013) Nurturing noticing. In J. M. Bergsleithner, S. N. Frota and J. K. Yoshioka (eds) *Noticing and Second Language Acquisition: Studies in Honor of Richard Schmidt* (pp. 169–180). Hawai'i: National Foreign Language Resource Center.

Storch, N. and Aldosari, A. (2010) Learners' use of first language (Arabic) in pair work in an EFL class. *Language Teaching Research* 14 (4), 355–375. doi:10.1177/1362168810375362.

Swain, M. and Lapkin, S. (1998) Interaction and second language learning: Two adolescent French immersion students working together. *The Modern Language Journal* 82 (3), 320–337.

Swain, M. and Lapkin, S. (2000) Task-based second language learning: The uses of the first language. *Language Teaching Research* 4 (3), 251–274. doi:10.1177/136216880000400304

Swan, M. (2005) Legislation by hypothesis: The case of task-based instruction. *Applied Linguistics* 26 (3), 376–401. doi:10.1093/applin/ami013

Thomas, M. and Reinders, H. (2015) *Contemporary Task-Based Language Teaching in Asia*. London: Bloomsbury Publishing.

Willis, D. and Willis, J. (2007) *Doing Task-Based Teaching*. Oxford: Oxford University Press.

Willis, J. (1996) *A Framework for Task-Based Learning*. Harlow: Longman.

Zhou, Y. (2016) Applying task-based language teaching in introductory level Mandarin language classes at the college of the Bahamas. *International Journal of Bahamian Studies* 22, 34–42.

4 Some Principles for Interactive Task Design: Observations from an EFL Materials Writer

Curtis Kelly

Teaching English as a foreign language (EFL) in non-English speaking countries presents context-specific challenges. In Asia, motivation to learn English can be low and learners have limited opportunities to speak the language outside of class. Both of these problems, however, can be addressed through the use of well-designed tasks. If tasks are interesting, learners are likely to engage, and if the tasks are carefully structured, the language they elicit can be as spontaneous as interactions in the real world. This chapter proposes principles for designing interactive classroom tasks that the author has used over three decades of writing and publishing task-based EFL materials in Japan and other East Asian contexts. Although the principles were generated within Asian EFL contexts, they might also inform task design in other contexts.

The Role of Tasks in an EFL Context

In the sixties, the traditional lecture-test curriculum for medical students was replaced with a problem-based approach. In doing so, the teaching of medicine saw improved clinical practices and lives were almost certainly saved (Albanese & Mitchell, 1993). Subsequently, task-based learning moved into various realms of education. Thanks to the work of researchers like Prabhu (1987), Long (1985, 2015), Skehan (1996, 2009), Robinson (2011) and Ellis (2003, 2009), this has come to include task-based language teaching (TBLT).

Whereas students studying English as a Second Language (ESL) in English-speaking countries might have daily opportunities to use English in real interactions with native speakers outside of the classroom, this is not the case for students of EFL in countries where the only opportunities a learner might have are within the walls of the classroom. In countries like Japan, Thailand, Saudi Arabia and Russia, where learners tend to have few naturalistic encounters with English, opportunities for genuine interaction in the language, the use of tasks in L2 instruction can create and simulate real interactions, reducing the distance between the classroom and the real world. In addition, well-designed tasks can have a profound effect on learner motivation and engagement in EFL contexts. In the last 20 years, non-English speaking countries all over the world have been adding EFL classes to primary school curricula and beyond (Butler, 2011), and interest in the impact of tasks on learners' engagement in language use in the L2 classroom has greatly increased (e.g. Lambert, 2017; Lambert *et al.*, 2017).

Learning a language in a country where the language is rarely used can be an uphill battle. Unless students experience an immediate need to learn particular language forms in order to communicate something, it can be much harder for them to retain these forms. However, tasks can create such immediate needs in the second language classroom, especially if the tasks are personalized. For example, Lambert and Zhang (2019) found that using tasks which create personal investment in the learning process might be especially important for the acquisition of pragmatic devices in an L2, more so than was previously recognized.

> If the tasks used in TBLT do not engage learners at a personal level and generate the use of pragmatic devices in completing them, learners can hardly be expected to master these pragmatic devices incidentally. (Lambert & Zhang, 2019)

A deficit of immediate personal need in using language can also impact motivation to learn. In fact, EFL environments have been characterized as 'motivational wastelands' (Berwick & Ross, 1989: 206). A task-based approach has the potential to activate the need for language use and foster motivation.

As an EFL textbook writer who has published with Pearson, Cambridge, Oxford, Macmillan, Longman, National Geographic Learning (previously Cengage) and other publishers, I have been involved in TBLT lesson design for almost 40 years. Interestingly, the examples that best fit the discussion in this chapter come from one of first books the author wrote, Kelly and Kelly's (1991) *The Snoop Detective School Conversation Book*. It provides an early example of how TBLT principles were put into practice in a successful course for East Asian EFL learners. As a materials writer, addressing the issue of learner engagement through task design is of particular importance to me professionally. For 20 of my 40 years in Japan, I had the opportunity to work in universities filled with low-proficiency English learners, almost all of whom had poor study habits and low levels of motivation. It was extremely difficult to get these students to pay attention, complete homework, or even come to class on a regular basis. Only when the language teaching activities were student-centered, success-oriented, and inherently interesting to the students did they commit to doing them. In every case, these involved the use of tasks in the syllabus.

In this chapter, I outline principles of task design that I have discovered through years of lesson crafting and teaching in Japanese universities. The observations are based on 25 years of in-class and post-course questionnaires, where students commented on how interesting, doable, and effective for their language learning the tasks illustrated in this chapter were. The feedback turned out to be surprisingly consistent. The focus of the chapter is on tasks designed for an East Asian EFL context. The main tasks provided extended interactive oral communication activities (20 minutes or more of class time) for use with high beginner to intermediate level students who can be considered representative of the majority of language learners in many EFL contexts. The principles provide guidance in how to (a) engage students, (b) control language targets and (c) solve typical classroom management problems such as keeping the learners focused on the completion of the task in the target language. The principles cover task design as well as support for learners' during their performance. While these principles were developed within East Asian EFL contexts, they are likely to be applicable to the design of interactive L2 speaking tasks for learners at the intermediate levels in other teaching contexts as well.

Principles of L2 Task Design

Principle 1. Design inherently interesting tasks

Teachers know that motivation and engagement are crucial for learning. While much of language teaching involves pushing students to study through the pressures of tests and grades, activities are needed that pull learners into learning. This raises the question of:

> … what makes some tasks inherently more motivating than others. From a practitioner's point of view, this is a crucial aspect of task design and implementation as it relates directly to improved instructional practice and the quality of learners' performance in the classroom. (Lambert *et al.*, 2017: 666)

There are a number of reasons why students might engage with particular tasks. These include the physical, social or personal needs that drive language use (Lambert, 2017) as well as proficiency-related, environmental, and instructional factors. Together these factors combine to create the inherent interestingness of a task.

To design engaging tasks, it is important to determine what is interesting or important to learners by looking at their lives and behaviors. One way is to do a needs analysis (Hillman & Long, Chapter 8, this volume; Oliver, Chapter 9, this volume) to identify engaging topics related to their personal lives (Lambert *et al.*, 2017; Phung, 2017). However, another way might be to employ general-interest tasks that involve a game element such as solving mysteries interactively (Butler, 2017; González-Lloret, Chapter 4, this volume). Cognitively challenging games are fun, independently of the language learning opportunities that they provide. They can motivate interaction and increase the incidental acquisition of interactive competence in the target language.

Kelly and Kelly's *The Snoop Detective School Conversation Book* (1991) was published by MacMillan Language House in Japan. It consists of a series of information gap mysteries, where learner pairs are given different sets of information to compare in order to work through a series of steps to solve crimes and earn points for their detective work. Figure 4.1 provides an example of an information-gap task sequence that tertiary-level Japanese students and teachers have evaluated as quite engaging over nearly three decades. Appendix 4.1 provides a second example of such a lesson. In the example in Figure 4.1, students are put in pairs and look at either the A or B page. Student A has photos of a party after a crime has occurred and Student B has photos of the party before a crime occurred. By comparing the

Figure 4.1 'Murder' task sequence from Kelly and Kelly (1991)

scenes in the photos, they can solve three mysteries: (1) who is the victim? (2) who is the thief and where are the jewels? and (3) who is the murderer and how was it done?

Other task sequences in the book involve rescuing people, disarming bombs (see Appendix 4.1), identifying counterfeits and apprehending thieves. After each task, learners record their answers in a checklist box in the upper right of the page and are awarded different values of detective points for each correct answer which they also record in the back of the book (see Figure 4.4 below). They can thus track their progress on completing tasks in non-linguistic terms over the course. The focus of attention is on solving the mysteries and the language used is incidental to this process.

All of the tasks in the main task sequences of Kelly and Kelly (1991) fit within Ellis' definition of a task:

(1) The primary focus is on meaning.
(2) There is a gap in information.
(3) Learners use their own linguistic and non-linguistic resources.
(4) There is an outcome other than the display of language (Ellis, 2018a: 106).

Furthermore, in order to maximize engagement, the task sequences in Kelly and Kelly (1991) consists of 'pedagogic tasks', mysteries, which focus on interactional authenticity rather than 'real-world tasks' that mirror real-world situations (Ellis, 2018a: 104). These tasks also have a linguistic focus in that they are constrained by the nature of the information the pairs of students need to compare in order to successfully arrive at the task outcomes. For example, students can hardly arrive at the outcomes of the tasks in the sequence in Figure 4.1 without successfully describing and identifying the faces, clothes and furniture involved at an appropriate level of detail.

For most learners in Japan and East Asia, working to solve mysteries like this one is inherently interesting. When using these tasks in class, it is frequently hard to get learners to stop working on them even after the end-of-class bell has rung. The students also request more information gap mystery tasks of this sort. These are good indications that these task sequences are inherently interesting and generate motivational intensity and engagement in language use (Lambert, 2017). By contrast, many of the typical information-gap tasks used in EFL teaching seem rather dull and mechanical. For example, when a pair of students are given menus showing food offerings with some prices are left blank on the respective students' materials, students are simply required ask each other how much each food item costs in order to fill in the blanks. The outcomes to such tasks are not particularly motivating as ends in themselves.

Principle 2. Design tasks of increasing difficulty in each sequence

A common problem with tasks is that more proficient students finish sooner than less proficient students and are left with nothing to do. More proficient students can often quickly complete a task that might take much longer for the rest of the class. Some textbooks have 'When you Finish' expansions for further language practice, but these can be perceived as a punishment for completing tasks rather than as a reward for doing so. One way to overcome this problem is to design task sequences which consist of multiple tasks of increasing difficulty. The *Murder* task sequence (Figure 4.1) illustrates how this might be done. In finding the victim, other than dealing with the minor surprise element of ambiguity caused by the mirror, learners just exchange information on what the six characters look like and match this information with their names. If learners need support, this can be scaffolded in the pre-task stage using a vocabulary guide (see Principle 3 and Figure 4.3 below). By providing resources such as these, even the weakest learners can complete the first task in the sequence. Then, finding the thief in the second task is a little harder, since inferences about the white bag must be made. Finally, finding the killer, the man missing a necktie, is usually the most difficult because students often fail to provide the required level of detail the first time through. Learners are typically required to revisit the task content and describe it in more detail, often pushing their L2 strategies and resources in doing so. Lambert (2019) discusses how describing items in more detail in order to arrive at task outcomes might positively impact language use. This method of graduated tasks makes low-proficiency learners in the class successful to some degree and keeps high-proficiency learners speaking for the full length of the time allocated to the task sequence.

The level of cognitive challenge of tasks in Kelly and Kelly (1991) was gauged by how quickly learners can do the task in their native language. Language tasks were made more or less difficult by: (a) including a little ambiguity, such as the mirror image in the *Murder* mystery; (b) making the answers less obvious, as with the missing necktie; and (c) requiring an inference to arrive at a solution, such as figuring out the white bag was probably used to carry the jewels. These factors are in line with Robinson's (2010) definition of task complexity as they relate to cognitive factors in task design rather than interactive or learner factors (Robinson, 2010: 245). Increasing difficulty by requiring a higher level of L2 proficiency in terms of lexical and syntactic knowledge was avoided, since proficiency-related affect can increase language anxiety and decrease the willingness to communicate (Hashimoto, 2002; Yashima *et al.*, 2018). A higher-level proficiency is useful in completing these task sequences, but lower-level learners also become empowered by the fact it is possible for them to complete at least some of the tasks in each sequence, and do relatively well in the course, in spite of their limited proficiency.

Principle 3. Provide language support separate from task sequences

The presentation-practice-production (PPP) framework is ubiquitous in EFL and ESL materials (see Lambert, Chapter 2, this volume), but it does not reflect the way the brain learns language (Long, 2015; Skehan, 1996; Willis, 1996; Sato, 2010). In PPP, language forms are presented first, practiced in exercises and finally used in a communicative activity. PPP assumes that students need to learn language forms first, before they have a felt need for them, and then automatize them through the extensive focused practice of completing a communicative task (DeKeyser, 2007). Unfortunately, just as one does not typically pick up a knife and look for something to cut, we do not learn isolated language forms and then look for ways to use them. Learning is driven by the physical, social and emotional needs (Paradis, 2004: 24–27) that are associated with the interactionally and pragmatically authentic language use that tasks are capable of generating in the classroom (Ellis, 2003).

Nevertheless, the explicit linguistic support provided by the PPP model may be helpful to learners of different needs and individual differences, if it is provided separately from tasks within a course of instruction (Ellis, 2018b: chap. 10). Kelly and Kelly (1991) provide supporting language materials to teachers in a separate section of book from the main task sequences so that teachers can make these resources accessible before, during, or even after students complete the task sequences. The aim is to facilitate learners in noticing and potentially using new forms when there is a communicative need for them. In other words, learners can acquire this language *through* task performance rather than *for* task performance (Ellis, 2003). For example, the vocabulary guide for the *Murder* task sequence (Figure 4.2) is available as a separate reference that teachers can allow learners to use before, during or after they complete each sequence, whenever deemed useful for reaching the task outcomes and interactive goals of the unit.

After providing engaging tasks (Principle 1 above), the cognitive and linguistic challenges of the tasks in Kelly and Kelly (1991) were carefully balanced with the cognitive challenge being the primary consideration (Principle 2 above). When learners are not overloaded linguistically, they can engage in completing tasks which drive the need for language and its incidental acquisition. To achieve this, just enough language support is provided to enable learners to get the task done, and it is provided in a different part of the book independent of the task sequence (Principle 3). Teachers can thus choose to use it or not based on the motivation, aptitude and proficiency levels of the specific group that they are using the materials to teach.

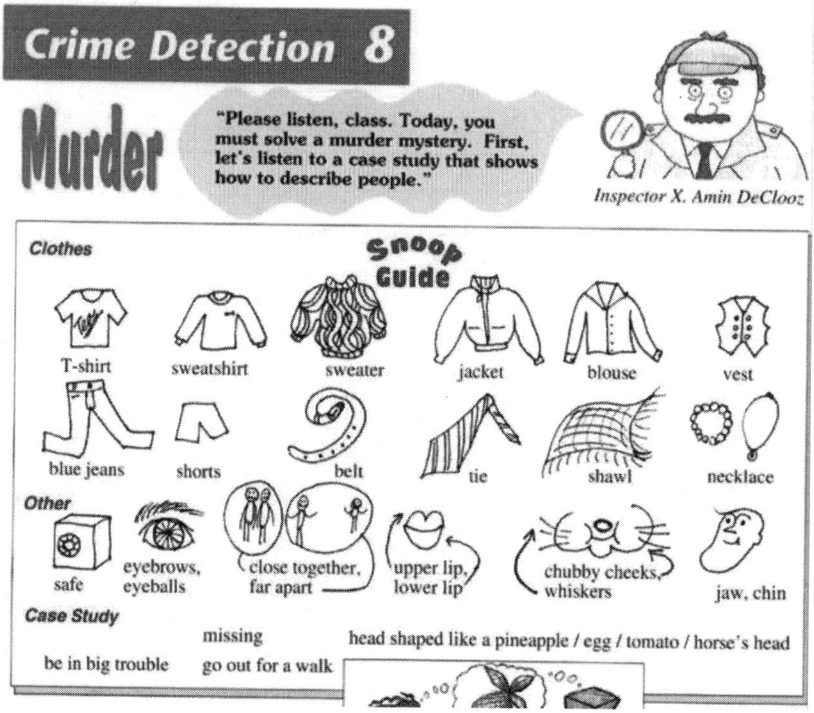

Figure 4.2 'Murder' vocabulary guide (Kelly & Kelly, 1991)

Principle 4. Structure tasks to promote target language use

As discussed in other chapters in the present volume, while some L1 use in connection with task performances might be beneficial (Ahmadian & Mansouri, Chapter 14, this volume; Kim, Cho & Ren, Chapter 15, this volume), a common problem that teachers in EFL contexts face is learners using more of the L1 than necessary, perhaps even completing the entire activity in their native language or using it to fill critical gaps which might otherwise have pushed their L2 resources in productive ways. However, careful task design can be used to optimize target language use on tasks. One way to achieve this is by constraining the language needed. For example, in the *Murder* task sequence (Figure 4.1), the language that is needed is restricted to clothing, faces, and furniture. This limiting of the linguistic demands that tasks make on learners brings the challenge of the task within reasonable limits for completion in the target language, particularly when linguistic support is available (see Principle 3 above). Another design feature that allows teachers to monitor student target language use and progress is to build in a written component to speaking tasks, such as filling in a chart with the partner's answers to questions. In Kelly and Kelly's (1991), 'Stakeout' task sequence, for example, where learners have to report complex narratives involving many characters at different locations in a crime scene, they are provided with a chart to record and organize the events in the different parts of the story chronologically in order to support their oral narration of these events and help them identify the culprits in a robbery. However, even with these types of support, it may still be difficult for many lower-proficiency EFL learners to use the target language when it is intended (see Newton & Bui, Chapter 3, this volume). Teachers have an important in situ role in this respect. If teachers have a sound understanding of the principles of TBLT (Ellis, Chapter 7, this volume), they will be able to intervene at critical points to mediate learners' language use by providing scaffolding and feedback to support and encourage attempts at using the target language while at the same time empowering them to complete the task by allowing judicious use of their L1.

Principle 5. Offer language for pragmatically appropriate interaction

Pedagogic tasks, in spite of the interaction that they generate, frequently lack in the range of devices used to create pragmatic meanings. Lambert and Zhang (2019) demonstrate how learner-generated task content can encourage advanced speakers of English and Chinese as foreign languages to use pragmatic devices such as vague language (e.g. *maybe, I think, more or less, possible*) to create pragmatic meaning in their task performances (e.g. tentativeness, self-protection, being collaborative/corporative) that does not tend to occur in comparable tasks based on teacher-generated task content. Kelly and Kelly (1991) take a different approach that they found better suited to their work with lower-level L2 learners.

In Kelly and Kelly (1991), the tasks were based only on teacher-generated content and pragmatic exchanges associated with appropriate communication on tasks were structured into the design of the tasks themselves. To scaffold such exchanges, task instructions reminded learners of the need to communicate appropriately and providing some guidance in how to do so as they complete tasks. For example, learners might be explicitly reminded to introduce themselves at the beginning of a task and examples of how to do this might be provided (e.g. 'My name is X', 'Hi, I'm Y but call me Z'). Putting a few helpful phrases on the task page can also draw learners' attention to ways that they can facilitate the pragmatic appropriateness of their interactive language use on tasks (e.g. 'Do you mind if I start?' 'I think it's your turn now' etc.). In short, simply reminding learners of different pragmatic dimensions of language use in each task sequence and giving them some examples of how to do so, might play an important role in helping them develop pragmatic competence through task performance.

Principle 6. Offer language for negotiating meaning

Negotiation of meaning refers to speakers working together to make their exchanges comprehensible to one another. One speaker might ask for a clarification on what the other said, repeat it back to confirm it, or request that the partner speak more slowly. Being able to negotiate understanding is vital to effective task completion both inside and outside of the classroom. Learners will undoubtedly need this kind of language when doing task sequences like the ones offered here. If the language to do this is not a part of their linguistic repertoire, they may be forced to use their L1 for this purpose instead of developing the ability to negotiate meaning in the L2.

As in Principle 5 above, language for negotiating meaning might be productively structured into the design of the tasks themselves (e.g. 'I'm sorry, I don't understand', 'What did you say?', 'Could you repeat that?' etc.). Adding such linguistic cues on the task page provides an opportunity for learners to acquire these important L2 skills within the context of specific task demands. For example, if a task involves writing down names, email addresses, or products, students might be provided with expressions such as 'How do you spell that?' or 'Could you say that again?' to facilitate their performance on the task and help them develop their skills for negotiating meaning in the L2. Teachers may also like to explain to their students why it is useful to develop the skill of negotiating for meaning in their L2 (cf. Sato, Chapter 13, this volume).

Principle 7. Keep instructions short and simple

It is important to use short and simple task instructions, especially for low- and intermediate- level learners. Using detailed or complicated instructions may result in learners misinterpreting what they are expected to do or ignoring the instructions all together. In either case, learners would end up doing the task in whatever way they interpret it rather than in the way that it was intended. The instructions for Step 2 of the *Murder* task sequence (Figure 4.1) and the instructions for the *Bomb* task sequence (Appendix 4.1) provide examples of short, simply worded instructions that communicate only the information that learners need to do the task. Such instructions also have the practical advantage of providing teachers with limited abilities in learners' L1 the flexibility of being able to translate some or all the instructions into the L1 for lower-level learners (see Principle 8 below). This flexibility can get learners on task more quickly and help learners perform task sequences in the way intended by the teacher or materials designer who wrote them.

Principle 8. Create adaptable tasks

Unlike traditional exercises, tasks rarely work the way teachers and materials writers think they will when they are designing them.

Regardless of clarity in design and instructions, what was intended to take three minutes might turn out to take twenty with some groups. Tasks need to be flexible and allow teachers to adapt them as they unfold with different groups of learners based on their levels of proficiency and motivation as well as their aptitudes. For a textbook, this is where a *Teacher's Guide* plays an important role. The *Teacher's Guide* should explain how much time each activity requires, indicate what pre-task and post-task activities can be skipped to save time, offer ways to modify the level, and provide expansion options. In regard to the latter, as textbook writer Marc Helgesen points out, the expansions in the *Teacher's Guide* are often the most creative: activities the authors wanted to put in but more conservative publishers kept out (Helgesen & Kelly, 2014).

In general, picture-based, multilayered tasks are particularly adaptable. For example, a time-saving (or level-lowering) adaptation for the *Murder* task sequence in Figure 4.1 would be for the teacher to describe each person in Step 1, rather than Student B. The *Bomb* information gap in Appendix 4.1 could also be simplified by telling the students to compare just what is next to the doors in Step 1, not the doors themselves, and also telling them that the room view and diagram in Step 2 are not at the same perspective. On the other hand, Step 3 could be more challenging by giving the activity in grayscale rather than color so that all of the wires become the same shades of grey (e.g. use high-speed mono photocopier handouts rather than the original book). Lambert (2019) provides a detailed discussion of how such subtle adjustments in the similarity between the items that learners must identify in order to complete a task can positively impact the language that they use.

Principle 9. Embed tasks in a macro-structure

Lambert (Chapter 2, this volume) provides a good picture of instructional frameworks for using tasks in L2 instruction. From the material writer's perspective, the PPP, Pre-task/Post-task (Skehan, 1996; Ellis, 2003) and simplify, stabilize, automatize, restructure, complexify (SSARC) frameworks (Robinson, 2010) represent either a partial or full textbook unit. These frameworks allow materials developers to write modules, but they do not solve the problem of a larger, macro-structure for the task sets over a semester or a year-long syllabus. Students in many EFL contexts can benefit from being oriented to task work and given an active role in setting their goals and tracking their progress in completing tasks over entire duration the course.

First, orienting learners to what is expected of them at the very beginning of the course might be helpful in some contexts where learners have limited experience with completing tasks. Figure 4.3 provides a page from the beginning of Kelly and Kelly (1991) which provides learners with an illustrated guide on how to do tasks at the very beginning of the

Figure 4.3 Orientation Material from Kelly and Kelly (1991)

course. This aspect of macro-structure at the beginning of the course is intended to provide scaffolding learners can use to get started in completing tasks effectively and to help them understand what is expected of them in terms of classroom behaviors. This page can easily be referred back to later if the instructor needs to re-establish behavioral norms.

In addition, providing an overall theme to the course that links the units together into some larger meaning beyond using language for its own sake can increase the learners' sense of ownership and commitment. This is particularly true in contexts where learner engagement and attendance present a problem. In Kelly and Kelly (1991), the individual task sequences or textbook units are organized with the macro-theme of 12 detective courses in the *Snoop Detective School* taught by three professors. The crime-solving information-gap task sequences represent the field work required for each course, and students track their progress towards graduation by filling task outcomes in the chart shown in Figure 4.4. After completing the textbook, they tally their detective points and receive a diploma with a detective level based on the number of mysteries that they solved. The motivation to acquire these points, combined with the intrinsic interest and game-like qualities of the task sequences (see Principle 1 above) typically results in learners being in class and ready to work on time, and sometimes results in difficulty getting them to stop working on the tasks at the end of the class period.

In line with this goal-tracking macro-structure, there is also an optional entrance ceremony before the first unit, where students introduce themselves to each other, and a graduation ceremony after the last, where they write messages to each other on yearbook pages in the back of the textbook, thereby creating a keepsake for the course. As the

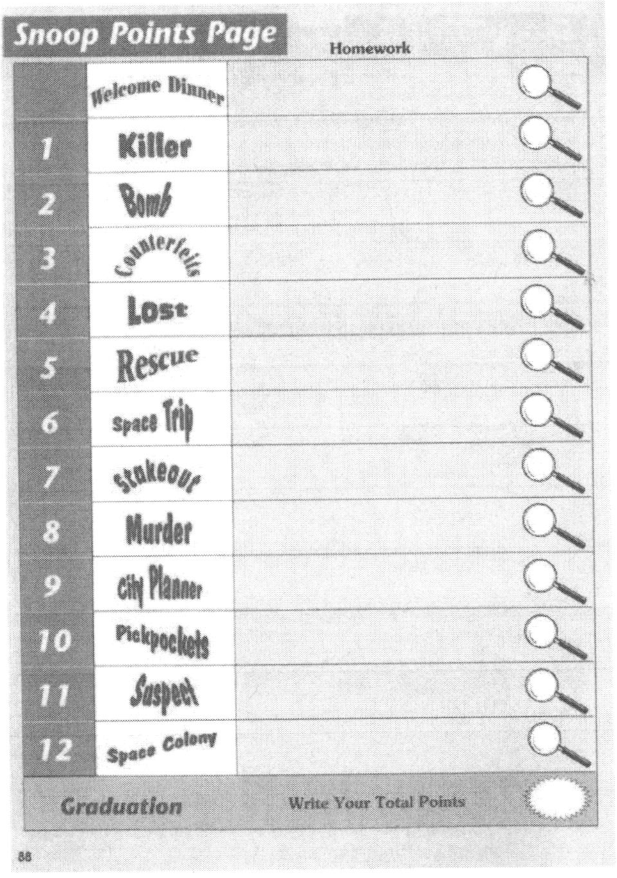

Snoop Points Page	Homework	
Welcome Dinner		
1 Killer		
2 Bomb		
3 Counterfeit		
4 Lost		
5 Rescue		
6 Space Trip		
7 Stakeout		
8 Murder		
9 City Planner		
10 Pickpockets		
11 Suspect		
12 Space Colony		
Graduation	Write Your Total Points	

Figure 4.4 Points page from Kelly and Kelly (1991)

main task sequences are primary, however, teachers can choose whether to use these additional resources or not depending on their learners and the amount of time available for the course.

Although such an extended framework might seem superficial to some trained L2 instructors, for learners in many contexts, especially younger learners, learners who do not have strong linguistic backgrounds, or learners who do not see themselves as being particularly 'good' at languages when taught as lists of grammar rules and vocabulary items, the use of tasks in conjunction with a non-linguistic macro-structure might provide a more comprehensible purpose in L2 courses. A fictional master framework, such as the detective school, can function metaphorically as well, and the role of metaphors in shaping learner concepts and behavior should not be underestimated. Metaphors exert their influence 'by instantiating frame-consistent knowledge structures', courses in a detective school that are metaphoric of the language curriculum and 'inviting structurally consistent inferences' that front the intellectual challenges that correlate to a less-visible target of language growth (Thibodeau & Boroditsky, 2011: 10).

Conclusion

As demonstrated by the other chapters in the present volume, the use of tasks in L2 instruction is supported by and relatively extensive body of empirical research and is gaining popularity in a variety of instructional contexts internationally. However, designing effective tasks is typically more challenging for teachers than designing traditional exercises. While a large body of literature has evolved that defines the role of tasks in the L2 curriculum and measures the effects of different tasks on language use, there is less information available about how tasks have been successfully used in published textbook materials. This chapter has offered some basic principles and examples of how this has been done in a textbook written nearly three decades ago in ways that are consistent with the principles of TBLT and which educators might wish to consider in designing their own tasks materials in diverse contexts internationally.

References

Albanese, M.A. and Mitchell, S. (1993) Problem-based learning: A review of literature on its outcomes and implementation issues. *Academic Medicine* 68 (1), 52–81.

Berwick, R. and Ross, S. (1989) Motivation after matriculation: Are Japanese learners of English still alive after exam hell? *JALT Journal* 11 (2), 193–210.

Butler, Y. (2011) The implementation of communicative and task-based language teaching in the Asia-Pacific region. *Annual Review of Applied Linguistics* 31, 36–57.

Butler, Y. (2017) Motivational elements of digital instructional games: A study of young L2 learners game designs. *Language Teaching Research* 21, 735–750.

DeKeyser, R. (2007) Skill acquisition theory. In B. VanPatten and J. Williams (eds) *Theories of Second Language Acquisition: An Introduction* (pp. 94–112). New York: Routledge.

Ellis, R. (2003) *Task-Based Language Teaching and Learning.* Oxford: Oxford University Press.

Ellis, R. (2009) Task-based language teaching: Sorting out the misunderstandings. *International Journal of Applied Linguistics* 19 (3), 221–246.

Ellis, R. (2018a) Taking the critics to task: The case for task-based teaching. *New Perspectives on the Development of Communicative and Related Competence in Foreign Language Education* 28, 23.

Ellis, R. (2018b) *Reflections on Task-Based Language Teaching.* Bristol: Multilingual Matters.

Hashimoto, Y. (2002) Motivation and willingness to communicate as predictors of reported L2 use: The Japanese ESL context. *Second Language Studies* 20 (2), 29–70.

Helgesen, M. and Kelly, C. (2014, March) *DIY NeuroELT – Making your textbook more brain-friendly.* Presentation at the TESOL 2014 International Convention & Language Expo, Portland, OR.

Kelly, C. and Kelly, E. (1991) *The Snoop Detective School Conversation Book: Information Gap Mysteries for Classroom Use.* Linguaphone Japan.

Lambert, C. (2017) Tasks, affect and second language performance. *Language Teaching Research* 21 (6), 657–664.

Lambert, C. (2019) *Referent Similarity and Nominal Syntax in Task-Based Language Teaching.* Singapore: Springer Nature.

Lambert, C., Philp, J. and Nakamura, S. (2017) Learner-generated content and engagement in second language task performance. *Language Teaching Research* 21 (6), 665–680.

Lambert, C. and Zhang, C. (2019) Engagement in the use of English and Chinese as foreign languages: The role of learner-generated content in instructional task design. *Modern Language Journal* 103 (2), 391–411.

Long, M.H. (1985) A role for instruction in second language acquisition: Task-based language teaching. In K. Hyltenstam and M. Pienemann (eds) *Modelling and Accessing Second Language Acquisition* (pp. 77–99). Clevedon: Multilingual Matters.

Long, M. (2015) *Second Language Acquisition and Task-Based Language Teaching.* Oxford: Wiley Blackwell.

Paradis, M. (2004) *A Neurolinguistic Theory of Bilingualism.* Amsterdam: John Benjamins.

Phung, L. (2017) Task preference, affective response, and engagement in L2 use in a US university context. *Language Teaching Research* 21, 651–666.

Prabhu, N. (1987) *Second Language Pedagogy* (Vol. 20). Oxford: Oxford University Press.

Robinson, P. (2010) Situating and distributing cognition across task demands: The SSARC model of pedagogic task sequencing. In M. Putz and L. Sicola (eds) *Cognitive Processing in Second Language Acquisition: Inside the Learner's Mind* (pp. 243–268). Amsterdam: John Benjamins.

Robinson, P. (2011) Second language task complexity, the cognition hypothesis, language learning, and performance. In P. Robinson (ed.) *Second Language Task Complexity: Researching the Cognition Hypothesis of Language Learning and Performance* (pp. 3–37). Amsterdam: John Benjamins.

Sato, R. (2010) Reconsidering the effectiveness and suitability of PPP and TBLT in the Japanese EFL classroom. *JALT Journal* 32(2), 189–200.

Skehan, P. (1996) Second language acquisition research and task-based instruction. In J. Willis and D. Willis (eds) *Challenge and Change in Language Teaching* (pp. 17–30). Oxford: Heinemann.

Skehan, P. (2009) Modelling second language performance: integrating complexity, accuracy, fluency and lexis. *Applied Linguistics* 30, 510–532.

Thibodeau, P. H. and Boroditsky, L. (2011) Metaphors we think with: The role of metaphor in reasoning. *PloS One* 6 (2), e16782.

Willis, J. (1996) *A Framework for Task-Based Learning.* Essex: Longman.

Yashima, T., MacIntyre, P. D. and Ikeda, M. (2018) Situated willingness to communicate in an L2: Interplay of individual characteristics and context. *Language Teaching Research* 22 (1), 115–137.

Appendix 4.1 'Bomb' Task Sequence from Kelly and Kelly (1991)

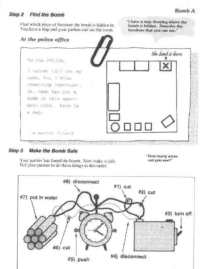

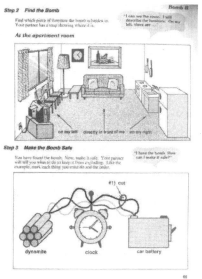

5 Using Technology-Mediated Tasks in Second Language Instruction to Connect Speakers Internationally

Marta González-Lloret

One of the main affordances of second or foreign language (L2) technology-mediated tasks is that they facilitate engagement among speakers of the L2 that are geographically remote, providing international education with a framework to foster intercultural understanding. This chapter presents successful technology-mediated tasks, undertaken by researchers in a variety of contexts, for the teaching of languages and the acquisition of intercultural competence. Several essential questions will be addressed to inform practitioners that are interested in incorporating technology-mediated tasks in their L2 classrooms. Issues and challenges of applying L2 technology-mediated tasks and recommendations to overcome them will be addressed. Finally, the chapter suggests research that is needed in the future to better understand the nature of technology-mediated tasks, their implementation, and the advantages that they have for international L2 instruction.

Introduction

In a growing multilingual world, learners across the globe need to be prepared for a society and a workforce in which a large part of communication is with people in other places, and mostly mediated by technology. Being able to use these modes of communication and understand authentic electronic discourses and engagement in digital communities are essential to prepare learners for a successful career and life in our technology-saturated world. In addition, to prepare technology-competent citizens, we need to educate our learners for an increasingly globalized world in which multilingualism is 'a normal and unremarkable necessity of everyday life for the majority of the world's population' (Romaine, 2008: 385). Being multilingual is usually equated with being able to speak a language, that is, to have language fluency, accuracy and complexity. We know, however, that being a competent speaker of a language involves more than being fluent. A capable speaker needs to engage in *appropriate* language use to effectively accomplish a communicative act. A speaker that is grammatically competent but inappropriate will be regarded as impolite or unfriendly (Thomas, 1983), and this may have critical consequences, especially in some situations such as business interactions, formal introductions, interviews, etc. As Björkman (2011) points out 'the aim in real high-stakes interaction is to communicate in a practical and functional fashion and achieve the desired outcome. In such settings, one needs to acquire an appropriate pragmatic competence to achieve effectiveness in communication' (2011: 923). Communicative competence has now been redefined 'in terms of cross-cultural understanding, intercultural and critical communicative competence' (Liddicoat & Crozet, 2000: 3). This chapter advocates that incorporating Technology-mediated Task-based Language Learning/ Teaching (TMTBLT) in the English as a Second Language (ESL) or English as a Foreign Language (EFL) classroom is an excellent approach to developing language competency (fluency, accuracy and complexity), language appropriateness (intercultural competence) as well as the digital and electronic communication skills required to succeed in a multilingual globalized society.

Task-Based Language Teaching

TBLT is based on an educational philosophy of experiential learning or 'learning by doing' (Dewey, 1938/1997) where the language is learned by doing something with it, rather than treating it as the object of learning. As Ellis (2009) points out, there are multiple versions of TBLT with different programmatic understandings of how to implement it. There are also multiple definitions of tasks which vary from more traditional language learning activities to things people do in everyday life outside of a classroom (i.e. Ellis, 2003; Long, 1985; Skehan, 1998). This is not uncommon in new fields of study. Although concepts of tasks and task-based curricula have existed for more than three decades (e.g. Candlin & Murphy, 1987; Prabhu, 1987), the field is still actively researching some of its basic underpinnings such as task complexity (as an essential characteristic of a task) and task sequencing (e.g. Robinson, 2011).

It is important to emphasize that, although the main focus of TBLT is communication, the goal of TBLT is not just the development of communicative effectiveness (to get the point across) but also to produce language that is fluent, accurate and complex. In addition, recently, several researchers (East, 2012; González-Lloret & Ortega, 2018; Taguchi & Kim, 2018) are advocating for language that is also *appropriate*. That is, tasks should also help learners become interactionally competent users, aware of the socio-pragmatics and intercultural norms of the L2.

Although some issues still need to be resolved, in general, TBLT researchers and practitioners agree that tasks can function as the building blocks of a curriculum. Task are understood (with some variation) as experiential (based on things that people need to do with language), communicative in nature, goal oriented, focused on meaning, (although language can be the focus of tasks; Ellis, 2009) and as authentic, contextualized and relevant to learners' needs as possible.

With these task characteristics in mind, the version of TBLT adopted in this chapter is one that considers all programmatic stages in the implementation of TBLT; from conducting a needs analysis (NA) (Long, 2015) to the development and implementation of materials, and learner assessment and program evaluation (Norris, 2009). It is also one that pays attention, not only to learning (and assessing) the language needed to conduct the task, but also the interactional, socio-pragmatic and intercultural issues that would allow for an appropriate and successful achievement of the task. This chapter advocates that technology can help realize such a version of a TBLT curriculum, in which learners engage in doing things with the language through tasks that are goal oriented, meaningful and as authentic as possible, that bring rich input, authentic language and intercultural interaction with other speakers of the language.

Technology-Mediated Tasks

One of the main affordances of second or foreign language (L2) technology-mediated tasks is that, if well designed, they can facilitate engagement among speakers of the L2 that are geographically remote, providing educators with a framework to help engage students in intercultural exchanges to foster active participation and interaction as well as opportunities for negotiation of differing perspectives and opinions, disagreement, resolution and consensus building (Meskill, 1999) as well as intercultural understanding (e.g. Belz, 2007; O'Dowd, 2003; Vinagre, 2010), which may then in turn help develop tolerance, mutual respect and an ethic of global citizenship, elements proposed by the United Nations (2015) in their General Assembly in their agenda for world transformation.

Tools for Interaction

Through technology, learners can engage in rich input and intercultural interaction that is often impossible face-to-face because of geographical, political or economic reasons. However, not all technologies are equally effective at promoting L2 and intercultural development; just bringing technologies into the language learning classroom is not going to produce learning. It is essential that their design, implementation and evaluation are guided by solid research on second language acquisition and intercultural development.

Early connections between technology and tasks explored the nature of the interaction that happened when a task was mediated by technology (mostly computer-mediated communication, CMC), providing recommendations on how to maximize the amount and quality of the interaction (Chapelle, 2001; Doughty & Long, 2003; Ortega, 2009; Skehan, 2003). A different strand of research concentrated on the effects of task design (type of task, difficulty, number of participants, etc.) on the quantity and quality of learners' interaction (Blake, 2000; Keller-Lally, 2006; Smith, 2003). The results of these first studies were quite inconclusive and the debate on these issues continues (Monteiro, 2014; Yilmaz & Yuksel, 2011). A few studies incorporated tools other than CMC to explore tasks through, for example, glosses (Plass *et al.*, 1998), video (Levy, 1999), web-based spaces (e.g. González-Lloret, 2003) and tasks delivered through interactional multimedia software (e.g. Schrooten, 2006). These studies suggested the potential that these tools had to enhance comprehension as well as to produce the rich interaction believed to promote language and cultural learning.

In an effort to move the interaction from within the classroom walls to engage learners in communication with other speakers, telecollaborative projects (teletandem) became and remain popular. During telecollaboration, learners from two institutions meet through CMC tools to discuss, negotiate and create some type of artifact (poster presentations for a conference, policies for a new building, a travel itinerary, etc.) using their L2. The collaborative projects usually occupy a large part of the course syllabus and have a strong intercultural learning goal. The tasks in these telecollaborative projects include discussion tasks, exploration of different cultural artifacts, presentations, development of websites, blogs, etc. These telecollaborative projects engage learners in authentic interaction, provide lots of language input and help develop cross-cultural awareness and sociocultural competence. See Helm (2015) and O'Dowd (2016) for recent reviews of the field.

In the last few years, the interest in technology-mediated tasks has spiked, as demonstrated by review studies (Lai & Li, 2011; Thomas, 2013) as well as volumes on TBLT and technology addressing both practical and theoretical matters (Al-Bulushi, 2010; González-Lloret & Ortega, 2014; Thomas & Reinders, 2010).

The number of tools and different technologies that are now employed within technology-mediated TBLT has grown exponentially. Among these, games and simulations have gained special attention because of the strong connections between gaming principles and the concepts behind TBLT (González-Lloret, 2017). For example, the structure of most games is goal-oriented, based on the completion of tasks (best known as 'quests'), which are sequenced according to principles of complexity (contextual, organizational, algorithmic, etc.). In order to accomplish these tasks, participants need to actively engage with the game (e.g. collect items, battle characters, solve clues) and most of the time with other players, which means producing meaningful language (written and/or spoken) to try to complete the task and move on in the game. In addition, game players shape the games by the actions they take and the decisions they make, much like speakers shape a task once they are immersed in it. Game players learn to play mainly by playing (as well as talking to other players, reading about the game, sharing tips in online spaces, etc.) which fits with TBLT's main educational philosophy of experiential learning. Researchers working in this area include Sykes (2012, 2014) and Collentine (2013), who have conducted several studies in immersive virtual environments that they have created.

Finally, mobile devices (phones especially) are gaining the attention of research trying to understand how learners interact and collaborate in the L2 with each other, around them, and with them, when trying to complete a task. Two recent studies (i.e. Hellerman *et al.*, 2013; Holden & Sykes, 2012) suggest that the device is the center of a large part of the interaction, facilitating interaction among the participants and within the environment. They also suggest that the person directing the talk tends to take control over the device and information derived from this is then made public and available through talk to the all the group members, which produces rich and interesting interaction among participants.

Writing Tools

Although theoretical and research work on task-based writing has been neglected in comparison with the oral mode (Byrnes & Manchón, 2014), in the field of technology-mediated TBLT, written tasks have received quite a lot of attention in a multiplicity of platforms such as text-based synchronous CMC (i.e. chat) (Adams & Nik, 2014; Baralt, 2013; Collentine, 2010), asynchronous CMC such as wikis and blogs (Adams *et al.*, 2014; Oskoz & Elola, 2014), online storytelling (Solares, 2014) and fandoms (Sauro, 2014). Several of these studies have focused on task complexity (Adams & Nik, 2014; Adams *et al.*, 2014; Baralt, 2013; Collentine, 2010), as well as how best to implement these technologies within a TBLT framework.

In addition to synchronous CMC, research has investigated asynchronous tools such as wikis and the role of planning on the fluency, complexity and accuracy of the writing (Adams *et al.*, 2014). This research has found that planning time can push learners to write more and to direct their attentional resources towards complexity or towards accuracy, but it does not necessarily improve the quality of their production. According to the authors, this may be related to the nature of writing on a wiki (i.e. more informal than an essay, with a chance to easily compare versions) but more research is needed to confirm this. Oskoz and Elola (2014) also found that different types of writing focused student attention on different aspects of language. While learners in their study focused more on accuracy during a linguistically less complex task such as expository writing, working with a more complex task such as argumentation may trigger syntactic complexity.

Recently, new tools and spaces that encourage technology-mediated writing through tasks are appearing. Among these, Fandoms, fanfiction sites and interest groups (e.g. Fanfiction.net, Reddit.com) are gaining popularity. These are environments where people join to read and write, and where the task is writing a piece within the norms and constraints of the group. These spaces provide teachers and learners with an excellent environment to develop pre-tasks (or pedagogic tasks) that can help the learner produce a quality piece to share with other readers (see Chapter 2, this volume). These pedagogic tasks are the activities that facilitate the learning of the vocabulary, language structures, cultural components, technologies, etc. that students need in order to be able to tackle the task. Writing a piece in such an environment is a meaningful, authentic, goal-oriented task. Allowing learners to choose a genre and/or a topic of their interest can also increase their motivation and engagement with the writing, as well as provide them with a sense of agency, an important feature of language learning success (Duff, 2012; Chapter 3, this volume). For an example of a Fandom task see Sauro (2014) and Sauro and Sundmark (2016) where first-year university English learners engaged in blog-based role-play storytelling (often found in online fandoms) to each voice a character for a missing moment from Tolkien's novel *The Hobbit*. Their research suggests that the tasks facilitated analysis of literary text, use of creative writing techniques and lexical development.

These examples demonstrate that technology-mediated TBLT is possible, and that it can have a positive impact on language teaching. In addition, research in the field of CALL (Computer-assisted Language Learning) in general suggest that the use of technology reduces learner's anxiety, it is a strong motivator and provides access to input, negotiation and feedback in ways impossible in a traditional classroom (see Ziegler (2016) for a detailed review of the affordances of technology in TBLT and in SLA in general). However, not all technology is equal and for technology to be effective, we need to pay close attention to the design of tasks incorporating technological tools, as well as their implementation.

In the following section, I will highlight some principles and issues that we need to keep in mind when developing (or adopting) and integrating technology-mediated tasks into the L2 curriculum. What technologies are most in line with TBLT principles? What do we need to consider when incorporating technology and tasks? How do we assess students? How do we evaluate whether the technology-mediated tasks are effective for learning?

Development of Intercultural Competence

Focusing on the advancement of L2 intercultural awareness and competency through technology-mediated tasks, a group of researchers have looked into the affordances of virtual environments (VE), such as Second Life, where thousands of users interact socially. Results of research in this area suggest that students find tasks in these spaces useful and highly motivating, especially when the tasks are well designed and collaborative in nature (Canto et al., 2014; Gánem-Gutiérrez, 2014; Thomas, 2013). Tasks in VEs promote negotiation of meaning, including intercultural communication routines (Canto et al., 2014), and the possibility of a 'physical simulation of real-life tasks' (Deutschmann & Panichi, 2009: 34). In addition, VEs allow students to re-engage with characters and the task environment which may produce high levels of lexical complexity, but this is highly dependent on the type of input they encounter (Collentine, 2011). Finally, tasks in VEs generate opportunities for casual conversation and social discourse which are largely absent from a traditional language classroom and are, however, essential to the repertoire of a language learner (Peña & Hancock, 2006; Thorne, 2010). For an example of a task conducted telecollaboratively in Second Life between learners of Spanish in the Netherlands and a Spanish-teacher in Spain, see the NIFLAR (now TeCoLa) European Project. In this task, the participants visit an apartment to live together and discuss their likes and dislikes, as well as the differences and similarities in ways of living in their respective countries.

These projects demonstrate how, through tasks, learners are able to negotiate each other's understandings of the other's culture and their own in ways that would be almost impossible without the technology. In the remainder of the chapter, I will outline some recommendations, deduced from the existing research and practice, for designing, integrating and evaluating technology and tasks.

Recommendations for Design, Integration and Evaluation of Tasks

When incorporating technology into our language classroom, we need to identify the role of the tasks and the technology in our L2 curriculum. This will help us undertake decisions while designing, integrating and evaluating the tasks. There are five questions that can help us identify what to include in our curriculum:

(1) What tasks will student need to be able to do?
(2) What language is involved in the completion of those tasks?
(3) What sociocultural knowledge is needed to be appropriate (and not just grammatically accurate) when doing the tasks?
(4) What technologies are needed to accomplish the tasks (or can facilitate them)?
(5) What are the technological capacities of the participants (their 'digital literacies' (Shetzer & Warschauer, 2000), their access to technology and the internet, etc.) and of the institution (technology, access, support, training, etc.)?

The best method to find the answers to these questions is to conduct a well-developed needs analysis with a balance of sources and methods to help decide which tasks, what language and which technologies to include in the curriculum (see González-Lloret (2014) for an example).

What Technologies?

It is important to understand that technology is integral to technology-mediated TBLT, but without 'technological determinism' (Warschauer, 2004). We need to develop a critical capacity for the 'analysis of the affordances of technology, needs of language learners, and opportunities missed when technology is selected' (Chapelle, 2014: 329). Consequently, the addition of technology should be driven by the analysis of learners' needs and conditions for task success, and it should be as carefully planned as any other aspect of task design. Needs analyses help us focus on what tasks our students will need to be able to do, which ones they want to be able to do and what technologies support, enhance or are needed to complete those tasks.

In general, the technologies that best fit principles of task-based instruction are those that help learners engage in doing things with the language and with others; that is, those technologies that provide 'sites for interpersonal communication, multimedia publication, distance learning, community participation, and identity formation' (Kern, 2006: 162). As we have seen in the examples above, video, audio or text CMC, as well as synthetic/virtual environments (Second Life, Quest Atlantis, etc.) facilitate interaction with others in remote spaces. Multiplayer online games provide opportunities for realistic, goal oriented tasks, as well as authentic input and interaction. Wikis, blogs, collaborative documents and fanfiction sites allow students to work collaboratively and perhaps to share written artifacts which contribute to the creation and distribution of knowledge. This provides a meaning-oriented communicative purpose and an authentic audience for communicative L2 use.

When selecting technologies, we are looking to integrate those that can potentially help minimize students' fear of failure, or embarrassment. We aim for technologies that can raise students' motivation to take risks and be creative while using language to make meaning. Such technologies enable students to meet other speakers of the language in remote locations. This is key to unlocking transformative exposure to authentic language environments and cultural representations. Engaging in interaction with other speakers outside of the class (many times of the same age as the L2 learners) can expose them to authentic input and language that does not often occur in the class; language that may be more colloquial and age appropriate. In addition, learners can use the language for what language is intended: real communication with real people, which is often motivating and at times transformative in the way learners see the target language and the target culture. It is also essential to integrate technology-mediated tasks that incorporate social dimensions of L2 learning such as identity construction, how we conceptualize privacy and social spaces, the role of pragmatics in communication, etc. (González-Lloret & Ortega, 2018). This can lead to the acquisition of intercultural competence. We want learners to be socially and culturally appropriate (and not just fluent, complex and accurate) in their communication.

Given the rapid changes in technology and innovation, predicting what tools learners will need in the future to be able to accomplish a task is almost impossible. For this reason, it is essential to focus on the affordances that technological innovations offer for language learning. In this way, when technology changes, we can revisit whether these components are intact. For example, we see different social media platforms gain and lose followers. The use of Facebook among teenagers has declined by 30% in the last six years while the use of Snapchat has increased by 35% (Jaffray, 2018). However, the potential of social networks to connect speakers of a language and share media-reach input remains unchanged. The pedagogic activities in the language classroom can be minimally modified to accommodate a change of platform.

Integration

Each technology-mediated task will require different specifications for integration depending on the existing institutional resources and whether students need to learn to use the technology before engaging in the task. It is crucial that the technology integrated into the full programmatic cycle that shapes the TBLT curriculum from needs analysis all the way to explicit learning outcomes for assessment and evaluation. Pedagogic tasks to learn the technology should be interlaced with language tasks to help learners accomplish the final target task (see González-Lloret (2014: 43–44) for a framework and an example of integration).

Integrating multiple technology-mediated tasks in the curriculum implies a method of sequencing these tasks. The issue of task sequencing (based on task complexity) is one of the most researched in TBLT. The results of studies of technology-mediated task complexity to date suggest that complexity principles such as those in Robinson's Cognition Hypothesis (2001, 2011) do not necessarily transfer to technology-mediated environments (Adams & Nik, 2014; Baralt, 2013). It could be because producing language in a chat is quite different from speaking, and/or because what is complex when we speak may not be so when we write in a chat. It seems that when learners do not feel pressure to communicate (when they chat), they can develop their language complexity (Collentine, 2010).

When integrating technology-mediated tasks, there are some pedagogic choices such as the use of group work around one device, versus pair work sharing a device, or individual work, how to provide feedback effectively, etc. as well as practical considerations such as where to find institutions and other practitioners with whom to collaborate, how much time to dedicate in the curriculum to the advancement of digital skills, etc. As for the pedagogic choices, they need to be in line with methodological principles of TBLT, but they may vary according to teacher choice and the affordances of the context. It is also important to keep in mind that the task that we plan (task-as-workplan) may be different from the task that takes place once the students start working on it (task-as-process) (e.g. Ellis, 2003; Seedhouse, 2005) so as teachers, we can plan the tasks that we think will be most effective. For example, we may want to include tasks with content generated by our learners, which Lambert *et al.* (2017) suggest are more engaging. Once students start the task, they may divert, and all we can do is try to keep them as close as possible to the plan without interfering with their performance. For answers on some of these practical issues, it is recommended to examine existing models in the specialized academic journals such as *CALICO*, *Language Learning & Technology*, *System*, *EuroCALL Review*, *ReCALL* and other published work written to guide practitioners through technology-mediated implementation (González-Lloret, 2016).

Assessment and Evaluation

In most contexts, technology-mediated TBLT will require some type of student assessment, both formative (to provide learners and teachers with an idea of the student's progress) and summative (to evaluate language and knowledge gains at the end of the course).

Program evaluation is also needed to determine the effectiveness of the curriculum. Although extremely important, these aspects of a TBLT curriculum tend to get the least attention. In TBLT, assessment is usually designed to provide learners with formative feedback to keep them improving until they are able to fully perform the target task. Formative assessment serves a motivational function, and it offers a frame of reference for teachers and learners about the learner's progress and the effectiveness of the pedagogic tasks (Norris, 2009). In addition, summative assessment is necessary to evaluate whether learners have achieved the specific outcomes for the lesson, course, etc. As in other forms of instruction, task-based practitioners need to know whether learners can perform the task and how accurately, fluently and culturally appropriately they can do it. However, those using technology-mediated tasks also need to know how effectively learners can use the technologies required to accomplish the task. One approach would be observing a simulation of the task performed with a speaker of the target language, a computer or the instructor. When assessing students, it helps to have a well-developed rubric with the categories to assess and the values given to them according to the course learning objectives. For some practitioners, it may be enough to see that students can perform the task, while most may prefer a numeric, more specific characterization of the learner's performance. For example, at a basic level of language, if we want to assess students on whether they are able to make a hotel reservation through the internet in the L2 and how well they are able to perform the task, we could use a basic rubric, such as the one in Figure 5.1 (with a scale as detailed as needed) to assess their language competence (reading, writing), their digital competence (use of the site), as well as their pragmatic competence (appropriateness of a personal request). For more information on how to create rubrics to assess technology-mediated tasks, and examples of technology-mediated assessments, see González-Lloret (2016).

The final step in a TBLT curriculum would be the evaluation of the technology-mediated tasks (and/or the full curriculum). If we want to know whether integrating technology-mediated tasks was effective for language learning, it would be important to find out whether the tasks that we are implementing are producing the desired outcomes (which can be observed through formative assessment) and enhance these data with other data sources such as learners' surveys or interviews, class observation, learning journals, etc. Nielson (2014) provides an excellent example of the evaluation of an intermediate task-based online Chinese course. To assess students, she collected data on students' participation on all pedagogic tasks, their performance-based assessment of each task, as well as two online surveys. To evaluate the course and whether the performance-based assessment was accurately measuring language gains, the students also completed a standardized test (STAMP) to measure

	2 points	1 point	0 points
Task Performance			
Student was able to perform the task	Yes	Yes, with difficulties	No
Digital Competency			
Student was able to navigate the site to find relevant information	Yes	Found most of the information	no
Student was able to write to the hotel requesting an accommodation (e.g. quite room, high floor, two beds)	Yes	Difficulty finding where and how	No
Language Competency			
Student found a hotel and a room following the given characteristics [demonstrates comprehension of written text]	Yes	Yes, with difficulties	No
The language of the message was accurate with the correct grammatical structures and vocabulary	Yes, without language errors	Some language errors	Lots of language errors
Pragmatic Competency			
The message was polite, using the appropriate register	Yes	Not completely appropriate	Inappropriate
The message included all parts needed in a short message communication	Yes	Some missing	Inadequate

Figure 5.1 Example of rubric to assess technology-mediated task: making a hotel reservation

their language ability. All these data helped her pinpoint elements to improve such as some pedagogic tasks, performance-based tests, and rubrics that the instructors had developed and needed to be fine tuned.

Challenges and Recommendations for Solving Them

Depending on the institution, a progressive change that starts by including a few technology-mediated tasks within a more traditional communicative curriculum may be wise. This would allow the different constituents to become familiar with the new method in small doses and evaluate its effectiveness in comparison to other activities in the curriculum. Regardless of the speed of change, an essential component for the successful implementation of technology-mediated tasks is teacher education. The chances of program success are much larger when teachers understand the methodology, believe in its efficacy and implement it correctly in the classroom. Without the appropriate methodological education, teachers may revert back to the techniques and classroom resources that are familiar to them. In addition, proper training on the use of the incorporated technologies is crucial. Technology can be highly intimidating for teachers without proper training and institutional support.

The technological capacity of institutions (hardware, software, internet access, facilities and technical support) as well as the digital literacies of teachers and students (and parents for school-age learners) are also decisive factors in the development of materials and the success of the program. Technology-mediated tasks do not necessarily require the most modern equipment and connections. The pedagogic tasks developed need to fit the constraints of the educational contexts in which they are used. In schools in rural areas with limited internet connections, for example, students might have cell phones with free data that allow tasks to be undertaken through mobile devices rather than in a computer lab. Also, connecting with others using video tools (i.e. Skype, FaceTime) may require a much stronger connection than sending pictures to our collaborative partner school using WhatsApp, Snapchat or Instagram. Such pictures can be used to share linguistic landscapes in different communities for students to discuss in their language classroom at a later time. Both sets of tools can aid on the performance of the same task, and it is up to the developer to understand the context where the pedagogic tasks are going to be performed, and to consider that digital literacy and access is not just a geographical issue. Digital literacy and access will vary according to economic status, education level and age.

Finally, we need more research into the nature of technology-mediated tasks, their implementation and the advantages that they have for international L2 instruction at different ages. At the same time, we need examples of developed and implemented technology-mediated task curricula (that have been researched and evaluated) as models for other institutions and practitioners. Hopefully, as technology access becomes more pervasive in schools and universities, we will see such models to help the field of technology-mediated task L2 education grow theoretically and practically.

References

Adams, R. and Nik, A.N.M. (2014) Prior knowledge and second language task production in text chat. In M. González-Lloret and L. Ortega (eds) *Technology-Mediated TBLT: Researching Technology and Tasks* (pp. 51–78). Amsterdam: John Benjamins Publishing Company.

Adams, R., Amani, S., Newton, J. and Nik, A.N.M. (2014) Planning and production in computer-mediated communication (CMC) writing. In H. Byrnes and R. M. Manchón (eds) *Task-Based Language Learning* (Vol. 7, pp. 137–161). Amsterdam: John Benjamins Publishing Company. doi:10.1075/tblt.7.06ada.

Al-Bulushi, A. (2010) *Task-Based Computer-Mediated Negotiation in an EFL Context: The Ins and Outs of Online Negotiation of Meaning Using Language Learning Tasks.* Saarbrucken: VDM Verlag Dr. Muller.

Baralt, M. (2013) The impact of cognitive complexity on feedback efficacy during online versus face- to-face interactive tasks. *Studies in Second Language Acquisition* 35 (4), 689–725.

Belz, J.A. (2007) The development of intercultural communicative competence in telecollaborative partnerships. In R. O'Dowd (ed.) *Online Intercultural Exchange: An*

Introduction for Foreign Language Teachers (pp. 127–166). Clevedon: Multilingual Matters.

Blake, R.J. (2000) Computer-mediated communication: A window on L2 Spanish interlanguage. *Language Learning and Technology* 4 (1), 120–136.

Björkman, B. (2011) The pragmatics of English as a lingua franca in the international university: Introduction. *Journal of Pragmatics* 43, 923–925. doi:10.1016/j.pragma.2010.08.015.

Byrnes, H. and Manchón, R.M. (2014) Task-based language learning. Insights from and for L2 writing. An introduction. In H. Byrnes and R. Manchón (eds) *Task-Based Language Learning: Insights From and For L2 Writing* (pp. 1–23). Amsterdam; John Benjamins Publishing Company.

Candlin, C. and Murphy, D. (1987) *Language Learning Tasks.* Englewood Cliffs, NJ: Prentice Hall.

Cantó, S., de Graff, R. and Jauregui, K. (2014) Collaborative tasks for negotiation of intercultural meaning in virtual worlds and video-web communication. In M. González-Lloret and L. Ortega (eds) *Technology-Mediated TBLT: Researching Technology and Tasks* (pp. 183–212). Amsterdam: John Benjamins Publishing Company.

Chapelle, C. (2001) *Computer Applications in Second Language Acquisition: Foundations for Teaching, Testing, and Research.* Cambridge: Cambridge University Press.

Chapelle, C. (2014) Afterword: Technology-mediated TBLT and the evolving role of the innovator. In M. González-Lloret and L. Ortega (eds) *Technology-Mediated TBLT: Researching Technology and Tasks* (pp. 323–334). Amsterdam: John Benjamins Publishing Company.

Collentine, K. (2010) Measuring complexity in task-based synchronous computer-mediated communication. In M. Thomas amd H. Reinders (eds) *Task-Based Language Learning and Teaching with Technology* (pp. 105–130). London; New York: Continuum.

Collentine, K. (2011) Learner autonomy in a task-based 3D world and production. *Language Learning & Technology* 15 (3), 50–67.

Collentine, K. (2013) Using tracking technologies to study the effects of linguistic complexity in CALL input and SCMC output. *CALICO Journal* 30, 46–65.

Deutschmann, M. and Panichi, L. (2009) Instructional design, teacher practice and learner autonomy. In J. Molka-Danielsen and M. Deutschmann (eds) *Learning and Teaching in the Virtual World of Second Life* (pp. 27–43). Trondheim: Tapir Academic Press.

Dewey, J. (1938/1997) *Experience and Education.* New York: Simon & Schuster.

Doughty, C. and Long, M.H. (2003) Optimal psycholinguistic environments for distance foreign language learning. *Language Learning & Technology* 7 (3), 50–80.

Duff, P.A. (2012) Identity, agency, and second language acquisition. In S.M. Gass and A. Mackey (eds) *The Routledge Handbook of Second Language Acquisition* (pp. 410–426). New York: Routledge.

East, M. (2012) Addressing the intercultural via task-based language teaching: Possibility or problem? *Language and Intercultural Communication* 12 (1), 56–73.

Ellis, R. (2003) *Task-Based Language Learning and Teaching.* Oxford: Oxford University Press.

Ellis, R. (2009) Task-based language teaching: Sorting out the misunderstandings. *International Journal of Applied Linguistics* 19 (3), 221–246.

Gánem-Gutiérrez, G.A. (2014) The third dimension: A sociocultural theory approach to the design and evaluation of 3D virtual worlds tasks. In M. González-Lloret and L. Ortega (eds) *Technology-Mediated TBLT: Researching Technology and Tasks* (pp. 213–238). Amsterdam; Philadelphia: John Benjamins Publishing Company.

González-Lloret, M. (2003) Designing task-based call to promote interaction: En Busca de Esmeraldas. *Language Learning & Technology* 7 (1), 86–104.

González-Lloret, M. (2014) The need for Needs Analysis in technology-mediated TBLT. In M. González-Lloret and L. Ortega (eds) *Technology-Mediated TBLT: Researching Technology and Tasks* (pp. 23–50). Amsterdam: John Benjamins Publishing Company.

González-Lloret, M. (2016) *A Practical Guide to Integrating Technology into Task-Based Language Teaching*. Washington, DC: Georgetown University Press.

González-Lloret, M. (2017) Technology and task-based language teaching. In S. Thorne and S. May (eds) *Language and Technology. Encyclopedia of Language and Education*. (pp. 1–13). Cham: Springer International Publishing. doi:10.1007/978-3-319-02328-1_16-1.

González-Lloret, M. and Ortega, L. (2014) Towards technology-mediated TBLT: An introduction. In M. González-Lloret and L. Ortega (eds) *Technology-Mediated TBLT: Researching Technology and Tasks* (pp. 1–22). Amsterdam: John Benjamins Publishing Company.

González-Lloret, M. and Ortega, L. (2018) Pragmatics, tasks, and technology: A synergy. In N. Taguchi and Y. Kim (eds) *Task-Based Approaches to Teaching and Assessing Pragmatics* (pp. 191–214). John Benjamins Pub. Company.

Hellermann, J., Thorne, S.L., Lester, D. and Jones, A. (2013) Walking and talking as a group: Interactional practices for playing an AR game with a mobile digital device. *Bellaterra Journal of Teaching & Learning Language & Literature* 6 (2), 1–26.

Helm, F. (2015) The practices and challenges of telecollaboration in higher education in Europe. *Language, Learning and Technology* 19 (2), 197–217.

Holden, C. and Sykes, J.M. (2012) *Mentira*: Prototyping language-based locative gameplay. In S. Dikkers, J. Martin and B. Coulter (eds) *Mobile Media Learning: Amazing Uses of Mobile Devices for Teaching and Learning* (pp. 111–131). Pittsburg: ETC Press.

Jaffray, P. (2018) *Most popular social networks of teenagers in the United States from fall 2012 to fall 2018*. Germany: Statista. Retrieved from https://www.statista.com/statistics/250172/social-network-usage-of-us-teens-and-young-adults/.

Keller-Lally, A.M. (2006) Effect of task-type and group size on foreign language learner output in synchronous computer-mediated communication. Unoublish PhD dissertation, University of Texas at Austin, Ann Arbor.

Kern, R. (2006) Perspectives on technology in learning and teaching languages. *TESOL Quarterly* 40, 183–210.

Lai, C. and Li, G. (2011) Technology and Task-Based Language Teaching: A critical review. *CALICO Journal* 28, 498–521.

Lambert, C., Philp, J. and Nakamura, S. (2017) Learner-generated content and engagement in second language task performance. *Language Teaching Research* 21 (6), 665–680.

Levy, M. (1999) Theory and design in a multimedia CALL project in cross-cultural pragmatics. *Computer Assisted Language Learning* 12, 29–57.

Liddicoat, A. and Crozet, C. (2000) Teaching culture as an integrated part of language: implications for the aims, approaches and pedagogies of language teaching. In A.J. Liddicoat and C. Crozet (eds) *Teaching Languages, Teaching Cultures*. (pp. 1–18). Merlbourne: Language Australia.

Long, M.H. (1985) Input and second language acquisition theory. In S. Gass and C. Madden (eds) *Input and Second Language Acquisition*. Newbury House: Rowley.

Long, M. (2015) *Second Language Acquisition and Task-Based Language Teaching* (First Edition). Malden, MA: Wiley-Blackwell.

Meskill, C. (1999) Computers as tools for sociocollaborative language learning. In K. Cameron (ed.) *Computer Assisted Language Learning: Media, Design and Applications* (pp. 141–162). Lisse: Swets and Zeitlinger.

Monteiro, K. (2014) An experimental study of corrective feedback during video-conferencing. *Language Learning & Technology* 18 (3), 56–79.

Nielson, K.B. (2014) Evaluation of an online, task-based Chinese course. In M. González-Lloret and L. Ortega (eds) *Technology-Mediated TBLT: Researching Technology and Tasks*. Amsterdam: John Benjamins Publishing Company.

Norris, J.M. (2009) Task-based teaching and testing. In M.H. Long and C.J. Doughty (eds) *The Handbook of Language Teaching* (pp. 578–594). Malden, MA: Wiley-Blackwell.

O'Dowd, R. (2003) Understanding the "other side": Intercultural learning in a Spanish-English e-mail exchange. *Language Learning and Technology* 7 (2), 118–144.

O'Dowd, R. (2016) Emerging trends and new directions in telecollaborative learning. *CALICO Journal* 33 (3), 291–310. doi:10.1558/cj.v33i3.30747.

Ortega, L. (2009) Interaction and attention to form in L2 text-based computer-mediated communication. In A. Mackey and C. Polio (eds) *Multiple Perspectives on Interaction in SLA: Research in Honor of Susan M. Gass*. New York: Erlbaum/Routledge/Taylor & Francis.

Oskoz, A. and Elola, I. (2014) Promoting foreign language collaborative writing through the use of Web 2.0 tools and tasks. In M. González-Lloret and L. Ortega (eds) *Technology-Mediated TBLT: Researching Technology and Tasks* (pp. 115–148). Amsterdam ; Philadelphia: John Benjamins Publishing Company.

Peña, J. and Hancock, J.T. (2006) An analysis of socioemotional and task communication in online multiplayer video games. *Communication Research* 33 (1), 92–109.

Plass, J., Chun, D., Mayer, R. and Leutner, D. (1998) Supporting visual and verbal learning preferences in a second-language multimedia learning environment. *Journal of Educational Psychology* 90 (1), 25–36.

Prabhu, N.S. (1987) *Second Language Pedagogy*. Oxford: Oxford University Press.

Robinson, P. (2001) Task complexity, task difficulty, and task production: exploring interactions in a componential framework. *Applied Linguistics* 22 (1), 27–57.

Robinson, P. (2011) Second language task complexity, the Cognition Hypothesis, language learning, and performance. In P. Robinson (ed.) *Researching Task Complexity: Task Demands, Task-Based Language Learning and Performance* (pp. 3–38). Amsterdam: John Banjamins.

Romaine, S. (2008) The bilingual and multilingual community. In T.K. Bhatia and W.C. Ritchie (eds) *The Handbook of Bilingualism* (pp. 385–405). Oxford: John Wiley & Sons. Retrieved from http://public.eblib.com/choice/publicfullrecord.aspx?p=214149.

Sauro, S. (2014) Lessons from the fandom: Technology-mediated tasks for language learning. In M. González-Lloret and L. Ortega (eds) *Technology-Mediated TBLT: Researching Technology and Tasks* (pp. 239–262). Amsterdam; Philadelphia: John Benjamins Publishing Company.

Sauro, S. and Sundmark, B. (2016) Report from Middle-Earth: Fan fiction tasks in the EFL classroom. *ELT Journal* 70 (4), 414–423. doi:10.1093/elt/ccv075.

Schrooten, W. (2006) TBLT and ICT: Developing and assessing interactive multimedia for task-based language teaching. In K. van den Branden (ed.) *Task-Based Language Education: From Theory to Practice* (pp. 129–150). Cambridge: Cambridge University Press.

Seedhouse, P. (2005) "Task" as research construct. *Language Learning* 55 (3), 533–570.

Shetzer, H. and Warschauer, M. (2000) An electronic literacy approach to network-based language teaching. In M. Warschauer and R. Kern (eds) *Network-Based Language Teaching: Concepts and Practice* (pp. 171–185). Cambridge: Cambridge University Press.

Skehan, P. (1998) *A Cognitive Approach to Language Learning*. Oxford: Oxford University Press.

Skehan, P. (2003) Focus on form, tasks, and technology. *Computer Assisted Language Learning* 16, 391–411. doi:10.1076/call.16.5.391.29489.

Smith, B. (2003) Computer-mediated negotiated interaction: An expanded model. *The Modern Language Journal* 87, 38–57.

Solares, M. E. (2014) Textbooks, tasks, and technology: An action research study in textbook-bound EFL context. In M. González-Lloret and L. Ortega (eds) *Technology-Mediated TBLT: Researching Technology and Tasks* (pp. 79–114). Amsterdam: John Benjamins Publishing Company.

Sykes, J.M. (2012) Synthetic immersive environments and second language pragmatic development. In C.A. Chapelle (ed.) *The Encyclopedia of Applied Linguistics*. Oxford: Blackwell Publishing Ltd. doi.wiley.com/10.1002/9781405198431.wbeal1136.

Sykes, J.M. (2014) TBLT and synthetic immersive environments: What can in-game task restarts tell us about design and implementation? In M. González-Lloret and L. Ortega (eds) *Technology-Mediated TBLT: Researching Technology and Tasks* (pp. 149–182). Amsterdam; Philadelphia: John Benjamins Publishing Company.

Taguchi, N. and Kim, Y. (eds) (2018) *Task-Based Approaches to Teaching and Assessing Pragmatics*. John Benjamins Pub. Company.

Thomas, J. (1983) Cross-cultural pragmatic failure. *Applied Linguistics* 4, 91–112.

Thomas, M. (2013) Task-based language teaching and CALL. In M. Thomas, H. Reinders and M. Warschauer (eds) *Contemporary Computer-Assisted Language Learning* (pp. 341–358). New York: Continuum.

Thomas, M. and Reinders, H. (eds) (2010) *Task-Based Language Learning and Teaching with Technology*. London: Continuum.

Thorne, S.L. (2010) The intercultural turn and language learning in the crucible of New Media. In S. Guth and F. Helm (eds) *Telecollaboration 2.0: Language, Literacies and Intercultural Learning in the 21st Century* (pp. 139–164). Bern; New York: Peter Lang.

United Nations (2015) *Transforming our world: the 2030 agenda for sustainable development* (General Assembly resolution No. A /RES/70/1). Retrieved from http://www.un.org/en/development/desa/population/migration/generalassembly/docs/globalcompact/A_RES_70_1_E.pdf.

Vinagre, M. (2010) Intercultural learning in asynchronous telecollaborative exchanges: A case study. *The Eurocall Review* 17. http://www.eurocall-languages.org/uploaded/EUROCALL_Review/review17.pdf.

Warschauer, M. (2004) Technological change and the future of CALL. In S. Fotos and C. Brown (eds) *New Perspectives on CALL for Second and Foreign Language Classrooms* (pp. 15–25). Mahwah, NJ: Lawrence Erlbaum Associates.

Yilmaz, Y. and Yuksel, D. (2011) Effects of communication mode and salience on recasts: A first exposure study. *Language Teaching Research* 15, 457–477.

Ziegler, N. (2016) Taking technology to task: technology-mediated TBLT, performance, and production. *Annual Review of Applied Linguistics* 36, 136–163. doi:10.1017/S0267190516000039.

6 Using Tasks within Neoliberal Educational Environments

Lindy Norris

This chapter examines tasks, and the implications for their use, within educational environments that are increasingly shaped by the values of the market-based economy and neoliberal ideology. The chapter begins with a brief description of aspects of neoliberal educational policy and reform that impact teachers' work and students' learning and achievement. Attention is then focused on tasks and task-based language teaching (TBLT). Characteristics of tasks are identified and examined with a view to investigating their compatibility within the neoliberal educational environment. Examples from the Australian educational context are used to illustrate this relationship. The chapter includes a discussion of challenges and constraints, but also of the possible benefits, associated with prioritising tasks within school language learning contexts that are constrained by the forces of neoliberalism.

Introduction

In a volume dedicated to the use of tasks in language learning and teaching, in contexts that are diverse and international, a discussion of the influence of neoliberalism in education is salient. So what is this thing called neoliberalism? According to Flubacher and Del Percio it:

> ... can best be described as a unifying or umbrella term to address a broad range of social, cultural and political transformations that reflect the priorities and values of a market-based economy, increasingly global in reach and integration, yet local and often personal in its workings. (2017: xi)

In essence, a set of economic principles has come to colonise very many aspects of our lives including education. Global and local educational environments are now routinely shaped by, and subject to, the values of neoliberalism. What this means for language education and for the use of tasks, and task-based approaches, is the subject of this chapter and will be explored in detail.

Ellis (2009: 222) in a discussion of how task-based language teaching challenges mainstream views of language teaching and learning, highlights the importance of 'nurturing the learner's natural language learning capacity' rather than 'making a systematic attempt to teach the language bit by bit'. Such an approach would appear to be at odds with the neoliberal educational agenda with its bureaucratisation and its focus on top-down conformity for school systems, for schools and also for students. Ellis (2018) also articulates principles and practices associated with the use of tasks. He stresses the need for teacher involvement and originality. He also emphasises the importance of learner reliance on their own linguistic and non-linguistic resources. Principles such as these also seem not to cohere with the conformity that is often characteristic of neoliberal education. These examples suggest competing values between the theoretical positioning of tasks and the expectations of education within the neoliberal environment. These tensions will be the subject of examination and critique within the following discussion.

Practical considerations are also significant and will be examined. The use of tasks has implications for teachers' work, particularly with respect to curriculum design, development and enactment, and also for assessment. The alignment of these areas with neoliberal policy and curriculum reform will be investigated and disconnects identified and discussed. It will be argued that managing language classrooms and curricula, in the face of neoliberal educational expectations, can present significant challenges for schools and for language teachers and their learners.

The chapter also addresses the possible benefits associated with prioritising the use of tasks, even within what is perceived as a hostile educational environment. Strategies to contest neoliberal discourses, and support the use of tasks in language learning, will be proposed.

All examples used within the discussion are from the Australian educational context. It is argued, however, that the issues and ideas presented and explored here may resonate more broadly for language educators working in global contexts that are impacted by neoliberal ideology and practices.

Neoliberalism and Education

In the last few decades, education systems all over the world have been impacted by the rise of neoliberalism and associated political, economic and cultural agendas (Connell, 2013). Education is now described as a commodity (Gao, 2017) or as an industry (Lingard *et al.*,

2013) that is influenced by 'market logic' (Connell, 2013: 102). As a result, the educational environment has become profoundly different, particularly with respect to policy, and to the imposition of standards, and the use of testing regimes and accountability processes.

Down and Sullivan (2019) describe the arena in which education policy is now made as consisting of neoliberal politicians, businessmen, measurement experts, economists and education system managers. The injection of 'out of education' stakeholders results in a significant shift with governments, not educators, defining curriculum content and creating curriculum standards to control what is taught in schools. In addition, the specification of curriculum standards is nearly always accompanied by measurement and accountability strategies often enacted through mandated testing (Ross & Gibson, 2006).

Intensified testing regimes have become a central part of the neoliberal agenda in education and are the subject of considerable critical commentary in the literature (Connell, 2013; Down & Sullivan, 2019; Lingard *et al.*, 2013). There are increased levels of control built into educational systems. This results in intensified pressure on schools and teachers, together with a narrowing of curriculum and a skewed focus on testing and test-based accountability.

In such circumstances there is a focus on what is testable. Teachers teach to the test and towards satisfying stringent accountability requirements. In such an educationally reductive environment the capacity for teachers to be able to develop curricula that are appropriate to their actual learners is both undermined and diminished. The question then becomes what does this mean for the use of tasks and TBLT? Willis and Willis (2007) make the point that task-based teaching is not designed with tests in mind. They assert that engaging actual learners in real language use in the classroom, as preparation for language use in the real world, is the focus. It is possible for teachers to accommodate this focus using criterion-referenced, real or simulated task-based performance tests (Bachman & Palmer, 1996; Ellis, 2003; Long, 2015). This is often not easy, however, within the neoliberal educational environment. Curriculum and assessment constraints, and the emphasis on norm-referenced testing measures and the comparison of students, suggest that task requirements and TBLT assessment practices, may not sit comfortably within the neoliberal educational agenda.

Neoliberalism: Changing Roles and Relationships in Schools

Neoliberalism has impacted education in other ways. With the redefinition of education as commodity, schools increasingly conduct themselves more like firms or companies (Connell, 2013). The neoliberal school is different, and within it, roles and relationships are changing. Principals and members of school administrative teams assume roles more akin to business managers than those traditionally ascribed to school leadership positions. This is highlighted by Lynch *et al.* (2015) who comment on the difficulties of balancing increasing performativity and new managerialist demands with the more traditional ethical and moral dimensions of leadership roles in education.

Redefined roles can also require a re-adjustment of relationships between members of the school community. This is particularly significant with respect to teachers who can find themselves isolated from decision making and thus in a different relational space with respect to school leadership, and sometimes also with their peers. Connell (2013: 207–208) links this to what she describes as schools 'being tied more tightly into a system of remote control … [where] there is an inevitable de-professionalisation of teachers'. This can be observed in areas such as the relational distance between teachers and the artefacts of teaching (such as curriculum, textbooks and resources) as well as in relationships with the learners themselves.

Interestingly, Connell (2013: 104) comments further on relationships in schools. She describes education as 'care' and as necessitating encounter between 'people capable of encounter; that is, people with significant autonomy'. She challenges the extent to which the neoliberal school is able to accommodate this, both with respect to teachers' work and also students' learning. Teachers' capacity to shape student experience can be curtailed by compliance and accountability requirements. There may also be restrictions on learner autonomy. Learners may have limited ability to engage in tasks if they are constrained in how they are able to use their own linguistic and non-linguistic resources in the enactment of the language curriculum.

Defining Tasks and Exploring their Characteristics

The previous sections of this chapter identify characteristics of the neoliberal educational environment that have the potential to influence the application of tasks and task-based teaching approaches in contemporary school environments. In this section the discussion will shift and the characteristics of tasks and task-based teaching will be examined.

Ahmadian (2016: 377) describes TBLT as both innovative in terms of language teaching and also a thriving area of investigation in the field of second language acquisition (SLA). The focus in this chapter is not on tasks and SLA research, but on the use of tasks and task-based teaching in school language learning contexts. The discussion draws extensively (though not exclusively) on the large body of work developed in this area, over several decades, by Rod Ellis.

In task-based teaching, tasks serve as the organising principle for a course (Ellis, 2018). They form the 'hub' for a full range of learning processes (Bygate, 2016: 386). Task-based teaching, however, is not rigid. Ellis (2009, 2018) makes the point that multiple versions exist, and that they are practised in a variety of ways in different language learning and teaching contexts. But what about the nature of tasks themselves? What are tasks? Whilst there is considerable debate within the literature about the definition of a 'task' (Long, 1985; Nunan, 1989; Bygate *et al.*, 2013), there is a general consensus that one characteristic has to be a focus on meaning.

Ellis, however, goes further, and with respect to the discussion here, it is the Ellis definition that will be applied in the present chapter. He states that for a language teaching activity to be a 'task' it must satisfy the following criteria:

- The primary focus is on meaning.
- There is some kind of 'gap' (i.e. a need to convey information, to express an opinion or to infer meaning).
- Learners rely mainly on their own linguistic and non-linguistic resources.
- There is a clearly defined communicative outcome.

(Ellis, 2009; Ellis & Shintani, 2014)

A task, therefore, is quite different from other exercises and activities utilised within a language learning context. Discrete-point tests, language rehearsal activities, and the completion of worksheets and workbook exercises where language is segmented and there is a 'focus on forms' (Long & Robinson, 1998; Long, 2000), are not tasks.

Ellis (2003, 2009, 2018) has discussed other features of tasks and task-based teaching extensively. It is not the intention here to critique this work in detail, but rather to identify a number of additional features, that are likely to impact the use of tasks in neoliberal influenced school classrooms. According to Ellis (2018: 160), all tasks involve the same kind of interactional processes (such as the negotiation of meaning and form, scaffolding, inferencing and monitoring) that arise in naturally occurring language use. Tasks also require detail in planning and execution, and teachers must be involved in the development of the task and associated materials. Ellis also comments on the need for originality (Ellis, 2018: 174). For teachers then, the use of tasks requires planning and action that goes beyond what may be articulated in curriculum documentation, or the textbook and assessment packages, that are prevalent and often mandated in the neoliberal educational environment.

For learners, too, the implications associated with task use go further. Involvement in interactional processes, such as those described above, requires personal responsibility and investment in the task process, and can require learner-generated content (Lambert *et al.*, 2017). It also means that to some extent at least, how learners perform a task will be unpredictable (Ellis, 2018: 1).

It can be seen, therefore, that task criteria and features can take tasks and their use beyond and outside of the compliance, conformity and accountability constraints often associated with neoliberal curricula and associated educational practices. The discourses of tasks in language, and neoliberalism in education, seem to be somewhat at odds. Tasks as real communicative use of language, by individual learners, contrasts sharply with education as commodity, situated within the neoliberal national enterprise.

The Compatibility of Tasks and Neoliberal Education: Practical Considerations

The discussion thus far has been primarily focused on the theoretical dimensions of neoliberalism and the use of tasks. The discussion now moves to a more detailed exemplification of practical issues and challenges arising from the confluence of tasks and neoliberalism. The section will be framed by three significant dimensions of teachers' work: curriculum and instructional programs, teacher and learner roles and responsibilities and assessment and accountability. Data informing this section are qualitative and are drawn primarily from teacher report, (their stories and commentaries), sourced through professional learning programs conducted by the author between 2016 and 2018. Classroom observation and the shadowing of teachers have also contributed valuable insights and information with respect to the interface between the use of tasks and the meeting of neoliberal influenced curriculum requirements. Various forms of educational documentation pertaining to the Australian curriculum, to jurisdictional requirements and to specific schools have also been analysed to inform the discussion in this section.

Curriculum and Instructional Programs

The Australian educational context is strongly influenced by neoliberalism. A visit to the homepage of the Australian Curriculum, Assessment and Reporting Authority (ACARA) reveals this through the three areas of responsibility identified and described on the site:

- Australian Curriculum
  'The Australian Curriculum sets the expectations for what all young Australians should be taught, regardless of where they live in Australia or their background'.
- NAP (National Assessment Program)
  'NAP provides the measure through which governments, education authorities and schools can determine whether or not young Australians are meeting important educational outcomes'.

- *My School*
  'The *My School* website is a resource for parents, educators and the community to find important information about each of Australia's schools. *My School* contains data on a school's student profile, NAPLAN (National Assessment Program Literacy and Numeracy) performance, funding levels and sources and other financial information'.

  (ACARA, 2018)

Curriculum is top-down and prescriptive, assessment is a measure foremost for the use of governments, and schools are positioned with respect to each other, and in terms of performance and the provision of financial information. Language teachers report feeling pressured and constrained by this situation. They also comment on their limited freedom to be able to develop in-school instructional programs that are flexible and that can accommodate the needs of specific learners. There is a significant level of frustration because schools demand programs that are 'set in stone' with respect to content, delivery timeframes, and assessment regimes. All this information is collated by schools, (and often using templates that are not task-based language teaching friendly), and is communicated to parents, as well as students.

When asked about how task-based teaching fits within this particular way of doing things, teacher responses identify significant concerns. Many feel that they don't have the time to develop and include tasks in a meaningful way because of prescribed curriculum content, limited language teaching time allocations and onerous sector and school accountability requirements. Some teachers also feel pressured by parents who use their 'customer' status to justify surveillance of what teachers do. Some state that it can be easier, and less stressful to acquiesce to the textbook or a prescriptive, clearly laid out instructional plan than to teach using tasks. Interestingly, teachers also report that school administrative or leadership teams often do not understand the implications of a task-based approach. Teachers who use tasks share their stories of being challenged by administrators because their instructional programs do not fit the 'norm', and because classrooms are noisy and can appear disorganised. And then there are those teachers who admit to not understanding task-based teaching and who are comfortable with a more traditional syllabus, or curriculum, that they can easily follow step by step. Oliver and Bogachenko (2018, Chapter 10, this volume) report similar findings. Teacher confusion and concern, and different levels of awareness, impact the application of task-based teaching approaches.

Curriculum documentation and teacher commentary suggest a significant disconnect here between how neoliberal curriculum is structured and managed compared with task-based teaching. The lack of teacher control stands out. This contrasts markedly with the need for teacher control in task design. Tasks involve considerable detail. Teachers need to be involved in the development of their task materials, and a high degree of originality should be evident (Ellis, 2018). The neoliberal curriculum can be beyond teacher control, it is often 'other-directed' (Ellis & Shintani, 2014: 53). Thus, significant characteristics of task-based teaching, as it relates to curriculum design, often cannot be satisfied within the neoliberal educational environment.

Teacher and Learner Roles and Responsibilities

How teachers see themselves, and their roles and responsibilities, in connection with curriculum design and delivery, requires further explication. As previously discussed, the neoliberal educational environment can shift and change language teacher roles and responsibilities. For language teachers, professionally respected control can become professionally expected compliance. For teachers who wish to use tasks and task-based teaching, this has been shown to be challenging. Teacher roles and responsibilities are, however, influenced in other ways. Conversations with teachers and classroom observation are particularly telling.

Many teachers see their primary professional responsibility to be the delivery of the explicit curriculum. They feel that introducing tasks, as defined by Ellis, requires deviation from the curriculum, and an alteration to classroom practices. This appears to be of particular concern for secondary school teachers preparing students for high-stakes examinations. Regardless of possible benefits associated with language use and the development of communicative ability, these teachers either use tasks sparingly, or avoid them altogether, in order to 'get through' curriculum content, rehearse for assessment processes, and adhere to systemic and school-based 'quality' and accountability requirements.

Roles and responsibilities are also determined by teachers' own teaching philosophy and theoretical understandings of second language acquisition (SLA) and language learning. Interestingly, this can be associated with particular languages and also different cultures of learning (Cortazzi & Jin, 2013). Conversations with Chinese teachers, and observations of Chinese teaching, for example, suggest that the primacy of knowledge of the rules of language results in a focus on forms being prioritised over meaning. This naturally restricts the use of tasks, even when teachers profess to want their students to be able to achieve clearly defined communicative outcomes. This concurs with Ellis (2009: 242) who states that when teachers see their role to be one of facilitating knowledge-learning rather than skill development a task-based approach to language teaching is not readily compatible.

In the neoliberal educational climate where managerialism has consumed teacher responsibility for teachers' work and replaced it with an onerous 'tick box' accountability regime, prioritising the teaching of grammar can also seem more manageable. With teachers reporting their working environments to be increasingly stressful, the added complexity of creating the conditions for task-based teaching is often a secondary consideration.

For teachers in Australian primary schools, there are additional considerations that work against task-based language teaching. The Australian government requires national testing for English literacy and for numeracy (NAPLAN). These tests are an annual assessment for students in Years 3, 5, 7 and 9. They are referred to as 'an everyday part of the school calendar' (ACARA, 2018). The 'everyday' focus of NAPLAN, however, negatively impacts the teaching and learning of languages other than English in a number of ways. English literacy is paramount, and this results in a narrowing of subject offerings in the primary school curriculum. Students have reduced opportunities to learn other languages. Resources and time allocations for such languages have also diminished. Significantly, the status of languages, and of their teachers, has been substantially weakened. Since the inception of NAPLAN tests in 2008, language teachers report a diminution in their roles and responsibilities, together with significant difficulties in teaching languages effectively due to constrained circumstances in schools. Too often language learning looks nothing like tasks. Characteristics observed include a focus on list learning and the memorisation of vocabulary, and a narrow and repetitive concentration on topics such as the 'F words' – food, festivals, folktales and the family. 'Drill and kill' classroom exercises are prevalent, and the use of worksheets ('worksheetitis') is ubiquitous. 'Busy work' and activities described by Long (2000, 2015) as having a focus on forms, predominate. None of these activities support the use of tasks. Language learning in classrooms may be continuous (learners have things called language lessons) but the limitations referred to above make it unlikely that learning will be cumulative with communicative outcomes being regularly achieved.

Therefore, in language teaching in Australia, instead of there being task-based teaching, too often there is an 'aphasiac' approach evident in student learning. This results in learners experiencing difficulty in putting words together in sentences, as there are limited opportunities for exchange of information in the language being learnt. It needs to be emphasised, however, that blame must not be conclusively attributed to the teachers. In primary schools particularly, the dominant position of standardised high-stakes English literacy and numeracy tests – hallmarks of neoliberal testing regimes – means that the necessary conditions for task-based teaching often cannot be provided.

And what of learner roles and responsibilities within the neoliberal educational environment? Considerations here will relate to the characteristics of this environment for learners, and also learners' capacities and opportunities to satisfy Ellis' task criteria and characteristics within the neoliberal educational environment. Communication with language teachers, about their learners, provides useful insights into these areas.

Teachers often bemoan the 'tell me what to do, and I'll do it' student culture that they now encounter in the classroom. Teachers report that too often students expect that their role will be to learn the content of the curriculum documentation, or instructional plans, that are publicly available to school communities. Content is predetermined and so too are details associated with assessment practices and requirements. Teachers report that it is becoming more common for students to perceive their responsibility to be no more than satisfying the requirements of scheduled tests. Going beyond these requirements, or being asked to deviate from them can, according to language teachers, meet with resistance from students, and also invoke parental interference. Teachers see this situation both as a manifestation of new managerialist practices in schools, and also as part of the associated reduction of teacher autonomy and control.

There is also a significant qualitative dimension related to this neoliberal environment for learners. Learners who position language use, first and foremost, as being to satisfy assessment requirements are not necessarily concerned with authenticity or the nature of real language. Rather, their energies are focused on marks, and on satisfying basic achievement standards established by government jurisdictions and instrumentalities.

There are, of course, many teachers who refuse to acquiesce to the constraints of the neoliberal environment, and who nurture learner capacity and responsibility to engage effectively in the use of tasks. There are also many learners who, when given the chance, thrive on the use of tasks within their experiences of language learning. Tasks enable learners to know language as real, meaningful and useful. Tasks also provide a context for learners to recognise and take ownership of their own learning resources (linguistic and non-linguistic) and apply them to the negotiation of meaning and the achievement of clearly defined communicative outcomes. Learners do have capacity, and can be provided with opportunities, to satisfy Ellis' task criteria and characteristics. The extent to which different learning and teaching contexts facilitate this can, however, be influenced by neoliberalism.

Assessment and Accountability

It is perhaps in the area of assessment that the influence of neoliberalism is most pernicious for teachers' work and students' learning. There is an increased emphasis on formal assessments and tests. These are valued, and frequently to the exclusion of other evidence of learning and language use. Formal assessments are often predictable, over-scripted and over-scaffolded. Scaffolding involves using a range of conceptual, material and linguistic tools and technologies to lead students towards understanding (Scarino & Liddicoat, 2009). Scaffolding should be used to support student learning, and assist learners to develop the skills they need to scaffold their own engagement with, and negotiation of tasks. Within neoliberal influenced education practices, however, scaffolding is often appropriated (or misappropriated) to constrain rather than support the learning and use of language.

Learners, and their parents, often know well in advance, exactly what is to be tested, and how. They are provided with prescriptive, or 'tick box', marking keys which pre-determine, and usually limit, representations of what language learners can do.

None of this sits comfortably with the use of tasks. Tasks are integral within learning and teaching. Formal assessments or tests, on the other hand, often are not. These are external to learning and teaching. Ellis (2018) reminds us that how learners perform a task will always, to some extent at least, be unpredictable. Formal assessments and tests are frequently designed to increase predictability. They often require learners to produce well-rehearsed language rather than necessitating dynamic language use that is spontaneous and purposeful. Formal assessments also limit opportunities, sometimes inadvertently, for learners to engage in the types of interactional processes that arise in naturally occurring language use. The limiting of these sorts of interactions, an essential feature of tasks (Ellis, 2018), also supports the contention that tasks do not work easily within the readily contrived circumstances of much testing and assessment that is conducted in many neoliberal educational environments.

Another very different example of the impact of formal testing regimes on language learning and use also deserves comment. Language learning in the Australian context includes English as an additional language, as well as the indigenous languages of remote Aboriginal communities. Sam Osborne in the Sidney Myer Rural Lecture Series (Lester *et al.*, 2013: 6) reports that the western, neoliberal philosophical position that informs the education system in Australia is at odds with the 'axiologies, epistemologies, ontologies and cosmologies of Aboriginal and Torres Strait Islanders'. He identifies that what is argued within the nationalised curriculum as a 'good education' is narrow and collides with traditional learning cultures. This impacts learners within these cultures in debilitating ways. He incisively critiques the effects of neoliberal uniform testing regimes on learners in remote community schools. Benchmark testing of English literacy highlights the relatively poor performance of very remote schools in comparison to other schools across Australia. The continued application of these tests, however, has not resulted in any statistically significant change in scores (Lester *et al.*,

2013: 6). For many of the learners in these schools English is a second, third or even fourth language. Learners do not automatically see English as 'real' within their world, and the potential for authenticity in English language use is obfuscated because of nationalised curriculum demands, and formal assessment and testing regimes. It can be argued, therefore, that an enhanced focus on the use of tasks, *within* learning and teaching in these contexts, as opposed to the application of testing regimes *to* these learning and teaching contexts, may be beneficial. It is also argued that this is not a unique circumstance and that the impact and consequences of neoliberalism on language learning as described here, may well resonate in other parts of the global community.

In the neoliberal educational environment, it is difficult to separate assessment from measurement and from accountability. Places of language learning have become spaces of measurement. But it's not just students being measured. Teachers and schools are also held accountable for the progress, (or lack thereof), of every student in their charge. Teachers report accountability requirements as onerous. Some describe requirements such as having to enter data into school systems on a weekly basis. It is little wonder that for teachers such as these, dealing with the demands of task-based teaching may seem like crossing a bridge too far.

In neoliberal education environments quantification and datafication are overemphasised (Lingard *et al.*, 2013). The application of these mechanisms for assessment and accountability do not easily reflect the important qualitative aspects of language use displayed through tasks. Richness and complexity of language become difficult to capture, record and report in an environment where teachers' capacity to make autonomous judgements about their students' language performance is either secondary to, or subsumed by, an emphasis on competitive testing to meet systemic or national needs or directions. In such circumstances test-based accountability is too often prioritised over task-based performance, and quality in the neoliberal world of language learning and teaching is too frequently reported quantitatively with little reference to learners' real capacity to communicate.

Benefits Associated with Prioritising Tasks in the Face of Neoliberal Influences

The extent to which tasks can be prioritised within languages education, in contexts influenced by neoliberalism, will vary. Difficulties and disconnects have been identified but these do not automatically preclude the use of tasks and task-based teaching. Bao and Du (2015: 291) remind us that 'task-based language teaching is not a one-size-fits-all method, but rather interacts with various contextual factors in its application'. For language teachers this provides scope for diverse approaches to the use of tasks whilst maintaining definitional integrity and securing intended communicative outcomes.

In an environment characterised by compliance and conformity, deviation from a one-size-fits-all approach constitutes a strategy to contest neoliberal educational discourses in schools. Language teachers need to re-claim their professional status and authority, and question the 'pedagogical adequacy' (McGroarty, 2017: 229) of neoliberal educational reforms. Tasks offer an alternative. Pedagogical practices associated with the use of tasks and task-based teaching can accommodate the complexities of communication in the diverse and rapidly changing world that we live in. Task-based teaching can be interpreted in a way that goes well beyond the traditional linguistic-cognitive SLA that has been so influential in TBLT's history (Ortega, 2013). Factors associated with the 'multilingual turn' (May, 2013) can embed language learning, and tasks, in wider social and linguistic contexts that encompass language use beyond native speaker norms. In addition, 'technology-mediated TBLT' (González-Lloret & Ortega, 2014, Chapter 5 this volume) can be built into designing and doing tasks. These actions can substantially enhance the relationship between learners and the world around them. A bigger view of language can be generated. This will not only enable language learners to use their language identities to both inform and mediate language learning and use through tasks, it will also help teachers re-define their authority, and challenge neoliberal curriculum limitations.

What then will be the benefits of these actions? This final section will identify benefits associated with the use of tasks and task-based teaching. These are grouped into five areas for ease of discussion. This is not a definitive catalogue of benefits or approaches, but rather recognition of what is achievable (to varying extents depending on specific contextual factors) even in educational environments constrained by neoliberal forces.

Real Language and Real Communicative Outcomes

Tasks have clearly defined communicative outcomes that enable learners to use language to do things (Ellis, 2018; Bygate, 2016). For learners, there may be a sense of the real world and of authenticity, and although meaning making is primary, there can be opportunities to focus on form. Tasks require learners to engage in the same interactional processes that arise in naturally occurring language use (Ellis, 2018). Tasks can be designed for all learners, including beginning learners, and they can involve different degrees of language complexity. There is, therefore, the potential for learners, at all phases of development and at different levels of learning, to benefit from dynamic engagement with language through the use of tasks. There is also potential for teachers.

Norris (2009) provides encouragement suggesting that language teaching can evolve into a more meaningful endeavour with the use of tasks.

Technology Enhanced Language Use

Technology and tasks, when utilised together, may offer significant benefits for language learning. Internet connected devices and digital technologies are integral within the lives and learning processes of learners (González-Lloret & Ortega, 2014, Chapter 5, this volume). As such, making meaning and 'doing things' can be substantially enhanced through the use of multimodal technology supported communication. This is reality in many societies, and its application to language learning is obvious and enticing. Language use is extended beyond the classroom and beyond monolingual norms. Technologies generate new environments for communication and the use of tasks. Opportunities for real interconnectedness and for meaningful interpersonal and community interactions are increased. So too is access to authentic text that can be used in tasks and task-based teaching (González-Lloret & Ortega, 2014, Chapter 5, this volume).

Developing Interculturality

An important benefit associated with tasks, and one that is enhanced through the use of technology, is the fostering of intercultural communication. Tasks can provide opportunities for learners to negotiate the complexity of the relationships between speakers and the world around them through participating in meaning making. Tasks can challenge learners to understand and respect the actual uses to which language is put in diverse cultures and discourse domains (Norris, 2009: 591), and they can afford opportunities for learners to critically reflect on their own language and culture in relation to those of others (Kramsch, 1993; Liddicoat & Scarino, 2013). Within contemporary global society (which ironically, is strongly influenced by neoliberal forces), using tasks to develop interculturality might be beneficial.

Language Learning Skills and Strategies

Tasks can reshape language learning for 'tell me what to do and I'll do it' learners. They can provide opportunities for learners to exercise conscious choice in how they negotiate tasks and achieve desired communicative outcomes. Learners can assume a significant role in regulating their own language learning. The strategies they use, and the resources they deploy – linguistic and non-linguistic – are essential to successful task achievement. For Ellis (2018), these characteristics are intrinsic to tasks. For learners, they mark the growing autonomy of being a successful language learner.

Meaningful Assessment

Tasks can make assessment much more meaningful than tests and other mechanisms regularly used in neoliberal educational environments. Tasks are not decontextualised – they are a part of the learning process. They require authentic performance where learners negotiate some form of gap to achieve a communicative outcome. Learners' language use is meaning focused and purposeful. Importantly, teachers are able to see directly what learners can do with the language, and the extent to which learners are developing the ability to communicate effectively (Ellis, 2018). This is a far cry from the standardised testing regimes that are endemic within neoliberal contexts.

A review of the benefits of tasks and task-based teaching highlights the contrast between the reductive and constraining features of neoliberal educational practices and the rich and diversified practices and opportunities offered through the use of tasks. It is acknowledged that for language teachers the scenario is not either/or. Just as learners are required to negotiate meaning through different languages, their discourses and cultures, so too language teachers need to negotiate the different priorities and values expressed in neoliberal and task discourses, and use these to develop pedagogies that are appropriate for, and manageable within, their specific contexts.

Conclusion

This chapter has explored key characteristics of both neoliberal educational practices and those of tasks and task-based teaching. The compatibility of the two approaches has been examined with a number of disconnects being identified. It has been argued that teachers can position themselves to contest neoliberal values, and that task-based teaching can provide the flexibility for teachers to target their own priorities, and tailor task-based teaching to suit their own specific circumstances. It is hoped that the articulation of possible benefits of task-based teaching can support this process and give teachers the courage to assert their professional authority in respect of language teaching, and to build programs that assist their language learners in their development of communicative competence through the use of tasks.

We began this chapter with Flubacher and Del Percio (2017) defining neoliberalism. It is fitting then to conclude with the support of their words:

> As language educators we need to be able to do more than ... bemoan the regimes of compliance in which we now work. (Flubacher & Del Percio, 2017: xiv–xv)

We need to disrupt the neoliberal narrative. We must discourage uncritical acceptance of the rhetoric of neoliberal discourses. New stories need to be generated and these must reflect the multiple versions of teaching and learning with tasks. Our story endings, however, should be similar and feature the sharing of successes. Both language teachers and language learners deserve opportunities to enact their responsibilities both with respect to task design and task achievement.

References

Australian Curriculum, Assessment and Reporting Authority (ACARA) (2018) See https://www.acara.edu.au/

Ahmadian, M. (2016) Task-based language teaching and learning. *The Language Learning Journal* 44 (4), 377–380. DOI: 10.1080/09571736.2016.1236523.

Bachman, L. and Palmer, A. (1996) *Language Testing in Practice*. Oxford: Oxford University Press.

Bao, R. and Du, X. (2015) Implementation of task-based language teaching in Chinese as a foreign language: Benefits and challenges. *Language, Culture and Curriculum* 28 (3), 291–310. DOI: 10.1080/07908318.2015.1058392.

Bygate, M. (2016) Sources, developments and directions of task-based language teaching. *The Language Learning Journal* 44 (4), 381–400. DOI: 10.1080/09571736.2015.1039566.

Bygate, M., Skehan, P. and Swain, M. (eds) (2013) *Researching Pedagogic Tasks: Second Language Learning, Teaching and Testing*. London: Routledge.

Connell, R. (2013) The neoliberal cascade and education: An essay on the market agenda and its consequences. *Critical Studies in Education* 54 (2), 99–112. DOI: 10.1080/17508487.2013.776990.

Cortazzi, M. and Jin, L. (2013) *Researching Cultures of Learning: International Perspectives on Language Learning and Education*. London: Palgrave Macmillan.

Down, B. and Sullivan, A. (2019) 'Classroom ready' teachers: Gaps, silences and contradictions in the Australian report into teacher education. In A. Sullivan, B. Johnson and M. Simons (eds) *Attracting and Keeping the Best Teachers: Issues and Opportunities* (pp. 39–61). Singapore: Springer.

Ellis, R. (2003) *Task-based Language Learning and Teaching*. Oxford: Oxford University Press.

Ellis, R. (2009) Task-based language teaching: Sorting out the misunderstandings. *International Journal of Applied Linguistics* 19 (3), 221–246. https://doi-org.libproxy.murdoch.edu.au/10.1111/j.1473-4192.2009.00231.x.

Ellis, R. (2018) *Reflections on Task-Based Language Teaching*. Bristol: Multilingual Matters.

Ellis, R. and Shintani, N. (2014) *Exploring Language Pedagogy through Second Language Acquisition Research*. London: Routledge.

Flubacher, M. and Del Percio, A. (eds) (2017) *Language, Education and Neoliberalism*. Bristol: Multilingual Matters.

Gao, S. (2017) The commodification of language in neoliberalising China: The cases of English and Mandarin. In M. Flubacher and A. Del Percio (eds) *Language, Education and Neoliberalism* (pp. 19–36). Bristol: Multilingual Matters.

González-Lloret, M. and Ortega, L. (2014) Towards technology-mediated TBLT. In M. González-Lloret and L. Ortega (eds) *Technology-Mediated TBLT: Researching Technology and Tasks* (pp. 1–22). Amsterdam: John Benjamins Publishing Company.

Kramsch, C. (1993) *Context and Culture in Language Teaching*. Oxford: Oxford University Press.

Lambert, C., Philp, J. and Nakamura, S. (2017) Learner-generated content and engagement in second language task performance. *Language Teaching Research* 21 (6), 665–680. DOI: 10.1177/1362168816683559.

Lester, K., Masnutjukur, M., Osborne, S. and Tjiaya, K. (2013) *Red Dirt Curriculum: Re-imagining Remote Education*. Paper presented at Sidney Myer Rural Lecture Series, 18 September, Alice Springs: Sidney Myer Fund. https://www.researchgate.net/publication/271769490.

Liddicoat, A. and Scarino, A. (2013) *Intercultural Language Teaching and Learning*. New York: Wiley-Blackwell.

Lingard, B., Martini, W. and Rezai-Rashti, G. (2013) Testing regimes, accountability and education policy: Commensurate global and national developments. *Journal of Education Policy* 28 (5), 539–556. DOI: 10.1080/02680939.2013.820042.

Long, M. (1985) A role for instruction in second language acquisition: Task-based language teaching. In K. Hyltenstam and M. Pienemann (eds) *Modelling and Assessing Second Language Acquisition* (pp. 77–100). Clevedon: Multilingual Matters.

Long, M. (2000) Focus on form in task-based language teaching. In R. Lambert and E. Shohamy (eds) *Language Policy and Pedagogy: Essays in Honour of A Ronald Walton*, (pp. 179–191). Philadelphia: John Benjamin.

Long, M. (2015) *Second Language Acquisition and Task-based Language Teaching*. Chichester: Wiley Blackwell.

Long, M. and Robinson, P. (1998) Focus on form: Theory, research, and practice. In C. Doughty and J. Williams (eds) *Focus on Form in Classroom Second Language Acquisition* (pp. 15–41). Cambridge: Cambridge University Press.

Lynch, K., Grummell, B. and Devine, D. (2015) *New Managerialism in Education: Commercialisation, Carelessness and Gender*. Basingstoke: Palgrave MacMillan.

McGroarty, M. (2017) Neoliberal reforms in language education: Major trends, uneven outcomes, open questions. In M. Flubacher and A. Del Percio (eds) *Language, Education and Neoliberalism* (pp. 229–242). Bristol: Multilingual Matters.

May, S. (ed.) (2013) *The Multilingual Turn: Implications for SLA, TESOL, and Bilingual Education*. Oxon: Routledge.

Norris, J. (2009) Task-based teaching and testing. In M. Long and C. Doughty (eds) *The Handbook of Language Teaching* (pp. 578–594). Wiley Online Library: Wiley-Blackwell.

Nunan, D. (1989) *Designing Tasks for the Communicative Classroom*. Cambridge: Cambridge University Press.

Oliver, R. and Bogachenko, T. (2018) Teacher perceptions and use of tasks in school ESL classrooms. In V. Samuda, K. Van den Branden and M. Bygate (eds) *TBLT as a Researched Pedagogy* (pp. 72–95). Amsterdam: John Benjamins. DOI. org/10.1075/tblt.12.04oli.

Ortega, L. (2013) Ways forward for a bi/multilingual turn in SLA. In S. May (ed.) *The Multilingual Turn: Implications for SLA, TESOL, and Bilingual Education* (pp. 32–53). Oxon: Routledge.

Ross, E. and Gibson, R. (eds) (2006) *Neoliberalism and Education Reform*. New Jersey: Hampton Press.

Scarino, A. and Liddicoat, A. (2009) *Teaching and Learning Languages: A Guide*. Carlton, Victoria: Curriculum Corporation.

Willis, D. and Willis, J. (2007) *Doing Task-Based Teaching*. Oxford: Oxford University Press.

7 Teacher-Preparation for Task-Based Language Teaching

Rod Ellis

This chapter begins by summarizing the problems that teachers in Asia have experienced in trying to implement task-based teaching as a prelude to emphasizing the need for teacher-preparation programmes. The chapter then reviews a number of studies that have reported on teacher-preparation programmes for task-based language teaching (TBLT) at both pre-service and in-service levels and identifies the factors that need to be considered in designing such programmes. The chapter also draws on education research that points to a number of key principles for effective teacher education. Finally, the chapter describes the content of an in-service teacher preparation programme for teachers working in school contexts in Asia.

Introduction: Problems in Implementing Task-Based Language Teaching

The introduction of communicative-oriented approaches, including task-based language teaching, into state schools has been mandated by the educational authorities of many countries (Lai, 2015). However, several studies (e.g. Adams & Newton, 2009; Butler, 2011; Carless, 2004) have pointed to the problems that teachers – especially those in Asian contexts – face in implementing TBLT in their classrooms. Structural problems arise from classroom-level and societal-institutional level constraints (Butler, 2011). Included in the former is the large class size that many teachers in Asia are confronted with and that make small group work – a major feature of task-based language teaching – difficult to manage (Li, 1998; Samimy & Kobayashi, 2004). Societal-institutional problems include the structural syllabus that teachers are required to teach to. In some settings (e.g. Japan) a structural syllabus is officially mandated even when TBLT is the recommended approach. A further problem is the continuation of traditional forms of discrete item language testing that emphasize linguistic accuracy. Understandably, teachers teach to the test, abandoning tasks in favour of explicit language teaching. As Butler (2011) concluded, if TBLT is to thrive 'not only are changes in the exam system required, but also drastic changes toward learning and assessment in general in society are needed' (2011: 46).

There are other kinds of problems facing the implementation of TBLT but these are perhaps more amenable to solution by teachers. The beliefs and attitudes that students bring to the classroom can lead to resistance to TBLT. Also, students may treat tasks as 'fun activities' rather than as serious activities that can help them learn the language (Foster, 1998). Students' limited speaking abilities in the target language may result in over use of their mother tongue (L1) when performing tasks. Alternatively, they may be so focused on achieving the task outcomes that they resort to pidgin-like use of the target language (Seedhouse, 1997). Such problems, if they arise, will seriously impede the effectiveness of TBLT. But they are not insuperable.

Finally, there are problems relating to the teachers themselves. Teachers do not always have a clear grasp of what a 'task' is. Hu (2013), for example, noted that the Chinese public school teachers of English he investigated had very different ideas of what a task was with some simply equating it with exercises in their text book. Even if teachers do have a good understanding of what a task is, they may still be reluctant to try TBLT if they lack confidence in their own oral proficiency in the target language. And even if they are prepared to try, they may be wedded to a traditional view of language teaching as a result of their own experiences of learning a language in the classroom or their prior teacher training. Teachers implementing TBLT frequently express concern about their students' grammatical development (East, 2014; McDonough, 2015; McDonough & Chaikitmongkol, 2007; Watson-Todd, 2006) and wonder where grammar fits in. A further problem is teachers' concerns that planning TBLT lessons imposes too great a workload on them. East (2014), for example, found that this was one of the main 'negative characteristics' that teachers in an in-service teacher education programme in New Zealand mentioned. This problem is very real given the lack of published task-based teaching materials. As a result of these problems, teachers tend to fall back on traditional teacher-centred modes of teaching (Butler, 2004; Jeon & Hahn, 2006) or resort to a weak form of TBLT (i.e. task-supported language teaching).

Several commentators (Butler, 2011; Littlewood, 2007, 2014) have pointed to the conflicts that exist between TBLT and culturally embedded traditional teaching approaches. They point to Confucian notions that emphasize knowledge as residing in books and the teacher as the primary sources of knowledge and suggest that such notions are incompatible with TBLT which emphasizes experiential learning. Samimy and Kobayashi (2004), for example, claimed there is a cultural mismatch between communicative language teaching and the Japanese culture of learning. However, this problem is overstated. Butler (2011) noted that the cultural backdrop of Asian language classrooms varies considerably and that in some cases – for example, primary school classrooms in Japan – it is well suited to the introduction of TBLT. Lai (2015) also warned against 'essentialist statements about cultural inappropriateness of TBLT in Asia' (2015: 14). She queried whether TBLT was in fact antithetical to Confucian values and noted that many of the problems documented in evaluation studies of TBLT in Asia can also be found in non-Asian contexts.

This brief review of studies that have evaluated the introduction of TBLT in Asia (and elsewhere) suggests a number of conclusions:

(1) TBLT is not necessarily incompatible with culturally shaped perceptions of what constitutes effective language teaching.
(2) There are, however, problems in implementing TBLT successfully.
(3) Some of these problems (e.g. how to manage large class sizes) are not specific to TBLT.
(4) Other problems, however, are TBLT specific. They concern structural/institutional issues, students and teachers' belief systems about what teaching and learning a language involves and issues to do with the pedagogical knowledge needed to implement TBLT (e.g. how to conduct TBLT with students with limited speaking ability).
(5) TBLT is unlikely to be successfully implemented unless the problems are addressed and teachers are given assistance in overcoming them.

These conclusions indicate the need for courses (both pre-service and in service) that prepare teachers for TBLT. Long (2016) and Ellis (2009) discuss a number of 'non-issues' that various critics of TBLT have raised in order to re-assert the legitimacy of more traditional approaches to language teaching. However, both Long and Ellis, acknowledge that one of the 'real issues' is the need for teacher education for TBLT and point to how little attention has been paid to this.

Teacher-Preparation TBLT Programmes

There is a very substantial literature on tasks and on task-based language learning (see Ellis, 2003; Long, 2015; Samuda & Bygate, 2008. In contrast, very little has been published on programs preparing teachers to teach TBLT [1]. As van den Branden (2016) noted, the teacher has been largely ignored by researchers and in theoretical discussions of TBLT – a fact he considered surprising given the central role the teacher has to play.

Undergraduate Level Courses

There are – understandably – no complete TBLT undergraduate programmes. However, TBLT has figured in some Batchelor level programmes. Rosessingh (2014) made the point that in countries such as Canada, where teachers need to be equipped to work in linguistically diverse classrooms, task-based teaching provides the obvious way of melding subject content to language development. She described a 3 hrs × 12 week course for pre-service elementary school teachers where students completed different types of tasks (e.g. *jigsaw tasks* and *word sorts*) that modelled how task-based teaching could be implemented in their future elementary classrooms. Rossesingh reported that the students taking this course evaluated it extremely positively.

Ogilvie and Dunn (2010) noted that 'teacher education programs can provide a safe, secure environment in which to experiment with novel approaches' (2010: 164). They designed a 37 hour introduction to TBLT for second language education minors at a Canadian university, drawing on constructivist theories of learning to encourage the students to reflect on and modify their pre-conceived beliefs about language teaching and learning. They collected data to evaluate its effectiveness by asking the students to give their views in writing about a series of TBLT and Present, Practice, Produce (PPP) lesson plans and also to complete a questionnaire. In addition, they interviewed a subset of the students after they had completed their teaching practicum. There was evidence of a change in the students' views about language instruction. Initially, reflecting their prior experiences of teacher-centred language instruction, they favoured PPP and were critical of TBLT. By the end of the course some of the students expressed more favourable views about TBLT and, in particular, were less sure about the importance of explicit grammar instruction and error correction. However, the post practicum interviews indicated that the students had implemented TBLT only sparingly. Ogilvie and Dunn suggested that this failure to uptake TBLT was due to the trainee teachers' epistemological frame (i.e. 'communication as an end, rather than the means of developing communicative ability' (2010: 172), the cultural norms of the classrooms they taught in, and the lack of support for TBLT from the mentors in their schools. The general conclusion of this study was that 'only after greater attention is devoted to issues of implementation will the principles of TBLT be regularly put into practice' (2010: 176).

Another undergraduate course, this time for 15 English language majors in Japanese university, is reported by Jackson (2012). The course consisted of a set of task-based units designed to train the students to undertake TBLT. The training units focused on planning a lesson, conducting a teaching demonstration, observing lessons, and undergoing debriefing afterwards. Evaluation was carried out by eliciting retrospective comments on the activities involved in each unit, analysis of the discourse of the final debriefing session, and a questionnaire about language teaching administered to students who completed the units and to another group of students who did not. Jackson reported that there were no statistically significant differences in the two groups of students who completed the questionnaire but that the group that completed the units rated statements related to TBLT more highly. Also, these students demonstrated an ability to elaborate, synthesize and critique practical knowledge and ideas concerning the use of tasks.

Masters-level Programmes

I have not been able to find any complete masters-level TBLT programmes. TBLT is covered in general methods courses and also a few programmes offer specific courses on TBLT.

The course I developed as part the Master in Teaching English as Second or Other Language (MTESOL) at the University of Auckland aimed to familiarize students with the theories and research that inform task-based learning and teaching. The course assignments required students to design a task and then to teach and evaluate it. In this way, it strove to build a nexus between research and practice. In Ellis (2015) I reported the results of the trainee teachers' evaluations of their tasks. I showed how asking teachers to design and evaluate a task helped to develop their content pedagogical knowledge of task-based language teaching.

The course that Jonathan Newton teaches in the MA programme at Victoria University of Wellington adopts a similar approach. The course content is described as follows:

> In the course we will draw on research and classroom perspectives to explore teaching through tasks, including a focus on the design of tasks, TBLT methodology and on the practical and contextual issues that teachers face when implementing tasks in specific learning contexts. Course members will have opportunities to apply ideas from the course to their particular teaching context whether it be teaching beginners or advanced learners, children or adults, ESOL/EFL or other second languages. (Downloaded from https://www.victoria.ac.nz/lals/study/postgraduate/attachments/Task-based-Language-Teaching.pdf on 7th October, 2017)

Newton's course explicitly addresses the problems that teachers face in implementing TBLT and the need to adapt it to suit specific teaching contexts.

In-service Training for TBLT

The Flemish government's Educational Priority Policy is directed at enhancing the quality of Dutch language education at primary, secondary and adult levels and, in particular, at enabling pupils-at-risk and adult immigrants to benefit from the educational and occupational opportunities open to them. The policy aimed to replace the traditional teacher-centred and audiolingual approach with TBLT. Responsibility for facilitating this was assigned to the Centre for Language and Education at the Katholieke Universiteit of Leueven, which undertook the design of programmes and the training of teachers. This constituted what is probably the most concerted effort to introduce TBLT into state school classrooms. Details of the approach adopted can be found in Van den Branden (2006).

Van den Branden (2006) viewed the traditional approach of in-service training used in the initial stage of the Flemish project where teachers attended short sessions dominated by the in-service trainers as not very successful. Although the teachers responded enthusiastically to the new ideas presented to them, they failed to implement them once back in their classrooms. Van den Branden went on to report a different approach in a project for teachers from Educational Priority Policy Schools (i.e. schools with a growing influx of migrant pupils) (Linsen, 1994). A key feature of the training offered was that it combined a theoretical account of TBLT with a presentation of task-based syllabuses that were ready to be tried out in the teachers' classrooms. The project adopted a snowball approach, with key teachers who attended the training sessions forming teams in their schools. Another important feature of the project was the support provided by school counsellors, who were also trained in the theory and practice of TBLT. The evaluation of the training showed that it clearly influenced both the teachers' beliefs about how to address the language needs of pupils and their actual practices.[2] It also pointed to a particular problem that the teachers faced – namely, selecting tasks at the right level of difficulty for their pupils. Van den Branden noted that the same problem is evident in a number of other studies evaluating the introduction of TBLT in Flanders.

A further problem noted by Van den Branden (2006) was the difficulty that the teachers had in maintaining control over what happens in the task-based classroom. He observed that the advantage of traditional, explicit approaches based on linguistic syllabuses is 'the psychological comfort they can give to teachers by spelling out to the teacher in full detail what is to be taught' (2006: 230). One of the aims of the in-service training was to combat this problem by developing teachers' confidence in using tasks.

A general finding of the evaluation studies carried out as part of the Flemish in-service training projects was that 'incorporation of task-based principles into daily classroom practice appeared to be a slow process' (Van den Branden, 2006: 233). This suggests the need for an approach that is school-based and provides practice-oriented coaching. That is, instead of withdrawing teachers for short in-service training sessions, the trainers and counsellors need to visit the teachers in their own schools. Van den Branden reports on a longitudinal study involving the introduction of task-based teaching in Dutch-medium primary schools in Brussels that adopted this approach. The study found that the teachers were appreciative of the support they received. They recognized the value of linking the training to actual tasks that they could use in their classrooms and of the post-lesson discussions where a trainer provided feedback on a lesson

Van den Branden concluded that 'on the whole, after 13 years, the implementation of task-based language education in Flemish education … has been a success, especially in primary education' (2006: 244). This was evident in several key ways – for example, the teachers' stronger orientation to functional language goals and the higher level of involvement and motivation evident in the students. He emphasized the importance of the sustained effort with school-based teams of teachers and the collaborative contributions of school counsellors, syllabus developers, in-service trainers, school inspectors and educational policy makers, who had a common set of principles and understanding of TBLT.

Erlam (2015) reported on teachers' responses to a year-long Teacher Professional Development Languages Programme funded by the New Zealand Ministry of Education. The teachers came from both elementary and secondary schools and taught a variety of foreign languages. There were three main components. The teachers were encouraged to take advantage of an opportunity to improve their own language proficiency. They were then enrolled in a Stage 3 university-level course introducing them to task-supported language teaching. They were asked to design their own tasks and evaluate them in terms of published criteria for a task (Ellis & Shintani, 2014). The final component of the programme took place in the teachers' own schools. The teachers were visited and observed four times during the year by facilitators, who helped the teachers apply and evaluate what they had learned in the university-level course. In the year following completion of the professional development programme, Erlam interviewed 48 teachers about the impact of this on their teaching and, in particular, their use of tasks. She reported that a substantial number of the teachers claimed that their teaching had changed substantially after participating in the programme. They stated that they used tasks regularly and that, as a result, their teaching had become more learner-centred and more motivating for both the students and the teacher. However, most of the teachers also mentioned difficulties they experienced in implementing TBLT, in particular the lack of task-based resources and how to find or make tasks of a suitable level of complexity for their students. Some of the teachers also admitted they lacked a clear understanding of TBLT while others said that their ability to implement TBLT was limited because of their students' lack of language proficiency. Erlam concluded that the majority of the teachers demonstrated 'significant learning' about TBLT and how to implement it but she felt that they needed further help in choosing suitable tasks.

In another article, Erlam (2016) focused on the same teachers' understanding and conceptualization of what a task is. She found that the tasks the teachers designed were primarily output-based (i.e. there were few input-based tasks) and had a grammatical focus (i.e. they were form focused tasks). The teachers found it difficult to craft tasks for low proficiency learners. They conceived of the 'gap principle' in terms of a gap in the students' language knowledge rather than in terms of an information or opinion gap. Their tasks did not always have a clear communicative purpose and they had a very unclear idea of what Ellis and Shintani (2014) meant by 'learners utilize their own linguistic resources' when they perform a task. Erlam concluded that the teachers needed more help to understand the difference between students functioning as 'language learners' and 'language users' – a distinction essential for grasping the rationale for task-based teaching.

Key Factors in Successful TBLT Teacher-preparation Programmes

Drawing on these evaluations of TBLT training courses, I have identified a number of factors that seem likely to contribute to their success. I have classified these factors into three major groups (see Table 7.1). The factors address quite concrete issues relating to the design and implementation of teacher-preparation programmes. Clearly, however, attending to all of them is a demanding undertaking. It is unlikely that most teacher-preparation programmes will be able to take account of all these factors, especially those relating to (c) – teachers' uptake of TBLT in their classrooms. The TBLT courses that figure in master's level programmes, for example, may not include a practical teacher component. I offer the list as a guide the development of programmes.

In the following section I consider what we can learn about what constitutes 'effective practice' in teacher education by drawing on educational research that has examined the relative effectiveness of different approaches to preparing teachers.

Effective Practice in Teacher-Preparation Programmes: General Principles

Richards (1990) distinguished two broad approaches to teacher education. In the micro-approach, 'teaching is viewed as a kind of technology' (1990: 8). The aim here is to identify the specific techniques and strategies associated with effective teaching – for example, the teacher's

Table 7.1 Factors influencing the success of teacher preparation programmes for TBLT

Type of factor	Factors
A: Factors relating to the content of a teacher-preparation programme	1. It is important to address and challenge teachers existing beliefs about teaching and learning. 2. Central to TBLT is the concept of 'task'. Thus it is essential that teachers are made aware of the difference between a 'task' and 'exercise'. 3. It is important to provide teachers with an actual task-based syllabus and the materials needed to teach it. 4. Theory and research is directly related to practical issues involved in the design and implementation of tasks. 5. Specific attention should be paid to task complexity in order to help teachers select tasks that are at an appropriate level for their students. 6. To overcome the general perception that a task is necessarily a speaking task, particular attention should be paid to making teachers aware of the importance of input-based tasks, especially with low proficiency students. 7. A component of the programme needs to directly address the kinds of problems teachers are likely to experience when they implement TBLT in their classrooms. For example, teachers should be introduced to strategies and techniques for handling mixed ability students in their classrooms.
B: Factors relating to the methodology of a teacher-preparation programme	1. The methodology of the preparation programme should be compatible with the principles of TBLT. This can be best achieved by ensuring that a large proportion of the programme is itself task-based (i.e. the programme emphasizes the kind of experiential, discovery learning that is central to TBLT by limiting lecturing and requiring teachers to complete tasks that address key issues about TBLT). 2. Teachers should be required to design their own tasks and, if possible, to also evaluate them by teaching them.
C: Factors relating to teachers' uptake of TBLT in their classrooms	1. Where possible training should be school based rather than in a training institution and should take the form of practice-oriented coaching. 2. Teachers will need the support of school-based mentors who are well-versed in the principles and practices of TBLT. 3. There needs to be ongoing support not just from the trainers but also from principals of schools and inspectors. 4. Teachers need the opportunity to receive feedback on their use of tasks through reflective discussions with their trainers and other teachers. 5. To enhance the effectiveness of a teacher-preparation programme, teachers who attend a preparation programme need to become leaders of a team of teachers in their schools. 6. Above all, teachers need support for the sustained effort that is required to implement TBLT successfully.

use of questions. Richards suggested that from this perspective the goal of teacher training is to impart these strategies to teachers. Richards questioned this approach as focussing on low-level skills. He noted that many aspects of teaching, such as classroom management, cannot be reduced to discrete components. In the alternative approach – the macro-approach – teacher education is based on a set of general principles that distinguish effective and ineffective teaching (e.g. the importance of structuring activities and assigning tasks in order to achieve specific learning objectives). Richards argued that both the micro- and the macro-approaches are needed to ensure a balance between a 'training' and 'education' view of teacher preparation programmes. Applied to TBLT, Richard's view of teacher-preparation points to the need to both equip teachers with tools (e.g. tasks) and techniques (e.g. how to focus on form in task-based lesson) and to ensure that they have a full understanding of the learning and educational theories that give support to TBLT.

Borg (2011) noted 'it is widely accepted that teacher education is more likely to impact on what teachers do if it also addresses their beliefs' (2011: 370). There is little chance of teachers adopting the techniques of TBLT if these do not accord with their beliefs about what constitutes effective teaching. Teachers' existing belief systems are robust, making change difficult to achieve. Borg investigated the impact that completing a Diploma in English Language Teaching to Adults (DELTA) had on the general beliefs about teaching of six experienced teachers. He concluded that it did not lead to any deep and radical reversal of beliefs and suggested that this was because the course did not confront and challenge the teachers' existing beliefs sufficiently. Thus, one of the main aims of teacher education (as opposed to teacher training) must be to help participants make explicit their existing beliefs and enable them to reflect on them critically and modify them.

An effective teacher-preparation programme for TBLT, then, needs to equip teachers with the specific techniques and materials they will need and also to help them understand the theoretical rationale for TBLT in such a way that it encourages the evaluation and modification of their existing beliefs systems. In other words, crucial to the success of a teacher-preparation programme is the nexus between theory and practice. It is how to achieve this nexus that underlies attempts at the identification of general principles that should inform the design and delivery of teacher-preparation programmes. Table 7.2 below lists the eight general principles that Darling-Hammond (2006) (cited in Ingvarson et al.'s (2014) report for the Australian Council for Educational Research) proposed. I have modified them slightly to emphasize their applicability to TBLT. These principles are equally relevant to pre-service and in-service programmes.

A comment on Principle (2) is in needed. As framed by Darling-Hammond, this requires taking account of the social and cultural context in which teachers will work, the curriculum they are asked to teach to, and the pedagogical practices and methods of assessment linked to them. The problem here – as I noted in the opening section of this chapter – is that these often conflict with the principles and practices of task-based language teaching. Thus, if TBLT it to be successfully implemented it may be necessary for teachers to challenge the existing curriculum, pedagogic practices and the methods of assessment that exist in their particular social and cultural context. One way of

Table 7.2 General principles of effective teacher education for TBLT

Principles	Description
1. Coherence	The programme should be based on a clear, common vision of good teaching grounded in an understanding of language learning.
2. A strong core curriculum	This should be grounded on knowledge of child and adolescent development along with knowledge of how children and older learners learn languages. It should also take account of the social and cultural context and the pedagogy and the methods of assessment of task-based language teaching.
3. Extensive, connected clinical experiences	These need to support the ideas and practices presented in simultaneous course work in the core curriculum.
4. Explicit strategies	These should address the trainees' deep-seated beliefs and assumptions about teaching and learning and also help trainees to learn about the experiences of language learners' and teachers different from themselves.
5. Well-defined standards of practice	These should be used to guide and evaluate course work and clinical work.
6. An inquiry approach that connects theory and practice	An inquiry approach aims at addressing real problems of practice and developing reflective practice through examining cases, methods, and analyses of language teaching and learning and research on instructed language learning.
7. Strong school-university partnerships	In a strong school-university partnership there are shared knowledge and beliefs about task-based language teaching that provide a context for trainees to learn how to practise TBLT within a professional community.
8. Assessment based on professional standards	These are needed to provide the means of evaluating the skills and abilities central to effective task-based language teaching while recognizing that teachers' expertise is necessarily developmental.

facilitating this is by establishing a strong partnership between the training institute and the teachers' schools (Principle (7)). This, however, may not always be possible especially in in-service teacher education programmes (see, for example, the problems that arose in implementing TBLT in Malaysia as reported in Hall, 2015). Perhaps, then, a corollary to Principle (2) is needed:

> In a strong core curriculum for TBLT, teachers should be introduced to strategies that they can use to modify and adapt TBLT for use in a social and cultural context which does not readily support its principles and practices.

Designing a Teacher Preparation Course for TBLT

It is, of course, one thing to identify a list factors and general principles that are needed for a teacher preparation programme to be effective. It is entirely another to ensure that this can be achieved. Very considerable resources will be required, and these are unlikely to be available in many contexts. At best, then, the factors and principles can serve as a checklist that programme designers can refer to with the aim of doing the best job they can with the resources available.

Invargson *et al.* (2014) pointed out that 'subject-matter knowledge and pedagogy ... should not be treated separately, but as intimately related' so that 'methods should be taught in the context of the content to be taught' (2014: 8). In other words, the aim should be to develop the pedagogical content knowledge based on both the practice of TBLT itself and in the subject area that provides its principal theoretical underpinning – namely, second language acquisition. A second major consideration is the importance of ensuring the availability of mentors trained in TBLT who can provide the in-school support that trainee teachers will need during their teaching practice and, also, when they start their first jobs as teachers. Context more than training determines how teachers teach, and unless teachers are able to work in a school context that is supportive of TBLT, there is little chance of its successful implementation. All too often, the top-down advocacy of TBLT by a Ministry of Education is not accompanied with any clear plan for a teacher-preparation programme. Nor is consideration given for how teachers trained in TBLT are to cope with the resistance that they may well find when they enter schools where the teachers are unfamiliar with TBLT and may be unconvinced of the need for it.

I have not been able to find many proposals for teacher preparation programmes for TBLT and those I have found focus on in-service rather than pre-service teachers. Lai (2015) suggested the following:

(1) TBLT be presented as a set of provisional specifications for teachers to consider rather than an approach that they are expected to implement.
(2) Teachers need to be engaged in the active design of tasks.
(3) Teachers need adequate access to task-based teaching materials
(4) The training needs to be institutionalized with teachers given help in translating the training into practice.

Lai emphasized the desirability of presenting TBLT as a set of possibilities and of exploring with teachers how they might adapt TBLT to make it more viable in their own classrooms. Her proposal emphasizes in-school support for teachers, but she acknowledged that the manpower resources to enable trainers to visit teachers in their schools is often not available in Asia.

The importance of situating training within the teachers' own institutions is also emphasized by Viet *et al.* (2015). They outlined a school-focused professional programme consisting of four cyclical stages:

(1) Orientation – prior to formally meeting the teachers they should be provided with input-based tasks that introduce them to task-based language teaching.

(2) Activation – involving school or local-centre meetings where teachers articulate their new understandings in structured discussions among themselves facilitated by a local adviser. The discussion should focus on how to introduce the innovation into their own contexts and how to address potential problems.

(3) Application – the teachers collaborate, with assistance, in developing tasks or task-like activities by adapting activities in their textbooks which could be inserted into the production phase of PPP lesson.

(4) Piloting – the teachers pilot the jointly created tasks in their own classes and write reflective notes of their experiences. The notes would then provide the input for the next 'Orientation' stage.

In this proposal, therefore, there is no withdrawal training programme. This has obvious merits but some disadvantages too. One is the practical problem of assuring that there are sufficient experienced trainers to make regular visits to the teachers' schools. Another is the lack of a 'strong core curriculum' that introduces teachers to how theories of language learning and good education support the practice of TBLT (Principle 2 in Table 7.2). In Viet *et al.*'s proposal the emphasis is on practice. However, newly acquired practical skills that are not grounded in theory challenging teachers fundamental beliefs about learning and teaching are unlikely to thrive.

There is another reason why I think an introductory withdrawal programme is desirable. As I pointed out in Ellis (2009), there are a number of common misconceptions about task-based language teaching that are best addressed and discussed head on. For example, many teachers conceptualize TBLT as invariably putting students into groups to perform speaking tasks. While group work and speaking tasks have a major place in TBLT, they are not in fact defining features. Tasks can involve listening or reading and be performed by the teacher working with the whole class or by students individually as in the Communicational Language Teaching Project (Prabhu, 1987). If teachers assume that TBLT consists entirely (or even primarily) of small-group speaking tasks (e.g. Zheng & Borg, 2013), they may be reluctant to implement it, especially if their students lack speaking ability. Unless such misconceptions are dealt with, there is little chance of TBLT succeeding.

Thus, while accepting the need for school-based programmes, I would also argue there is a case for an introductory TBLT withdrawal programme and would like to suggest what such a programme might consist of, drawing on my *Introduction to Task-Based Teaching* (Ellis, 2019). An outline of the contents of the book can be seen in Table 7.3. This course was designed for use in in-service courses with teachers who have no background in TBLT and who are used to a structural syllabus and explicit language teaching. I have no expectancy that the book will

Table 7.3 Contents of *Introduction to Task-Based Teaching* (Ellis, 2019)

Preface
Chapter 1: What is task-based language teaching?
Chapter 2: Some key concepts
Chapter 3: Choosing tasks
Chapter 4: The methodology of a task-based lesson
Chapter 5: Doing focus on form
Chapter 6: Assessing students using tasks
Chapter 7: Addressing problems in task-based teaching
Glossary

result in the immediate introduction of TBLT. I hope, however, that it can motivate teachers to experiment with task-based language teaching and equip them with the tools for doing so.

The starting point of the course – and surely of any teacher-preparation programme – is to help teachers form a clear understanding of what a 'task' is. As we have seen (e.g. Oliver & Bogachenko, 2018; Erlam, 2016; Carless, 2004) teachers frequently have only a vague idea of what constitutes a task. So I would start by pointing out that tasks (e.g. debates; role plays) have always had a place in language teaching and thus are not an exotic novelty. I would then invite teachers to compare two activities – one a standard dialogue and the other a spot-the-difference activity - and ask them to judge which of these activities satisfies Ellis and Shintani's (2014) four criteria for defining a task. To build on this I would show how a standard cloze exercise can be redeveloped as a task by creating a gap and introducing a communicative purpose for performing the activity. This leads into an example of the kind of language use that results from performing a task. Finally, I would introduce task-supported language teaching as an alternative to task based. From the start, then, I acknowledge that many teachers may feel more comfortable with using tasks if they are linked to the kind of structural syllabus with which they are familiar.

There is no theory to begin with – rather the purpose is to introduce teachers to the kinds of activities that figure in task-based and task-supported language teaching. However, theory is important (Principle 2 in Table 7.1). As noted above, if task-based teaching is to take root, teachers need to understand the rationale for it and to evaluate their beliefs about how languages can be best learned in a classroom. At this point, then, I would introduce the key theoretical concepts that underpin the use of tasks. The crucial difference between incidental and intentional language learning is explained and linked to the two ways of using tasks in task-based and task-supported language teaching. Finally, these two types of teaching would be considered in relation to general principles drawn from theories of education. I continue to make a strong case for task-based language teaching but also acknowledge the theoretical basis of task-supported teaching.

Next, I would address the factors that teachers need to consider in deciding what tasks to use with their students. I would show how tasks can be distinguished in terms of two key dimensions (i.e. real-world versus pedagogic tasks; focused versus unfocused tasks) and then discuss different ways of classifying tasks. I would illustrate the difference between input-based and output-based tasks and point out the importance of the former for students with limited proficiency. Next, I would discuss the three types of gap in a task (information, opinion or reasoning), the nature of the task outcome (closed versus open) and whether the content of the task is teacher or student generated. In each case, examples of actual tasks are provided. I have several aims here. One is to make teachers aware of the range of tasks types available to them. A second is to address the common misunderstanding that tasks always involve speaking. A third – and arguably the most important – is to show how these different types of tasks vary in the demands they place on students and how tasks can be broadly matched to students' levels of development. I also would point out how the design features of specific tasks can influence their complexity. Finally, I would outline how teachers can use tasks in a specific purpose and general purpose course, focusing on how to select and sequence tasks to suit the abilities of their students. In this way I try to address the difficulty that teachers frequently experience in judging the complexity of a task (Van den Branden, 2006; Erlam, 2016).

Having dealt with task selection and the design of task-based courses, I then focus on the methodology of task-based teaching, describing the various options available for the pre-task, main task and post-task stages of a lesson. My aim here is to help teachers construct lesson plans around tasks and to show the importance of scaffolding the main task by preparing students to perform it. I also show that follow-up activities can include quite traditional form-focused activities directed at the linguistic problems that the students experienced while they performed a particular task. I illustrate the various options by showing how they can figure in lessons built round actual tasks. For this reason I do not refer directly to research that has investigated tasks and task-based teaching. I instead point to concrete ideas drawn from both research and the pedagogical literature. For the main task phase, I discuss the different roles that students and teachers will need to adopt, emphasizing the need to function primarily as communicators. I also point out that attention to linguistic form can occur in all stages of the lesson, including the main task phase, and in this way cater to both incidental and intentional language learning. My two underlying aims are to help teachers to see the variety of task-based lessons possible and to guard against the common misconception that in task-based teaching there is no focus on form (Ellis, 2009).

Focus on form is an essential feature of TBLT although its importance is often not recognized by even experienced TBLT educators (e.g. Willis & Willis, 2007). As defined by Long (1991, 2015), focus on form consists of the online strategies that teachers can use to draw students' attention to form as they perform a task. I describe the various pre-emptive and reactive strategies that teachers and students use to address the communicative and linguistic problems that arise while they perform tasks.[3] The focus is on the strategies themselves, each of which is illustrated in examples taken from classroom interaction, rather than on the theory that supports focus-on-form.

Next, I introduce teachers to how they can assess students in TBLT. I start by contrasting discrete-point testing – the kind of test that many teachers will be most familiar with – and task-based testing. I describe how to set about designing an assessment task and different ways in which the students' performance of an assessment task can be evaluated. I show how an assessment scale can be used to provide a measure of how successfully students have achieved the outcome of a task, if the task is a closed one, and also how to measure the quality of the students' production as they perform a task. I distinguish formative and summative assessment, pointing out that tasks are ideally suited to the former. Finally, I discuss how students can self-assess their own performance of a task. In many teaching contexts, of course, teachers are not free to determine their own method of assessment (see my discussion of the structural impediments for TBLT at the beginning of this chapter). My hope is that if teachers have a solid understanding of how tasks can be used for assessment purposes they will at least start to introduce assessment tasks into their teaching.

Finally, I address the problems that teachers commonly face when they try to implement TBLT in their classrooms. My understanding of these problems derives in part from the literature on TBLT and also from my experience of running workshops in different part of the world, where teachers commonly ask specific questions. The approach I adopt is to explain each problem and then suggest possible ways of addressing it. For example, for the problem '*How do teachers know what learners have learned in task-based language teaching?*' I point out that when learning is incidental, it is not possible to identify the specific bits of language that learners have acquired in a task-based lesson because this kind of learning is highly individual and is a slow, accumulative process. I also offer a concrete suggestion for investigating whether learners have acquired some new language (i.e. listing key vocabulary items at the beginning of the lesson, establishing that the students do not yet know them, and then showing them the same list at the end of the lesson and asking if they now know some of them). In other words, I continue emphasizing that learning occurs incidentally through using language while offering suggestions to assuage teachers' doubts about incidental learning.

In writing *An Introduction to Task-Based Language Teaching* I was very much aware of the factors that need to be considered in designing effective teacher-preparation programmes (see Table 7.1) and the general principles that can guide the development of such programmes (Table 7.2). My aim was to offer a practical and theory-informed account of TBLT, to help teachers' to develop a clear understanding of what a task is, to provide copious examples of actual tasks that teachers can try out in their classrooms, to put forward guidelines to help teachers select tasks at an appropriate level of complexity for their students, and to address the kinds of problems teachers are known to experience. Throughout the book, I include activities designed to encourage teachers to reflect on key issues raised in the text, to design their own tasks, and to prepare lesson plans. Of course, the book does not constitute a complete teacher-preparation course, as this would require the all-important in-school component. My hope is that it can lay the groundwork for such a component.

In writing this book, I was very much aware of the likelihood that in many cases teachers will not make an immediate shift to full TBLT and that the best that might be hoped for in the Asian classrooms I am most familiar with is a hybrid approach involving both traditional types of teaching associated with a structural syllabus (perhaps involving tasks as in task-supported language teaching) and, in some lessons, task-based teaching. In the book's conclusion I explore this idea of a hybrid approach.

Conclusion

I began this chapter by discussing the various impediments to the implementation of TBLT in state schools in Asia. This provided the basis for arguing the need for well-thought out teacher preparation programmes. Previous studies of such programmes have pointed to the factors that are the key to their success (see Table 7.1). Drawing on research in teacher education more generally, I identified a number of general principles that can guide the design of preparation programmes (see Table 7.2). It is, however, clear that problems are likely to remain. In particular, the structural/institutional issues mentioned in the chapter's opening section are unlikely to be resolved in the short term. Policy makers may mandate TBLT but at the same time wish to adhere to a structural syllabus and explicit language teaching. Traditional tests may stay in place. In such a context – and in my experience in Asia it is the dominant context – pure TBLT cannot flourish. It is necessary to seek some kind of compromise.

One such compromise might be to accept that task-supported language teaching should be accepted as the best way for moving forward. Long (2015), no advocate of task-supported language teaching, acknowledged that it might serve as a waystage towards the full implementation of TBLT in some contexts. Viet *et al.* (2015) argued the same. There are, however, other possibilities.

First, in many Asian countries (China, Japan, Korea, Malaysia, the Philippines) English starts at the elementary school level. Here there is a real opportunity for fully fledged TBLT to take root. It will be an enormous pity if these countries attempt to mimic the way English has been traditionally taught at secondary level in elementary classrooms. Also, educational practice at the elementary level has always been more open to the kind of experiential learning that TBLT aims to provide. Furthermore, as I have pointed out elsewhere (Ellis, 2017), the fact that the early stages of learning are essentially agrammatical (i.e. they involve the acquisition of words and chunks rather than rules), the case for choosing an initial approach that does not place grammar at its core is all the stronger. Perhaps then emphasis should be placed on introducing TBLT in elementary schools in Asia and teacher preparation directed also at this level.

Second, even teachers, who claim to be shackled by a structural syllabus, a text book that treats language as a set of objects to be mastered, and a test that prioritizes grammar and multiple-choice comprehension questions, have some choices available to them. They do not have to be so shackled in every lesson. If TBLT is to make strides, it is most likely to start by teachers having the confidence and knowledge to experiment with tasks in one-off classes or perhaps in a 15-minute slot at the end of a traditional lesson. Such experimentation does not necessitate resorting to task-supported language teaching. There is room for at least the occasional task-based lesson and, once teachers realize its potential, the seed can grow. As Van den Branden (2006) noted it takes time for task-based teaching to flourish. In contexts where learners have clearly specifiable language needs – as in González-Lloret and Nielson's (2015) task-based Spanish course for US border patrol officers – or in contexts such as Belgium where the structural, institutional impediments to introducing TBLT have been addressed, the aim should be to prepare teachers for full task-based teaching. In state schools in Asia (elementary schools being the exception), however, the aim should be the lesser and more realistic one of ensuring teachers have the understanding and the practical means to give tasks a try.

Notes

(1) Van den Branden *et al.*'s (2009) *Task-Based Language Teaching: A Reader* contains just one article (by Van den Branden) on training teachers for TBLT.
(2) The relationship between beliefs and practice is a complex one. See Breen *et al.* (2001) for a thoughtful examination of this. Their study showed that 'there is an underlying and consistent pattern in the ways they think about their work and the ways in which they act in the language class' (2001: 496). It follows that when teacher educators aim to induct teachers into a new approach (such as TBLT) it is important that the teachers adopt new ways of thinking. The Flanders teacher development programme was successful because it achieved this.
(3) Long (2015) considers that focus-on-form involves reactive strategies (e.g. recasts) only. However, drawing on research by Ellis *et al.* (2001), I argue that it can be pre-emptive as well as reactive (e.g. teachers and students sometimes pre-empt linguistic problems).

References

Adams, R. and Newton, J. (2009) TBLT in Asia: Opportunities and constraints. *Asian Journal of English Language Teaching* 19, 1–17.

Borg, S. (2011) The impact of in-service teacher education on language teachers' beliefs. *System* 39 (3), 370–380.

Breen, M., Hird, B., Milton, M., Oliver, R. and Thwaite, A. (2001) Making sense of language teaching: Teachers' principles and classroom practices. *Applied Linguistics* 22, 470–501.

Butler, Y. (2004) What level of English proficiency do elementary school teachers need to attain to teach EFL? Case studies from Korea, Taiwan, and Japan. *TESOL Quarterly* 38 (2), 245–278.

Butler, Y. (2011) The implementation of communicative and task-based teaching in the Asia-Pacific region. *Annual Review of Applied Linguistics* 31, 36–57.

Carless, D. (2004) Issues in teachers' reinterpretation of a task-based innovation in primary schools. *TESOL Quarterly* 38, 639–662.

Darling-Hammond, L. (2006) *Powerful Teacher Education: Lessons From Exemplary Programs*. San Francisco: Jossey-Bass.

East, M. (2014) Encouraging innovation in a modern foreign language initial teacher education programme. What do beginning teachers make of task-based language teaching? *The Language Learning Journal* 42, 261–274.

Ellis, R. (2003) *Task-Based Language Learning and Teaching*. Oxford: Oxford University Press.

Ellis, R. (2009) Task-based language teaching: Sorting out the misunderstandings. *International Journal of Applied Linguistics* 19, 221–246.

Ellis, R. (2015) Teachers researching tasks. In M. Bygate (ed.) *Domains and Directions in the Development of TBLT* (pp. 247–270). Amsterdam: John Benjamins.

Ellis, R. (2017) Towards a modular curriculum for using tasks. *Language Teaching Research*.

Ellis, R. (2019) *Introducing Task-Based Language Teaching*. Shanghai: Shanghai Foreign Language Education Press.

Ellis, R. and Shintani, N. (2014) *Exploring Language Pedagogy Through Second Language Acquisition Research*. London: Routledge.

Ellis, R., Basturkmen, H. and Loewen, S. (2001) Learner uptake in communicative ESL lessons. *Language Learning* 51, 281–318.

Erlam, R. (2015) 'New tricks': Teachers talk about task-based language teaching. *Babel* 50, 4–11.

Erlam, R. (2016) I'm still not sure what a task is: Teachers designing language tasks. *Language Teaching Research* 20, 279–299.

Foster, P. (1998) A Classroom perspective on the negotiation of meaning. *Applied Linguistics* 19, 1–23.

González-Lloret, M. and Nielson, K. (2015) Evaluating TBLT: The case of a task-based Spanish program. *Language Teaching Research* 19 (5), 525–549.

Hall, S. (2015) Gaining acceptance of task-based teaching during Malaysian rural in-service teacher training. In M. Thomas and H. Reinders (eds) *Contemporary Task-Based Teaching in Asia* (pp. 156-169). London: Bloomsbury.

Hu, R. (2013) Task-based language teaching: Responses from Chinese teachers of English. *TESL-EJ* 16, 1–21.

Ingvarson, L., Reid, K., Buckley, S., Kleinhenz, E. and Masters, G. (2014) *Best Practice Teacher Education Programs and Australia's Own Programs*. Canberra: Department of Education.

Jackson, D. (2012) Task-based language teacher education in an undergraduate program in Japan. In A. Shehadeh and C. Coombe (eds) *Task-Based Language Teaching in Foreign Language Contexts* (pp. 267–285). Amsterdam: John Benjamins.

Jeon, I.J. and Hahn, J.W. (2006) Exploring EFL Teachers? Perceptions of task-based language teaching: A case study of Korean secondary school classroom practice. *Asian EFL Journal* 8, 123–139.

Lai, C. (2015) Task-based language teaching in the Asian context: Where are we now and where are we going? In M. Thomas and H. Reinders (eds) *Contempory Task-Based Teaching in Asia* (pp. 12–29). London: Bloomsbury.

Li, D. (1998) It's always more difficult than you planned. Teachers' perceived difficulties in introducing the communicative approach in South Korea. *TESOL Quarterly* 32, 677–703.

Linsen, B. (1994) Met vallen en opstaan: de intrioductie van taakhericht taalonderwijs. Een praktijkbeschrijving uit bet basisonderwijs in Vlaanderen. In S. Kroon and T. Vallen (eds) *Nderlands als teweede taal in het onderwijs. Parktijkbeschrijvingen uit Nederland en Vlaanderen* (pp. 131–59). 'S Gravenhage: Nderelandcse Taalunie Voorzetten 46. Cited in K. Van den Branden (2006).

Littlewood, W. (2007) Communicative and task-based language teaching in East Asian classrooms. *Language Teaching* 40, 243–249.

Littlewood, W. (2014) Communication-oriented teaching: where are we now? Where do we go from here? *Language Teaching* 47, 249–362.

Long, M. (1991) Focus on form: A design feature in language teaching methodology. In K. de Bot, R.B. Ginsberg and C. Kramsch (eds) *Foreign Language Research in Cross-Cultural Perspective* (pp. 39–52). Amsterdam: John Benjamins.

Long, M. (2015) *Second Language Acquisition and Task-Based Language Teaching*. Malden, MA: Wiley Blackwell.

Long, M.H. (2016) In defence of tasks and TBLT: Nonissues and real issues. *Annual Review of Applied Linguistics* 36, 5–33.

McDonough, K. (2015) Perceived benefits and challenges with the use of collaborative tasks in EFL contexts. In M. Bygate (ed.) *Domains and Directions in the Developments of TBLT* (pp. 225–246). Amsterdam: John Benjmain.

McDonough, K. and Chaikitmongkol, W. (2007) Teachers' and learners' reactions to a task based EFL course in Thailand. *TESOL Quarterly* 41, 107–132.

Ogilvie, G. and Dunn, W. (2010) Taking teacher education to task: Exploring the role of teacher education in promoting the utilization of task-based teaching. *Language Teaching Research* 14, 161–181.

Oliver, R. and Bogachenko, T. (2018) Teacher perception and use of tasks in school ESL classrooms. In V. Samuda, K. van den Branden and M. Bygate (eds) *Task-Based Language Teaching as a Researched Pedagogy* (pp. 72–95). Amsterdam: Johns Benjamins.

Prabhu, N.S. (1987) *Second Language Pedagogy*. Oxford: Oxford University Press.

Richards, J. (1990) The dilemma of teacher education in second language teaching. In J. Richards and D. Nunan (eds) *Second Language Teacher Education* (pp. 3–15). Cambridge: Cambridge University Press.

Roessingh, H. (2014) TBL and teacher preparation: Toward a curriculum for pre-service teachers. *TESL Canada Journal* 31, 157–174.

Samimy, K. and Kobayashi, C. (2004) Toward the development of intercultural competence: Theoretical and pedagogical implications for Japanese English teachers. *JALT Journal* 26, 245–261.

Samuda, V. and Bygate, N. (2008) *Tasks in Second Language Learning*. Basingstoke: Palgrave Macmillan.

Seedhouse, P. (1997) The case of the missing "no"; the relationship between pedagogy and interaction. *Language Learning* 47, 547–83.

Van den Branden, K. (2006) Training teachers: Task-based as well? In K. van den Branden (eds) *Task-Based Language Education: From Theory to Practice* (pp. 217–248). Cambridge: Cambridge University Press.

Van den Branden, K. (2016) The role of teachers in task-based language education. *ARAL* 36, 164–181.

Van den Branden, K., Bygate, M. and Norris, J. (eds) (2019) *Task-Based Language Teaching: A Reader*. Amsterdam: John Benjamins.

Viet, N., Canh, L. and Barnard, R. (2015) "Old wine in new bottles': Two case studies of task-based language teaching in Vietnam. In M. Thomas and H. Reinders (eds) *Contemporary Task-Based Language Teaching in Asia* (pp. 68–86). London: Bloomsbury.

Watson-Todd, R. (2006) Continuing change after innovation. *System* 34, 1–14.

Willis, D. and Willis, J. (2007) *Doing Task-Based Teaching*. Oxford: Oxford University Press.

Zheng, X. and Borg, S. (2013) Task-based learning and teaching in China: Secondary school teachers' beliefs and practices. *Language Teaching Research* 18 (2), 205–221.

Part 2: Approaches to Using Tasks

8 A Task-Based Needs Analysis for US Foreign Service Officers: The Challenge of the Japanese Celebration Speech

Kyoko Kobayashi Hillman and Michael H. Long

Foreign language classes for diplomats must equip them to handle a variety of important tasks in their work overseas. A needs analysis (NA) was conducted for Foreign Service Officers (FSOs) assigned to the US embassy and consulates in Japan. In Stage 1, use of multiple sources and methods identified 68 target tasks for FSOs in Japan (and presumably, with some modifications, diplomatic postings elsewhere). In Stage 2, an analysis of target discourse (ATD) was carried out for one of the most complex of the target tasks, 'Delivering a celebration speech'. The celebration speech was selected because of the challenge it presents for TBLT or any other communicative approach to language teaching, due to the subtle pragmatic knowledge and appropriate sociolinguistic choices required for a formal occasion in Japanese. The ATD revealed the typical structure of such speeches. Sub-tasks were identified with high interrater reliability, along with their corresponding linguistic features. The results were distilled to produce two prototypical exemplars to serve as input for the design of task-based materials.

Introduction

Government employees around the world often require proficiency in two or more languages to do their work. Because this work focuses on the real-world tasks they must perform, task-based language teaching (TBLT) is a viable approach to language training for many such occupations (Long, 2015a, 2015b; Long *et al.*, 2019).

123

In some cases, basic L2 abilities will suffice in such contexts. For example, González-Lloret and Nielson (2014) described the design and implementation of a Task-Based Language Teaching (TBLT) program in L2 Spanish for the US Border Patrol Academy (BPA), and its evaluation through three follow-up studies. Target tasks for the BP agents – such things as conducting an emergency vehicle stop, inspecting bus passengers' identification documents and communicating with immigrants who have been abandoned by smugglers – were identified through a NA that used data from several sources, including observations of the real-world tasks performed by experienced agents (domain experts). Series of initially simple, gradually more complex, *pedagogic tasks* were then designed for modules of task-based materials, sequenced by increasing task complexity, not linguistic complexity. Although classroom instruction did not include planned explicit grammar teaching, grammatical accuracy and lexical complexity achieved by the TBLT student group were found to be comparable to that of students in an earlier grammar-based course for BP agents, and more relevant to their duties in the field. As for overall proficiency improvement, results showed that final test scores for 256 trainee agents who completed the eight-week TBLT course were statistically significantly better than their test scores before they began the course. A survey administered to students enrolled in the TBLT course and agents who had completed it showed positive reactions to their learning experiences. These are typical findings in TBLT course evaluations (Bryfonski & McKay, 2017; Long, 2015a: 341–365, 2015b).

In other cases, for example, military linguists, intelligence personnel and diplomats, more advanced proficiency may be required. In the United States, that can often mean Level 3, so-called 'Professional ability', on the Inter-Agency Language Roundtable (ILR) scale. It is hard for many government employees to reach Level 3, especially in a foreign language (often their second, third or fourth) typologically distant from their L1 (usually English), and when their age and the limited number of hours they can invest in language study may not be ideal. Hence, there is interest in improving the effectiveness and efficiency of language classes to meet their and their country's needs. TBLT is currently being explored as a viable solution, such as in pilot courses at the US Foreign Service Institute (Matar, 2014; Touré & Nicolai, 2015).

The first step in creating a TBLT program for adults is to conduct a learner needs analysis (NA). Designers of courses for children who as yet lack identifiable needs can skip this step, select high interest pedagogic tasks for the age concerned, and focus on TBLT methodology and pedagogy (see, e.g. Shintani, 2013). The frequency and rigor of NAs have considerably improved in recent years, with a growing literature now available on NA methodology (see, e.g. Brown, 2009, 2016; Gilabert, 2005; Lambert, 2010; Long, 2005, 2013, 2015a: 85–204, 2020; Malicka *et al.*,

2017; Serafini *et al.*, 2015). The study reported here was a standard, two-stage, task-based NA conducted for US foreign service officers (FSOs) in Japan: (i) identification of target tasks, and (ii) analysis of target discourse (ATD). In Stage 1, 68 target tasks were identified using multiple sources and methods. One of the most complex, delivering a celebration speech, was then deliberately selected for the ATD demonstration, due to the challenge it presents for any communicative approach, not just TBLT. It is especially tricky because its successful performance in Japanese entails knowledge of specific formulaic expressions and a command of the appropriate register and pragmatics. Following standard procedure, the results of the ATD were distilled to produce prototypical exemplars of celebration speeches to serve as input for the design of task-based materials.

The Study

A NA for TBLT has two parts. First, target tasks are identified for a specified group of learners, such as physicians, undergraduate computer science students, bio-science post-docs, traffic policemen, hospital porters, restaurant chefs, insurance sales people, airline flight attendants, tour guides, automobile mechanics and so on. Reliability and validity are increased when use is made of multiple sources of information, multiple methods for tapping those sources, and triangulation among methods and sources (Long, 2005, 2015a: 117–168; Serafini *et al.*, 2015). Second, an analysis of target discourse (ATD) is carried out on genuine samples of language use for performing the most critical (essential), important, and/or most frequent tasks for their work.

Identification of Target Tasks

Published written source

To identify the communicative needs of the FSOs, a published written source, the *Dictionary of Occupational Titles*, was consulted first to obtain a general overview of FSO job requirements. Next, written introspections were gathered from experienced FSOs (domain experts). Finally, to assess the generalizability of the initial findings, an on-line survey was conducted of a larger group of FSOs. As usual, the three components were sequenced from 'open' to 'closed'. Earlier deployed methods, in this case, written introspections, provided qualitative data that allowed more in-depth understanding (but were labor intensive to collect and analyze), which informed later deployed methods, in this case, the online questionnaire survey. The questionnaire resulted in shallower, but easier to analyze, quantitative data. It allowed wider coverage of the learner group's membership, effectively testing the generalizability of the earlier findings.

The *Dictionary of Occupational Titles (DOT)*, published by the United States Employment Service, includes very general overviews of tasks performed, and performance standards required, in several thousand occupations (US Department of Labor, 2011). The *DOT* is gradually being supplanted by its online successor *O*Net*, the *Occupational Information Network*, which is more easily accessed and, like the *DOT*, free of charge, but as yet covers fewer occupations. The *DOT* describes the FSO as a generalist with a broad range of responsibilities, including representing the interests of the US government and US nationals and providing various services to US citizens and foreigners who wish to enter the US.

Written introspections

To further specify tasks for FSOs that require use of Japanese, written introspections were sought via e-mail from current or former employees of the US Department of State. Spoken or written introspections by insiders are valuable when designing a language course because, as 'open' procedures, they can reveal information about tasks known to domain experts, and sometimes only to domain experts, because of their first-hand experience with the work. The tasks they identify are likely to be those perceived as meaningful and relevant for job performance by the people who actually do the job (emic categories), rather than a list of tasks enshrined in 'closed' questionnaire items (etic categories) presented to them by outsiders only for approval or rejection.

Twelve FSOs out of the 17 contacted replied to the request, for a response rate of 70.6%. The mean length of their foreign service at the time of the replies was 15.1 years. Their Japanese language proficiency on the US government's Inter-Agency Language Round Table (ILR) five-level proficiency scale ranged from ILR 2 to 4 for speaking, and ILR 0+ to 4+ for reading (roughly CEFR B1/2 to C2). Their mean speaking and reading scores were ILR 3.27 and ILR 3.12, respectively. Their Japanese language-learning experiences with the Foreign Service Institute (FSI) varied. While three had been posted to Japan twice, the rest had been assigned there only once. Each had previously worked in the US embassy in Tokyo or in one of the consulates elsewhere in Japan. The request to the informants for written introspections was that they provide a list of specific tasks performed in Japanese while in a typically three-year assignment in Japan and write down key words and expressions they encountered.

Based on their responses, 43 different target tasks were identified, but some, including 'Meeting with officials, representatives, journalists and academics for substantive talks', were too general (closer to task-*types* than target tasks) and needed to be broken down and made more specific, resulting in a total of 50 target tasks. Fifteen were related to interactions with contacts outside the embassy or consulate, such as 'Accompanying US politicians and military officials on courtesy calls with Japanese counterparts', 'Ordering a product or service from a vendor' and 'Visiting military bases'. Three concerned interactions with embassy and consulate staff members, e.g. 'Obtaining directions from a receptionist or guard'. Two tasks were directly related to interactions with foreigners who wish to enter the United States, most obviously, 'Conducting a visa interview'. Four involved interactions with mass media, including 'Explaining US policy', and 'Appearing on a TV show'. Seven miscellaneous tasks were folded into more general categories of wider applicability: 'Making courtesy thank-you calls to companies that hosted visiting US engineers', for example, became part of 'Conducting site visits to factories, companies and small businesses'. Twelve tasks, e.g. 'Checking in and out at hotels', and 'Making restaurant reservations', concerned individuals' private lives, although they could also be job related.

At the level of task type, the most frequently listed was 'Meeting with officials, representatives, journalists and academics for substantive talks'. The second most frequent was 'Talking with office receptionists or building guards to obtain directions and information'. Five task types were the joint third most listed: 'Delivering speeches and/or remarks at events in Japanese', 'Talking about everyday issues (traffic, weather, food, travel, etc.) with guests or contacts on official occasions and at receptions', 'Conversing with Japanese staff', 'Talking with restaurant wait-staff for reservations and orders' and 'Talking with shop owners and/or employees'. Fewer informants responded to the second question related to words and expressions frequently used in Japan. Those that did mostly offered formulaic expressions commonly used to build rapport, such as *otsukare sama desu* and *gokuroo sama desu* (well done; good job). A possible reason for the fewer replies to the second question is that all informants but one had left Japan some time before the study, their official ILR scores notwithstanding. FSO informants still in Japan were likely to produce better information on language and tasks, as they were less reliant on their memory.

Online questionnaire survey

Based on the written introspections, the pilot version of a questionnaire was distributed to 12 FSOs who had served in Afghanistan or Nigeria, as a result of whose suggestions a further 18 tasks were added to the list, for a final total of 68. The 68-item questionnaire was then administered to a larger group of 67 FSOs in Japan in the form of an online survey posted on a website.[1] The instrument was carefully designed to avoid possible bias or misunderstanding. For example, items were piloted, and any that proved ambiguous, overly complex, or too abstract were removed (For additional considerations when writing items for needs analysis questionnaires, see Long, 2015a: 152–156). Also, mostly closed items were employed, given the likely quantity of data, although a few open-ended questions were retained. To ensure anonymity, questions pertaining to individual details of the FSO respondents were minimal, concerning only their length of employment in the Foreign Service, posting experiences in Japan, learning experiences at FSI, and highest ILR ratings for Japanese. Questions were as concise as possible, including just three choices for the frequency with which respondent had performed the tasks: Never, Once or twice and More than twice. The results, therefore, reflected only the FSOs' perceptions regarding their performance of the tasks, not the actual frequencies with which each task was performed. Completing the survey took five to ten minutes, a short period designed to increase response rate.

The online survey was returned by 32 FSOs out of the 67 contacted, a response rate of 47.8%. Nineteen had been in the service from a few months to 10 years, ten for 11–20 years and three for 21 years or longer. While 22 had taken Japanese classes at the main FSI campus in the US, 10 had never studied Japanese at that location. Of the 22, nine had studied only at the main FSI campus, and two only at the FSI's overseas branch in Japan. The remaining 11 had studied at both sites. Average ILR speaking and reading scores were 2.90 and 2.32, roughly B1 and A2, respectively, ranging between ILR 0 + and 4 for speaking, and ILR 0 and 4 for reading, roughly A1 to C1.

The frequency with which FSOs reported having performed each task was tallied. At least half the respondents reported having performed 19 more than twice. All had performed three of the tasks more than twice: 'Talking with restaurant wait staff', 'Talking with a shop owner and/or employee' and 'Conversing for shopping and other daily life use'. 'Talking with taxi drivers' was the next most frequent task, which all respondents but one reported having performed more than twice. The task the fifth largest number of FSOs had performed was 'Making a reservation at a restaurant'. These five tasks were categorized as interactions for semi-private use. The task that the sixth largest number of FSOs had performed more than twice was 'Talking about everyday issues (traffic, weather, food, travel, etc.) with guests or contacts at receptions', which was categorized as interaction with contacts outside the embassy and consulate. Two tasks performed inside the embassy and consulate, 'Talking with an embassy and/or consulate driver', and 'Communicating with embassy and/or consulate Japanese staff verbally', had been performed more than twice by over 80% of respondents.

Tasks performed more than twice were broken down by respondents' Japanese proficiency level: those performed by FSOs with relatively higher (ILR 3 or above) or lower (ILR 0 – 2+) proficiency. The lower group reported having performed all the tasks for inside the embassy and consulate and in their semi-private lives more than twice. Although many tasks had only been performed by the higher proficiency group, e.g. 'Conducting site visits to factories, companies, and small businesses', and 'Accompanying US politicians and military officials on courtesy calls with Japanese counterparts', four pertinent to consular work, 'Conversing with a visa applicant', 'Taking an oath when notarizing documents', 'Conducting a visa interview' and 'Conversing with Japanese police and prison officials about American citizen issues', were found to have been performed more by the lower group. Although the proficiency information did not necessarily indicate the level required to perform specific tasks, it is potentially useful for TBLT curriculum design. Other needs analyses, too, have found that target tasks for the same population can change as proficiency increases. For example, a needs analysis conducted (and subsequently repeated) for an ESL program for Latino migrant workers in the United States (Nielson, 2010) reported predominantly simple tasks, such as 'Following street directions' and 'Using public transport', as priorities for the most recent arrivals, generally those with lowest L2 proficiency, whereas some longer-term residents with higher proficiency were interested in such tasks as 'Registering a child in school' and 'Opening a bank account'. In the interest of relevance to student needs, such differences should obviously be reflected in the resulting task syllabus.

Discourse Analysis (DA) and Analysis of Target Discourse (ATD)

Stage 2 of a task-based NA involves analyzing genuine samples of spoken and/or written language use surrounding performance of the most important of the target tasks identified in Stage 1. This is referred to as an analysis of target discourse (ATD), as distinct from a conventional discourse analysis (DA). There are significant differences between the two.

A conventional DA is expected to meet four criteria (Sinclair & Coulthard, 1975: 15–17): (i) a descriptive apparatus with a finite set of categories, specified *a priori*, (ii) categories that are operationalized clearly and explicitly, (iii) comprehensive coverage, without recourse to a 'wild card' category like 'miscellaneous' or 'other' to deal with data not handled by the main system and (iv) two or more levels of analysis, with categories at higher levels 'consisting of' categories at lower levels (e.g. in the Sinclair and Coulthard analysis of classroom lessons, lesson > transaction > exchange > move > act), with one or more impossible combinations of categories, to preclude pseudo-analyses which implicitly suggest that the target discourse can have any structure or no structure at all, i.e. to eliminate analyses with no predictive power.

An ATD has different goals and is not subject to the same constraints (for discussion and five examples, see Long, 2015a: 181–204). The objective is not a comprehensive, hierarchical DA, but a flatter, serial analysis focusing on just those segments, aspects and features of language use that are relevant for some issues outside the discourse itself. For example, a researcher might be interested in the relationships between types of errors made by L2 learners, types of negative feedback those error types elicit, and types of uptake following the feedback, or in relationships between types of teacher questions (referential/display, open/closed, etc.) and the accuracy and complexity of student responses. Conversations between native and non-native speakers in the classroom or outside of the classroom obviously involve far more than just those two types of exchanges but, rightly or wrongly, the researcher may only be interested in the role of negative feedback or of question types in SLA, and not in the position of such exchanges in conversation as a whole or in anything else in the interaction.

DAs and ATDs defined this way are usually readily distinguished but are not mutually exclusive. Some DAs serve an applied function, as was the case with Sinclair and Coulthard's analysis of classroom lessons. The purpose of an ATD in TBLT is to identify commonalities in genuine samples of language use surrounding successful performance of target tasks. The results are distilled to produce prototypical models, with any idiosyncrasies removed. These models then use *elaborated* (not linguistically simplified) input. Therefore, task-based teaching materials retain unknown, but domain-appropriate, language that learners require to meet their specialized needs, instead of losing such items as a by-product of linguistic simplification because they are (often) of lower frequency, as is customary with commercially published generic materials. (For details and examples of prototypical models and input elaboration, as well as research findings, see Bartlett, 2005; Long, 2015a: 169–204; O'Connell, 2015; O'Donnell, 2009.)

Analysis of Target Discourse (ATD): Delivering a Celebration Speech

At the level of *target task-type*, both the written introspections and the on-line survey data consistently pointed to the importance of formal public speeches of various kinds, a finding consistent with that of previous NAs for diplomats (Kim, 1999; Yalden, 1987; Yazawa, 2013). The task-type in Japanese is a particularly challenging one for FSOs, and also for TBLT, given the attention to linguistic accuracy and pragmatic appropriateness required as intrinsic dimensions of task-based abilities for what are often very formal occasions in Japan. It is possible to follow street directions, buy a cell phone, report a traffic accident or understand the information in a university lecture without anything approaching native-like command of past time reference, the English article system or the ability to appreciate subtle asides the lecturer may include, but delivering a formal speech in Japanese requires grammatical accuracy, appropriate lexical choice and, above all, selection of the correct register, including use of the appropriate formulaic expressions and honorifics.

English native speakers' experiences delivering speeches in Japanese in formal situations were gathered via semi-structured interviews with two FSOs and an employee closely associated with foreign affairs, specializing in Japan, each with advanced Japanese proficiency and an average of 22 years of service in the US State Department.[2] All three informants reported that Japanese honorific expressions were the most difficult linguistic aspect of delivering speeches, including brief remarks. They also noted how Japanese speeches mainly consisted of lengthy formulaic expressions with the requisite honorific forms and that the speeches themselves did not necessarily include many substantive points. Accordingly, they began delivering their speeches, including some suddenly requested on the spot, with frequently used formulaic expressions, including those for conveying gratitude. In the interviews, the informants pointed out that these formulaic expressions are closely related to the organization and flow of the speech. Some expressions are always used either at the beginning or the end. All three informants appeared to have managed to include the original messages that they wanted to convey successfully, while managing to follow the regular flow of Japanese speeches and with the frequently used formulaic expressions. Nevertheless, delivering speeches in formal situations, such as at receptions and important social events, is clearly a challenging target task type for FSOs, and for TBLT. At the level of *target task*, the particular example selected for analysis was 'Delivering a celebration speech'.

As noted above, an ATD constitutes the second part of a task-based NA. ATDs produce *prototypical models* of L2 use for doing important target tasks identified during Stage 1. Given the extremely high level of formality required for the delivery of a celebration speech in Japanese, it is better if materials used in class are based on speeches delivered by native Japanese speakers. However, the possibility of obtaining celebration speeches delivered by Japanese diplomats is low, because diplomats seldom deliver speeches as diplomats in their home country. Therefore, materials specifically designed for FSOs in Japan need to be developed using native speech samples collected at anniversary events that are then modified for an individual FSO's requirements according to his or her position. The raw data used for the ATD in this study consisted of six celebration speeches delivered by native Japanese speakers. The six speeches, ranging in length from one to six minutes, were audio-recorded at three anniversary events hosted by a Japanese government agency and a Japanese international organization.

Classification of Sub-tasks and Inter-rater Reliability

A Japanese celebration speech is a monologue that differs from conversational interaction in a number of ways, including the lexical items and expressions likely to be used for formal occasions. While some speakers deliver speeches without prompts or notes, others read from prepared scripts. In contrast to conversational data, speeches are typically made up of complete sentences, possibly because they reflect both spoken and written language (Fukasawa & Hillman, 2012; Hillman & Fukasawa, 2009). Therefore, each of the six speeches was transcribed in sentence form. Sentences were analyzed in terms of T-units, defined as one main clause plus any subordinate clauses attached to or embedded in it (Crookes, 1990; Foster et al., 2000). Most sentences in the data consisted of one main clause with several long subordinate clauses, including relative clauses and adverbial clauses. The subordinate clauses were examined closely for how they helped convey a speaker's main message. The clauses were divided into separate units when it was obvious that the speaker had shifted the content of the message from one clause to another within a single sentence, and when the clauses were juxtaposed using connectives. There were many cases in which speakers used verb conjugations, (gerundial te-forms and infinitival forms meaning and in English, as in eat and drink, and go and see, and ga and keredomo, meaning but in English) to connect two verbs to reinforce the message in the main clause. Those were not divided into separate T-units. A new unit was created only when the speaker clearly established a new message in the juxtaposed position.

The speeches were then analyzed into sub-tasks. A sub-task is 'a differentiated process which, while having a number of steps and an outcome, is dependent on or part of another major target task' (Gilabert, 2005: 184). The frequencies of sub-tasks were tallied across the six speeches. As shown in Table 8.1, 24 sub-tasks were found in the six celebration speeches that constituted the data for this part of the study.

Crookes (1986, 1990) noted that a system that describes particular activities and behaviors is required to demonstrate consistency among raters trained according to that system. He considered it necessary to validate an ATD (in his case, of the introductions to scientific journal articles) in the same manner. Following Crookes's procedure, two experienced Japanese language instructors were individually trained using one of the speeches in the data set. They then separately each rated two additional speeches, Speech 1 and Speech 3. Using SPSS,

Table 8.1 Description of sub-tasks

	Sub-task	Description	Expressions	Total # identified
1	Greet audience*	The speaker directly greets the audience using common greeting expressions.	minasan, konbanwa	2
2	Introduce self***	The speaker introduces him/herself mentioning his/her name and title/position of affiliated organization.	watakushi wa ~ (affiliation) no (name) de gozaimasu, ~to mooshimasu	5
3	Introduce affiliation	The speaker introduces him/herself as a representative of an affiliated group to justify why he/she is delivering the speech.	~o daihyoo itashimashite,	1
4	Congratulate organizers***	The speaker politely or directly congratulates the organizers.	oiwai o mooshiagetai to omoimasu, oiwai o mooshiageru shidaidegozaimasu, omedetoo gozaimasu, oyorokobi o mooshiagemasu	12
5	Thank organizers*	The speaker directly expresses his/her gratitude to the organizers of the event.	arigatoo gozaimasu, kyooshuku o shiteorimasu, junbi shite itadaki	2
6	Thank organization**	The speaker expresses his/her gratitude to the organization that is recognized at the event.	kansha o mooshi agetai, onrei o mooshiageru, arigataku omou	4
7	Thank audience *	The speaker expresses gratitude to the general audience.	arigatoo gozaimashita	2
8	Welcome audience	The speaker welcomes the audience.	kangei itashimasu	1
9	Recognize honor of invitation	The speaker mentions the honor he/she feels in speaking at the event.	kooei ni zonjite iru	1
10	Express respect to organization**	The speaker expresses respect to the organization.	keii o hyoo suru	3
11	Excuse lack of preparation	The speaker makes an excuse for his/her lack of preparation for the speech.	~monndesu kara, ~ (sas)etekimashita, nani mo yooi sezuni	1
12	Explain significance of the occasion*	The speaker provides a brief overview and explains the timing of the event and/or the importance of the timing.	masani hajimaroooto shiteimasu, seedai ni kooshite kaisai saremashita, choodo ~ nen desu ne	3
13	Comment on occasion**	The speaker makes comments about what he or she thinks related to the occasion.	subarashiku ii, ureshiku omotte orimasu, kokoro zuyoku omotte iru	9

(Continued on next page)

Table 8.1 Description of sub-tasks (Continued)

14	Explain organization's importance**	The speaker mentions the organization's achievements, contributions and reputation in detail.	*katsudoo wa takaku hyooka sareteiru, juuyoona yakuwari o ninatte orareru, (organization) ga attareba koso*	7
15	Recognize other important guests*	The speaker directly mentions the names of other important guests at the occasion.	*(guests' names) ni oide o itadakimashita, (guests' names) kara mo ohanashi gozaimashita*	2
16	Explain current situation*	The speaker refers to what is currently happening.	*~te orimasu, ~te iru tokoro de arimasu, yoku iwareru*	10
17	Comment on current situation	The speaker makes comments about what he or she thinks is related to what is currently happening.	*~to omotte orimasu, ~to iufuuni omotte iru, ~to omou*	6
18	Commit to cause	The speaker commits or promises to support the cause or goal.	*ochikai shitai to omoimasu*	1
19	Request audience agreement	The speaker asks for the audience's agreement.	*ikaga de shoo ka*	1
20	Explain historical overview	The speaker explains historical facts.	(vocabulry related to history) *~ nen, ~jidai*	3
21	Share past experiences	The speaker mentions his/her past experiences.	*katteha, omoide wo tsukurasete itadakimashita*	1
22	Anticipate future development	The speaker mentions future perspectives and expresses prospects for future development.	*sarannaru hiyaku o mezashite, kongo no dantai no katsudo*	1
23	Request cooperation*	The speaker requests cooperation.	*renkei kyooryoku o shinagara, gokyooryoku o yoroshiku onegai o mooshiagetai to omou shidai degozaimasu*	2
24	Pray for future success***	The speaker wishes for the future success of the organization and the audience.	*gokenshoo gokatsuyaku o gokinen mooshiage, ~wo kokoro kara gokinen mooshiage, kinen mooshiage*	6
	TOTAL			86

***The sub-task occurred in five to six speeches.
**The sub-task occurred in three speeches.
*The sub-task occurred in two speeches.

values of Cohen's kappa for inter-rater reliabilities for the speeches were 0.79 and 1.0, respectively. Values higher than 0.60 are deemed reliable, given that this is a conservative measure that corrects for chance agreement (Chaudron *et al.*, 1988; Crookes, 1986; Long & Ross, 1993). These results demonstrated that the classification system could be used with confidence to analyze genuine speeches as a basis for developing prototypical speeches to include in teaching materials.

The number of times each sub-task appeared across the six speeches was tallied. All six used 'Congratulate organizers' at the beginning, somewhere between the first and fourth unit. Five of the speeches included this sub-task twice, once at the beginning and once at the end. Four of the six speeches ended with it. By including congratulatory expressions at both the beginning and end of speeches, speakers showed they clearly found it important to recognize the organizers of the events in question. The next most frequently used sub-tasks were 'Introduce self' and 'Pray for future success', although one speech (#4) did not include either. The self-introduction occurred at the beginning of speeches and made speakers' names and organizational affiliations clear to their audiences. The sub-task 'Pray for future success' occurred towards the end of all five speeches, appearing one to two units before the closing.

The sub-task, 'Thank organization' was used in the main body of three speeches. There was no pattern to the preceding or following sub-task. A distinction was made between 'Thank organizers' and 'Thank organization' because some units expressed gratitude specifically to those who had organized the events, while others focused on the organizations behind the events. Three other sub-tasks appeared in three speeches: 'Comment on occasion', 'Explain organization's importance' and 'Express respect for organization'. The comments observed in the data were directly related to the events hosted, with speakers expressing their view of the events. They also mentioned contributions of the organization to the public, so as to emphasize the important role it played. For this sub-task, speakers directly used a collocation, *keei o hyoo suru* (to express one's respect) only seen in formal situations.

Some sub-tasks were obligatory, but most were optional, as, in most cases, was their position within a speech. Seven sub-tasks only appeared in two speeches: 'Greet audience', 'Thank organizers', 'Thank audience', 'Explain significance of occasion', 'Recognize other important guests', 'Explain current situation' and 'Request cooperation'. The sub-task 'Greet audience' appeared at the beginning of two speeches as *minasama/minasan konbanwa* (Good evening, everyone). 'Thank audience' was used at the end of two speeches as *arigatoo gozaimashita* (Thank you very much). Ten other sub-tasks were observed scattered across the speeches, showing variation in the content of the celebration speeches and optional sub-tasks speakers could use.

The overall flow of a celebration speech, shown in Figure 8.1, includes the 11 sub-tasks from the description table. The three most frequently observed, found in five of the six speeches, appear in rectangles. The sub-task 'Congratulate organizers' is used at both the beginning and end of a speech. Two other sub-tasks, 'Introduce self' and 'Pray for future success', are positioned at the beginning and towards the end of the speech flowchart, reflecting the results found in the ATD. Thus, moves in the four rectangles form the basis of the speech. The next four most frequently found sub-tasks, each in three

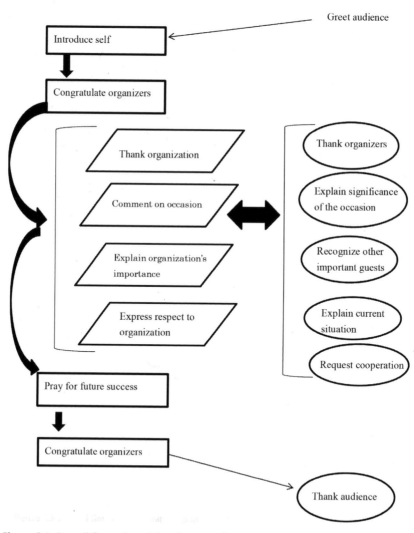

Figure 8.1 Overall flow of a celebration speech

speeches, are listed in parallelograms. Lastly, the seven sub-tasks found only in two speeches are listed in ovals. The sub-tasks 'Greet audience' and 'Thank audience' can be included in a speech at the beginning and end, respectively. The other sub-tasks in the parallelogram-shaped and oval-shaped boxes can be included in the order individual speakers prefer between the framing sub-tasks 'Congratulate organizers' and 'Pray for future success'.

Linguistic Features: Nouns, Verb Phrases and Collocations

Vocabulary items and collocations must also be examined when developing teaching materials, especially for advanced learners (Long et al., 2018), for most of whom command of the relevant lexis and collocations (plus a foreign accent), not basic grammar, is what differentiates them from native speakers. Specialized vocabulary must be recognized in language for specific purposes programs, and identified using genuine language samples. The use of elaborated, not linguistically simplified, input means that relevant, often low frequency, domain-specific items can be retained in task-based materials – one of many advantages of TBLT (Long, 2016).

When analyzing linguistic features in the data, which included both spoken and written language, the focus was on three categories: nouns, verb phrases, and collocations. Reading Tutor (Kawamura et al., 2009), a web-based vocabulary judgment tool, was used to examine the difficulty level of nouns. The program classifies lexical items into six categories: Beyond Categorization (BC), N1, N2, N3, N4 (high to low) and others, based on the proficiency levels of the Japanese-Language Proficiency Test (JLPT; The Japan Foundation/ Japan Educational Exchanges and Services, 2012). In the JLPT, N1 denotes the highest proficiency level, and N4 the least proficient.[3] The nouns classified by the judgment tool as BC are rare items not found in the vocabulary lists for N1 through N4. Approximately 35% were BC, including sub-technical terms (e.g. *shikiten* as ceremony) that were related to celebration events, as well as names of people and locations. A proportional increase in frequency was expected as the difficulty of nouns increased (N1 > N2 > N3 > N4), but the second most frequently occurring nouns belonged to the N2 category (approximately 28%). The smaller proportion of N1 than N2 nouns was consistent across the speech samples. The proportion of N3 to N4 nouns followed the original expectation, although there was variability across speeches. Overall, the data showed that the vocabulary required of FSOs is highly specialized, including items mostly at the BC level.

The second category concerned verb phrases. Verb phrases with a respectful or a regular verb form were used with roughly the same frequency across the six speeches (50.6% and 49.4%, respectively). However, there was some variability in their proportions from one speech to the next. As reported in the interviews with FSOs, honorific expressions were perceived to be a difficult aspect of Japanese. The results from native Japanese speakers may suggest helpful resources reflecting variation in native Japanese speakers' use of honorifics. The variation depends on an individual speaker's judgement as to the number of respectful forms in their verb phrases to include, and how to do so.

Lastly, collocations and formulaic sequences were examined. They can play an important role in formal Japanese expressions, including polite expressions. Collocations are not easily acquired by non-native speakers, even advanced learners, for a variety of reasons, including L1 – L2 differences, semantic ambiguity, the time that may occur between encounters (such that a memory trace from the first instance has faded by the time the item occurs again), and the fact that many errors (*_make a photo_, *_the government _announced_ war on crime_) do not cause breakdowns in communication (Boers & Lindstromberg, 2012; Wray, 2012; Yamashita & Jiang, 2010). Twelve collocations from the speeches (Figure 8.2) were selected and analyzed for proficiency level using Reading Tutor. Understandably, the results were closely related to those for their constituent nouns and verb phrases.

Prototypical celebration speeches

Overall, analyses of linguistic features showed that the six speeches contained numerous specialized vocabulary items, collocations and honorific expressions. The ATD provided rich information for developing teaching materials and pedagogic tasks. Although lower frequency and looser combinations of words may inhibit acquisition of collocations and formulaic expressions, due to the use of linguistic simplification in conventional teaching materials, those frequently found in the speech data can be focused on in task-based materials, which eschew simplification in favor of elaboration.

Based on the overall flow of a celebration speech (Figure 8.1), together with the analyses of linguistic features, including the specialized lexis and collocations (Table 8.2), two prototypical examples of celebration speeches were developed (Table 8.3). Both include the eight sub-tasks occurring most frequently in the data. The second includes additional sub-tasks from the oval-shaped boxes. The occasion for both speeches is a reception honoring the 100th anniversary of the arrival of cherry trees in Washington, DC. The possible location of the reception is in Japan, although the speeches could also be delivered to the local Japanese community in Washington, meaning FSOs learning Japanese at FSI can easily identify with the situation.

Table 8.2 Collocation list

	Japanese verb phrase	English translation	Collocations
1	申し上げる *mooshiageru*	to say humbly	お祝い/お慶び/ごあいさつ を 申し上げる N3 N2 N3 N3 *oiwai/oyorokobi/goaisatsu o mooshiageru* to say humbly a celebration/a pleasure/a greeting
2	ご祈念 申し上げる *gokinen* *mooshiageru*	to say a prayer humbly	（ますますの）ご発展ご健勝 を ご祈念申し上げる N2 BC* *(masumasu no) gohatten gokenshoo o gokinen* *mooshiageru* to say a prayer humbly for your (further) development and good health ご健勝ご活躍 を ご祈念申し上げる BC N2 BC *gokenshoo gokatsuyaku o gokinen mooshiageru* to say a prayer humbly for your good health and success
3	いただく *itadaku*	to receive humbly	お出で/お越し/ご紹介/ご尽力 を いただく N3 BC N3 BC N4 *oide/okoshi/goshookai/gojinryoku o itadaku* to receive humbly your arrival/coming/introduction/endeavors
4	賜る *tamawaru*	to be granted humbly	ご尽力 を 賜る BC N1 *gojinryoku o tamawaru* to be granted humbly your endeavors
5	させて いただく *saseteitadaku*	to let me do humbly	お祝いのことば/ ごあいさつ と させていただく N3 N4 N3 N4–N3 *oiwai no kotoba/ goaisatsu to sasete itadaku* to let me humbly make (this) celebration address/ greeting
6	表する *hyoosuru*	to express (one's respect)	敬意 を 表する N2 BC *keei o hyoosuru* to express one's respect
7	存じる *zonjiru*	to think/feel humbly	光栄 に 存じる BC N2 *kooei ni zonjiru* to feel humbly honored
8	担う *ninau*	to play (a role)	役割 を 担う N2 N1 *yakuwari o ninau* to play a role
9	受ける *ukeru*	to receive	感銘 を 受ける BC N3 *kanmei o ukeru* to be deeply impressed
10	目指す *mezasu*	to aim	（更なる）飛躍 を 目指す BC N2 *(saranaru) hiyaku o mezasu* to aim towards (further) progress
11	作る *tsukuru*	to create	思い出 を 作る N2 N4 *omoide o tsukuru* to create memories
12	築く *kizuku*	to build	伝統 を 築く N2 N1 *dentoo o kizuku* to build traditions

*BC: Beyond categorization.

Table 8.3 Prototypical speeches (PTS)

PTS 1

Function	Speech
Introduce self	わたくしは、アメリカ政府のスミスと申します。 *watakushi wa amerika seefu no sumisu to mooshimasu.* I am (humble) Smith from the US government.
Congratulate organizers	この度は、ワシントンDCの桜の植樹100周年の祝賀会、本当におめでとうございます。 *konotabi wa washinton DC no sakura no shokuju 100shuunen no shukugakai, hontoo ni omedetoo gozaimasu.* Today, I extend my sincere congratulations on this gathering honoring the 100th anniversary of the cherry tree planting in Washington DC.
Thank organization	このパーティーを主催された桜まつり基金のみなさまのご尽力に心からお礼を申し上げます。 *kono paatii o shusai sareta sakuramatsuri kikin no minasama no gojinryoku ni kokoro kara oneri o mooshiagemasu.* I humbly offer my deep appreciation for the endeavors (polite) of everyone from the Sakura Festival Foundation hosting this party.
Comment on occasion	美しい桜の花を通して、日本とアメリカがこのように交流できることを、本当にうれしく思っております。 *utsukushii sakura no hana o tooshite, nihon to amerika ga konoyooni kooryuudekirukoto o, hontooni ureshiku omotteorimasu.* I am very happy that Japan and the US can enjoy cultural exchanges like this through beautiful cherry blossoms.
Explain organization's importance	桜まつり基金は、桜まつりを始め、桜の管理やその歴史について広く一般の人々に向けて情報を発信されるなどして、日米関係の更なる発展に大きく貢献されてきたと思っております。 *sakura matsuri kikin wa, sakura matsuri o hajime, sakura no kanri ya sonorekishi nitsuite hiroku ippan no hitobito nimukete joohoo o hasshin sareru nado shite, nichibei kankei no saranaru hatten ni ookiku kooken saretekita to omotte orimasu.* I think that the Sakura Festival Foundation has greatly contributed to the further development of the Japan-US relationship through the Sakura Festival, the care of the cherry trees, and widely providing information to the general public regarding the history of the trees.
Express respect to organization	ここに、この歴代の桜まつり基金の皆様に深く敬意を表したいと思います。 *kokoni, kono rekidai no sakuramatsuri kikin no minasama ni fukaku keii o hyooshitai to omoimasu.* I express my deep respect for everyone here involved with the Sakura Festival Foundation.
Pray for future success	最後になりますが、ここにお集まりの皆様のますますのご健勝、日米交流のますますの発展を祈念して、お祝いのあいさつとさせていただきます。 *saigo ni narimasu ga, koko ni oatsumari no minasama no masumasu no gokenshoo, nichibei kooryuu no masumasu no hatten o kinen shite, oiwai no aisatsu to sasete itadakimasu.* Lastly, I pray for the continued good health of everyone gathered here, and the further development of the Japan-US cultural exchange, and conclude with these humble celebration remarks.
Congratulate organizers	今日は本当におめでとうございます。 *kyoo wa hontoo ni omedetoo gozaimasu.* I sincerely congratulate you today.

(Continued on next page)

Table 8.3 Prototypical speeches (PTS) (Continued)

PTS 2

Function	Speech
Greet audience	みなさん、こんばんは。 *minasan, konbanwa.* Good evening, everyone.
Introduce self	わたくしは、アメリカ政府のスミスでございます。 *watakushi wa amerika seefu no sumisu de gozaimasu.* I am (humble) Smith from the US government.
Congratulate organizers	この度は、ワシントンDCの桜の植樹100周年の祝賀会、本当におめでとうございます。 *konotabi wa washinton DC no sakura no shokuju 100shuunen no shukugakai, hontoo ni omedetoo gozaimasu.* Today, I extend my sincere congratulations on this gathering honoring the 100th anniversary of the cherry tree planting in Washington DC.
Thank organization	このパーティーを主催された桜まつり基金の皆様のご尽力に心からお礼を申し上げます。 *kono paatii o shusai sareta sakuramatsuri kikin no minasama no gojinryoku ni kokoro kara oneri o mooshiagemasu.* I humbly offer my deep appreciation for the endeavors (polite) of everyone from the Sakura Festival Foundation hosting this party.
Comment on occasion	美しい桜の花を通して、アメリカと日本がこのように交流できることを、心からうれしく思っております。 *utsukushii sakura no hana o tooshite, nihon to amerika ga konoyooni kooryuudekirukoto o, kokoro kara ureshiku omotteorimasu.* I am happy from the heart that Japan and the US can enjoy cultural exchanges like this through the beautiful cherry blossoms.
Recognize other important guests	今日は、日米協会のxx会長を始め、日米商工会議所の代表の方々も、この祝賀会にお出でくださいました。 *kyoo wa, nichibei kyookai no xxkaichoo o hajime, nichibei shookoo kaigisho no dairyoo no katagata mo, kono shukugakai ni oide kudasaimashita.* Today, we are honored at this celebration by the attendance of dignitaries including Mr.xx, President of Japan-US Society, and representatives from the US-Japan Business Council.
Explain organization's importance	桜まつり基金は、桜まつりを始め、桜の管理やその歴史について広く一般の人々に向けて情報を発信されるなどして、日米関係の更なる発展に大きく貢献されてきたと思っております。 *Sakura matsuri kikin wa, sakura matsuri o hajime, sakura no kanri ya sonorekishi nitsuite hiroku ippan no hitobito nimukete joohoo o hasshin sareru nado shite, nichibei kankei no saranaru hatten ni ookiku kooken saretekita to omotte orimasu.* I think that the Sakura Festival Foundation has greatly contributed to the further development of the Japan-US relationship through the Sakura Festival, the care of the cherry trees, and widely providing information to the general public regarding the history of the trees.
Explain current situation	ここ最近十年ほどの間に、ワシントンDC地域の日系企業の数が減り、桜まつり基金の経済的な支援をお願いするのに、多方面に働きかけておられると伺っております。 *koko saikin juunen hodo no aida ni, washinton DC chiiki no nikkei kigyoo no kazu ga heri, sakura matsuri kikin no keezaitekina shien o onegai suru noni, tahoomen ni hatarakikakete orareru to ukagatte orimasu.* I hear that because the number of Japanese businesses in the Washington DC area has declined in the past ten years, the Sakura Festival Foundation has worked diligently from numerous angles to request financial support for the festival.

(Continued on next page)

Table 8.3 Prototypical speeches (PTS) (Continued)

Express respect to organization	ここに、この基金の皆様のご努力に深く敬意を表したいと思います。 *kokoni, kono rekidai no sakuramatsuri kikin no minasama no godoryoku ni fukaku keii o hyooshitai to omoimasu.* I express my deep respect for everyone's efforts here involved with the Sakura Festival Foundation.
Request cooperation	また、引き続き、桜まつり基金へのご支援を賜りますように、今日ご出席の皆様のご協力をどうぞよろしくお願い申し上げます。 *mata, hikituzuki, sakura matsuri kikin eno goshien o tamawarimasu yooni, kyoo goshusseki no minasama no gokyooryoku o doozo yoroshiku onegai mooshiagemasu.* I humbly request the cooperation of all of you attending today to continue your support of the Sakura Festival Foundation.
Pray for future success	最後になりますが、ここにお集まりの皆様のますますのご健勝、日米交流のますますの発展を祈念して、お祝いのあいさつとさせていただきます。 *saigo ni narimasu ga, koko ni oatsumari no minasama no masumasu no gokenshoo, nichibei kooryuu no masumasu no hatten o kinen shite, oiwai no aisatsu to sasete itadakimasu.* Lastly, I pray for the continued good health of everyone gathered here, and the further development of the Japan-US cultural exchange, and conclude with these humble celebration remarks.
Congratulate organizers	今日は本当におめでとうございます。 *kyoo wa hontoo ni omedetoo gozaimasu.* I sincerely congratulate you today.
Thank audience	ありがとうございました。 *arigatoo gozaimashita.* Thank you very much.

Discussion and Conclusions

The development of TBLT materials is guided by the results of a two-stage, task-based NA: identification of target tasks and an ATD. The materials eventually consist of series of progressively more complex *pedagogic tasks*, which gradually introduce, and require, use of more and more of the language identified by the ATD. The NA for FSOs reported here was conducted using multiple sources of information and multiple methods of tapping that information. Following an initial overview provided by the DOT, FSOs' written introspections, collected via email, together with a pilot survey, generated a detailed list of target tasks. A closed, on-line questionnaire survey then elicited data efficiently from a larger number of domain experts (experienced FSOs), implicitly testing the generalizability of findings from the smaller sample. A simple three-choice scale as part of the questionnaire produced frequency data for task performance. Future studies of this kind should add a measure of task criticality, as critical tasks are not always the most frequent. Information on respondents' Japanese proficiency allowed some inferences about which tasks are typically handled by FSOs with higher L2 abilities, but such data cannot reveal whether any of the tasks are performed satisfactorily. Discovering that would require task-based, criterion-referenced performance tests, not continuation of the current use of what are largely irrelevant global 'proficiency' measures with no known relationship to target task performance.

Although not usually as onerous as the example described here, developing TBLT modules for a program is more labor-intensive than the procedure followed by most commercial textbook authors, who rely on intuitions to write generic course books supposedly suitable for everyone, but in fact for no-one in particular. However, once developed, TBLT materials can be refined and re-used on numerous occasions. They are likely to encourage students to study more diligently because course content is visibly relevant to their frequently occurring job requirements, their personal lives, and real-world L2 communicative needs. Evaluations of TBLT programs routinely report such positive student (and teacher) responses (see, e.g. Bryfonski & McKay, 2017; González-Lloret & Nielson, 2014; Long, 2015a: 350–365; Van den Branden, 2006). Information gathered from domain experts and an ATD make it possible to create materials that are better appreciated as students move on to their real-world jobs and find themselves able to use the L2 to perform their duties satisfactorily.

Acknowledgements

The authors thank the FSOs who provided invaluable information for this study. Thanks are also due to Dr Nozomi Fukasawa, who gave permission for use of some previously analyzed data. Any errors and limitations are our own.

Notes

(1) The internet survey tool, SurveyMonkey was used for creating the questionnaire for this study (SurveyMonkey, 2014).
(2) The original interview data were gathered to investigate the needs for Japanese public speaking for foreign professionals who had worked in Japan or worked for Japanese companies abroad (Hillman & Fukasawa, 2012).
(3) Due to a change in 2010, the JLPT currently has five levels of proficiency, from N1 through N5. In 2017, levels N2 and N3 of Reading Tutor were combined, and N5 added, to reflect the revised five levels of the JLTP (N1 - N5), meaning it still has six categories.

References

Bartlett, N.J.D. (2005) A double shot 2% mocha latte, please, with whip: Service encounters in two coffee shops and at a coffee cart. In M.H. Long (ed.) *Second Language Needs Analysis* (pp. 305–343). Cambridge: Cambridge University Press.

Boers, F. and Lindstromberg, S. (2012) Experimental and intervention studies on formulaic sequences in a second language. *Annual Review of Applied Linguistics* 32, 83–110. DOI: 10.1017/S0267190512000050.

Brown, J.D. (2009) Foreign and second language needs analysis. In M.H. Long and C.J. Doughty (eds) *Handbook of Language Teaching* (pp. 269–293). Oxford, England: Wiley-Blackwell.

Brown, J.D. (2016) *Introducing Needs Analysis and English for Specific Purposes*. New York: Routledge.

Bryfonki, L. and McKay, T.H. (2017) TBLT implementation and evaluation: A meta-analysis. *Language Teaching Research* doi/full/10.1177/1362168817744389.

Chaudron, C., Crookes, G. and Long, M.H. (1988) *Reliability and validity in second language classroom research*. Technical Report No.8. Honolulu, HI: Center for Second Language Classroom Research, Social Science Research Institute, University of Hawai'i at Manoa.

Crookes, G. (1986) Towards a validated analysis of scientific text structure. *Applied Linguistics* 7 (1), 57–70.

Crookes, G. (1990) The utterance, and other basic units for second language discourse analysis. *Applied Linguistics* 11 (2), 183–199.

Foster, P., Tonkyn, A. and Wigglesworth, G. (2000) Measuring spoken language: A unit for all reasons. *Applied Linguistics* 21 (3), 354–375.

Fukasawa, N. and Hillman, K.K. (2012) Components and development patterns of Japanese *shikiji* speeches: Characteristics of one genre in Japanese public speaking. *Journal of Technical Japanese Education* 14, 27–34.

Gilabert, R. (2005) Evaluation the use of multiple sources and methods in needs analysis: as case study of journalists in the Autonomous Community of Catalonia (Spain). In M.H. Long (ed.) *Second Language Needs Analysis* (pp. 19–76). Cambridge: Cambridge University Press.

González-Lloret, M. and Nielson, K.B. (2014) Evaluating TBLT: The case of a task-based Spanish program. *Language Teaching Research* 19 (5), 525–549.

Hillman, K.K. and Fukasawa, N. (2009) Characteristics of business speech in Japanese and its application possibility to Japanese language education. *Proceedings of the International Conference on Japanese Language Education* (p. 273). Sydney, Australia.

Hillman, K.K. and Fukasawa, N. (2012) Needs analysis regarding public speaking for foreign speakers of Japanese. *Proceedings of the International Conference on Japanese Language Education* (p. 275). Nagoya, Japan.

Kawamura, Y., Kitamura, T. and Hobara, R. (2009) Reading tutor. See http://language.tiu.ac.jp/ (accessed March 2014).

Kim, M. (1999) Language training at the school of language studies. *Proceedings of the 10th International Colloquium on Program Management*. The Japan Foundation Japanese Language Institute, Kansai, Japan.

Lambert, C. (2010) A task-based needs analysis: Putting principles into practice. *Language Teaching Research* 14 (1), 99–112.

Long, M.H. (2005) Methodological issues in learner needs analysis. In M.H. Long (ed.) *Second Language Needs Analysis* (pp. 19–76). Cambridge: Cambridge University Press.

Long, M.H. (2013) Identifying language needs for TBLT in the tourist industry. In G. Bosch (ed.) *Teaching Foreign Languages for Tourism: Research and Practice* (pp. 21–44). Berlin: Peter Lang.

Long, M.H. (2015a) *Second Language Acquisition and Task-Based Language Teaching*. Oxford: Wiley-Blackwell.

Long, M.H. (2015b) TBLT: Building the road as we travel. In M. Bygate (ed.) *Domains and Directions in the Development of TBLT* (pp. 1–26). Amsterdam: John Benjamins Publishing Company. DOI: 10.1075/tblt.8.01lon.

Long, M.H. (2016) In defense of tasks and TBLT: Non-issues and real issues. *Annual Review of Applied Linguistics* 36, 5–33.

Long, M.H. (2020) Needs analysis. (Revised and updated version). In C. Chapelle (ed.) *The Concise Encyclopedia of Applied Linguistics* (2nd edn). Oxford: Wiley-Blackwell.

Long, M.H. and Ross, S. (1993) Modifications that preserve language and content. In M. Tickoo (ed.) *Simplification: Theory and Application* (pp. 29–52). Singapore: SEAMEO Regional Language Centre.

Long, M.H., Granena, G. and Montero, F. (2018) What does Critical Period research reveal about advanced L2 proficiency? In A. Benati and P. Malovrh (eds) *The Handbook of Advanced Proficiency in Second Language Acquisition* (pp. 51–71). Oxford: Wiley.

Long, M.H., Lee, J. and Hillman, K.K. (2019) Task-based language learning. In J.W. Schwieter and A. Benati (eds) *Cambridge Handbook of Language Learning*. Cambridge: Cambridge University Press.

Malicka, A., Gilabert Guerrero, R. and Norris, J.M. (2017) From needs analysis to task design: Insights from an English for specific purposes context. *Language Teaching Research* 23 (1), 78–106. https://doi 10.1177/1362168817714278.

Matar, T. (2014) *Task based assessment and ALERT (Awareness Language and Emergency Response Training)*. Paper presented at Assessment LEARN (Language Education and Resource Network): Applications and implications of the ILR skill level descriptions, Chevy Chase, MD.

Nielson, K. (2010) Results of the first stage of an initial needs analysis for CASA de Maryland. Unpublished manuscript. College Park, MD: University of Maryland, PhD Program in Second Language Acquisition.

O'Connell, S. (2015) A task-based language teaching approach to the police traffic stop. *TESL Canada Journal/ Revue TESL du Canada* 31 (8), 116–131. https://doi.org/10.18806/tesl.v31i0.1189.

O'Donnell, M.E. (2009) Finding middle ground in second language reading: Pedagogic modifications that increase comprehensibility and vocabulary acquisition while preserving authentic text features. *The Modern Language Journal* 93 (4), 512–533. https://doi.org/10.1111/j.1540-4781.2009.00928.x.

Serafini, E.J., Lake, J.B. and Long, M.H. (2015) Needs analysis for specialized learner populations: essential methodological improvements. *English for Specific Purposes* 40, 11–26.

Shintani, N. (2013) The effect of focus on form and focus on forms instruction on the acquisition of productive knowledge of L2 vocabulary by young beginner learners. *TESOL Quarterly* 47 (1), 36–62.

Sinclair, J. McH. and Coulthard, M.R. (1975) *Towards an Analysis of Discourse: The English Used by Teachers and Pupils*. Oxford: Oxford University Press.

SurveyMonkey. (2014) See https://www.surveymonkey.com/ (accessed June 2014).

The Japan Foundation/Japan Educational Exchanges and Services. (2012) See http://www.jlpt.jp/e/about/levelsummary.html (accessed March 2014).

Touré, A. and Nicolai, K. (2015) Designing a new task-based curriculum with job-relevant foreign affairs performance tasks. *Proceedings of the Sixth International Conference on Task-Based Language Teaching* (p. 116). Leuven, Belgium.

US Department of Labor. (2011) See http://www.occupationalinfo.org/18/188117106.html (accessed March 2014).

Van den Branden, K. (2006) *Task-Based Language Education: From Theory to Practice*. Cambridge: Cambridge University Press.

Wray, A. (2012) What do we (think we) know about formulaic language? An evaluation of the current state of play. *Annual Review of Applied Linguistics* 32, 231–254.

Yalden, J. (1987) Three case studies. In J. Yalden (ed.) *Principles of Course Design for Language Teaching* (pp. 102–168). Cambridge: Cambridge University Press.

Yamashita, J. and Jiang, N. (2010) L1 influence on the acquisition of L2 collocations: Japanese ESL users and EFL learners acquiring English collocations. *TESOL Quarterly* 44, 647–668.

Yazawa, M. (2013) *Supeechi o koa toshita shokuu karano senmon nihongo doonyuu: gaikookan, koomuin koosu no jissen to sonogono tenkai* (Introduction to specialized Japanese for basic learners through delivering speeches: Implementation and additional development of a course for diplomats and public officials). *Journal of Technical Japanese Education* 15, 7–12. The Society for Technical Japanese Education.

9 Developing Authentic Tasks for the Workplace Using Needs Analysis: A Case Study of Australian Aboriginal Vocational Students

Rhonda Oliver

This chapter provides a description of how authentic tasks can support vocational skill learning while promoting second language learning. The target cohort are Aboriginal, vocational, high school students from remote locations in Western Australia who have English as their second language or dialect. At the time of the study they were attending a boarding school – the research setting for this study – which is located a considerable distance from their homes. Using an ethnographic approach, classroom observations supplemented with interviews with teaching staff were used to document suitable tasks and the students' engagement with these. The findings show the important contribution that a needs analysis makes to the selection of tasks – enabling them to be contextually relevant and culturally appropriate and to serve the learners' long-term needs.

Introduction

This chapter examines the use of tasks and a task-based approach in a unique context, namely a school for older adolescent Australian Aboriginal students, many of whom speak Standard Australian English (SAE) as their second language or dialect. To maintain confidentiality the pseudonym Kutja School is used, with Kutja being derived from Nintirringkutja – a traditional language used near where the school is located – and meaning learning to speak the local community language. Kutja School aims to prepare students for work and life beyond school, developing vocational skills, functional literacy and the type of communicative competence in SAE that will enable them to successfully transition to life outside the classroom. This is particularly important for the current cohort as 'Young people who do not successfully make the transition from education to work are at risk of long-term disadvantage' (Steering Committee for the Review of Government Service Provision, 2016: 7.14). Aboriginal people living in regional and remote areas have a greater risk of such disadvantage as without appropriate skills they will experience continuing inequality and poor quality of life (e.g. low socio-economic status, high levels of unemployment, ill health and rates of death) (Australian Bureau of Statistics [ABS], 2016a, 2016b; Cameron et al., 2017).

Despite the concerted efforts of many teachers in various schools, including those at Kutja, there is ongoing concern that the transition from such vocation programs to life beyond school is less than successful (e.g. Windley, 2017), and there have been repeated calls to assess their outcomes (Hunter, 2010). There is also a need to identify activities that do not work within such programs (Hunter, 2010: 2) and those that are effective based on thorough research, rather than solely on government reports or quantitative evaluations. This is the approach taken in the current study where a qualitative and in-depth exploration and documentation of effective tasks is made.

This research was possible, and data collection successfully completed, which is not always the case when non-Aboriginal people undertake investigations in Australian Aboriginal settings. Our success stemmed from the long-term connection my colleagues and I have had with Kutja School. Over a period of nine years, we have developed strong relationships with the staff (Aboriginal and non-Aboriginal) and many of the students. During multiple visits to the school we have investigated different aspects of the school's vocational program with a particular focus on how this can support the students' acquisition of SAE from a TBLT perceptive. Our first major line of investigation involved a thorough needs analysis (NA) (see Long, 2015, Chapter 8, this volume), focusing especially on those needs that fall within the language and literacy domain (see Oliver et al., 2012). Following this investigation, we provided professional development to the teachers, and we have continued to support them as they implement a task-based language approach within their classrooms. In this chapter, the selection and development of tasks to address learner need (as identified by Oliver et al., 2012) are described.

Tasks are, therefore, the key focus of this chapter. Although tasks have an everyday meaning, from a TBLT perspective the term is much more specific. As Nunan (2004) states, tasks are:

> a piece of classroom work that involves learners in comprehending, manipulating, producing or interacting in the target language while their attention is focused on mobilizing their grammatical knowledge in order to express meaning. (Nunan, 2004: 4)

That is, tasks are more than just exercises or activities that focus on the forms of the target language (e.g. grammatical or lexical items). They also involve more than a functional goal and instead they have both an authentic as well as a linguistic focus. Furthermore, tasks are dynamic, having a meaning focus which includes a 'gap' that needs to be addressed, and one that learners must do using their own language resources, although ultimately the overall desired outcome is non-linguistic, rather than linguistic (Ellis, 2003). However, for tasks to be effective, they should be selected and/or designed in ways that are culturally, as well as contextually, relevant for the learners. By ensuring such relevance, tasks can support a diversity of learners from a range of backgrounds (East, 2017). This is particularly important for the learners in the present study who represent a distinct group of people, not only being Aboriginal learners, but also those who come from remote locations where many live a more traditional lifestyle and who speak a language or dialect other than Standard Australian English (SAE).

Building on the previous NA undertaken at the school (see Oliver *et al.*, 2012, also 2013a, 2013b), the goal of the current study is to examine if and how it is possible to incorporate culturally and contextually relevant tasks that meet the needs of the Aboriginal Vocational Education and Training (VET) students who are learning English as an additional language/dialect.

Context

Kutja is a boarding school that caters for Aboriginal students. It is located a considerable distance from many of the students' homes in a small town an eight-hour drive south-east from the capital city, Perth, Western Australia. In addition, many of the students come from central and far north Australia and travel considerable distances (i.e. thousands of kilometres) to attend the school.

Kutja School is an independent school overseen by a board representing Aboriginal parents who hold Christian values. It was first established as a mission training school in 1954, and in 1990 the board took over the running of the training program. Eventually in 1993 the whole property was 'deeded' to the board. The school is led by a principal who had previously worked as a teacher at Kutja School for more than a decade. There are approximately 20 staff connected to the school and boarding house. Over half of the staff are trained teachers, and the rest have trade qualifications or are unqualified support staff. Unlike the situation in many remote Aboriginal schools where there is a high turnover of staff, most of the teachers have been at this school long term (over 15 years). Although the majority of staff members have Anglo-Australian backgrounds, three are Aboriginal, and there are also staff from other countries.

Kutja School operates as a working farm and includes over 1000 acres of land. The campus consists of classrooms and workshops where trade skills are taught. The school is a Registered Training Organization (RTO) and workplace experience is an integral part of the program. The school focuses on the vocational areas of General Construction, Business and Administration, Hospitality, Tourism, Stock and Station (Rural Operations), Automobile Mechanics, Metals and Engineering and Land, Parks and Wildlife. As well as providing training in these VET subject areas, the students are taught English as their second language, mathematics and religion. The students also do sport, cooking and participate in a bush ranger program (a youth-based community and conservation program). Aptly, as a VET school, it has as its motto 'training for life' and the aims of the program are to:

- help students to gain a wide range of employability skills
- help students with planning a career
- increase self-esteem and confidence in students
- help students develop communication skills with people outside the school.

(From school website – not cited for ethical reasons)

With these aims and given the non-English speaking background of the students, the context is an ideal one for the implementation of a TBLT approach.

Enrolment at the school ranges from 50 to 70 Aboriginal high school students, aged from approximately 15 to 19 years. As noted, the students travel considerable distances to attend Kutja School and come from a range of areas, with a high proportion coming from remote communities where Aboriginal culture and oral traditions remain strong. The general locations include the Kimberly, Pilbara, goldfields and central desert areas of Western Australia, but students also come from other locations including larger regional areas. The languages spoken by the students include traditional languages (e.g. Ngariyin, Kija, Jaru, Walmarjarri) but also Kriol (a particularly type of creole spoken in northern Australia), Aboriginal English (as distinct dialect of Australian English) and, generally with less proficiency, Standard Australian English. In fact, it was because of the students' ongoing struggle with 'English' that our initial research was undertaken (i.e. Oliver *et al.*, 2012, 2013a, 2013b). Our reconnaissance highlighted the ongoing struggles the students seemed to have communicating in English, particularly outside the classroom setting and because of this we instigated our NA.

Needs Analysis

According to Long (2015), the foundation of TBLT is a NA and this guided what we did in our previous research at the school. The current study examines the development of relevant tasks. The literature shows that although early attempts at NA shifted the focus from grammatical structures to what learners needed to do with language, the initial checklist of needs was largely informed by intuition and the unit of analysis remained linguistic (Gilabert, 2005; Long, 2005). As such early NAs often failed to consider the context in which learners would use the target language, and they did not take into account the various factors that would affect the students' second language learning (Oliver *et al.*, 2013). Yet according to Long (2005), to be effective a task-based syllabus should be based on systematic and evidence-based analysis of need, including actual workplace communication (Long, 2005) which is of particular relevance for the target cohort – VET students. In the NA we undertook at Kutja School (Oliver *et al.*, 2012, 2013a, 2013b), and as suggested by Cowling (2007) and Long (2005), we collected data from a wide range of sources using different methods. In particular, we focused on gathering data to enable us to document the English language and literacy challenges that Aboriginal high school VET students encounter to ascertain ways that these needs could be addressed. In this way tasks could be developed that fostered the development of their skills, especially communicative skills, to enable them to participate effectively in the workplace.

The data we collected was analyzed thematically (see Oliver *et al.* (2012) for details) and our findings documented. Based on the evidence we collected, from the teachers, community members, potential employers and the students themselves, we identified that the learners needed to develop the following skills, including being able to understand and use appropriate language (oral and written) pertaining to:

- vocational terms (e.g. knowing the English words for tool names and workplace procedures, including both formal and more colloquial expression 'Get me a 2.4!');
- safety (e.g. understanding equipment and product warnings such as recommendations about the need for protective gear);
- workplace duties (e.g. being able to indicate they understood instructions or being able to ask for clarification if they were unsure);

- socializing at work (e.g. using appropriate greetings, sharing personal information and engaging with workplace humor);
- satisfying functional needs and wants related to their transition to life beyond the classroom (e.g. doing banking, filling in forms, communicating with health care professionals).

Our findings showed that the teachers often identified oral language and written literacy skills as needs to be addressed, while the vocational teachers suggested skills beyond language. However, potential future employers were less concerned with VET and written literacy skills: they were most concerned with their potential Aboriginal employees being confident to engage orally in English. As one stated '*we can teach them the skills they need for the job, we can't teach them to be confident to talk to us*'. Somewhat surprisingly, even though some of the employers were located in places with high Aboriginal populations, they were not aware that the students spoke anything but English, adding to the potential for misunderstandings in the workplace.

Related to the need to communicate with confidence, other needs identified included developing:

- behaviors that suggested they had a strong 'work ethic' showing they were enthusiastic to work and could manage their time independently;
- translanguaging abilities (i.e. being able to move fluidly from one language or dialect to another based on their audience – Aboriginal and non-Aboriginal);
- interaction skills to capably communicate with bosses, fellow non-Aboriginal workers and clients – a need emphasized particularly by Aboriginal community members.

For the students, this final point was a crucial issue for them as it meant overcoming the personal and cultural feelings of *shame*. Shame is an Aboriginal English term that describes an overwhelming feeling of embarrassment or shyness (Grote & Rochecouste, 2012; Malcolm & Grote, 2007). It can often occur when talking with *white fellas*. Hence, the students interviewed for the NAs described their need to develop their confidence to '*talk to white fellas*' and they described to us their desire to have many more opportunities to do so.

These findings were the foundation for the direction the school chose to follow. To support them in achieving this, and at the request of the school leadership team, we provided professional development (PD) to teachers at Kutja. This PD aimed to raise the teachers' awareness of their learners' needs and help them explore how to address these needs using TBLT. The intention was to help teachers develop the skills necessary to create or select learning tasks of their own which were relevant to their specific teaching areas and to the needs of their learners. The term 'tasks' was used not only because it aligned with our own beliefs about how second language can be effectively acquired, but also because the concept of *task* was something understood by all the participants – students, teachers and employers.

A task-based approach, which focuses on the needs of the learners and is bottom up (rather than top-down) in its design, has raised some controversy in Australia. National documentation (ACARA website, 2018) states that:

> The Australian Curriculum sets the expectations for what all young Australians should be taught, regardless of where they live in Australia or their background.

Yet at Kutja School, the context of the learners (including their language background) and their needs are primary considerations for effective instruction. This pedagogical position is led by the principal, who is supported by the board and by the families who chose to have their children enrolled at the school. It is also reflected in such actions as the decision by the principal to request exemption for the students from the state and national standardized testing – a mechanism which seeks to determine whether or not young Australians are meeting important educational outcomes. The decision to focus on meeting the needs of the learners means that teachers are strongly encouraged to use or select appropriate tasks for learning opportunities that prepare their students to transition from school. These tasks have a dual focus: authentic and underpinned by VET skills, but also addressing the linguistic needs of the learners, particularly related to the communication skills they need in the workplace and for life beyond the classroom.

Therefore, this study addressed the following research questions:

(1) What tasks do the teachers incorporate into their classrooms that address both the VET skills and language learning needs of their students?
(2) How are the tasks made or selected to be culturally and/or contextually relevant to the learners?

Method

Data collection and analysis

Using an ethnographic approach, regular visits were made to Kutja School where classroom observations were made and informal interviews undertaken with teachers and students. In this way, it was possible to document those tasks used at the School and, in particular, those that are either selected or developed that appeared to address the students' identified needs. Records, both written and photographed, were collated. These were interrogated to determine the match between needs and the tasks used. This was done in an iterative manner so that the documented tasks were examined and then re-examined, as necessary, during subsequent visits to the school. This interrogation was supplemented with field notes that were taken based on these observations and upon the information obtained during informal interviews undertaken with the teachers and students. The data from these notes provided information about the purpose and the outcomes of the tasks.

Findings

It was apparent that the teachers at Kutja select or develop tasks in close alignment with their students' needs. The observations suggest that while the VET teachers in particular have a vocational focus (authentic and real-life goals), the tasks they set are strongly underpinned by a meaning focus and consistently involve a communicative gap that the students work to resolve. Furthermore, the tasks are typically culturally and contextually relevant for learners and are targeted at addressing the students' transition to life in the workplace and beyond school.

In what follows, a small, representative sample of tasks, organized in terms of the need that they meet, has been selected to illustrate the way that tasks addressing the VET skills and language learning needs of students are incorporated into the teaching at Kutja School. These sample tasks also illustrate how tasks at the school were designed or selected to be culturally and contextually relevant to learners.

Vocational terms

Knowing the names of tools and other vocational-related vocabulary is important if students are going to function well in their chosen workplaces. Teachers were consistently observed using the English names of equipment in their daily practice, they labeled items in their workshops and asked students questions that required them to use this language. This authentic language use provides important pre-task conditions, namely opportunities for understandable input, for the students to engage in output production and a focus on form during meaning-based communication tasks.

Learner engagement in interactive tasks that supported the learning of vocational terms was also observed in classroom and workshop settings. For example, one task that addressed both the VET and language skills needed by students occurred in an automobile mechanics lesson. One of the more experienced students (Student A) was selected to provide directions to another newer student (Student B) about changing a spark plug in an excavator. The first step required them to

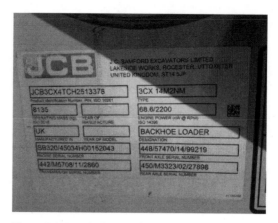

Figure 9.1 Excavator specifications

identify the key information from the specifications on a label located on the machine (Figure 9.1). Learners were then able to identify the right equipment and the correct spark plug to use, as outlined in the workshop manual. This was done collaboratively with Student A pointing to the key pieces of information in the text when Student B was uncertain. It was also a very active task – the pair found the appropriate manual together and then worked through the pages until the correct specifications were found. It was only in the final stages, when Student B actually worked to replace the spark plug that Student A stepped back and took a less hands-on approach – simply giving oral directions for Student B to follow in a one-way interactive instruction task (Figure 9.2). Such tasks provided students with an opportunity to learn both VET language and develop their communication skills through the negotiation of meaning, particularly when the meaning was unclear and when information was hard to locate or understand.

Another one-way instruction task was observed in a Stock-and-Station lesson. Here, however, instead of being undertaken as pair work task, it was done with one student providing the directions for a group to follow. The lesson began with the teacher revising the hand signals needed when undertaking fencing (Figure 9.3).

Student A stood some distance away and, after judging the post's position by eye, he conveyed directions to the group using the hand signals for how they could move it so that it aligned with other posts they had previously put in. Although Student A was not involved in interacting with the group verbally, the directions he gave created opportunities for the group to interact with each other, working together to ascertain his meaning in a purposeful way. It should be noted that, in this context, the teacher engaged as a member of the group and so was able to model language that other members used. Expressions such as

Figure 9.2 Student B following directions

Figure 9.3 Hand signals for fencing

'move it up a bit', 'move it to the left/right/sideways, etc.' were used and deliberations were undertaken with each other when they were not sure. It should be noted that under the pressure of lifting and moving a heavy post (Figure 9.4), the learners drew on their full language repertoire and at times used English, Aboriginal English and Kriol words to convey their meaning. One advantage of this particular task was the alignment between the students' home language – which is very gestural – and the provision of directions using hand signals. In this way, the task was both functionally and culturally relevant to the learners.

Safety

Understanding the language surrounding Occupational Health and Safety issues is imperative for all workers, but especially those working in an environment where the language used to convey this information

Figure 9.4 The group positioning the post

Figure 9.5 Safety poster

is not their first. This is the case for the students from Kutja School if they elect to work in non-Aboriginal workplaces. As in teaching vocational terms, teachers supported language learning connected with safety by first creating pre-task conditions. For example, safety signs written in English are located in all of the workshops and in most of the classrooms. Teachers frequently worked with their classes to recount the safety procedures that need to be followed. In addition, to assist learners in remembering key information, posters with mnemonics are used. Figure 9.5 provides an example.

In addition, teachers were observed in the VET classes enacting authentic workplace tasks to ensure the students remained safe. For instance, when a new welding task was about to be done in the metal work class, the teacher had one student (Student C) recount to the others what procedures they would need to follow and what safety equipment they would need to use. This was done especially for the new student who had joined the class as an instructional task, with Student C pointing to the safety poster, and the remainder of the class following his instructions – getting their safety googles and gloves, pointing to their steel cap boots, etc.

A more complex written task was observed during a class excursion to a not-for-profit training course provider. This visit was organized by school staff to ensure their students' competitiveness in the job market, specifically helping them to attain First Aid certificates that are useful for their curriculum vitae and in some cases essential requirements for employment (e.g. in the mining industry). The task was the actual multiple-choice assessment test, but it was done in a collaborative and interactive way that was culturally appropriate for this cohort. It was not the content that the students did not understand, but rather the way the test language was constructed that made the meaning unclear to them. To address this gap, the students read the test items together and discussed the meaning of the items as a group. Unfamiliar words were scaffolded by others in the group after the teacher modelled how this could be done on the first few instances. Examples supported by gestures and physical demonstration were also used. In these ways, learners initially unsure of the meaning of different items were supported in developing an understanding adequate to select the correct answer in the test. An authentic and necessary task thus addressed both the VET skills and language needs of the students and did so in a way that was culturally and contextually relevant.

Workplace duties

In the workplace, there is a need to perform requisite duties, but there is also a need to indicate that instructions are understood or, if they not, to ask for clarification. The latter can be particularly problematic for Aboriginal students because expressing non-understanding can induce the feeling of shame, an emotion that can have serious negative repercussions (as described previously). For example, when pushed too far outside their comfort zone by unfamiliar language and procedures, students at Kutja tend to react in ways that may be unacceptable in the workplace (e.g. being unresponsive, averting eye contact, walking away or swearing). Because the teachers and other staff members at the school are very familiar with the background of these students and their needs, and how shame can affect them, they are well equipped to respond appropriately. However, in the workplace non-Aboriginal workers and line managers may not have the same level of cultural awareness, and it is thus necessary for students to develop the language and confidence to express a lack of understanding and to overcome their feelings of shame in doing so. The school has put in a number of mechanism to help in this regard, and one place where a task-based approach is used for this purpose is in the cooking classes. These are not limited to students wishing to work in hospitality. Most students take these classes as a way to develop functional skills they need for everyday life outside of school.

An interesting aspect of the cooking classes is that they have been intentionally constructed, as indicated by the teachers, in a way whereby the students can practice the language needed to express non-understanding. At the time of data collection, two different teachers were responsible for the cooking lessons and both explicitly stated their desire to create a secure and non-threatening environment where, as one of teachers described it, students were 'comfortable to talk'.

The actual cooking lessons often followed a set routine where first the students watched a particular recipe demonstrated by the teacher – a practice not dissimilar to how the students would be taught many cultural activities from a young age in their own communities. Next, they would follow a recipe which was sometimes written on a white board (often only in dot point form because of the low level of written literacy of some of the students) or given as a set of oral instructions. Then the students worked in small groups making the food for themselves. Whilst cooking, the students were encouraged to talk about other aspects of their life, feelings and concerns, and the teacher often joined different groups in their conversations – as would occur in many workplaces. When the students were unsure of the next step in their cooking, they often tried to resolve the issues within their group, discussing what was needed in terms of ingredients or what step needed to be followed next. However, they were equally comfortable to call out to the teacher for help. Thus, these cooking classes provided the opportunity for the students to do real-world tasks in a way that they could learn to follow instructions and seek clarification when they were unsure. These were communication skills that were identified as a real need for this cohort of students.

Socializing at work

In the NA that preceded the current study (Oliver *et al.*, 2012, 2013a, 2013b), the need for Aboriginal students to be able and willing to chat informally with workmates was identified as crucial for the workplace. For example, the boss of a tyre workshop that took students from Kutja school for work placements described how 'Boys who were too quiet and who didn't join in at break times made everyone feel uncomfortable' (Adams & Oliver, 2019: 307–308). The students themselves identified the need to have more opportunities to practice talking with *white fellas* (i.e. non-Aboriginal people) (Oliver *et al.*, 2012).

To address this need, the school adapted some of their practices, doing so over time. More opportunities were created to have the students interacting with visitors to the school, and other opportunities were created where the students went off campus and 'talked for themselves' as one teacher described it. Prior to such activities, the teachers would ask more confident and capable students to model conversations for the other students. In one case, the focus was on oral interaction with non-Aboriginal people and culminated in a day of activities conducted on National Aboriginal and Islander Day of Celebrations (NAIDOC). As described in Adams and Oliver (2019), on NAIDOC day those students who were confident in talking with non-Aboriginal people were put in charge of running events on their own (e.g. telling traditional tales, leading spear throwing competitions, doing traditional art activities with visitors). At the same time, those who were not as confident worked in teams doing things that required less prolonged interaction (e.g. leading small children to pat the farm animals, helping visitors onto a tractor pulled train of carriages around the farm, serving cups of tea and coffee). Again, pre-tasks were undertaken in class before this event, and students had the opportunity during whole class and pair work activities to practice the language they would need for the actual tasks. These tasks and pre-tasks were conducted in such a way that addressed the needs of the learners and were contextually and, at times, culturally relevant to them.

Satisfying functional needs and wants

As described, the school aims to provide its students with 'training for life' and a key part of this is preparing students with those skills necessary for life outside of school. Various functional aspects of the teaching program were observed, each underpinned by the language needs of the students and authentic tasks enacted to allow students to develop skills to address their needs. The vast array of authentic tasks incorporated into the program included having students set up bank accounts and interact with bank staff, having them apply for Australian tax file numbers and passports, and providing them with ongoing opportunities to engage with non-Aboriginal health practitioners. Prior to the NA research, the staff often 'spoke for the students' when they engaged in such tasks. For example, one staff member described how he had previously done all the talking when students set up a bank account. Now he provides practice opportunities for how they will do this during his English and then mentoring classes and now 'stands back' at the bank to allow them to negotiate their own way through the process.

Another teacher was observed conducting a series of lessons on filling in forms. For example, she used input tasks to help them understand the genre of forms and the vocabulary used, and then she undertook information-gap tasks using a smart board where the students matched form-filling questions to possible answers. For the final two tasks, she had the students actually apply for their tax file number and their passport. Instruction thus satisfied functional needs, but in a meaning-based way.

Interacting with health professional staff is sadly a need that many Aboriginal people encounter too frequently in their adult lives. However, our previous NA indicated that many students at Kutja do not have the language or confidence to engage meaningfully with such staff. The school has for some time employed a nurse who has held a regular on-campus clinic. The students are encouraged to visit her if they have physical or emotional concerns. This provides them with opportunities to interact with her about their health. The current nurse has become engaged with helping the students in this regard by conducting in-class lessons on various topics related to young adults and engaging in activities where they can develop the vocabulary necessary for such interactions. Furthermore, she has become part of the social fabric of the school, and in doing so, she has increased the students' confidence to engage with her without *shame*. In this way, the clinic and other functional activities at the school provide an environment for authentic and real-life task engagement.

Conclusion

The evidence from the data presented in the current study demonstrates that it is possible to develop contextually relevant and culturally appropriate tasks for learners in diverse contexts based on a thorough needs analysis. For the Australian Aboriginal cohort observed, it was indeed possible to select and create authentic tasks that enhanced their successful transition to the workplace and to life beyond the classroom with the use of tasks that fulfill both functional as well as linguistic goals.

References

Adams, R. and Oliver, R. (2019) *Peer Interaction in Classrooms*. NY: Routledge.

Australian Bureau of Statistics [ABS] (2016a) National Aboriginal and Torres Strait Islander social survey. See www.abs.gov.au.

Australian Bureau of Statistics [ABS] (2016b) Schools, Australia. See www.abs.gov.au.

Australian Curriculum, Assessment and Reporting Authority (ACARA) (2018) See https://www.acara.edu.au/.

Cameron, R. Stuart, L. and Bell, T. (2017) Race based inequalities for Indigenous Australian's participation and engagement in VET: A targeted review of the research. *Journal of Vocational Education and Training* 69 (3), 311–332.

Cowling, J.D. (2007) Needs analysis: planning a syllabus for a series of intensive workplace courses at a leading Japanese company. *English for Specific Purposes* 26 (4), 426–442.

East, M. (2017) Task-based teaching and learning: Pedagogical implications. In N. van Deusen-Scholl and S. May (eds) *Second and Foreign Language Education* (pp. 1–11). Cham: Springer International Publishing. 10.1007/978-3-319-02323-6_8-1.

Ellis, R. (2003) *Task-Based Language Learning and Teaching*. Oxford: Oxford Applied Linguistics.

Gilabert, R. (2005) Task complexity and L2 narrative oral production. Unpublished doctoral dissertation, Universitat de Barcelona, Spain.

Grote, E. and Rochecouste, J. (2012) Language and the classroom setting. In Q. Beresford, G. Partington and G. Gower (eds) *Reform and Resistance in Aboriginal Education*. Crawley, WA: UWA Publishing.

Hunter, B.H. (2010) Pathways for Indigenous school leavers to undertake training or gain employment. Resource sheet no. 2. See www.aihw.gov.au/closingthegap.

Long, M.H. (ed.) (2005) *Second Language Needs Analysis*. Cambridge: Cambridge University Press.

Long, M.H. (2015) *Second Language Acquisition and Task-Based Language Teaching*. New Jersey: Wiley-Blackwell.

Malcolm, I.G. and Grote, E. (2007) Aboriginal English: Restructured variety for cultural maintenance. In G. Leitner and I.G. Malcolm (eds) *The Habitat of Australia's Aboriginal Languages* (pp. 153–180). Berlin & New York: Mouton de Gruyter.

Nunan, D. (2004) *Task-Based Language Teaching*. Cambridge: Cambridge University Press.

Oliver, R., Rochecouste, J. and Grote, E. (2013) *The Transition of Aboriginal and Torres Strait Islander Students into Higher Education*. Office of Learning and Teaching, Australian Government.

Oliver, R., Grote, E., Rochecouste, J. and Exell, M. (2012) Addressing the language and literacy needs of Aboriginal high school VET students who speak SAE as an additional language. *Australian Journal of Indigenous Education* 41 (2), 1–11.

Oliver, R., Grote, E., Rochecouste, J. and Exell, M. (2013a) A task-based needs analysis for Australian Aboriginal students: Going beyond the target situation to address cultural issues. *International Journal of Training Research* 11 (3), 246–259.

Oliver, R., Grote, E., Rochecouste, J. and Exell, M. (2013b) Needs analysis for task-based language teaching: A case study of Indigenous vocational education and training students who speak EAL/EAD. *TESOL in Context* 22 (2), 36–50.

Steering Committee for the Review of Government Service Provision (2016) Overcoming indigenous disadvantage: Key indicators 2016. Productivity Commission, Canberra. See http://www.pc.gov.au/research/recurring/overcomingindigenous-disadvantage/key-indicators-2016.

Windley, G. (2017) Indigenous VET participation, completion and outcomes: Change over the past decade (Research Report). Adelaide: National Centre for Vocational Education Research. See https://www.ncver.edu.au.

10 The Potential Use of Tasks in Post-Soviet Schools: Case Studies from Ukraine

Tatiana Bogachenko and Rhonda Oliver

This study explored the potential of implementing task-based language teaching (TBLT) in Ukraine. Using a case study methodology, it focused on three teachers from different schools within Ukrainian state education. Whilst their practices differed in substantial ways, particularly in relation to the use of communicative activities, each teacher employed some aspects of TBLT such as undertaking a needs analysis, making real life connections, providing a focus on form and utilising activities with a non-linguistic outcome. This provides a foundation for the development of locally appropriate tasks. However, reflecting post-Soviet educational practices, the teachers faced a number of difficulties – time restrictions, compulsory marking and working with different age levels. We suggest that local initiatives could serve as a starting point for the inclusion of TBLT (albeit in a modified version) in Ukraine and indicate ways to address practical challenges of implementation.

Introduction

Because of its sound theoretical and pedagogic foundation, TBLT has gained increasing popularity with language educators and has done so despite the fact that it often poses a challenge to existing teaching beliefs and practices. In fact, it has been claimed that TBLT has contributed to changes in language teaching and to education more generally (e.g. Ellis, 2009; Najjari, 2014; Ogilvie & Dunn, 2010). The key advantages of TBLT are that it provides an opportunity for language learners to focus on both meaning and form, facilitating the development of accuracy as well as fluency and complexity (Ellis, 2000) and fostering the development of communicative competence (Adams & Newton, 2009). Even so, its uptake has been less prevalent in some contexts than others, and overall it is still seen as an 'innovation'. Whilst initially appearing in the 1980s, TBLT has only started to be widely implemented in the last decade or so in such places as Hong Kong (Carless, 2007) and New Zealand secondary schools (East, 2012); and in universities in France (McAllister *et al.*, 2012), Thailand (McDonough & Chaikitmongkol, 2007) and Iran (Latif & Shafipoor, 2015). These cases do serve to illustrate the extent and diversity in the uptake of TBLT in a variety of educational settings.

There remains, however, a lack of research data about the implementation of TBLT, or at least the potential for this to occur, in the post-Soviet countries. This is not surprising given the overall scarcity of empirical educational research in that region (Fim'yar *et al.*, 2019; Smotrova, 2009; Tarnopolsky, 1996). Recently, however, Ukraine adopted the Common European Framework of Reference for Language Teaching (CEFR) (Council of Europe, 2001) and inherent in the related policy documents is the promotion of tasks for language learning. Thus, the uptake of the CEFR in Ukraine offers a unique opportunity to explore the potential of TBLT as an educational innovation, and to do so at the stage before it is implemented (Fullan, 2007). The current study is part of a larger research project that set out to explore how language teaching is being done in Ukrainian schools, what Ukrainian teachers believe about language pedagogy, particularly with respect to approaches that underpin TBLT, and how this aligns with the requirements and expectations outlined in educational documents and policies. To do this, a survey of the relevant policies and documents, teacher interviews, lesson observations and teacher focus groups were employed in the first two stages of the research study, providing data for the description of the 'macro' context of foreign language teaching (FLT) in Ukraine. The case studies presented here constitute the final phase of the project and involve an exploration of three different micro contexts of language teaching (i.e. three teachers and their classrooms) in Ukrainian state schools.

TBLT as an Innovation

Emerging from Communicative Language Teaching (CLT), tasks have been used in Europe, Asia, North and South America, New Zealand and Australia in second and foreign language teaching programs, academic and vocational programs, in communicative classrooms and in more forms-focused settings, with small and large classes, and with children, adolescents and adult learners. How tasks are used in this range of contexts varies considerably, as does the focus of the teaching (Carless, 2009), the types of tasks (e.g. Ellis, 2003) and the materials and resources that are used (Breen *et al.*, 2001; Najjari, 2014; Prabhu, 1987).

Some key features of task-based instruction are that it is needs based (Long, 2015), primarily involves a focus on meaning (Ellis, 2009; Skehan, 1998), includes focus-on-form (Long, 2015), requires learners to draw on their own language resources (Ellis, 2009), includes a 'gap' that necessitates interaction (Ellis, 2009), is based on the real-world activities (Skehan, 1998), is learner centred or learner directed (Long, 2015) and has a non-linguistic outcome (Ellis, 2009; Skehan, 1998). Depending on how many of these features are included, instruction can be described along a continuum of more or less task-like.

Inherent in TBLT is its flexibility to meet local needs. According to Long (2015), the foundation of TBLT is a needs analysis (NA), and based on the evidence from this, tasks can be designed or modified in ways that make them more compatible with the target context and learners (e.g. Carless, 2003, 2007, 2009; McAllister *et al.*, 2012; Van Gorp & Bogaert, 2006). By meeting the requirements of particular groups of learners, their motivation and enjoyment can be increased (e.g. Bao & Du, 2015; McDonough & Chaikitmongkol, 2007). Furthermore, learning outcomes can be improved because TBLT supports a shift from teacher-centred to learner-centred practices (e.g. Ellis, 2009; McAllister *et al.*, 2012; McDonough & Chaikitmongkol, 2007; Van Avermaet *et al.*, 2006). For example, in a French university, a task-based program that used small-group work helped students to become more confident in speaking (McAllister *et al.*, 2012).

Although it has many advantages, TBLT can be challenging for the stakeholders (Barnard & Nguyen, 2010; Butler, 2011; Kollmann, 2005). Shehadeh (2012) indicates that issues may arise at various levels. For example, at the institutional level, it may be difficult to reconcile the imperative for examinations with a task-based approach. Large class sizes can also create certain difficulties, as can teachers' and learners' beliefs about how languages should be taught and learnt (Shehadeh, 2012). To counter these issues, it is vital that stakeholder perceptions and current practices are examined as this provides the type of evidence necessary for successful task development and TBLT implementation (Long, 2005).

Investigating the utility of TBLT for post-Soviet schooling offers a unique context to explore such perceptions and practices. This is because, unlike in many parts of the world, the Soviet education system developed in isolation and heavily influenced the development of education and pedagogy in the independent states (see Bogachenko & Perry, 2015). However, there is now an openness towards ideas from the 'outside' motivated in part by the adoption of the CEFR. Ukraine is an example of this, combining its Soviet heritage with its own long-lasting and deep-rooted traditions and an appetite for innovation (Kuzio, 2003).

Examining Ukrainian stakeholder perceptions and practices – teachers' in particular – may shed light on how TBLT can be implemented in more 'traditional' and non-Western settings.

State Schools in Ukraine

Since independence from the Soviet Union in 1991, Ukraine has experienced large-scale social and educational change. FLT has been one of the priority areas for curriculum reform (Goodman, 2009; Mitter, 1992). This is not surprising given that competence in another language, particularly English, is deemed essential for the 'integration of the country into the world community and the international economy' (Tarnopolsky, 1996: 616). As a result, new FLT syllabuses reflecting the CEFR were developed in the early 2000s. In addition to this, English has become a compulsory subject in all Ukrainian schools and is now taught throughout the country commencing in the first year of primary school for all students.

However, in spite of the push for reform, there is evidence that language pedagogy has, essentially, remained unchanged (Koshmanova & Ravchyna, 2008; Smotrova, 2009), as has general pedagogy in Ukraine (Fim'yar *et al.*, 2019). Hence, although the Ukrainian curriculum is informed by the CEFR – a curriculum that supports the use of tasks – it does not seem that this is being translated into teaching practice. This claim was supported by the first stage of the research project where a discrepancy was found between the official curriculum and classroom reality, in particular in the areas of teacher and student roles and the use of communicative activities (Bogachenko, 2016). If TBLT is to be used in Ukraine, there is a need to establish how this can best be done. Given that there is a higher likelihood of an innovation being adopted if it does not require significant changes to the teachers' usual routine (Cohen & Ball, 2007), or in other words, builds on their existing practices (Wedell, 2009), the present case study research seeks to answer the following questions:

(1) Are there task-like practices already in place in school FLT contexts in Ukraine?
(2) What challenges might occur in language teaching classrooms in Ukrainian schools if TBLT is implemented?

Method

The method used here is case study research, which involves a detailed and contextualised inquiry into the phenomenon under investigation (Baxter & Jack, 2008), namely the potential for a TBLT approach to be adopted in Ukraine. Case study methodology was adopted to understand 'the particularity and complexity of a single case, coming to understand its activity within important circumstances' (Stake, 1995: xi). Research methods of an exploratory and descriptive nature were necessary for this purpose (Ellinger & McWhorter, 2016), including methods that capture the voices of the participants (Baxter & Jack, 2008).

Participants

The participants in this study were three teachers chosen using theoretical sampling (Merkens, 2004), that is, a representative sample was chosen based on the researcher's previous work in the target schools. Their circumstances constituted a maximum variation sample (Creswell, 2013) as the cases represented different school types, locations, teaching styles (most task like, least task like and somewhere between the two) and a range of teaching experiences. Pseudonyms are used for each teacher.

Procedure

Data for the three case studies were collected qualitatively by way of numerous lesson observations (20 per teacher), undertaken over a nine-week period (approximately three weeks per teacher) and repeated semi-structured interviews, occurring before and after each of the three-week observation periods. The data from these sources were recorded using extensive field notes and supplemented with audio recordings, photographs and the collection of artefacts (e.g. copies of teaching resources, teacher-created lesson plans and students' written work). The use of data from various sources provided triangulation (Brown, 2009) serving to substantiate the trustworthiness of the data.

Analysis

To begin the analysis, field notes were read and re-read several times and the key themes emerging from the data for each teacher were identified. These were used to write a detailed description of the three classrooms. To create a narrative that would represent the participants' voices, a four-step process, as set out in Smyth and McInerney (2013), was followed. This process involves the researchers: (1) immersing themselves in data to get a feel of what was said, (2) re-reading the data more closely to gain insights, (3) making choices as to what to include and translate this into the content and then (4) writing up the case. To capture the voices of the participants, quotes were selected that are illuminative of the particular case and translated into English. It should be noted, however, that lesson excerpts were not translated in order to showcase the extent of L1 and FL use by the teacher and students during the lesson. In addition, English grammatical and lexical errors were not corrected to provide an authentic representation (Smyth & McInerney, 2013).

Findings

The findings are reported in three sections. First, the three teaching contexts are briefly described to provide background information about each teacher and their school. Second, task-like elements that already exist in these contexts (including elements found in all three contexts and those encountered in only one or two of the classrooms) are presented. Next, the elements of TBLT that potentially can be challenging within these different contexts are described. Finally, the implications for TBLT implementation in Ukraine are outlined.

Teaching contexts

Oksana worked as a teacher in a specialised school located in a large city. At the time of the study, she had 11 years of FLT experience and described teaching children as her calling. She was known as an innovative teacher for her use of project work and technology. Her classroom was equipped for language learning: there was a tape recorder in the room, and the walls were decorated with posters that depicted famous landmarks from English-speaking countries. The room was small and could only seat up to 18 students. Oksana would normally have 8 to 12 students in her lessons, which is seen by local educators as providing more opportunities for each student to practice using the target language and lead to better learning outcomes. In addition to the prescribed textbooks, Oksana used a number of other resources including vocabulary and grammar reference books, CDs, readers and printouts. Oksana also brought her own laptop to school to use in her lessons.

The second teacher, Olena, was a recent university graduate and in her third year of teaching in a specialised school in a regional town. Her classroom was situated near that of other FLT teachers meaning that the noise level of her students, which can be a distraction to other subject teachers, was not a problem. Her classroom was even smaller than Oksana's and accommodated only 6 to 8 students. Olena had more resources than Oksana, including many visuals (e.g. posters, photos and flash cards) and reference books, most of which were provided by her school's administration. The FL department at that school was very supportive of teaching innovations, the use of technology and international collaboration. Workshops and various language-related events were frequently held in her school. Hence, Olena had more opportunities for professional development than many of her FLT colleagues in Ukraine.

On this basis, it was not surprising to observe that she encouraged pair and group work in every lesson. She also changed the layout of the classroom to facilitate learner cooperation and problem-solving. Unlike the others, she did not stop conversations in L1, but attempted to shift them to English while maintaining the focus on meaning.

The third teacher, Tamara, worked in a non-specialised school. She was in her fifties and had over three decades of teaching experience. While being open to new ideas and approaches, she appeared to have fewer opportunities for innovation than either Oksana or Olena, particularly because of the fewer hours available for FLT in her school (2–3 hours compared to 3–5 in specialised schools). Her students also had lower levels of English language proficiency than in the two other contexts. No authentic FL communication was observed to occur in her classes with the learning activities consisting mostly of reciting dialogues, text translation, and textbook-based questions and answers.

Task-like elements of the three teachers' current practices

There were a number of elements of the teachers' practices and beliefs that were task like and supportive of a TBLT approach. These included consideration of student needs, making connections to real-life language use, occasional lesson sequence resembling a focus on form (rather than formS through present-practice-produce [PPP]) and the incorporation of some activities with a non-linguistic outcome.

Student needs

Although no formal needs analysis was conducted by either the educational authorities or the schools, the three teachers appeared aware of their students' needs and interests and took these into account in their lesson planning. For instance, Oksana was mindful of her students' increased travel outside of Ukraine and their opportunities to talk to foreign tourists in their city. She encouraged her students to describe their travels and included the development of cultural awareness in her lessons through the use of historical accounts and comparison of various aspects of life such as schooling or eating out in different countries.

Oksana was mindful of her younger primary school students' (Years 1 to 4) need for physical movement. She employed poems and songs that were accompanied by gestures and body movement, such as pointing at various objects in the classroom. She also showed YouTube videos based on songs such as 'The Alphabet Song' and 'The Colours of the Rainbow', and her students sang along and danced. She explained that actions made remembering the songs easier for students and also catered for their need to move frequently during the long 45-minute lessons.

Like Oksana and Olena, Tamara emphasised the growing demand for FL skills. This motivated her to use more contemporary textbooks produced by foreign publishers which were provided through the support of parents and the school leadership team. At the same time, she also had a strong focus on explicitly teaching reading skills in her lessons and she did this using older, locally published books from the school library. She described how these skills were not given sufficient attention in more recent materials and she believed this did not prepare her students for a lifetime of reading.

Real-life connection

Through their awareness of and attention to the needs of their students, the teachers also appeared to make clear links to life outside the classroom. Some real-life activities involved Oksana's students searching for information for their project work on the internet. Like Tamara, Oksana also prioritised reading, but her emphasis was on reading for pleasure, selecting texts that her students liked. She also encouraged them to discuss the meaning of the text and to make connections to their everyday lives.

Of the three teachers, Olena was probably the most creative in the ways she made this real-life connection. For instance, when her Year 8 students read a text about the use of English as an international language and encountered the term 'native speaker', she initiated the following conversation about their experiences:

T: Did you have experience of speaking in English with a native speaker?

S1:   Yes, it was interesting to speak with native speaker because they have correct pronunciation and you can improve your own language.

T: When did you communicate?

S1:   Two years ago.

T: With whom did you communicate?

S1:   With my uncle's friend.

T: Which country was he from?

S1:   From England.

T: Kate, you were in Egypt. Did you communicate in English?

S2:   No, but I was in the camp, and there were two people from America, and they spoke English, and we communicated in it as well.

(Fieldnotes, Teacher 2, Lesson 7, Year 8 students)

Focus on form

In Ukrainian schools, language input in FLT is often pre-determined and based on set texts with a lot of drilling and chorus repetition, translation and reciting. Whilst Oksana was observed doing this, she was also seen deviating from the prescribed script and engaging in meaningful interaction, providing her students with a focus on form as needed (Long, 2015). For example, in the following exchange, she responds to one student's impromptu question and further explores the response of another:

> T: How are you?
> S1: I am happy and sleepy. How are you?
> S2: I am scared ... How are you?
> S3: I am wonderful. How are you?

The girl who was supposed to answer next asked the teacher:

> S4: А як сказати «холодно»? (*What is the word for 'cold'?*)
> T: Cold (*the teacher put her arms around herself and started shaking to imitate being cold*).
> S4: I am cold. How are you?
> S5: I am angry.
> T: На кого це ти злий? (*Who are you angry with?*)
> S5: На папу. (*With my dad*)
>   (Fieldnotes, Teacher 1, Lesson 2, Year 1 students)

Olena provided even more opportunities to focus on form. She would start each lesson quite informally asking the students in English what they did on the weekend, whether they watched the news, how their maths test went, etc. She encouraged student-initiated meaning making and used these exchanges to draw attention to the form of English. This happened even with seemingly 'unrelated' and spontaneous comments made by students in their L1 to which she responded by prompting them to translate into English:

> S: Муха летает (*There is a fly flying around [in the classroom]*).
> T: Say it in English.
> S: A fly flies?
> T: Now at this moment, what tense should be used?
> S: A fly is flying.
>   (Fieldnotes, Teacher 2, Lesson 3, Year 11 students)

Non-linguistic outcomes

While most class activities were explicitly language focused, with a clear objective related to the use and acquisition of grammar forms, it was found that two of the teachers utilised a different approach in some of their lessons. Note, however, that neither referred to having a 'non-linguistic outcome' in any of their comments, suggesting that this outcome may have been a by-product of their experimenting with communicative approaches. For example, one of Olena's lessons was built around the topic 'Food'. She started the lesson with a brainstorming activity asking students to work in groups and write down as many words as possible for different types of food (e.g. 'everything connected with bread'; 'things that you add to food'; 'now make a list about fish'). Next, the students worked in groups to create a menu for their school canteen. The activity was essentially meaning focused with a non-linguistic outcome – a menu for their school lunches. This was followed by students presenting their suggestions and providing feedback on each other's ideas. The teacher asked: 'What do you think? Would you like to have this menu at school?' In Oksana's classroom, a non-linguistic outcome resulted from the project work she did with her students. This involved research undertaken by the students on a particular topic (e.g. 'The Fire of London') then a presentation where they exchanged information with their peers.

Potential challenges and implications for using tasks effectively in Ukrainian schools

While the observations in the previous section show some potential for the use of tasks in these Ukrainian classrooms, other observations revealed potential challenges in implementing TBLT. These included the compulsory nature of marking, an overall tendency for noise avoidance, classroom management, time constraints, high teacher workload and lack of facilities and resources in schools.

Compulsory marking

Following the educational practices implemented during the Soviet period, marking has been an important part of the pedagogy in Ukraine, and this was also the case for the three teachers observed in this study. For example, during and at the completion of each lesson, Oksana spent considerable time marking her students' work. She recorded and signed the marks in the school register and in the students' diaries. She said she did this to monitor students' progress and in order to report to the school authorities and parents. For students, however, marking seemed to be an end in itself, rather than part of the learning journey. In their lessons they often asked, 'Will this be graded?', 'What mark did I get?'. Having received a low mark (2 out of 12) for their homework, students on two separate occasions started crying. Thus, the emphasis on marking appeared to distract the students from engaging with meaningful language use.

Olena highlighted another issue – namely that it is much harder for her to mark meaning-focused activities than those focused on 'forms'. She indicated that the centralised marking system (i.e. the one established by the Ministry of Education authorities and compulsory for all government educational institutions of a particular type) gives little direction to teachers regarding the assessment of meaningful language use and that it was especially difficult to mark oral activities such as discussions. As a result, her assessment regime had an accuracy rather than meaning focus. Tamara provided more marks during her lessons than the others. Her students' work was marked even after a small piece of work was done – for instance, she would give her student a mark for only a couple of sentences they had translated. She also used the promise of extra marks to motivate her students to work faster. For instance, she would set a competition to give a mark to the first student to finish a written exercise. This was done to address the time constraints she faced in a non-specialised school.

Overall, with the existing centrally developed marking rubrics used in Ukrainian state schools, assessing meaning-focused task activities in a fast and accurate manner may prove difficult. Furthermore, obtaining good marks appeared as a primary motivation for most students. For the effective use of tasks in instruction in Ukrainian schools, there is a need for feasible assessment practices.

Noise

By its very nature, TBLT can involve 'noisy' lessons. However, the physical layout and lack of noise insulation in schools and classrooms in Ukraine may make the use of tasks disruptive to others. This is especially the case if nearby classes are of a non-language type, involving little cooperation or discussion, such as Maths and Science. Hence, for TBLT to be successfully implemented, quieter practices may be needed (see Adams & Oliver, 2019; Ellis & Shintani, 2013 for examples, such as using input-based tasks, using reading tasks, and through the use of technology).

Classroom management

Existing beliefs about pedagogy, especially pertaining to classroom management, manifested in the teachers keeping strict order using a lock-step style of teaching. Even Olena, who followed the most task-like practices, reported that communicative activities (inherent in TBLT) require special classroom management skills, which she found challenging particularly with younger learners. When primary school students in her lessons had opportunities to talk or move in the classroom (e.g. to form groups), they were observed becoming off task and switching to their L1 a lot. For TBLT to be successfully implemented in Ukraine, teachers would need professional development to increase their repertoire of skills in this regard (see Adams & Oliver, 2019; Ellis & Shintani, 2013; Ellis, Chapter 7, this volume, for possible options).

Time constraints

The need to fulfil the curriculum requirements within the restricted lesson time of 45 minutes seemed to be an issue for each of the teachers. It was perceived that communicative group work took more time than activities outlined in the set textbooks. Creative, collaborative and meaning-focused activities were seen to fit poorly into the fast pace of the lessons. For example, and similar to the situation in other educational settings with centralised curriculum and prescribed textbooks (e.g. Carless, 2003 in Hong Kong), Oksana experienced significant issues finishing lessons on time. Given that classes are combined for a lesson if another teacher is away, she also felt compelled to have her students complete textbook exercises at the same time as their peers in other classes. Further, she described the need to do all these exercises because parents might complain about wasting money on these resources if they are not used. As a result, Oksana was frequently observed asking students to work faster. Similarly, Tamara was observed constantly reminding her students to keep up the pace. Her routine appeared motivated by her need to finish the lesson before the bell rang so that she would be able to move quickly to another part of the school for her next lesson. This was necessary in her school because the breaks between lessons had been shortened to accommodate the two shifts of students which in turn had been put in place to accommodate the growing enrolment numbers. In contrast, Olena's lessons were often double periods of 90 minutes duration and this provided a noticeable advantage, in particular allowing time for her to implement meaning-oriented language pedagogy and providing opportunities for group-work activities, discussions and games. Again, this was quite different from Oksana's students' project work, which was mainly done by the students, not in the classroom, but at home after school.

Limited class time can potentially undermine the introduction of an innovation, and in particular TBLT. Systemic level changes, such as adapting the timetable in ways more conducive for language learning (e.g. increasing the number of double periods), may address these problems, although the established beliefs and practices may render these options unrealistic. A more practical solution would be working with teachers and using their resources to develop contextually appropriate tasks that can be completed within the current timeframe.

Lack of facilities and resources

Although the three cases differed considerably in the availability of resources, teaching materials and facilities, all teachers described how they spend long hours developing or looking for resources and asking for materials. For example, Oksana's CD-player worked intermittently, and she had to bring her own laptop to school. Tamara had to move between four to six classrooms each day, moving upstairs and down again, which discouraged her from using additional resources to support her students' learning. Olena, however, was much more fortunate as the school administration and parents of her students were happy to provide additional resources.

The development of centrally accessible task resources, as described above and in Chapter 7 of this volume, would go some way to alleviating these issues as would working with teachers to show how tasks can be developed (and modified) based on readily available resources. This variety might also give teachers freedom to exercise the 'sense of plausibility' or decision-making regarding what is appropriate (or not) for their students (Prabhu, 1987: 107), especially when working across age groups. Although the development of such resources may require input from local teachers to facilitate contextual appropriateness, the concomitant time and financial commitment may well be beyond the current resource abilities of post-Soviet schools.

High workload

Similar to other studies (e.g. Zhang, 2007), in the Ukrainian context where there is a high workload associated with preparation, marking time and administrative duties, teachers face challenges incorporating interactive tasks in their FL classrooms. For example, Oksana felt using tasks would be difficult because she taught students in Primary, Middle and Secondary school levels resulting in more preparation and marking time. She was also a mentor teacher meaning she had additional responsibilities such as providing support for a set group of students, helping them academically and in terms of their wellbeing, often during the break times. Again, systemic-level changes would be needed to address this issue. In the shorter term, however, professional development work could be undertaken with teachers (and textbook developers) to develop task resources that could reduce teacher workload. Compiling and sharing these centrally, as suggested by Ellis (Chapter 7, this volume) and above, may lead to supplementary resources that teachers could access and modify to suit the needs of their particular learners, while also still addressing the curricular requirements. However, it may be useful to introduce both focused and unfocused tasks (Ellis, 2003) so that teachers could choose the ones with which they feel more confident. What is clear from the current study is the need to incorporate an approach that recognises diverse settings and various possibilities, even when they function as a part of one centralised system.

Conclusion

The current study conducted in three different classrooms in Ukraine revealed a number of issues that can potentially both support and undermine the use of tasks in Ukrainian schools. There were considerable challenges inherent in these settings including limited facilities and resources, as well as issues related to post-Soviet educational practices such as the use of a centrally developed compulsory marking system and low noise tolerance. Even so, although the Ukrainian classrooms were quite 'traditional', some elements can be described as 'task-like' and these may serve as the foundation for implementing tasks in a way compatible to the current context, thus enabling a starting point for innovation (Wedell, 2009).

Furthermore, the teachers appeared open to innovation and, particularly, to communicative approaches. All three were aware of their students' needs, including language needs and the need to engage in real-life activities. Despite the fact that needs analyses are not generally conducted in Ukrainian schools and that both the program and the textbooks are centrally prescribed, the teachers appeared to make some adjustments to accommodate their students' needs, interests and future plans. They were also all aware of the growing opportunities to use FL outside the classroom. In addition, Olena demonstrated that it was possible to provide focus-on-form in a Ukrainian teaching context, and both Olena and Oksana utilised some activities with non-linguistic outcomes. Together these attributes could serve as a starting point for the development of locally appropriate tasks.

Undoubtedly, however, more empirical research is needed to provide a better understanding of how task-like elements can be used as a platform for further development of task-like and potentially task-based practices. This would include consideration of the potential challenges and the ways to address those, such as how to incorporate the requisite marking, appropriate classroom management strategies, and the development of the necessary resources for teachers. It is possible that local initiatives may provide a possible way forward for the development of these aspects.

References

Adams, R. and Newton, J. (2009) TBLT in Asia: Constraints and opportunities. *Asian Journal of English Language Teaching* 19, 1–17.

Adams, R. and Oliver, R. (2019) *Teaching Through Peer Interaction*. New York: Routledge.

Bao, R. and Du, X. (2015) Implementation of task-based language teaching in Chinese as a foreign language: Benefits and challenges. *Language, Culture and Curriculum* 28 (3), 291–310.

Barnard, R. and Nguyen, G.V. (2010) Task-based language teaching (TBLT): A Vietnamese case study using narrative frames to elicit teachers' beliefs. *Language Education in Asia* 1, 77–86.

Baxter, P. and Jack, S. (2008) Qualitative case study methodology: Study design and implementation for novice researchers. *The Qualitative Report* 13 (4), 544559.

Bogachenko, T. (2016) Contextualising educational innovation: Task-based language teaching and post-Soviet classrooms in Ukraine. Unpublished doctoral dissertation, Curtin University, Perth WA.

Bogachenko, T. and Perry, L. (2015) Vospitanie and regime change: Teacher-education textbooks in Soviet and post-Soviet Ukraine. *Prospects: Quarterly Review of Comparative Education* 45 (4), 549–562.

Breen, M.P., Hird, B., Milton, M., Oliver, R. and Thwaite, A. (2001) Making sense of language teaching: Teachers' principles and classroom practices. *Applied Linguistics* 22 (4), 470–501.

Brown, J.D. (2009) Foreign and second language needs analysis. In M.H. Long and C.J. Doughty (eds) *The Handbook of Language Teaching* (pp. 269–293). Oxford: Blackwell.

Butler, Y.G. (2011) The implementation of communicative and task-based language teaching in the Asia-Pacific region. *Annual Review of Applied Linguistics* 31, 36–57.

Carless, D. (2003) Factors in the implementation of task-based teaching in primary schools. *System* 31, 485–500.

Carless, D. (2007) The suitability of task-based approaches for secondary schools: Perspectives from Hong Kong. *System* 35, 595–608.

Carless, D. (2009) Revisiting the TBLT versus P-P-P debate: Voices from Hong Kong. *Asian Journal of English Language Teaching* 19, 49–66.

Cohen, D.K. and Ball, D.L. (2007) Innovation and the problem of scale. In B. Schneider and S. McDonald (eds) *Scale-Up in Education: Ideas in Principle* (Vol. 1, pp. 19–36). Lanham, MD: Rowman & Littlefield.

Council of Europe (2001) *Common European Framework of Reference for Languages: Learning, Teaching, Assessment*. Cambridge: Press Syndicate of the University of Cambridge.

Creswell, J.W. (2013) *Qualitative Inquiry and Research Design: Choosing Among Five Approaches* (3rd edn). Los Angeles, CA: SAGE Publications.

East, M. (2012) *Task-Based Language Teaching from the Teachers' Perspective: Insights from New Zealand*. Amsterdam: John Benjamins.

Ellinger, A.D. and McWhorter, R. (2016) Qualitative case study research as empirical inquiry. *International Journal of Adult Vocational Education and Technology* 7 (3), 1–13.

Ellis, R. (2000) Task-based research and language pedagogy. *Language Teaching Research* 4 (3), 193–220.

Ellis, R. (2003) *Task-Based Language Learning and Teaching*. Oxford: Oxford University Press.

Ellis, R. (2009) Task-based language teaching: Sorting out the misunderstandings. International *Journal of Applied Linguistics* 19 (3), 221–246.

Ellis, R. and Shintani, N. (2013) *Exploring Language Pedagogy Through Second Language Acquisition Research*. London: Routledge.

Fim'yar, O., Kushnir, I. and Vitrukh, M. (2019) Understanding Ukrainian pedagogical sciences through textbook analysis of four 'Pedagogy' textbooks [Special issue]. *European Educational Research Journal*. Advance Online Publication. https://doi.org/10.1177/1474904119866516.

Fullan, M. (2007) *The New Meaning of Educational Change* (4th edn). Abingdon: Routledge.

Goodman, B. (2009) The ecology of language in Ukraine. *Working Papers in Educational Linguistics* 24 (2), 19–39.

Kollmann, V. (2005) Aspects of current English language teaching practices with a special focus on task. (Unpublished doctoral dissertation). Edith Cowan University, Joondalup, WA.

Koshmanova, T. and Ravchyna, T. (2008) Teacher preparation in a post totalitarian society: An interpretation of Ukrainian teacher educators' stereotypes. *International Journal of Qualitative Studies in Education* 21 (2), 137–158.

Kuzio, T. (2003) *EU and Ukraine: A Turning Point in 2004? Occasional Papers No. 47*. Paris: European Union Institute for Security Studies.

Latif, F. and Shafipoor, M. (2015) Task-based language teaching in General English classrooms: A case study in Engineering Faculties in Iran. *Mediterranean Journal of Social Sciences* 6 (4), 587–593.

Long, M.H. (2005) Overview: A rationale for learner needs analysis. In M.H. Long (ed.) *Second Language Needs Analysis* (pp. 1–16). Cambridge: Cambridge University Press.

Long, M.H. (2015) *Second Language Acquisition and Task-Based Language Teaching*. Oxford: Wiley-Blackwell.

McAllister, J., Narcy-Combes, M.-F. and Starkey-Perret, R. (2012) Language teachers' perceptions of a task-based learning programme in a French University. In A. Shehadeh and C.A. Coombe (eds) *Task-Based Language Learning and Teaching in Foreign Language Contexts: Research and Implementation* (pp. 313–342). Amsterdam/Philadelphia: John Benjamins.

McDonough, K. and Chaikitmongkol, W. (2007) Teachers' and learners' reactions to a task-based EFL course in Thailand. *TESOL Quarterly* 41 (1), 107–132.

Merkens, H. (2004) Selection procedures, sampling, case construction. In U. Flick, E. von Kardorff and I. Steinke (eds) *A Companion to Qualitative Research* (pp. 165–171). London: Sage.

Mitter, W. (1992) Education in the period of revolutionary change. In D. Philips and M. Kaser (eds) *Education and Economic Change in Eastern Europe and the Former Soviet Union* (pp. 15–28). Cambridge: Cambridge University Press.

Najjari, R. (2014) Implementation of task-based language teaching in Iran: Theoretical and practical considerations. *Procedia – Social and Behavioral Sciences* 98, 1307–1315.

Ogilvie, G. and Dunn, W. (2010) Taking teacher education to task: Exploring the role of teacher education in promoting the utilization of task-based language teaching. *Language Teaching Research* 14 (2), 161–181.

Prabhu, N. (1987) *Second Language Pedagogy*. Oxford: Oxford University Press.

Shehadeh, A. (2012) Broadening the perspective of task-based language teaching scholarship: The contribution of research in foreign language contexts. In A. Shehadeh and C.A. Coombe (eds) *Task-Based Language Learning and Teaching in Foreign Language Contexts: Research and Implementation* (pp. 1–20). Amsterdam/Philadelphia: John Benjamins.

Skehan, P. (1998) Task-based instruction. *Annual Review of Applied Linguistics* 18, 268–286.

Smotrova, T. (2009) Globalization and English language teaching in Ukraine. *TESOL Quarterly* 43 (4), 727–732.

Smyth, J. and McInerney, P. (2013) Whose side are you on? Advocacy ethnography: Some methodological aspects of narrative portraits of disadvantaged young people, in socially critical research. *International Journal of Qualitative Studies in Education* 26 (1), 1–20.

Stake, R.E. (1995) *The Art of Case Study Research*. Thousand Oaks, CA: Sage.

Tarnopolsky, O.B. (1996) EFL teaching in the Ukraine: State-regulated or commercial? *TESOL Quarterly* 30, 616–622.

Van Avermaet, P., Colpin, M., Van Gorp, K., Bogaert, N. and Van den Branden, K. (2006) The role of the teacher in task-based language teaching. In K. Van den Branden (ed.) *Task-Based Language Education: From Theory to Practice* (pp. 175–196). Cambridge: Cambridge University Press.

Van Gorp, K. and Bogaert, N. (2006) Developing language tasks for primary and secondary education. In K. Van den Branden (ed.) *Task-Based Language Education: From Theory to Practice* (pp. 76–105). Cambridge: Cambridge University Press.

Wedell, M. (2009) *Planning for Educational Change: Putting People and their Contexts First*. London: Continuum.

Zhang, Y.E. (2007) TBLT innovation in primary school English language teaching in mainland China. In K. Van den Branden, K. Van Gorp and M. Verhelst (eds) *Tasks in Action: Task-Based Language Education from a Classroom-Based Perspective* (pp. 68–91). Newcastle: Cambridge Scholars Publishing.

11 Task Design and Implementation for Beginning-Level Elementary School Learners in South-Brazil: Challenges and Possibilities

Priscila Fabiane Farias and
Raquel Carolina Souza Ferraz D'Ely

This chapter examines some challenges and possibilities for designing and implementing a task cycle for beginning-level English as a Foreign Language (EFL) learners in an elementary school classroom in the south of Brazil, following Skehan's (1996) framework and Ellis' (2003) modular approach for task implementation. Results reveal that deciding on target and pedagogical tasks and supporting tasks for beginners were two primary challenges that pointed to the important roles of needs analysis and a clear instructional framework in using tasks. Additionally, findings show that implementing task-as-a-workplan into task-as-a-process also creates challenges such as difficulties in input processing and output production by beginning-level learners. In this sense, the results highlight the pivotal role teachers have in task implementation. By reflecting upon the challenges and possibilities of using tasks with beginners in the Brazilian context, the chapter aims to provide insights for teachers using tasks in other contexts.

Introduction

In the Brazilian context, task-based language teaching (TBLT) has been gaining increasing importance, with several authors investigating the impact of tasks in foreign language teaching/learning (Xavier, 2004;

Guará-Tavares, 2009, 2011; Ferreira, 2013; Pereira, P., 2015; Specht & D'Ely, 2017; D'Ely & Farias, 2017; D'Ely *et al.*, 2019). Since 1998, the federal educational curricular documents for Brazilian schools have recommended the use of tasks (Brasil, 1998) with foreign language teachers being encouraged to focus on teaching language through socially constructed interaction and with a focus on meaning making.

However, implementing tasks in classrooms is not always easy (e.g. Foster, 2009; Long, 2016; East, 2017). As the results predicted are not always realized in practice, some researchers have argued for a distinction between *task-as-a-workplan* and *task-as-a-process* (Breen, 1989; Ellis, 2003; Foster, 2009; Samuda, 2015). Foster (2009) discusses 'the unpredictable nature of what learners focus upon when using the L2' (2009: 250) and points to the need for research that scrutinizes the process of how tasks are actually implemented. The current chapter discusses some challenges that were faced in designing and implementing a task-cycle in an elementary school classroom in the south of Brazil.

Key Constructs in TBLT

Although previous literature related to needs analysis focuses on the field of English for Specific Purposes (West, 1994), more recently there has been an interest in understanding the relevance of a needs analysis for general second and foreign language learning (see Hillman & Long, Chapter 8, this volume; Oliver, Chapter 9, this volume). Long (1985, 2015, 2016) describes the needs analysis process as a way to establish target and pedagogical tasks that are relevant and meaningful for a specific group of learners. The author describes target tasks as being real-world tasks that learners need for daily life. In turn, these are the basis for the pedagogical tasks as the teacher adapts them to accommodate for the classroom environment. Long also describes the needs analysis process as an adaptable approach that embodies TBLT principles 'whose realization will vary systematically at the level of *pedagogic procedures* to take account of individual differences among teachers, learners, languages, and settings' (Long, 2015: 92). In this way, a needs analysis is the starting point in task development and implementation (Nunan, 2004; Willis & Willis, 2007; Long, 2015). As Long (2015) explains, 'objective and felt needs should be cross-validated and triangulated among teachers, learners, and external sources' (2015: 129) before syllabus design, and more specifically task design, takes place. If one considers how tasks are used in the learners' natural environments, then tasks can be specifically developed to address the needs of those learners.

Once selected, a framework is needed to enable teachers 'to implement task-based instruction on a more systematic and principled basis' (Skehan, 1996: 38). Skehan (1996, 2016) proposes a three-stage framework consisting of pre-tasks, mid-tasks and post-tasks to achieve teaching goals (see Lambert, Chapter 2, this volume). Pre-task activities aim at either introducing new elements or reorganizing the existing elements in the learners' language systems in order to prepare them for the task properly. They are used to ease the processing load learners may encounter. This can be done by either teaching or making salient language that will be relevant during main task performance. Mid-task activities, on the other hand, focus on developing or improving linguistic performance. As Skehan (1996) explains, 'the main factor affecting performance during the task is the choice of the task itself' (1996: 55). Hence, tasks should neither be too difficult, as this causes processing overload, nor too easy, as learners make little effort and end up with few linguistic gains. Finally, post-task activities serve the purpose of aiding the learner in focusing their attention on those aspects that were not attended to during task completion. Post-tasks may also be used as reflective tools for assessment or as an opportunity for repeating the task, aiming at improvement.

Since its publication, several studies have attempted to investigate the utility of implementing Skehan's framework. In Brazil, Pereira, G. (2015) designed and implemented a cycle of tasks under Skehan's framework with a group of elderly EFL learners enrolled in a language course in a Brazilian university. The aim was to investigate participants' perceptions regarding the implementation of the cycle of tasks. Eight participants answered perception questionnaires about the classes and took part in an interview at the end of the cycle. Her findings revealed that Skehan's framework is a useful tool for balancing the level of difficulty of the tasks and also provides a way of balancing learners' attention between meaning and form which overall suggest the benefits of its use with beginner learners.

Another study, carried out in Brazil by Afonso (2016) aimed at investigating seventeen 9th grade students' perceptions regarding the implementation of a cycle of tasks. The tasks were designed according to Skehan's (1996) framework for task implementation, with the purpose of preparing them to read the first chapter of 'Harry Potter and the Sorcerer's Stone'. At the end of each class, learners answered a questionnaire. At the end of the cycle they also engaged in interviews. The results of this study also provided support for using Skehan's framework to offer learners' opportunities to communicate their ideas effectively.

Based on this research, the current study uses Skehan's framework for designing and implementing a task-cycle aimed at language development (among other goals) in a Brazilian EFL beginner classroom. The choice of the word 'cycle' in the current study is used to reflect the connection between the tasks – how one leads to another. Within each task, the learners are also encouraged to revisit their previous learning and reflect upon their development. This also reflects Skehan's (1996) view of language learning that is cumulative and non-linear. He suggests it is a process that involves the development of complex metalanguage systems involving 'cycles of analysis and synthesis revisiting some areas that require complexification, learning others in a simple, straightforward manner, developing others by simply relexicalizing that which is available syntactically' (1996: 58).

Using tasks for language development also allows for moments of thinking about language structure within meaning-oriented communication. This has been referred to as *focus-on-form*, a term originally coined by Long (1991). It involves drawing learners' attention to linguistic problems as they arise in communication. That is, it is a pedagogical intervention in which form receives attention during task performance. Specifically, whilst the learner's attention is mainly concerned with language meaning, there is a 'brief switch of attention from meaning to form (…) usually triggered by a communication problem, either receptive or productive, and thus is, by definition, reactive' (Long, 2015: 317). It is different from its counterpart *focus-on-forms* which as Long (2015) suggests, underpins language teaching where language itself is the object of study and attention.

Because focus-on-form is reactive, the emphasis on a grammar point 'is operating in tandem with the learner's internal syllabus, in that the focus-on-form was triggered by a problem that occurred in the student's performance, not by a pre-set syllabus having prescribed it for that day's lesson' (Long, 2015: 28).

In contrast, Ellis supports non-reactive and pre-emptive opportunities for focus-on-form. These may consist of a focus on specific linguistic features, either initiated by a student or the teacher. Hence, the difference between Long and Ellis's positions lies with how focus-on-form originates in class: while the reactive kind derives from a communication problem or the desire of the teacher to call attention to a 'better way' of expressing an idea; pre-emptive focus-on-form derives from attention to form even if there was no apparent communicative gap. In Ellis' view, pre-emptive focus-on-form can be beneficial, and it can frequently occur in task-based classes (see Ellis *et al.*, 2001). Ellis also makes a case for focus-on-forms arguing that 'both focus-on-form and focus-on-forms can result in the kind of L2 knowledge (implicit or automatized explicit knowledge) that enables learners to communicate fluently and accurately' (Ellis, 2017: 515).

One way of encouraging focus-on-form within tasks is through the use of focused tasks. Ellis (2009, 2017) differentiates tasks as either 'unfocused' or 'focused'. Unfocused tasks are not concerned with any specific aspect of the language, and, in this sense, 'provide learners with opportunities for using language in general communicatively' (Ellis, 2009: 223). Focused tasks, on the other hand, are designed to offer 'opportunities for communicating using some specific linguistic feature' (Ellis, 2009:

223), that is, the task itself is designed to elicit pre-determined linguistic features.

Ellis (2017) defends the use of focused tasks as complementary options in language programs as they help the learner in becoming aware of language in both functional and semantic ways, reinforcing accurate communication. Ellis (2017) also endorses the relevance of a particular type of focused task: namely the consciousness-raising task (CRT) (Ellis, 1991, 1997). According to Ellis, CRTs which have a linguistic feature as the topic of a task, aim at developing metalinguistic understanding of rules or regularities of a target feature, noting that they are not the focus of a complete syllabus, but instead can be used 'as a means for developing explicit knowledge of specific features that are problematic to learners on the grounds that such knowledge might facilitate attention to these features in subsequent input and output' (Ellis, 2017: 511).

Studies have shown the importance of using CRTs in a communicative classroom setting as an aid to develop learners' language learning with more explicit grammatical knowledge whenever gaps appear (Takimoto, 2006; Eckerth, 2008; Roscioli et al., 2015). According to Roscioli et al. (2015), by making use of CRTs in a task-based classroom environment, whenever a linguistic problem appears, 'learners could be helped by being exposed to explicit knowledge through the use of consciousness-raising tasks and, consequently, improve performance and, maybe, acquisition' (2015: 92).

Although there may be no consensus about the use of focused tasks in task-based teaching, there is also no single way of doing TBLT. Thus, there is need for 'a pluralistic research agenda capable of addressing the multi-faceted nature of task-based instruction' (Ellis, 2017: 127).

The Project

The study presented in this chapter was conducted with a group of fourteen foreign language Brazilian learners enrolled in the 7th grade of a public school located in the south of Brazil. The learners' ages varied from 12 to 13 years old at the time of data collection. Eight main instruments were used for data collection, namely, two pre-tests, two post-tests, post-task questionnaires and interviews, teacher/researcher's diary notes and learners' performance data from the cycle of tasks developed for the study.

Data collection was carried out in three phases during normally scheduled class periods. In the first phase, the teacher-researcher engaged in a needs analysis using class discussions and observations. The second phase began with two pre-tests. Pre-Test 1 was a Grammaticality Judgment Test (GJT) (Loewen, 2009) and Pre-Test 2 was a narrative writing activity. After the cycle of tasks was implemented, Post-Test 2 was administered. Post-Test 2 was another narrative writing activity.

Table 11.1 General research design

Phases	Instruments
Phase 1	– Needs Analysis period
Phase 2	– Pre-test 1
	– Pre-test 2
	– Cycle of tasks
	– Post-test 2
Phase 3	– Questionnaires
	– Interviews
	– Post-test 1

The third phase included of the use of the post-questionnaires, interviews, and the application of Post-Test 1, which was the same GJT used in Pre-Test 1. Table 11.1 summarizes the research design. The total amount of time for the data collection was 6 months.

During the first phase of the study, participants' profiles were investigated, listing their personal background and experiences as well as language proficiency. The specifics of the learning context were scrutinized in an attempt to understand learners' needs and possible requirements. This information was then compared to the recommendations outlined in the Brazilian federal documents that guide foreign language education. Hence these data informed the needs analysis which underpinned the design of the cycle of tasks.

The needs analysis was undertaken three months prior to data collection. Learners' answers to a profile questionnaire provided the following information: (a) in terms of language proficiency, learners were categorized as false beginners and their experience with English accounted for one year of studying English at school (since 6th grade) once a week for 45 minutes as well as sometimes making use of language learning apps and games; (b) in terms of how much contact with English the learners had in their lives, data revealed English was rarely present in their routines, mostly appearing when being online, such as engaging in social networks, using apps or playing games, as well as watching movies and television series; (c) in relation to the themes the learners were interested in discussing in class, the topics included football, books and music; (d) during debates and class activities, the teacher-researcher also identified issues around gender, difficulties dealing with emotions, and difficulties related to using group work in class as themes emerging from the class discussions selected to be tackled in the tasks.

It is also important to highlight that the recommendations encapsulated in the Brazilian educational documents (Brasil, 1998; Brasil, 2017), as well as the school syllabus for 7th grade, were also considered during the needs analysis process. According to these two documents, teaching foreign languages involves preparing learners for being agents of transformation through discourse. The documents recommended that a communicative focus be used for encouraging language development and preparing learners to use the foreign language effectively by actively participating in a social context. In addition, the textbook *Alive!* (2012), which was used in the school during the year of 2016 and which was produced in Brazil for elementary learners, was divided into 8 units that offered different possibilities in terms of topics and structural content. All made use of a communicative and functional approach to language learning. Unit 3, for instance, is entitled 'Special Women' and aimed at promoting learners' communication about past events by making use of the simple past while discussing gender issues.

Based on the information gathered, most important to the design of the task cycle were: (i) learners' proficiency (beginners); (ii) the expectation of a communicative focus when teaching English; (iii) the need to discuss a theme relevant to the learners' lives; (iv) the need to approach a relevant target task to learners' routine, that is, a real-world linguistic outcome to be achieved; and, (v) the need to fit the expectations derived from the educational documents, the school syllabus and the textbook, which together reflected the course content and material. All these aspects are further explored in the results section of this chapter.

At the end of the needs analysis process, the cycle of tasks was designed. It tackled issues concerning the representation of gender in the Brazilian society, and it was divided into seven tasks: the first two parts of the pre-task phase; Tasks 3, 4 and 5 part of the mid-task phase; and the last two tasks, constituting the post-task phase. At the end of the cycle, it was envisioned that the learners would be able to write narratives that would address the theme under discussion (gender representation), by making use of language within a transformative discursive perspective.

Having designed the cycle of tasks, after the second and third phases of the study, which included the implementation of the task-cycle, both quantitative and qualitative analyses of the data were undertaken. Language development was analyzed considering: (a) teacher-researcher's perception during the implementation of the cycle of tasks, (b) learners' performance in two pre-tests and two post-tests, (c) learners' perceptions after the implementation of the cycle of tasks.

The following section focuses on discussing some challenges and possibilities that arose from the design and implementation of the task cycle.

Some Observations from Designing and Implementing the Task Cycle

Some key challenges encountered in designing and implementing the task cycle in the context of a Brazilian public school are now explored together with the choices that were made to overcome them.

Task Design Challenges

Challenge 1: Selecting target and pedagogical tasks

During the needs analysis stage, it became apparent that the learners were unclear about their needs when learning a foreign language. This was not surprising considering they were all young beginners, with very little experience as foreign language learners. In addition, their experience in public elementary school in Brazil was based on syllabi which are pre-determined by teachers and experts, with little input from learners. Therefore, one of main challenges that arose from designing tasks for this specific context was to select the target and pedagogical tasks that resembled the real world and were relevant to the students' lives. In order to address this challenge, information from the needs analysis questionnaires and discussions, from the federal educational documents and from the textbook were considered.

In the needs analysis, learners reported that they used English mostly on the internet, typically engaging in social networks, playing games, using apps and watching movies and television series. For most games and social networks mentioned, one skill that seemed to normally be required from learners was to write stories, that is, to either create stories for their own characters in games or to write about their own life as part of their social networking. This information was balanced with the federal educational documents and with the textbook, both of which recommend the practice of the writing ability in foreign language classes and which also suggest that teacher attempt to develop story-telling skills with students. Therefore, considering all these aspects, writing narratives for digital media was the target-task selected for the task-cycle. The idea, therefore, was to offer learners an opportunity to write stories in the target language that would later be shared through social networking, preparing them for engaging in an activity that is part of their daily lives, whilst also learning English as a foreign language.

Having determined the target task, the pedagogical tasks chosen (that is, what they would actually do in the classroom) were interviewing and writing narratives about people in their school, taking into account the themes being discussed in class. As previously mentioned, this theme was gender representation. Hence, after having worked on preparatory tasks, learners were asked to interview someone in their school that had dealt with overcoming stereotypes concerning gender representation. With the data from the interview, learners wrote narratives. The stories the learners wrote were later posted on a Facebook page, mirroring the popular page *Humans of New York*. A similar page was created on Facebook to share with the school community (more details about the pedagogic task are given in the next section).

Challenge 2: Adapting tasks for beginners

Another challenge that arose was how to prepare beginning learners to tell stories in the foreign language. This challenge required linguistic scaffolding as well as careful planning and preparation prior to implementing the pedagogical tasks. The framework used in the study drew on Skehan (1996) and Ellis (2003). The task cycle created aimed to prepare beginner learners to engage in their final target/pedagogical tasks by building their knowledge about the theme being discussed, about the genre of narratives, and about the language they needed. In this way, the task cycle was intended to calibrate the cognitive load of different tasks, as learners moved through the cycle, and equip them with the necessary tools to engage in the target/pedagogical task. Table 11.2 summarizes the task cycle developed.

The pre-tasks aimed at presenting learners with content and language related to the theme in order to prepare them to engage in the subsequent tasks and allow them to 'have clearly activated schemas when the real task is presented' (Skehan, 1996: 54). The pre-task phase was comprised of two tasks. Task 1 took the form of a game. During the game, learners were asked to answer questions about their tastes and routines. After the game, the whole class analyzed the answers, reflecting on pre-conceived ideas about gender representation. The questions were asked and answered in English and the discussion after the game was also done in English. In Task 2, learners then watched an advertisement involving gender representation. After watching the video, they answered questions in Portuguese related to the advertisement, particularly about the main message conveyed and the language used. The questions were asked and answered in Portuguese to avoid overloading learners with content and language at the same time.

The mid-phase was comprised of three tasks. These tasks were intended to align to Ellis's (2003) modular approach, with a communicative module, seen as the main component, and a code-based module, seen as a secondary element, which can be taught 'by means of focused tasks such as structure-based production tasks, interpretation tasks, and

Table 11.2 The task cycle designed for the study

The cycle of tasks

Pre-task phase	Task 1	Unfocused task	Brainstorming Game
	Task 2	Unfocused task	#LikeAGirl
Mid-task phase	Task 3	Focused Interpretation task	Yes, They Can
	Task 4	Focused Consciousness-raising task	I Wanna See You Be Brave
	Task 5	Unfocused Production task	Humans of CA – On the move
Post-task phase	Task 6	Focused Reviewing task	Humans of CA - Reviewing
	Task 7	Unfocused task	What Did We Learn

consciousness-raising tasks' (2003: 236). Task 3 presented learners with texts to be read and comprehension questions to be answered. Three pieces of news that discussed gender representation were introduced in Task 3 and the learners focused their attention on comprehending the texts, which were all in English, in order to successfully answer the questions that followed.

Task 4 then focused on the simple past. The past was chosen as it is a common feature used to write stories, and it also reflected the content of the school syllabus for the 7th grade. When performing Task 4, the learners engaged in three steps designed to prompt them to develop rules pertaining to the use of the simple past. First of all, they worked on two oral and written comprehension activities that discussed the stories of two women who challenged gender stereotypes in their lives. These stories served as input in terms of content, but they also had all verbs in the simple past highlighted and differentiated from each other (i.e. regular or irregular verbs), and according to whether they were part of an affirmative and a negative sentence. Then, in the second part of Task 4, the learners were asked to summarize, in English, the stories they had read about the two women. They were given a word limit and encouraged to use words from the original texts if necessary. Next, the learners read a third story also about a woman who challenged gender stereotypes and that also presented the past tense as input. The questions that followed this text required learners to analyze the language that was used in an attempt to understand how the grammatical rule system worked. Therefore, this time, learners were required to go back to the story and explicitly focus-on-form as they attempted to understand and describe simple past rules considering the story they were reading. By the end of Task 4, learners had been exposed to and engaged with a considerable amount of input in English. In addition, they had the opportunity to: (1) develop content knowledge and collect information about the main theme, (2) develop linguistic knowledge and learn vocabulary to express themselves about the theme and (3) create their own rules for the use of the simple past when writing a story. They were also given the chance to write a short summary based on their readings. In this way, the learners had the chance to notice the input, convert it to intake, compare it to their own mental hypothesis about language, and integrate the intake into their own mental representation of the target language grammar.

In Task 5, learners were asked to produce their own narrative to check whether they were able to make successful use of this knowledge in a less controlled manner. Although they were not explicitly told to use the simple past to tell their stories, it was expected that they would choose to do so, since they had been exposed to this grammatical feature during the previous tasks. In order to write their stories, the learners collected data at school by conducting interviews on gender representation. They used the information from the interviews to write the first version of their narratives.

Finally, the post-task phase was comprised of two tasks. In Task 6, the learners wrote the second and final draft of their narrative texts. The texts were reviewed by the teacher who provided feedback, including reactive focus-on-form. Where necessary, the teacher explicitly called learners attention to grammatical choices they had made and asked them to find alternative ways to express their ideas. In Task 7, they then shared, commented and reflected on the content of each other's texts. In this way, the post-task phase was intended to give learners the chance to reflect on how language works, particularly when it came to telling stories, and to test the hypotheses they had developed. Additionally, this phase provided the chance to notice gaps in their language knowledge and engage in metalinguistic processes during task completion (Swain, 1995). Learners were thus provided with the possibility of learning by doing (learning to write by writing).

Task Implementation Challenges

The implementation of the task-cycle showed that in spite of careful planning, challenges emerged in situations related to learners' low proficiency level and lack of practice in output production that required informed decision-making on the part of the teacher-researcher.

Challenge 3: Facilitating understanding of authentic input

The teacher-researcher used English most of the time during task-cycle implementation and also the input from the tasks themselves was all taken from authentic sources that made use of English. Low proficiency learners found it difficult to comprehend the information in this input.

Task 2 for example required students to answer comprehension questions about an advertisement that (among other goals) discussed the impact of gender stereotypes on girls. It was presented in the form of a video and follow up comprehension questions of oral input were presented to students in two activities. Nunan (2004) highlights the value in exposing learners to authentic input as a way of offering them a chance to deal with meaningful real-life messages, but this can have a negative impact if learners' level of proficiency does not match the input. The input in Task 2 had not been calibrated or adapted at all since it corresponded to an authentic advertisement broadcasted on American television produced with an American audience in mind. As an attempt to ensure learners would be able to comprehend relevant information from input in order to complete the task, the teacher engaged in a pre-paratory discussion with learners prior to task completion. An excerpt from the teacher-researcher's diary notes is presented below as a way to illustrate the strategies used during this preparation period.

Diary notes – Day 3
I showed them an image from the video of Task 2 and asked them what they thought the video could be about. Students were very focused on the image and how the girl was kicking the box. I called their attention to the words written on the box: 'can't be brave'. Some of them did not know what Brave means, and related it to the word 'brava' which can mean angry, in Portuguese. I told them it meant courageous, so, together, we translated the sentence as 'não pode ter coragem'. They were still confused but guessed the video would be about girls proving they are brave since the girl in the image is kicking the box, and there is an X crossing the sentence 'can't be brave'.

As this diary excerpt indicates, students engaged in processes of forming hypothesis about what the word 'brave' could mean. Their first guess was to a false cognate in Portuguese. When the teacher told them to think of 'courageous' as a possible translation for 'brave' (also possible in Portuguese), students then attempted to translate the whole sentence and relate their translation to the given image. Multimodality, in this case, served as a tool to engage in meaning making (Heberle, 2000) as the image assisted learners in enhancing their comprehension. Students thus learned new vocabulary in context in preparation to the following task.

Another way of dealing with input-processing difficulty was presenting and teaching reading strategies prior to task completion. The texts used in Task 3 corresponded to pieces of news taken from authentic websites that were most likely directed to a native audience. Learners were instructed to pay attention to the images, titles or other information that was not in the body of the text, to focus on the familiar words first, and to keep the questions they had to answer in mind while reading. They were reminded that it was not necessary to understand the whole text and given other strategies aimed at meaning-mapping and form-meaning relations. Thus, the teacher prepared the learners for the tasks through pre-task discussions in the classroom context to facilitate successful task completion.

Challenge 4: Facilitating comprehensible output

Although the whole task-cycle served as a scaffold aimed at preparing learners to engage in the main task, learners still struggled to write texts telling the stories they had planned to tell. Teacher feedback through focus-on-form was used as a strategy to aid learners in this respect. For example, on the first version of her narrative, Participant 4 wrote '*When Roberta was a child, suffered prejudice*'. Possibly influenced by her knowledge of Portuguese in which it is possible to use a verb without a precedent subject, the learner did not include the subject 'she' in her second clause to indicate who suffered prejudice. In reaction, the teacher asked the learner 'who suffered prejudice', highlighting it was not clear from her sentence who the subject was. Participant 4's second version of her narrative indicates that she benefited from this reactive feedback as she rewrote her sentence in the following way: '*When Roberta was a child, she suffered prejudice*'. Moreover, the results from pre-test × post-test comparisons also seem to indicate improvement, as follows:

(1) statistically significant difference (= <.000) between pre-test 1 (M = 46.74, SD = 10.61) × post-test 1 (M = 79.21, SD = 13.06), which means participants were better able to identify appropriate use of the simple past structure after task-cycle implementation;
(2) statistically significant difference (= <.001) between pre-test 2 (M = 37.44, SD = 13.2) × post-test 2 (M = 6.21, SD = 3.68) for accuracy, which means participants produced narratives with less errors in the post-test phase;
(3) statistically significant difference (= <.001) between pre-test 2 (M = 155.86, SD = 53.43) × post-test 2 (M = 220.93, SD = 34.41) for outcome, which means the narratives produced for the post-test 2 where closer in achieving the expected outcome than the ones produced for the pre-test 2.

Thus, although much was accomplished by the learners during task cycle because of careful planning and task design, the decisions made by the teacher during task implementation as well as the support offered were critical to the effective use of tasks in this context. The teacher seemed to be a key agent in TBLT who made informed decisions during task design and implementation.

Conclusion

The Brazilian public-school context presents challenges in using task in language teaching. One is the limited exposure of learners to the target language. Even when the learners who participated in this study reported that they had exposure to English when using the internet in their daily lives, Brazilian children typically cannot communicate in English successfully. Therefore, designing and implementing tasks that are relevant to learners' routines and contexts, and that are appropriate to beginners in terms of language and task complexity, is not an easy task.

This chapter has described some of challenges related to the design and the implementation of a cycle of tasks for beginning-level learners of EFL studying in a Brazilian elementary school. The project highlights the crucial role of a needs analysis, a task-based framework and focus on form in successfully using tasks in this context. The chapter also points to the pivotal role that teachers have in effective task implementation in terms of in situ support and informed decisions in facilitating successful task performance.

Developing and implementing a task cycle in this context involved a time commitment and structure not commonly available to Brazilian teachers, especially those working in public schools, and perhaps to teachers elsewhere. To make TBLT feasible in diverse contexts such as Brazilian public schools, teachers need opportunities to familiarize themselves with TBLT in undergraduate courses and continuing education programs. They also need to be provided with time to prepare appropriately for activities specific to their context and their learners' needs. Finally, there is also a need for more task-based materials for specific contexts such as Brazilian schools that may be adapted to the needs and specificities of each teacher and his or her learners.

References

Afonso, J.C. (2016) What role do tasks play in an EFL environment? Unfolding 9th grade learners' perceptions on the implementation of a cycle of tasks on the first chapter of Harry Potter and the Sorcerer's Stone. Unpublished Masters thesis, Universidade Federal de Santa Catarina.

Brasil (1998) *Parâmetros Curriculares Nacionais*. Brasília/DF: MEC/SEF.

Brasil (2017) *Base Curricular Nacional Comum*. Brasília/DF: MEC/SEF.

Breen, M. (1989) The evaluation cycle for language learning tasks. In R.K. Johnson (ed.) *The Second Language Curriculum*. Cambridge: Cambridge University Press.

D'Ely, R.C.S.F., Motta, M.B. and Bygate, M. (2019) Strategic planning and repetition as metacognitive processes in task performance: Implications for EFL learners' speech production. In Z. Wen and M.J. Ahmadian (eds) *Researching Second Language Task-Performance and Pedagogy: Essays in Honor of Peter Skehan*. Amsterdam: Johns Benjamin Company.

D'Ely, R.C.S.F. and Farias, P.F. (2017) Teste-Tarefa: o que está por trás da implementação de um teste na perspectiva de um ensino baseado em tarefas? Desvendando a percepção dos alunos sobre essa situação de avaliação. In L.M.B. Tomitch and V.M. Heberle (eds) *Perspectivas Atuais de Aprendizagem e Ensino de Línguas* (1st edn) (pp. 201–236). Florianópolis.

East, M. (2017) Research into practice: The task-based approach to instructed second language acquisition. *Language Teaching* 50 (3), 412–424.

Eckerth, J. (2008) Investigating consciousness raising task: Pedagogically targeted and non-targeted learning gains. *International Journal of Applied Linguistics* 18 (2), 119–145.

Ellis, R. (1991) Grammar teaching-practice or consciousness-raising. In R. Ellis (ed.) *Second Language Acquisition and Second Language Pedagogy*. Clevedon: Multilingual Matters.

Ellis, R. (1997) SLA research and language teaching. Oxford: Oxford University Press.

Ellis, R. (2003) *Task-Based Language Learning and Teaching*. Oxford: Oxford University Press.

Ellis, R. (2009) Task-based language teaching: Sorting out the misunderstandings. *International Journal of Applied Linguistics* 19, 221–246.

Ellis, R. (2017) Position paper: Moving task-based language teaching forward. *Language Teaching* 50 (4), 507–526.

Ellis, R., Basturkmen, H. and Loewen, S. (2001) Doing focus-on-form. *System* 30, 419–432.

Ferreira, G.M. (2013) O Uso De Estratégias De Comunicação (Ec) Em Tarefas Orais Em Língua Inglesa (Li). *Unpublished Masters thesis,* Universidade de Brasilia.

Foster, P. (2009) Task-based language learning research: Expecting too much or too little? *International Journal or Applied Linguistics* 19, 247–263.

Guará-Tavares, M.G. (2009) The relationship among pre-task planning, working memory capacity and L2 speech performance: A pilot study. *Linguagem & Ensino* 12, 165–194.

Guará-Tavares, M.G. (2011) Pre-task planning, working memory capacity and L2 speech performance. *Organon* 26, 245–266.

Heberle, V.M. (2000) Critical reading: Integrating principles of critical discourse analysis and gender studies. *Ilha do Desterro* 38, 139–154.

Loewen, S. (2009) Grammaticality judgment tests and the measurement of implicit and explicit L2 knowledge. In R. Ellis, S. Loewen, C. Elder, R. Erlam, J. Philp and H. Reinders (eds) *Implicit and Explicit Knowledge in Second Language Learning, Testing and Teaching.* Bristol: Multilingual Matters.

Long, M.H. (1985) Input, interaction and second-language acquisition. In H. Winitz (ed.) *Native Language and Foreign Language Acquisition* (pp. 259–278). Annals of the New York Academy of Sciences. New York: New York Academy of Sciences.

Long, M.H. (1991) Focus-on-form: A design feature in language teaching methodology. In K. de Bot, R.B. Ginsberg and C. Kramsch (eds) *Foreign Language Research in Cross-Cultural Perspective.* Amsterdam: John Benjamins.

Long, M. (2015) *Second Language Acquisition and Task-Based Language Teaching.* Oxford: Wiley-Blackwell.

Long, M. (2016) In defense of tasks and TBLT: Nonissues and real issues. *Annual Review of Applied Linguistics* 36, 5–33.

Menezes, V., Tavares, K., Braga, J. and Franco, C. (2012) *Alive!: inglês, 7° ano.* São Paulo: Editora UDP.

Nunan, D. (2004) *Task Based Language Teaching.* Cambridge: Cambridge University Press.

Pereira, G.D. (2015) The development and implementation of tasks to elderly learners of English as a foreign language. Unpublished Masters thesis, Universidade Federal de Santa Catarina.

Pereira, P.S.L.A. (2015) A produção oral de inglês como LE em uma escola pública de Natal: uma experiência com a Abordagem Baseada em Tarefas. Unpublished Masters thesis, Universidade Federal do Rio Grande do Norte.

Roscioli, D.C., Toassi, P., Farias, P.F. and D'Ely, R.C.F.S. (2015) The relationship between explicit learning and consciousness-raising tasks within a communicative language context. *Belt Journal* 6, 81–99.

Samuda, V. (2015) Tasks, design, and the architecture of pedagogical tasks. In M. Bygate (ed.) *Domains and Directions in the Development of TBLT.* Amsterdam: John Benjamins.

Skehan, P. (1996) A framework for the implementation of task-based instruction. *Applied Linguistics* 17, 138–162.

Skehan, P. (2016) Tasks versus conditions: Two perspectives on task research and their implications for pedagogy. *Annual Review of Applied Linguistics* 36, 34–49.

Specht, A.L. and Dely, R.C.S.F. (2017) Planning oral narrative tasks: Optimizing strategic planning condition through strategy instruction. *Acta Scientiarum* 39, 203–212.

Swain, M. (1995) Three functions of output in second language learning. In G. Cook and B. Seidlhofer (eds) *Principle and Practice in Applied Linguistics.* Oxford: Oxford University Press.

Takimoto, M. (2006) The effects of explicit feedback and form-meaning processing on the development of pragmatic proficiency in consciousness-raising tasks. *System* 34, 601–614.

Xavier, R.P. (2004) O desenvolvimento da compreensão oral e em leitura em um programa temático baseado em tarefas. *Revista Brasileira de Linguistica Aplicada* 4 (1), 117–154.

West, R. (1994) Needs Analysis in language teaching. *Language Teaching* 27 (1), 1–19.

Willis, D. and Willis, J. (eds) (2007) *Doing Task-Based Teaching.* New York: Oxford University Press.

12 Teachers' Responses to an Online Course on Task-Based Language Teaching in Mexico

Maria-Elena Solares-Altamirano

This study explores teachers' responses to an online task-based language teaching (TBLT) course. Nine Mexican in-service foreign language (FL) teachers participated in a 12-week professional development course on TBLT. The course aimed to prepare teachers for using TBLT principles. The course content and methodology are assessed using Ellis's factors for successful teacher preparation programmes in TBLT (Chapter 7, this volume). Rather than assessing the course, the study aims to illustrate how teachers experienced their instruction in terms of their responses to the instructional design and to TBLT itself. Pre- and post-course questionnaires and written self-assessments resulting from teachers' reflections constituted the data collection methods. Findings indicate teachers gained awareness of their own teaching beliefs and of the second language acquisition (SLA) principles underlying TBLT. Participants also developed practical skills to use of tasks in FL instruction. The main problems that emerged for teachers were limited knowledge of different task types, insufficient awareness of the value of L2 input in TBLT and skills for implementing focus-on-form. Teachers also identified insufficient time to create and implement TBLT lessons while completing structure-based syllabi in their contexts. The chapter concludes with a summary of important features of online TBLT teacher preparation courses.

Introduction

The terms '*task*' and '*task-based language teaching*' first appeared in the 1980s with Breen and Candlin (1980), Long (1985) and Prabhu's (1987) groundbreaking work in instructed second language acquisition

(ISLA). Tasks have since then been used in SLA research to promote input processing, language production, negotiation of meaning, interaction and focus-on-form. Research on TBLT has also explored areas such as the implementation of TBLT curriculum design (Candlin, 2001; Ellis, 2003; Skehan, 1998), task difficulty (Robinson, 2007; Skehan, 1996) and teachers' and learners' responses to TBLT courses (Carless, 2004; McDonough & Chaikitmongkol, 2007; Schart, 2008). More recently, due to the proliferation of online education, technology-mediated TBLT has also been investigated (see González-Lloret, Chapter 5, this volume, for an overview). TBLT research in FL contexts, however, has concentrated on European and Asian countries (Lambert, 2010; McDonough & Chaikitmongkol, 2007; Schart, 2008). This leaves the Latin-American context relatively underexplored. Similarly, regardless of the role teachers play as agents of change in educational innovation (Markee, 1997), little research exists on teachers' response to online professional development courses. Some educators (Avermaet *et al.*, 2006; Prabuh, 1987; Samuda, 2001; Willis, 1996) have described the role of teachers in TBLT. However, as Van den Branden (2006) emphasizes, there is little evidence on whether teachers can be trained to use tasks effectively in their classes in line with current approaches to TBLT. What does successful teacher education in TBLT involve? How do in-service foreign language teachers respond to TBLT? What are teachers' main challenges in adopting TBLT? What demands do online TBLT teacher education impose on course designers? And, what advantages does it offer? These questions are explored in this chapter within the context of an online TBLT teacher education course in Mexico.

The Mexican Educational Context

The teaching of English as a foreign language (EFL) has a central position in the Mexican language curriculum. English is taught as a compulsory subject in middle and tertiary education. English proficiency is also a graduation requirement in most university study areas. Solares-Altamirano (2010) explains that this is justified by the role of English as an international language, as the lingua franca for science and technology, and as a means to have a better career and pay. In Mexico most FL teachers are underpaid and frequently teach in many schools in order to guarantee a reasonable income. This leaves little time for them to continue their professional development. Although most language teachers claim they teach based on Communicative Language Teaching (CLT) principles, Solares-Altamirano (2010) notes that 'the majority have been using grammar-based syllabuses for years, building and reinforcing their beliefs about teaching as a form-focused, content-transmission, teacher-centred job' (2010: 54). This form of teaching, added to the limitations of education in the public sector, justifies investigation of teacher education and language teaching in Mexico. In contrast to Asian and European countries where TBLT was made mandatory in state schools, TBLT has not had the same impact in Mexico where TBLT is only included in some teacher training courses and TESOL bachelor programmes as an optional subject or as part of general methods and approaches courses. At the postgraduate level, the current literature suggests no TBLT courses exist. Hence, teachers are less familiar with tasks and TBLT procedures than other approaches to FL instruction.

In another paper, Solares-Altamirano (2014) explains that the EFL context in Mexico is 'task-supported' rather than 'task-based'. Samuda and Bygate (2008) describe the former as 'a context where tasks are used to enrich the syllabus or to provide additional learning opportunities. However, tasks are not used for assessment purposes and the syllabus may be defined by categories other than tasks' (2008: 59). Most Mexican FL teachers become acquainted with TBLT by working with the latest language textbooks in the market, which present this approach as an advance in language teaching. This textbook-bound content has led to confusion among FL teachers: they are uncertain as to whether TBLT seeks to replace CLT or whether it is simply a way to implement it more effectively. Despite the importance of English proficiency in Mexico, the low quality of education, particularly in the public sector (large classes, underqualified teachers, low salaries, and lack of material resources), often results in English language teaching that is little more than wasted hours and unproductive work for both teachers and students.

Theoretical Framework

Can teachers' professional development be promoted through an approach that focuses on the effective use of tasks in their teaching? Solares-Altamirano (2010) explored this question by developing a 12-week online course. The stated course objective was as follows: 'Through direct experience in learning tasks, participants will analyse and implement the principles of TBLT in order to assess its usefulness in their specific teaching context'. With experiential learning and learner-centredness being amongst the main principles of TBLT (Breen & Candlin, 1980) it seems logical that the best way to inform teachers about TBLT is by letting them experience this approach. Above all, the researcher's main objective when designing this course was to make participants cognizant of how the latest second language acquisition (SLA) findings are incorporated into TBLT. Markee (1997) claims that SLA theory is seldom accessible to practising teachers because of its distance from the reality of the classroom and the specialized way such theory is written in. To overcome this, there is a need to make such knowledge comprehensible to teachers. Solares-Altamirano's (2010) proposed that a TBLT framework for teacher education be understood as an educational philosophy based on social constructivist principles.

Samuda and Bygate (2008) indicate that the 'principles underlying ... what we now call tasks ... owe their genealogy to the developments in general education over the last century' (2008: 18), such as Dewey (1975), Freire (1970) and Kolb (1984). Solares-Altamirano's framework is also informed by Wallace's (1991) reflective model of professional education, Waters' (2005) model for teacher education, Puren's (1998) model of teacher development and Schweitzer's (1999) performance-based model for curriculum design and assessment. To incorporate new knowledge in teacher education Puren (1998) suggests teachers' previous theoretical and practical knowledge should be accounted for, as should be their feelings and beliefs about teaching. Thus, the course encourages teachers to reflect on and assess their pre-conceived beliefs about language teaching and learning. Key to the effective use of tasks in teacher education in this approach are learning experiences that are learner-centred, experiential, meaningful, collaborative and that involve learner engagement in active mental activity (Avermaet et al., 2006).

Ellis' concerns (Chapter 7, this volume) about the structural, student- and teacher- related problems for implementing TBLT are particularly relevant for the study presented in this chapter. They are summarized in Table 12.1. Most of the problems in the table are relevant to Mexican L2 instructional contexts. Structural syllabus and linguistic accuracy-based tests prevail in Mexican educational institutions.

Table 12.1 Problems in implementing task-based language teaching (Ellis, Chapter 7, this volume)

Structural problems	Classroom-level constraints: working with large classes, mixed L2 proficiency levels.
	Societal-institutional level constraints such as prevalence of ... – structural syllabuses – linguistic accuracy-based tests
Teacher-related problems	– vague understanding of 'tasks' – reluctance to undertake TBLT due to insufficient L2 oral proficiency – reluctance to forgo traditional language teaching practices due to own L2 learning experiences – concern about their students' grammatical development – struggle with the workload that planning TBLT lessons demands

Student-related problems	– beliefs about FL learning
	– misunderstanding of tasks as 'fun' rather than 'learning' activities.
	– limited oral proficiency in the L2, frequently leading to:
	  – over-use of students' L1 when performing tasks
	  – pidgin-like use of the L2 in students' effort to achieve task outcomes

Based on models in teacher education (Richards, 1990; Borg, 2011), Ellis (Chapter 7, this volume) also outlines factors that may influence the success of teacher preparation programmes in TBLT. These are outlined in Table 12.2. Ellis suggests that the factors outlined in the table can serve as a checklist that programme designers can refer to in the design

Table 12.2 Factors influencing the success of TBLT teacher preparation programmes (Ellis, Chapter 7, this volume)

Factor	Description
Content should …	1. reflect SLA principles underlying TBLT (Borg, 2011) 2. challenge teachers existing beliefs about teaching and learning 3. explain the concept of 'task' and differentiate tasks from exercises 4. provide teachers with a task-based syllabus and materials* 5. relate theory and research to practical issues (i.e. design & implementation of tasks) 6. address task complexity* 7. clarify tasks are not only speaking tasks, but also input-based tasks* 8. address classroom problems teachers experience when they implement TBLT (e.g. mixed-ability learners)*
Methodology should …	9. be compatible with TBLT principles: emphasis on experiential, discovery learning, (limiting lecturing) 10. require teachers to design, teach and evaluate their own tasks
Teachers' uptake of TBLT in their classrooms requires …	11. school-based training rather than drawing teachers from their workplace for training. 12. practice-oriented coaching 13. the support of school-based mentors well-versed in TBLT* 14. ongoing support from trainers, school principals and inspectors* 15. teachers' feedback on their use of tasks through reflective discussions with trainers and teacher colleagues 16. teacher trainees become future leaders of teacher teams in their schools* 17. support for the sustained effort to implement TBLT successfully*

*Factors with asterisk indicate those that were 'absent' or 'partially dealt with' in the analysed course design.

of teacher preparation programmes in TBLT. They are used in this way in the present study to assess an online TBLT teacher preparation programmes in Mexico and identify important features of content, methodology and delivery of online teacher preparation courses on TBLT more generally.

The Teacher Development Course

The course analysed in this chapter constitutes one of the modules within the ALAD (*Actualización en Lingüística Aplicada a Distancia*) Online Diploma Course at ENALLT (*Escuela Nacional de Lengua Lingüística y Traducción*), UNAM. It commenced in 2007 and has run annually since that time. This module is offered in English, most of the other modules are in Spanish. The course is promoted via the ALAD and ENALLT web pages, the UNAM Gazette, direct invitations to language centres in public and private schools and mail-lists of FL teacher associations. Entry requirements stipulate (a) being an in-service FL teacher with previous training in language teaching, (b) having a minimum of three years' teaching experience and (c) paying a fee of 4150 Mexican pesos ($181 USD) for the module. Provided the participants are fluent in English, the course is available to anyone meeting these requirements. Scholarships are granted to all UNAM teachers which constitute approximately 80% of participants in course. Teachers enrol in the course voluntarily, either because they want to improve their qualifications or for professional development. The number of participants external to UNAM, who are located out of the capital city, and who teach FLs other than English has increased in the last few years.

Online distance education is regarded as a means of (a) reaching a larger number of teachers with fewer material resources, (b) overcoming teachers' scheduling and distance constraints and (c) letting teachers gain professional development without leaving their workplace (cf. González-Lloret, Chapter 5, this volume).

The course structure and thematic content were determined by means of conducting a needs analysis among UNAM teachers. As indicated in Solares-Altamirano (2010), teachers' needs included those that can be described as both theoretical and methodological. Needs were classified into topic areas which later became course units. Following Schweitzer's (1999) performance-based model for curriculum design and assessment, the course structure and content were built around the main task, namely Implementing TBLT. The knowledge and skills required to reach that outcome were derived from the teachers' identified needs. The specific content of the course is summarized in Table 12.3.

Online components of the course include: (1) a *folder for reflections*, equivalent to a personal journal where participants individually wrote their insights on different assignments; (2) a *forum*, for interactive discussions among participants; (3) *interactive activities* that promoted interaction between participants and course content; (4) a *gallery* where participants' work was shared; (5) *evaluation criteria* to ease self-regulation and to guide performance and outcomes (Duggleby, 2000). Recent updates and improvements were made to the course in 2017 including two skype tutorials, a screencast-o-matic presentation (https://screencast-o-matic.com/), a free-access podcast on TBLT and a FAQs (Frequently Asked Questions) section.

Teachers' responses to the course instructional design and to the way TBLT has influenced their cognition, practice and effective use of tasks is the focus of this chapter. The study addresses the question of how in-service foreign language teachers respond to the instructional design of a TBLT course and to TBLT itself.

Method

Participants

The participants were nine in-service teachers. Six were teachers of English as a foreign language, and three were teachers of Spanish as a foreign language. Five of the participating teachers were males and four were females. Their average age was 44 (30–57, Standard Deviation

Table 12.3 Course implementation and data collection methods

Week	1-2	3-4-5	6-7-8	9-10-11	12
	Unit-1 What is TBLT?	**Unit-2** What is a task?	**Unit-3** Models for language teaching	**Unit-4** Implementing TBLT	**Unit-5** Assessing TBLT
PRE-QUESTIONNAIRE	Content: Historical background to TBLT; differences/similarities between CLT and TBLT; key concepts of TBLT (method, approach, methodology, syllabus); incidental and intentional learning.	Content: Defining 'task'; criterial features of tasks; difference between 'tasks' and 'exercises'	Content: Analysing my teaching; the TBLT lesson; the role of grammar in TBLT.	Content: Advice for implementing TBLT; teachers' experiences with TBLT; implementing TBLT.	Content: Criticisms against TBLT; teachers' role in promoting innovation. **POST-QUESTIONNAIRE**
	Teachers identify the SLA principles underlying TBLT	Teachers' develop their ability to design tasks	Teachers plan a TBLT lesson	Teachers are guided on the implementation of the task and lesson they prepared.	Teachers agree/disagree with criticisms against TBLT based on their implementation in Unit 4.
	Forum Discussion TBLT vs CLT	*Forum Discussion* Tasks vs Exercises	*Forum Discussion* What model does your lesson follow?		
		Gallery Task Design	*Gallery* TBLT Lesson	*Gallery* Implementing TBLT	
	FOLDER FOR REFLECTIONS				**WRITTEN SELF-ASSESSMENTS**

Note: Bold CAPITALS indicate methods for data collection: 9 pre- and 9 post-questionnaires; 9 written self-assessments.

(SD) 7.81). Their average teaching experience was 19 years (7–28, SD 6.73). Four held a BA degree, and five held a post-graduate degree. All participants were full-time teachers except one. They taught four-skill courses to teenagers and adults at all proficiency levels. These participants came from public and private sectors and were recruited as they registered for their first optional module in the ALAD Diploma course. The course designer/researcher was the tutor for this group. Participants were asked for their consent to participate in the study.

Data collection and analysis

Pre- and post-course questionnaires with closed and open questions constituted the first data collection method. The pre-course questionnaire included three open questions aiming to identify participants' expectations about the course, queries about TBLT and teaching philosophies and methodologies. Answers given in the pre-course questionnaire were returned to participants, together with a post-course questionnaire, to permit them to re-read and assess their initial answers.

Written self-assessments resulting from participants' online folder for reflections constituted the second data source for the study. The folder in this course is equivalent to a journal or diary (Richards & Ho, 1998). Lee (2009) states 'A diary study must involve more than just making regular introspective entries … in order to be a study, there must be a careful analysis of the data, either by the diarist herself or himself … or the researcher' (2009: 230). Entering written insights into teachers' folders along the course aimed to encourage participants to write reflectively on their teaching beliefs and practices concerning TBLT and help them keep record of learning experiences, reactions and thoughts. By the end of the course, as one of the activities in Unit 5 (see Table 12.3), participants were asked to analyse information in their folders and write a self-assessment of their growth concerning TBLT.

Data analysis involved categorization of answers in questionnaires, coding of data in written journals and the iterative process of qualitative research (Creswell, 2003; Denzin & Lincoln, 2000; Heigham & Croker, 2009). Common patterns and themes were identified in participants' answers to questionnaires and in written journals. Table 12.3 displays the point at which data collection methods were used during course implementation.

Findings

The findings of the study are presented in two sections. The first section illustrates how teachers experienced the online instruction. This section is guided by those factors outlined by Ellis in Table 12.2 as influencing the success of teacher-preparation programmes in TBLT. In the second section, the challenges teachers encountered in using of tasks are considered. Some of these problems correspond to those described by Ellis in Table 12.1.

Teachers' experiences of the programme

In terms of course content, extracts from questionnaires and written self-assessments show that teachers gained some awareness of the SLA principles underlying TBLT. Interestingly, in their testimonies, teachers exemplified concrete ways to put SLA principles into practice rather than repeating SLA principles or theoretical concepts.

Evidence was found for awareness of *The Input hypothesis* (Krashen, 1985) supporting learners' need for comprehensible spoken and written input.

- Questionnaire P4: *Today, when I think of a TBL lesson, I immediately consider what the input might be, whether the textbook input is appropriate and enough.*
- Self-assessment P4: *I learned that TBL lessons for beginners are feasible, the key: giving enough input.*

The 'Output Hypothesis' (Swain, 1985) encouraging learners' use of L2 for real purposes in order to learn it.

- Self-assessment P8: *I expose my students to real-life contexts more than before.*

The 'Interaction Hypothesis' (Gass & Varonis, 1994) supporting interaction providing opportunities for negotiation of meaning, which in turn facilitates second language acquisition.

- Questionnaire P6: *I have now [the] foundations to implement TBLT. Negotiation of meaning will be a 'must' in my lessons henceforth.*

The 'Noticing Hypothesis' (Schmidt, 1990) supporting the idea that addressing learners' attention to important linguistic patterns at some point in TBLT may help learners achieve greater levels of accuracy.

- Self-assessment P9: *The post-task stage should be led by the learners, it is something that increases their noticing level.*

Teachers also showed their satisfaction at building on their existing theoretical knowledge.

- Self-assessment P2: *I was fascinated to [read] theoretical material on TBLT. This time it would be different. It had been many years since I [studied] linguistic theory; this time, I would be more experienced.*

- Self-assessment P6: *Refreshing the differences between method and approach, curriculum and syllabus, reminded me of how languages are learnt. It was nice to remember how CLT started and even better to know it has the foundations for TBLT.*

There was also evidence of the challenge of teachers' beliefs about teaching and learning. Four out of nine participants' self-assessments presented teachers' perceptions as a sequence of challenges to their beliefs about:

(1) their role as teachers (from being the owner and provider of knowledge to becoming an additional resource for learners).
   - P7: *At the beginning of this module, the first challenge was to understand that my role as teacher had to change. I had to become just another resource for students to exploit in their learning process. Students become more active and independent in the development of that process by looking for information and drawing their own conclusions about how language works.*
   - P4: *In TBLT, the teacher has to be creative, alert to what is happening during the implementation of the task and make decisions in real time.*
(2) their way of teaching grammar (from presenting it explicitly and at the start of each lesson to presenting it incidentally throughout the lesson and only explicitly in the last stage).
   - P7: *The language focus was challenging because it is a lesson [stage] that [I had always presented in an] explicit way while TBLT puts it at the end of the lesson and in an indirect way.*
   - P1: *I realized a task does not end in the outcome. Language is also analysed and practised as much as necessary.*
(3) their misconceptions about TBLT (an approach that disregards grammar, is unsuitable for beginners, and difficult to implement).
   - P1: *I had a fuzzy idea about [TBLT], I [thought] that it was a technique for integrating projects. It seemed hard to implement, time-consuming, and suited for intermediate or advanced students.*
   - P4: *TBLT goes beyond following a prescribed syllabus. It implies considering many variables and acting accordingly.*
   - P7: *I realized that TBLT does not require me to look for different types of activities from those I had been using for years. I just needed to give them a different approach and place them in the appropriate part of the cycle.*

There was also evidence of teachers' awareness of the 'difference between tasks and other types of L2 learning exercises'. Extracts from questionnaires and written self-assessments show that teachers managed to understand this difference. The use of interactional multimedia software made the practice activities focused on this objective appealing, enjoyable and dynamic.

- P6: *Learning the difference between exercise and task clarified the concept I had of tasks. All the practice activities [to] identify tasks eased the process.*
- P1: *I did not believe tasks for beginners were possible. After transforming communicative activities into tasks, it was clear tasks can be created for any level.*

Teachers also related theory and research to practical issues such as the design and implementation of tasks. The statements below illustrate that teachers designed and implemented both tasks and TBLT lessons.

- P8: *I found it gratifying to be able to design and implement my own task.*
- P2: *It was up to that moment [planning a TBL lesson] that I understood all the process[es] TBLT involved.*
- P7: *The pre–task, the task and the language focus stages [were] highly clarifying. This is what I had been looking for! Suddenly with the practical aspect of the approach [everything] seemed less overwhelming.*

Questionnaire results also showed that planning a TBLT lesson, implementing it and getting feedback on its implementation were the most significant and challenging activities for teachers. It is clear from their responses that they perceived the activities related to task and lesson plan as a single task. The adjectives teachers used in the questionnaires to describe these activities were 'revealing' and 'rewarding'.

Teachers' self-assessments also show them moving toward methods in their teaching which are compatible with the principles of TBLT and designing their own tasks (see Table 12.2):

- P6: *Transforming exercises into tasks was an excellent way to put knowledge into practice. This was [an activity] I enjoyed and learned the most from.*
- P2: *We reflected on certain issues. We answered some questions [What is the teacher's role in the learning process?]. At that moment, [my answers] seemed complete, but right now they seem inadequate. This shows how much deeper I am thinking now about these problems. We moved onto another question [How do we learn a language?] in which I elaborated a bit more. The question was broad and controversial, we must be very knowledgeable to express a reasoned opinion.*
- P2: *As we progressed through the course, I noticed that the course initial statement, 'We will not only discover new things about TBLT but also about ourselves as learners and teachers', became true. I realized that as a language teacher and trainer I had been taking some things for granted.*

- P8: *From the reading material, my tutor's feedback, and discussions with my fellows, I learned that problem-solving is a good learning method. We learn a language by using it in real-life situations, which require interactive response to problematic scenarios.*
- P6: *We learned that the task was only part of the lesson. We needed to add some other elements [to build] a TBLT lesson. Thus, we learned that TBLT followed its own model. That unit ended with the planning of a TBLT lesson to be implemented in our classes. The implementation was the jewel in the crown. Evaluating the results of our lesson implementation gave us a broader idea of what TBLT can do for our students.*

Finally, the results from the questionnaires revealed that the forum was the component of the online course that participants valued most, mainly because of the feedback they received from peers and tutors, and because of the way it overcame their feelings of classroom isolation through sharing knowledge and experiences.

- P1: *Peers and tutors revised my work in forums and gave me information which helped me reflect on and improve the tasks I submitted.*
- P4: *In forum discussions, we looked at the same topic from different perspectives. My peers were experienced teachers with bright and clever ideas which I really appreciated.*

Skype sessions were the second most valued component for the teachers. They applauded the way these personalized sessions (a) enabled connection to individual teaching contexts and experience, (b) provided a clearer idea of their individual progress, and (c) enabled an immediate response to be provided to any questions that arose.

- P7: *[Skype] communication with the tutor was clarifying. [Skype sessions] gave me the chance to ask questions. Somehow the human contact made me feel more comfortable and gave me confidence.*

Self-assessments also revealed teachers' development of additional practical skills such as their ability to incorporate problem-solving techniques and to use group work more frequently.

- P6: *I have more tools to implement in my lessons. I can get different ideas to change what I have done in my teaching so far.*
- P8: *[Implementing TBLT] encouraged me turn individual tasks into collective ones, making the learning process more dynamic.*

Learners comments also suggest that participants engaged in careful thinking and critical assessment of TBLT. As a result, most were inclined to try TBLT and add it as an option in their repertoire. The course also made them aware of their role as active decision-makers who have to respond to their learners' specific needs and specific teaching contexts.

- P4: *I feel compelled to try [TBLT] in my courses and observe how it works. Although TBLT is not a new approach, I am a pioneer discovering unknown territory. It will take time and effort to build up a set of tasks to cover the course programmes I am supposed to complete each semester. I am eager to start.*
- P9: *The instructor must recognize the appropriate moment to implement [TBLT, or] to switch to more restricted [teaching]. [I will] continue looking for ways that promote optimal language acquisition.*
- P5: *Being a teacher means to reinvent oneself class after class. I have tried methods and approaches [which] claimed to be the perfect [ones]. Learning a language involves motivation from the learner and creativity from the teacher.*

Teachers' inclination to try TBLT was also greatly influenced by their students' responses.

- P5: *Implementing TBLT was a great experience. Students' engagement was immediate. They have more speaking time than myself in the classroom, [something] which I enjoy.*
- P7: *The most rewarding part of my learning process [was] witnessing how my students' motivation grew, how they got interested and how they gained independence.*
- P4: *[TBLT] is plenty of work. But I found this work very stimulating.*

Thus, if Ellis' list of factors from Table 12.2 is used for assessing the teacher preparation course in TBLT, participants might be argued to have experienced nine out of the 17 factors identified in Table 12.2 based on their self-reported experiences during the course (see Table 12.4). Except by 'practice-oriented coaching' reported by 7 out of 9 (80%) participants, 100% of them reported having experienced the remaining eight factors.

Below, the challenges that teachers experienced during the course are dealt with.

Limitations of the course in promoting the successful use of tasks

Despite the teachers' positive experiences described above, the course had some shortcomings. The first was making explicit the different task types available for L2 instruction. Focused versus unfocused tasks, real world versus pedagogic tasks and receptive versus productive tasks were introduced in the compulsory readings for the course. However, Ellis (2018) suggests providing information about different types of gaps in a task (information, opinion or reasoning), the nature of the task outcome (closed versus open) and whether the content of the task is teacher- or student-generated. Failure to explain these classifications hindered the participants' ability to develop appropriate TBLT lessons.

Table 12.4 Features of task-based instruction identified by participants

	TBLT Feature	Perceived by
Course content: – reflects SLA principles underlying TBLT. – challenges teachers existing beliefs about teaching and learning. – explains the concept of 'task' and differentiates tasks from exercises. – relates theory and research to practical issues, i.e. design & implementation of tasks. – accounts for participant's previous knowledge/experience.*	Course methodology: – emphasizes on experiential, discovery learning, (limiting lecturing). – requires teachers to design, teach and evaluate their own tasks. – focuses on the student-teacher.* – promotes collaborative learning.* Teachers' uptake is supported by: – school-based training rather than drawing teachers from their workplace for training. – teachers' feedback on their use of tasks through reflective discussions with trainers and teacher colleagues.	9 out of 9 (100%)
Course content: – offers much input.* – offers challenging tasks.*		8 out of 9 (90%)
Teachers' uptake is supported by: – practice-oriented coaching. – attention to teachers' specific teaching context and needs.*		7 out of 9 (80%)

*Factors with asterisk indicate other factors the researcher considered important to assess in the proposed TBLT instruction.

A second problem related to the lack of importance given to comprehensible input in TBLT. Teachers need to grasp more clearly the idea that exposure to abundant comprehensible input triggers incidental learning. A common weakness of most of the teachers' TBLT lesson plans was the insufficient amount of input provided for subject matter, lexis or grammar structures.

Teachers' ability to deal with grammar after the course was also limited. The incidental approach to grammar in TBLT was one of the features attracting teachers' interest. They emphasized that this was a challenge they wanted to face. Their submitted tasks and lesson plans were meaning focused and promoted interaction, but they explained that they considered it dishonest to force grammar structures into learners' input. The researcher realized that the teachers still had only a partial understanding of how to provide grammar incidentally. Thus, a deeper understanding of what incidental learning involves and the role of noticing activities might have been beneficial.

Teachers were also concerned with grammatical accuracy. During skype tutorials, for instance, the teachers appeared to be reassured when they discovered that grammar practice and structural rehearsals do not run counter to the principles of TBLT. As Ellis (Chapter 7, this volume) explains, 'follow-up activities can include quite traditional form-focused activities directed at the linguistic problems that the students experienced while they performed a particular task'. Teachers also seemed relieved to find that 'attention to linguistic form can occur in all stages of the lesson, including the main task phase and in this way cater to both incidental and intentional language learning' (Ellis, Chapter 7, this volume). Interestingly, most of the participants' task designs were focused tasks. As Ellis explains, 'many teachers may feel more comfortable with using tasks if they are linked to the kind of structural syllabus they are familiar with' (Chapter 7, this volume).

Finally, the questionnaire data reflect what teachers considered to be the main problems in implementing TBLT. Contextual and individual restrictions were mentioned.

- P4: *Students may be reluctant to move out of their comfort zone of receiving a 'formula'. Traditional exams will not [assist] this way of learning the language. School authorities may have to be convinced to consider the evaluation of outcomes according to the way students are taught.*
- P9: *Implementation of [TBLT] requires: the instructor's time to design or modify the activities in the textbook; preferably, learners need to have a linguistic repertoire to draw from when involved in tasks; teachers teaching beginners may find [it] complicated to implement [TBLT]. There needs to be willingness on the side of the learners to learn and experiment with the language. This involves motivation and solid self-esteem. It is the instructor's responsibility to provide an atmosphere [where] the learners feel empowered to embark on this type of instruction.*

Discussion

This chapter has explored the extent to which an online teacher-development TBLT course succeeded in equipping teachers with the necessary theoretical principles and pedagogical techniques to support their successful implementation of TBLT. Various aspects of course content, methodology and teachers' uptake were addressed in the course (see Table 12.4). Content factors include approaching SLA principles, challenging teachers' beliefs, explaining the differences between 'tasks' and 'exercises' and relating theory to practical issues. Methodology factors involve promoting experiential and discovery learning by engaging teachers in the design, teaching and evaluation of their own tasks. Factors under teachers' uptake embrace school-based training, practice-oriented coaching and the provision of feedback through reflective discussions. The advantages of online education were decisive to meet the conditions in teachers' uptake. Teachers comments during the course distinguished other strengths: (a) teachers gained in confidence to incorporate problem-solving techniques and collaborative work into their teaching, and (b) teachers' developed their reflective and critical assessment skills.

The limitations of the course included deficient attention to different task types, lack of emphasis on the value of L2 input in TBLT and insufficient development of teachers' skills for implementing focus-on-form. The researcher is also aware that what participants reported they have grasped does not necessarily imply so. Reported insights must be compared with participants' actual teaching practices. Grasping concepts and translating them into real practice, however, is not considered an immediate course result. It is a process that requires time of constant understanding and trying.

Despite its limitations and the number participants, teachers' testimonies suggest a positive response to instruction. Overall, it does seem that the course offers a practical and theory-informed understanding of TBLT. It achieves this by challenging the participants' existing beliefs about language learning, and it raises their awareness of contemporary SLA research.

While the course involves online instruction, the participants familiarity with technology-mediated tasks is also boosted. Online education allowed teachers from different contexts to share their insights and experiences, which was enriching for everyone, including the tutor. The appropriate selection and use of online resources also allowed for experiential and discovery learning, rather than limiting instruction to online lecturing.

Participants in the study were highly motivated teachers who enrolled in the course voluntarily. They all had considerable teaching experience. Whether teachers' responses to this preparation course would be the same for less motivated and less experienced teachers, or for teachers with little academic background, would require future research. The tutor's role in the outcome of the course is also an open question. However, the diversity of participants' profiles and their teaching contexts are typical of learners in the ALAD diploma course. The course has run for ten years, but this iteration was the first group to use skype tutorials. The researcher was impressed by the way skype sessions (a) reinforced the tutor-teacher relationship, (b) overcame the feelings of isolation that most participants experience by not living in the same city or not even being members of the UNAM community, and (c) became an opportunity to share all types of feelings, questions, fears, challenges or insights participants had about different course issues. Skype sessions were crucial to identify the participants' main challenges concerning TBLT in their specific contexts.

This was a single three-month course and whether teachers continue to implement TBLT or revert to their default teaching approaches has yet to be investigated. Clearly, further longitudinal studies are necessary. Future research might consider using Van den Branden's (2006) approach of preparing key teachers in different schools as TBLT instructors using a snowball technique, whereby they provide practice-oriented coaching and act as school-based counsellors. This could also involve the creation of a website where teachers can freely access and share their TBLT lessons and teaching materials and develop a communities of practice approach to continue exploring TBLT. And it may well be that previous participants are already promoting change in their establishments towards TBLT and developing their own support groups. Follow-up research should be conducted to ascertain whether or not this has occurred. Different proposals have also come from teachers participating in this online course to continue their TBLT development. Issues that future teacher-preparation courses need to address include: providing information about different task types available for L2 instruction; emphasizing the importance of comprehensible input and how it triggers incidental learning; developing teachers' strategies to promote noticing in their teaching. If the programme is delivered online, skype sessions should also be considered.

The purpose of this chapter is to contribute to our understanding of teacher cognition developed by way of a TBLT online course. Its value lies on the way the researcher and course designer was able to identify some of Ellis' factors in his suggested checklist (Chapter 7, this volume) before those factors were known or published. The course was first implemented in 2007. The paper has addressed how task-based instruction can be put into practice in online teacher education, and how some Mexican teachers responded. It was found that the course helped teachers in Mexico to understand TBLT and to implement it in their own teaching. Even so, they continued to struggle with some aspects of the approach. The paper has thus outlined some alterations that might be made to the TBLT teacher education course to rectify these shortcomings. In short, as Ellis (Chapter 7, this volume) states, 'It is, of course, one thing to identify a list factors and general principles that are needed for a teacher preparation programme to be effective. It is entirely another to ensure that this can be achieved'. It is hoped that the present chapter contributes to improved practice in this area.

Acknowledgements

The author thanks the teachers who participated in this study for providing priceless information to it. Testimonies were occasionally shortened due to word constraints. Book editors Drs Craig Lambert and Rhonda Oliver also deserve my gratitude for their sound suggestions and multiple revisions.

References

Avermaet, P.V., Colpin, M., Van Gorp, K., Bogaert, N. and Van den Branden, K. (2006) The role of teacher in task-based language teaching. In K. Van den Branden (ed.) *Task-Based Language Education: From Theory to Practice* (pp. 175–196). Cambridge: Cambridge University Press.

Borg, S. (2011) The impact of in-service teacher education on language teachers' beliefs. *System* 39 (3), 370–380.

Breen, M. and Candlin, C.N. (1980) The essentials of a communicative curriculum in language teaching. *Applied Linguistics* 1, 89–112.

Candlin, C. (2001) Afterthought: Taking the curriculum to task. In M. Bygate, P. Skehan and M. Swain (eds) *Researching Pedagogic Tasks: Second Language Learning, Teaching and Testing* (pp. 229–243). London: Longman.

Carless, D. (2004) Issues in teachers' reinterpretation of a task-based innovation in primary schools. *TESOL Quarterly* 38, 639–62.

Creswell, J. (2003) *Research Design: Qualitative, Quantitative, and Mixed Methods Approaches.* Thousand Oaks, CA: Sage.

Denzin, N. and Lincoln, Y. (2000) *Handbook of Qualitative Research.* Thousand Oaks, CA: Sage.

Dewey, J. (1975) *Interest and Effort in Education.* Toronto: Collier Books.

Duggleby, J. (2000) *How to be an Online Tutor.* Hampshire: Gower Publishing Limited.

Ellis, R. (2003) *Task-Based Language Learning and Teaching.* Oxford: Oxford University Press.

Ellis, R. (2018) *Reflections on Task-Based Language Teaching.* Bristol: Multilingual Matters.

Freire, P. (1970) *Pedagogy of the Oppressed.* Harmondsworth: Penguin Books.

Gass, S. and Varonis, E. (1994) Input, interaction, and second language production. *Studies in Second Language Acquisition* 16, 283–302.

Heigham, J. and Croker, R.A. (2009) *Qualitative Research in Applied Linguistics. A Practical Introduction.* London: Palgrave Macmillan.

Kolb, D. (1984) *Experiential Learning: Experience as the Source of Learning and Development.* Englewood Cliffs, NJ: Prentice-Hall.

Krashen, S. (1985) *The Input Hypothesis.* London: Longman.

Lambert, C. (2010) A task-based needs analysis: Putting principles into practice. *Language Teaching Research* 14 (1), 99–112.

Lee, M.S. (2009) Introspective techniques. In J. Heigham and R. Croker (eds) *Qualitative Research in Applied Linguistics* (pp. 220–241). London: Palgrave Macmillan.

Long, M. (1985) A role for instruction in second language acquisition: Task-based language teaching. In K. Hylstenstam and M. Pienemann (eds) *Modelling and Assessing Second Language Acquisition* (pp.77–99). Clevedon: Multilingual Matters.

Markee, N. (1997) Second language acquisition research: A resource for changing teachers' professional cultures? *Modern Language Journal* 81, 80–93.

McDonough, K. and Chaikitmongkol, W. (2007) Teachers' and learners' reactions to a task-based EFL course in Thailand. *TESOL Quarterly* 41, 107–32.

Prabhu, N. (1987) *Second Language Pedagogy.* Oxford: Oxford University Press.

Puren, C., Bertocchini, P. and Costanzo, E. (1998) *Se Former en Didactique des Langues.* Paris: Ellipses.

Richards, J. (1990) The dilemma of teacher education in second language teaching. In J. Richards and D. Nunan (eds) *Second Language Teacher Education* (pp. 3–15). Cambridge: Cambridge University Press.

Richards, J.C. and Ho, B. (1998) Reflective thinking through journal writing. In J.C. Richards (ed.) *Beyond Training Perspectives on Language Teaching Education* (pp. 153–170). Cambridge: Cambridge University Press.

Robinson, P. (2007) Criteria for classifying and sequencing pedagogic tasks. In M.P. García Mayo (ed.) *Investigating Tasks in Formal Language Learning* (pp. 7–26). Clevedon: Multilingual Matters.

Samuda, V. (2001) Guiding relationships between form and meaning during task performance: The role of the teacher. In M. Bygate, P. Skehan and M. Swain (eds) *Researching Pedagogic Tasks, Second Language Learning, Teaching and Testing* (pp. 119–140). Harlow: Longman.

Samuda, V. and Bygate, M. (2008) *Tasks in Second Language Learning*. Houndmills: Palgrave.

Schart, M. (2008) What matters in TBLT – task, teacher or team? An action research perspective from a beginning German language classroom. In J. Eckerth and S. Siekmann (eds) *Task-Based Language Learning and Teaching: Theoretical, Methodological, and Pedagogical Perspectives* (pp. 47–66). New York: Lang.

Schmidt, R. (1990) The role of consciousness in second language learning. *Applied Linguistics* 11, 129–158.

Schweizer, H. (1999) *Designing and Teaching an Online Course. Spinning Your Web Classroom*. Boston: Allyn & Bacon.

Skehan, P. (1996) A framework for the implementation of task-based instruction. *Applied Linguistics* 17, 38–62.

Skehan, P. (1998) *A Cognitive Approach to Language Learning*. Oxford: Oxford University Press.

Solares-Altamirano, M.E. (2010) Promoting teacher professional development through online task-based instruction. *International Journal of Virtual and Personal Learning Environments* 1 (4), 52–65.

Solares-Altamirano, M.E. (2014) Textbooks, tasks and technology: An action research study in a textbook-bound EFL context. In L. Ortega and M. González-Lloret (eds) *Technology-Mediated TBLT: Researching Technology and Tasks* (pp. 79–113). Amsterdam: John Benjamins Publishing Company.

Swain, M. (1985) Communicative competence: Some roles of comprehensible input and output in its development. In S. Gass and C. Madden (eds) *Input in Second Language Acquisition* (pp. 235–253). New York: Newbury House.

Van den Branden, K. (2006) Training teachers: Task-based as well? In K. Van den Branden (ed.) *Task-Based Language Education: From Theory to Practice* (pp. 217–248). Cambridge: Cambridge University Press.

Wallace, M.J. (1991) *Training Foreign Language Teachers*. Cambridge: Cambridge University Press.

Waters, A. (2005) Expertise in teacher education: Helping teachers to learn. In K. Johnson (ed.) *Expertise in Second Language Learning and Teaching* (pp. 210–229). London: Palgrave Macmillan.

Willis, J. (1996) *A Framework for Task-Based Learning*. Essex: Longman.

Part 3: Research on Using Tasks

13 Metacognitive Instruction for Collaborative Interaction: The Process and Product of Self-Regulated Learning in the Chilean EFL Context

Masatoshi Sato

The current study examined the impact of metacognitive instruction for collaborative interaction during communicative tasks. While task-based research shows considerable supportive evidence of tasks, there are many pedagogical obstacles to the implementation of tasks, especially in foreign language contexts. Further, research suggests that even when a task is found to be effective, learners' lack of engagement may hinder its effectiveness. Instead of focusing on the nature or implementation conditions of a task, the current study, undertaken with Chilean high school learners of English, explored their metacognition as a potential support. In this quasi-experimental study, the participants were in 11th grade ($N = 42$) and were divided into three groups. Learners in Group A ($n = 14$) were given *metacognitive instruction for collaborative interaction* (MICI) and paired communicative tasks, while Group B ($n = 14$) engaged in the tasks only. Group C ($n = 14$) served as the control group. Delivered over a seven-week period, MICI consisted of six stages each of which served to increase learners' metacognitive knowledge of collaborative peer interaction and to train them to use three collaborative strategies – appeal for help, clarification requests and comprehension checks. Interactions during the tasks were audio-recorded three times (over 10 hours in total) to identify which strategies were used. As the outcome measure, learners' comprehensibility was measured before and after the intervention, via picture description and sentence reading tests. The results showed that only Group A increased the frequency of strategy use over time. In addition, the learners in Group A improved their comprehensibility significantly more than those in Groups B and C. It is concluded that MICI facilitated self-regulated learning of adolescent English as a Foreign Language (EFL) learners in Chile, and that the effectiveness of peer interaction tasks was improved by providing metacognitive instruction as cognitive support.

Background

The current pedagogical practice of communicative language teaching and task-based language teaching (TBLT) often involves activities in which second language (L2) learners work together in order to complete them. On the one hand, empirical research generally supports the effectiveness of task-based interaction on L2 learning (see Loewen & Sato, 2018; Philp *et al.*, 2014; Sato & Ballinger, 2016). On the other hand, survey and observation research has reported that such activities may not necessarily bring about positive effects on learners' L2 development especially in real classroom settings, potentially due to students' lack of engagement with the task and/or their conversation partners (Sato, 2017). This may occur because learners may not consider communicative activities as beneficial for their learning (McDonough, 2004; Sato, 2013). Consequently, they may resort to their first language (L1) to complete the task (Azkarai & García Mayo, 2017). Further, learners may not see their classmates as a viable learning resource (Philp *et al.*, 2010). Even when they try to take advantage of peer interaction activities, their psychological state (e.g. feeling shy or embarrassed) may hinder their active participation in the task (Yoshida, 2013). In such an interactional environment, learners may fail to construct collaborative relationships found to be conducive to L2 learning (Sato, 2017; Storch, 2002). Consequently, interactional moves that are necessary for L2 development, such as input, corrective feedback and modified output, may be absent during task-based interaction (McDonough & Mackey, 2000; Sato & Lyster, 2007). Those factors, contributing to learners' lack of engagement, may not be resolved simply by manipulating task features or by implementing various task conditions.

To counter these pedagogical challenges in TBLT, the current study investigated the potential effects of metacognitive instruction both on learners' engagement during peer interaction activities and L2 development. In educational psychology research, metacognition – knowledge about learning (Flavell, 1976) – has been found to account for learning outcomes, particularly after factoring in other variables such as attendance rates, motivation, and even instructional methods (see meta-analyses in Donker *et al.*, 2014; Wang *et al.*, 1990). The impact of metacognition in those studies is explained by the learners' ability to plan what they are going to learn, self-monitor their learning processes and self-evaluate those learning processes after engaging in the task (Dinsmore *et al.*, 2008). Hence, successful metacognitive instruction arguably leads to self-regulated learning. Such pedagogical intervention, however, has been examined in a limited area in the field of second language acquisition (SLA), specifically in listening comprehension (Goh, 2008; Vandergrift & Baker, 2015). Hence, the current study developed metacognitive instruction – called *metacognitive instruction for collaborative interaction* (MICI) – as part of task-based performance and aimed to promote self-regulated learning during peer interaction activities.

The current study was conducted in the Chilean EFL context. In this context, typical primary- and secondary-level classes often contain more than 30 students, English is often taught primarily in the learners' first language (i.e. Spanish), and lessons tend to focus on grammar teaching and vocabulary memorization. Furthermore, lessons are teacher-centered and meaningful interaction between the students is limited (see Barahona, 2016). Even when a task from the textbook is designed to elicit communicative interaction between students, it is often decontextualized and grammar focused (e.g. role plays based on the thematic unit of the textbook, discussion tasks based on the text unrelated to the students' interests). This context presented an ideal background to the current investigation at two levels. First, students may not be accustomed to meaningful and contextualized interaction between each other. MICI was designed to raise their awareness of the benefit of the task for L2 learning and, consequently, to increase their engagement levels. Second, it was suspected that the students would not know how to benefit from the task. MICI entailed a strategy training component by which the students took advantage of the task for their own L2 development.

Literature Review

Task-based interaction and task engagement

Research has shown that TBLT is theoretically sound and pedagogically viable (see a meta-analysis in Bryfonski & McKay, 2017). Researchers have argued that task-based interactions are not only effective for L2 learners to improve L2 skills, but also that TBLT can be used as a curricular framework across L2 learning/teaching contexts (Bygate *et al.*, 2017; Ellis, 2018). Amid the ever-growing support for TBLT, however, research has reported some implementation issues, specifically in the area of learners' engagement. That is, even when learners are given a task proven to be effective, it may not lead to a positive change in their L2 knowledge if they did not engage with the task. Furthermore, the issues related to learner psychology in relation to task engagement have been reported both in cognitively-oriented and socially-oriented research.

From the cognitive-interactionist perspective, when L2 learners engage in a task, they can be exposed to beneficial input from their conversational partners. For example, García Mayo and Pica (2000) compared task-based interaction between English learners and native speakers of the target language. The results showed that the frequencies of input modification were comparable in the two types of interaction. It has also been found that learners provide corrective feedback to each other, which in turn positively affects L2 learning (Adams, 2007; Sato & Lyster, 2007). The most advantageous feature of task-based interaction is associated with output. When learners work on a task with their peers, as opposed to with the teacher or a native speaker, they feel more comfortable, and they are afforded more time to process their production. During task-based performance, therefore, learners produce an increased amount of output (Shehadeh, 2001) when trying out their linguistic hypotheses (Swain, 1985).

However, research has also shown that the frequency of peer feedback is often insufficient to lead to any substantial change in the partner's cognitive system (e.g. McDonough, 2004). Even when feedback is provided, its quality may be problematic. For instance, peer feedback may be segmented and/or unfocused and, thus, limited in the impact that it has on errors made and feedback provided on those errors (Adams *et al.*, 2011; Pica *et al.*, 1996). For instance, learners may not feel comfortable to provide feedback to their classmates, as it may appear socially inappropriate. Even when they provide feedback, they may not feel it appropriate to act as the language 'authority' by explicitly indicating that the error was made. In this regard, Lambert (2017) argues that affective factors such as a sense of personal investment in task content can influence engagement with the task (see also Philp & Duchesne, 2016). Lambert *et al.* (2017), for example, found that learner-generated task content results in more peer interaction and feedback than teacher-generated task content.

From sociocultural perspectives, during task-based interaction, learners may engage in scaffolding whereby 'students exteriorize their expertise and offer each other knowledge about language' (Swain *et al.*, 2002: 175). While scaffolding is generally considered as a support from a more capable individual (Lantolf & Poehner, 2011), Donato's (1994) classroom observations showed that peers were indeed capable of scaffolding bidirectionally—offering help to each other. Storch's (2002) seminal study further examined scaffolding and categorized learners' social relationships into four types based on the level of control or authority (i.e. equality) and engagement (i.e. mutuality). Among the four, when a dyad constructed either collaborative or expert/novice relationships, both of which entailed high levels of equality and engagement, peer interaction could bring about positive effects on language learning. More recently, Sato's (2017) socio-cognitive approach empirically showed that when learners form collaborative relationships, those learners tend to benefit from task engagement more than those who exhibited uncollaborative interaction patterns (see also Storch & Sato, 2019).

Metacognitive instruction and L2 learning

Metacognitive instruction is not designed to directly impact upon the development of learners' knowledge; rather, it provides them with cognitive support – metacognition – to enhance the content learning. Originally, metacognition was categorized into three types of knowledge by Flavell (1979): (a) person knowledge (the knowledge a person has about him/herself and others as cognitive processors); (b) task knowledge (the knowledge a person has about the information and resources needed to undertake a task); and (c) strategy knowledge (knowledge regarding the strategies which are likely to be effective in achieving goals and undertaking tasks). Brown (1987) then distinguished two components of metacognition – the knowledge of cognition and the regulation of cognition. The knowledge of cognition refers to the knowledge about a learner's own cognition or cognition in general (e.g. knowing specific communication strategies), while the regulation of cognition refers to a set of activities that enable learners to attain control on their thinking and learning, including planning, self-monitoring, and self-evaluation (see also Veenman, 2011). Therefore, the results of successful metacognitive instruction leads to self-regulated learning whereby learners 'set goals for their learning and then attempt to monitor, regulate and control their cognition' (Pintrich, 2000: 453).

Following Wenden's (1987) application of metacognitive research to SLA, several studies have investigated the effects of metacognitive instruction on L2 learning. For instance, in Vandergrift and Tafaghodtari's (2010) study, university-level learners of French were first instructed to predict the types of information they would hear before actually listening to it. They were then told to verify their predictions during listening. Results showed that the experimental learners not only outperformed the control group in listening comprehension, but they also exhibited heightened awareness of their learning processes (see also Goh & Taib, 2006; Rahimi & Katal, 2012). Later, Sato and Loewen (2018) used metacognitive instruction to increase the effectiveness of corrective feedback. In this study, prior to communicative activities undertaken with the teacher, learners were told that they would receive feedback on their grammatical errors. The analysis showed that learners who then received metacognitive instruction increased the accuracy of the target structure use during spontaneous oral production tasks. While the pedagogical potential of metacognitive instruction seems promising, the previous research has not examined its effects on task-based performance and certainly not with adolescent learners in a Chilean context – where the current study was undertaken.

The Current Study

Given the positive findings of peer interaction on L2 development, on the one hand, and the pedagogical and social challenges, on the other, the current study examined metacognitive instruction designed to enhance collaborative interaction during task performance. By implementing such an intervention, it was hoped that learners would become more aware that (a) their classmates can be a useful learning resource (*person knowledge*), (b) peer interaction activities can be helpful for their L2 learning (*task knowledge*) and (c) collaborative strategies increase the benefit of the task-based interaction (*strategy knowledge*). As a result, it was hypothesized that learners' general comprehensibility would be affected. This was because if learners engaged in problem-solving related to linguistic issues by using the taught strategies, they may become more aware of the nature of communication problems and ways in which they can be resolved. Accordingly, the following research questions were explored:

RQ1:   Does metacognitive instruction for collaborative interaction facilitate collaboration between adolescent Chilean learners of English?

RQ2:   Do peer interaction tasks promote the development of these learners' comprehensibility?

RQ3:   Does metacognitive instruction for collaborative interaction embedded in peer interaction tasks affect the development of these learners' comprehensibility?

Methods

Participants

Participants were 11th grade students from two secondary schools in Santiago, Chile ($N = 42$) whose ages ranged from 16–17 ($M_{age} = 16.3$; Standard Deviation (SD) = 0.6). Though the students had not taken any standardized test, the schools' averages of the nation-wide English test administered by the Ministry of Education (English SIMCE) indicated that one of the schools was at the 65th percentile and the other at the 68th percentile. Hence, the participants in our study were considered as beginner to lower-intermediate. They were all L1 speakers of Spanish who had studied English previously for a mean of 3.9 years ($SD = 0.2$). Prior to the intervention, the learners had not been accustomed to engaging in tasks with their peers. In fact, the initial classroom observations indicated that most of the classes were conducted in Spanish using teacher-fronted activities. All classes consisted of 39–42 students.

Design of the study

From the two intact classes, 42 learners volunteered for extra English lessons after regular instructional hours. The learners were assigned to one of the three groups. Learners in Group A (MICI: $n = 14$; 4 females and 10 males) were given *metacognitive instruction for collaborative interaction* (MICI), while Group B (PI-only: $n = 14$; 9 females and 5 males) were a *peer interaction* (PI) group who engaged only in the communicative tasks that were embedded in the MICI treatment. Group C (Control: $n = 14$; 9 females and 5 males) served as the control group. The experimental groups (Groups A and B) were given a series of information-gap tasks designed to elicit authentic, communicative interaction over seven lessons (45 minutes each totaling over 5 hours). In addition to the developmental measure pertaining to comprehensibility, the interactions were audio-recorded three times (Days 1, 3 and 7) during the course of the intervention. The control group took the pre- and post-tests and completed the three tasks for obtaining the strategy use data. The data were collected from the same pairs. Ten out of 45 minutes during task engagement from each data collection point were submitted to further analyses because the tasks involved constant changes of partners. In total, 10 hours of audio data (10 min × 7 pairs × 3 groups × 3 times) were transcribed. Figure 13.1 depicts the overall design of the study.

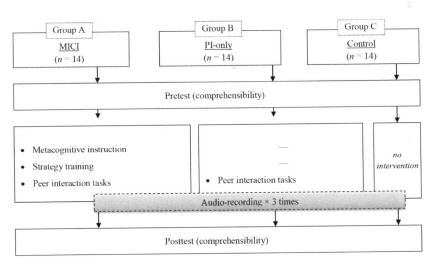

Figure 13.1 Design of the study
Note: MICI = metacognitive instruction for collaborative interaction; PI = peer interaction.

Instructional Target

Comprehensibility was chosen for the target of instruction, although previous task-based studies focused on narrower targets such as grammatical accuracy. This was because the intervention was designed to enhance collaborative interaction in general, and it was thought that its impact would be reflected in a more global measure.

Comprehensibility is defined as listeners' perceptions of how easy or difficult it is to understand speech (Derwing & Munro, 1997). Hence, comprehensibility is essential for successful communication. Research suggests that communicative interaction is a driving force for improving comprehensibility (Derwing *et al.*, 2008). It is important to note that comprehensibility is a different construct from accentedness (Trofimovich & Isaacs, 2012). In the current study, comprehensibility was considered more important than accentedness; there is no reason to sound like native speakers as long as learner speech is understood by others.

Materials

Peer interaction activities. The activities were information-gap tasks with topics and materials thought to be engaging for 11th graders. Topics for the seven lessons included Facebook, afterlife, virginity, tattooing, adoption, gay marriage and aliens. For each topic, learners were given a short reading of a controversial issue connected with the topic (e.g. privacy in Facebook), along with a list of interview questions. After individually reading the text, their task was to find out their classmates' personal opinions. The learners changed partners after 10 minutes. Every time they had a new partner, they needed to tell him or her what their previous partners had told them. Hence, while the amount of information to communicate kept increasing, they had the same amount of time to deliver the information and obtain new information (for more details see Sato & Lyster, 2012).

Metacognitive instruction for collaborative interaction (MICI). The metacognitive instruction focusing on collaborative interaction consisted of six stages, with an overall aim of enhancing self-regulated learning whereby 'learners manage, direct, regulate, guide their learning, i.e. planning, monitoring, and evaluation' (Wenden, 1987: 519). The three types of metacognitive knowledge – person, task and strategy – were targeted throughout the intervention.

Stage 1 (Awareness-raising) was designed to raise the learners' awareness of peer interaction in general as well as their interaction mindset (see Sato, 2017) that may facilitate or inhibit the effectiveness of peer interaction on L2 learning. The learners were first given a checklist pertaining to peer interaction (see Figure 13.2) which was translated into Spanish. The items in the checklist focused on general perceptions

Figure 13.2 Collaborative interaction checklist

of peer interaction, learner psychology, and corrective feedback during peer interaction. After individually completing the checklist by choosing an option from the spectrum (from A to E), the learners engaged in a discussion in pairs comparing and explaining their choices. Afterward, the teacher led a class discussion and explained the value of peer interaction, the importance of risk-taking during tasks, and the effectiveness of peer feedback.

Stage 2 (Understanding) introduced the learners to three collaborative strategies: Appeal for help, clarification request and confirmation check. The teacher explained the strategies and presented examples. Appeal for help was defined as learners' collaborative action to seek for help from their partner either directly or indirectly. Examples included: 'How do you say … in English?' 'Do you know how to say this?', etc. Clarification requests were explained as a collaborative action to indicate that there were linguistic issues related to either meaning of a word/sentence or forms of linguistic features such as grammar and pronunciation. Learners were given examples such as: 'Sorry, what did you say?' 'Can you repeat?' 'Do you mean "*the correct version of the incomprehensible/inaccurate utterance*"?' Importantly, clarification requests were operationalized in the current study differently from the interactional move of the same name that appears in the corrective feedback literature. As can be seen from the examples, in the current study clarification requests included any type of corrective feedback such as prompts and recasts (see Lyster *et al.*, 2013). Finally, confirmation checks were presented to the learners as a collaborative action to make sure that their partners understood what they said (e.g. 'Got it?' 'Is that clear?' 'Did you understand?' 'Am I making sense?' etc.).

Stage 3 (Analysis) and Stage 4 (Modeling) both involved the learners with a transcription analysis. First, for Stage 3 the researcher prepared a set of transcripts from his previous studies of peer interaction. The pairs of participants were then asked to identify the three strategies. Then, they were also told to look for other places in the transcripts where the three strategies could be effectively used. Finally (Stage 4), the teacher discussed the transcripts by pointing out the strategies as well as possible locations where the strategies could be implemented.

Stage 5 (Practice) was embedded within the communicative tasks where the learners were encouraged to use the taught strategies. In addition to trying out the strategies, the teacher encouraged them to monitor their own and their partners' use of the strategies.

Stage 6 (Evaluation) involved self- and other-evaluation of the strategy use. After each task, the paired learners reflected upon their strategy uses. The teacher instructed them to recall which strategies were used during the task and how many times they were used. The learners were also asked to come up with better ways of using the strategies, such as being more polite or giving more time for their partners to respond.

Stage 1 was implemented in the first intervention day prior to the learners' performing the task. Stages 2, 3 and 4 were implemented in the second day, while the learners engaged in Stages 5 and 6 for the second day and onward.

Data Collection and Analysis

Interaction data. Over 10 hours of audio-recorded data were first transcribed verbatim by a research assistant. Transcripts were verified by another research assistant to ensure their accuracy. In the transcripts, the three strategies were identified and their frequencies were tallied over the three data collection points; 20% of the transcripts were coded by two research assistants and the interrater reliability calculated by Cohen's kappa coefficient reached 0.96.

Inferential statistics were not run for the interaction data because of the sample size (i.e. 7 pairs in each group), the nature of the scores (i.e. ordinal), and the number of factors (i.e. group and time). The results of descriptive statistics are presented in the results section.

Comprehensibility pre and post-tests. Two tests were used to elicit two types of L2 skills. The first test was a picture description task that elicited the learners' spontaneous production skills. In this test, learners were provided with a series of six pictures that were connected chronologically. They were asked to describe the events in as much detail as possible. Similar but different sets of pictures were prepared for the pre- and post-tests. Thirty seconds of planning time was given, but there was no time limit to complete the test.

The second test was a sentence reading test. It was thought that the test, unlike the picture description test, would elicit controlled processing of L2 knowledge by allowing learners to access their explicit knowledge.

In the test, the learners were given 15 sentences to read aloud. The syntactic complexity and vocabulary were adjusted to the current learners' proficiency level. Two sets of 15 sentences were prepared for the pre- and post-tests.

The audio-recorded data were then prepared for the raters. For the picture description test, the first minute was extracted (see Derwing *et al.*, 2006), resulting in 84 one-minute speech samples (42 participants × 2 testing times). The samples were then randomized including group and time. As for the sentence reading test, 10 sentences were randomly chosen to avoid the raters' fatigue. Hence, in each of the 84 samples, there were 10 sentences embedded and the rater gave one score for each sample. The samples were randomized.

Four English-L1 raters rated the samples. They were all teaching English in Chile for an average of 6.4 years ($SD = 5.5$). Hence, they were familiar with English spoken by Chilean learners. They rated the speech samples using a 7-point Likert scale (1 = extremely difficult to understand; 7 = very easy to understand). The interrater correlation coefficients of the picture description test was 0.87 and the sentence reading test 0.86. Accordingly, the averages of the four raters were assigned to individual learners and these served as the scores of comprehensibility.

Statistical analyses were conducted using version 21.0 of the *Statistical Package for Social Sciences* (SPSS). In order to examine differential effects of the intervention on the development of comprehensibility, analyses of covariance (ANCOVAs) were conducted on the rated scores of the two tests, using the pre-test scores as covariates (Keselman *et al.*, 1998). The datasets met the assumptions of normality as well as the regression of slopes and homogeneity of variance. For *post hoc* pair-wise comparisons, Bonferroni corrections were applied, and the alpha level for all tests of significance was set at 0.05. Effect sizes and confidence intervals of the group differences were calculated based on the adjusted means. Effect sizes were calculated using Cohen's (1988) *d*.

Results

Strategy use

Table 13.1 reports the means and standard deviations of the strategy uses over time and Figure 13.1 visually depicts the findings. The results of the Appeal for Help strategy showed that the three groups were comparable at Time 1 (Day 1). However, the MICI group increased the use of this strategy over time (Time 2 = 3.14; Time 3 = 4.43). Such changes were not observed in either the PI-only group or control group. The results of the Clarification Request strategy showed a similar pattern with higher frequencies in the MICI group (Time 2 = 5.86;

Table 13.1 Frequencies of strategy uses of three groups over three times

	Time 1		Time 2		Time 3	
	M	SD	M	SD	M	SD
Appeal for help						
MICI (n = 7)	0.29	0.49	3.14	1.35	4.43	1.27
PI-only (n = 7)	0.14	0.38	0.71	0.76	0.57	0.79
Control (n = 7)	0.29	0.49	0.57	0.79	0.29	0.49
Clarification request						
MICI (n = 7)	0.57	0.53	5.86	1.95	6.43	0.98
PI-only (n = 7)	0.86	0.69	0.57	0.53	0.43	0.53
Control (n = 7)	0.71	0.76	0.71	0.76	0.57	0.53
Confirmation check						
MICI (n = 7)	0.29	0.49	4.86	1.07	2.71	1.11
PI-only (n = 7)	0.29	0.49	0.57	0.79	0.29	0.49
Control (n = 7)	0.29	0.49	0.57	0.79	0.43	0.79

Note: MICI = metacognitive instruction for collaborative interaction; PI = peer interaction.

Time 3 = 6.43), but not for the other two groups. Finally, the results of the Confirmation Check strategy differed from the other two strategies in that although the MICI group increased the frequencies from Time 1 (0.29) to Time 2 (4.86), there was a decrease from Time 2 to Time 3 (2.71). This pattern was similar for the other two groups, but not as pronounced.

Furthermore, the MICI learners used the strategies in effective ways. For instance, in Excerpt 1, the pair discusses decisions related to adoption. When Learner A3 realized that he did not know how to say 'decision' in English, he uses appeal for help by saying: 'how can you say "decisión"?' As a response, Learner A2 provides support by providing the correct word, which was followed by Learner A3's correct use.

Excerpt 1
A2:   Do you want another brother if he say no no if he say yes
A3:   Ah you, you ask about the, the opinion of your family
A2:   For me, is important
A3:   Yeah yeah is an, an important deci ... de ... **how can you say** 'decisión'?
A2:   Ehh ... Decision
A3:   Decision. Decision ... is an important choice, is the same...

In Excerpt 2, the pair discusses the existence of aliens. Being unsure of her utterances, Learner A4 uses a confirmation check ('Do you understand?'). Learner A5 admits that he did not understand his partner and politely asks her to repeat what she said. Due to the combination of

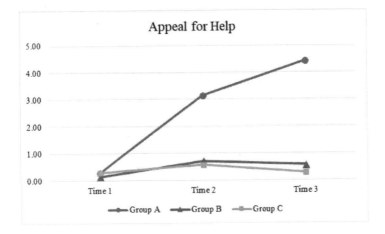

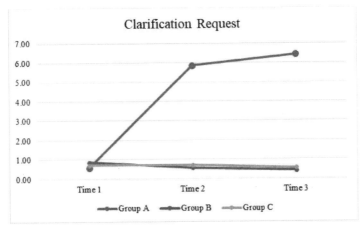

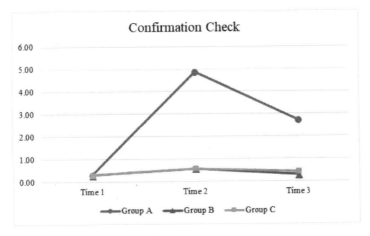

Figure 13.3 Strategy use for three groups

the two strategies, the communication breakdown, potentially caused by the word usage of 'crawl', was successfully identified and resolved.

Excerpt 2

A4:   I think the same because we, we are intelligence but we can crawl in the space we can crawl in the space like alien because I think that the spaceship of alien are better than the space spaceship of us. **Do you understand?**

A5:   Ehh ... **You can repeat please?**

A4:   I believe that aliens can travel in the universe because their spaceship are better than our spaceship, spaceship are *naves espaciales* [spaceships].

A5:   I agree.

Comprehensibility

In terms of changes in the comprehensibility of the three groups between the pre-tests and post-tests, the ANCOVA of the picture description scores yielded a statistically significant group effect, $F(2, 41) = 4.854$, $p = 0.013$, partial $\eta^2 = 0.203$, suggesting significant differences among the three groups at the time of post-test after factoring in the pre-test scores as the covariate. The *post hoc* pair-wise comparisons revealed that the MICI group outperformed both the PI-only ($p = 0.034$; $d = 3.89$; 95% CI [3.79, 3.98]) and the control groups ($p = 0.028$; $d = 4.03$; 95% CI [3.94, 4.13]). The difference between the PI-only and control groups did not reach a significance ($p = 1.000$; $d = 0.14$; 95% CI [0.05, 0.24]). The ANCOVA on the sentence reading scores did not show a significant main effect, $F(2, 41) = 1.006$, $p = 0.375$, partial $\eta^2 = 0.050$. Hence, follow-up pair-wise comparisons were not conducted. The descriptive statistics including effect sizes and their confidence intervals based on the pre-post comparisons are presented in Table 13.2 and Figure 13.4 visually presents the results.

Table 13.2 Group means and standard deviations of comprehensibility scores

	Pre-test		Post-test			
	M	SD	M	SD	d	d's 95% CI
Picture description						
MICI (n = 14)	4.54	.84	5.39	.68	1.12	[0.88, 1.43]
PI-only (n = 14)	4.50	1.22	4.38	1.50	0.09	[−0.39, 0.58]
Control (n = 14)	4.16	1.39	4.07	1.64	0.06	[−0.48, 0.60]
Sentence reading						
MICI (n = 14)	4.82	.89	5.02	.98	0.22	[0.11, 0.56]
PI-only (n = 14)	4.43	.77	4.75	1.01	0.37	[0.05, 0.69]
Control (n = 14)	4.30	1.13	4.32	1.14	0.02	[−0.43, 0.39]

Note: MICI = metacognitive instruction for collaborative interaction; PI = peer interaction.

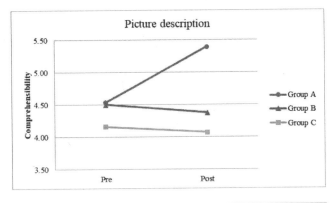

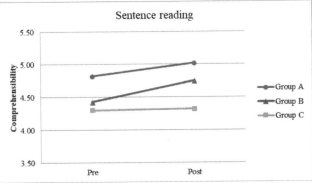

Figure 13.4 Developmental patterns of three groups on two comprehensibility tests

Discussion

The first research question asked about the impact of MICI on the learners' task-based performance. The results of strategy use suggest first that these L2 learners could be trained to interact in specific ways, supporting previous strategy training research (Ballinger, 2013; Fujii *et al.*, 2016; Nakatani, 2005; Sato & Ballinger, 2012). In contrast to previous research, strategy training in the current study was embedded within metacognitive instruction. Throughout the intervention, especially in Stage 1 (awareness raising), instruction aimed at enhancing learners' understanding of their classmates as a learning resource (*person knowledge*). Although the current study did not include a separate measure of the learners' metacognitive knowledge, it can be speculated that due to the intervention, they may have come to realize that they could help each other to complete the task (*task knowledge*). The metacognitive instruction was embedded in tasks requiring the learners to obtain information from their classmates and communicate it with the other classmates as quickly as possible. The analysis of the transcripts showed that the focused strategies did appear to help them complete the tasks successfully (*strategy knowledge*). As such, it is argued that the intervention might have increased the participants' understanding of: (a) the importance of peer interaction tasks in the classroom (*task knowledge*); (b) the ways in which tasks can be useful for acquiring their desired communicative skills (*strategy knowledge*); and (c) the fact that their classmates can help them achieve the goal (*person knowledge*).

While the use of appeals for help and clarification requests steadily increased, the learners' use of confirmation checks in the last data collection point (i.e. seventh lesson) decreased (see Table 13.1 and Figure 13.3). This may have occurred because this strategy functioned differently from the other two and over time lost their interactional utility. Specifically, once the learners became more skillful in using clarification requests, they may have realized that confirmation checks were unnecessary. They might have also become more trusting of their partners to ask for clarification if their utterances were unclear. In fact, the learners often used clarification requests in response to confirmation checks, as can be seen in Excerpt 2. It is also possible that confirmation checks became socially inappropriate over time. For instance, constantly repeating, 'Do you understand?' may appear rude or obtrusive in collaborative efforts to complete the task. From an SLA perspective, it may be that clarification requests are related to L2 development more so than confirmation checks. When learners are asked to clarify their utterances, they may restate what they have said, during which time they may engage in syntactic processing of their output (Swain, 1985). Moreover, they may engage in repeated production practice, which has been shown to positively affect L2 development in skill learning research (Lyster & Sato, 2013).

The second question addressed the impact of peer interaction tasks on the development of comprehensibility. The results indicate that, for these learners, solely engaging in the tasks was not effective for improving comprehensibility (see Table 13.2 and Figure 13.4) despite the fact that the tasks met the four criteria of a task proposed by Ellis and Shintani (2014) in that the learners' primary focus was presumably on meaning, there was an information gap embedded as opinion exchanges, learners relied on their own linguistic resources because there was no explicit form-based instruction during the intervention tasks, and the task's goal was not language-focused as the goal was to collect their classmates' personal opinions of a given topic. Given the developmental measure (comprehensibility) and the context of the current study (EFL), several explanations are possible. First, the learners in the PI-only group did not tend to notice linguistic issues during the tasks. Second, even when they noticed these issues, they understood each other due to their shared L1 background and, thus, did not clarify their partners' utterances. Third, even when they decided to signal linguistic issues, they often did not know how to initiate such an exchange. As a consequence, the development of their comprehensibility may not have been positively affected due to lack of engagement in negotiation of meaning or form. This aligns with previous research, such as that by Sato and Lyster (2012) who found that learners who engaged in communicative paired tasks improved their fluency only, while learners who were trained to give corrective feedback to each other improved in both fluency and accuracy.

The third research question focused on the effectiveness of MICI. The results showed that for the learners in the MICI group the intervention positively affected the development of comprehensibility but only for the spontaneous production test (see Table 13.2 and Figure 13.4). However, the positive impact did not transfer to reading out written sentences. These results are supported by previous research related to transfer-appropriate processing – a skill acquired in a certain context is best transferred to a similar context (see Lightbown, 2000). The learners in the MICI group improved their comprehensibility in the context of communicative interaction. Hence, the skill acquired in this context (i.e. producing more comprehensible utterances) may have transferred only to the spontaneous production test, but not to the sentence reading test. It is possible that these learners used different knowledge sources during the sentence reading tests: first encoding the written information, accessing their explicit knowledge to comprehend the sentences, and finally trying to produce the sentences phonologically accurately. While reading sentences aloud in a comprehensible manner may be an important skill, spontaneous production skills may be more useful for real-world use of the language.

In sum, the results of the study suggest that the MICI succeeded in helping the learners in Group A to engage in collaborative interaction. At the same time, those learners increased their comprehensibility during the spontaneous production task. However, metacognition is argued to provide cognitive support for learners to engage in behaviors that may be conducive to L2 learning. It is not argued to directly affect L2 learning. In the current study, the metacognitive instruction targeted collaborative interaction. Based on SLA research, especially that undertaken from a cognitive-interactionist perspective, collaborative interaction is purported to lead to more modified input, corrective feedback, and to modified output. From sociocultural perspectives, collaborative interaction involves more scaffolding between the learners, there is more mutual respect provided to each other and they are more likely to share the responsibility in completing the task.

Conclusion

The present study set out to address TBLT implementation issues. It focused on learners' lack of engagement during task-based interaction and ways to overcome this. This was achieved through metacognitive instruction encompassing communication strategies, and ways to increase learners' self-regulated learning and collaborative interaction during communicative tasks. The intervention was designed to tap into three types of metacognitive knowledge – personal, task and strategy. The study examined both the process (changes in interactional behaviors over time) and product (development of comprehensibility) of self-regulated learning. Methodologically, this is one of few studies that has attempted to reveal a causal relationship between collaborative interaction and L2 development, by drawing on cognitive and social perspectives. Overall, the study demonstrates a potentially important impact for the intervention (i.e. instructional support) for enhancing the ways in which learners engage in communicative tasks. In doing so, the study also demonstrates how instructed second language acquisition can apply theoretical and empirical research to the classroom L2 teaching (Loewen & Sato, 2017; Sato & Loewen, 2019).

The study, however, has several methodological limitations. Data pertaining to learners' metacognition and perceptions of the intervention were not collected. Future research may benefit from collecting data to determine the impact of (a) the changes in their person, task, and strategy knowledge, and (b) learner perceptions about MICI as an instructional framework. In so doing, the feasibility and sustainability of MICI as classroom instruction can be investigated. Another limitation relates to the design of the current study; namely, in order to obtain interaction data, the control group engaged with the tasks three times (albeit only for 10 minutes each time without changing partners), which might have contributed to the non-significant differences between the PI-only and control groups. In addition, although the learners' heightened metacognition may arguably support their continuous use of the focused strategies, it is an empirical question as to whether they would maintain their collaborative behaviors after the intervention. This may be addressed by implementing a longitudinal design. Finally, the study narrowly focused on the three strategies in the interaction data. Future studies could analyze other interactional moves and social relationships as possible outcomes of metacognitive instruction. For instance, learners may use less L1, produce more words, and take more turns, as a result of increased metacognition (see Dörnyei & Kormos, 2000).

Future task-based research should consider incorporating the psychology of the learners (e.g. metacognition) and go beyond L2-specific behaviors while investigating task-based performance. By knowing what types of learner psychology are related to interactional behaviors that SLA research has found to affect L2 development, researchers could examine ways in which those psychological states can be enhanced (e.g. higher motivation, more willingness to communicate, growth mindset, and collaborative mindset). If learners were prepared to fully engage with the task and their partner, positive effects of task engagement may persist regardless of the nature (e.g. simple vs. complex) or implementation conditions (e.g. planning time and task repetition) of the task. From a pedagogical perspective then, in addition to using effective tasks in the classroom, teachers will be able to support learners in taking an advantage of task-based experiences regardless of task types or implementation procedures.

Acknowledgements

This work was partially supported by the Fondo Nacional de Desarrollo Científico y Tecnólogico from the Ministry of Education of Chile (FONDECYT: 1181533) as well as PIA (CIE160009) from the Chilean National Commission of Science and Technology (CONICYT), awarded to the author as the co-investigator and associate researcher, respectively.

References

Adams, R. (2007) Do second language learners benefit from interacting with each other? In A. Mackey (ed.) *Conversational Interaction in Second Language Acquisition: A Collection of Empirical Studies* (pp. 29–51). Oxford: Oxford University Press.

Adams, R., Nuevo, A. and Egi, T. (2011) Explicit and implicit feedback, modified output, and SLA: Does explicit and implicit feedback promote learning and learner-learner interactions? *The Modern Language Journal* 95, 42–63.

Azkarai, A. and García Mayo, M.P. (2017) Task repetition effects on L1 use in EFL child task-based interaction. *Language Teaching Research* 21 (4), 480–495.

Ballinger, S. (2013) Towards a cross-linguistic pedagogy: Biliteracy and reciprocal learning strategies in French immersion. *Journal of Immersion and Content-Based Language Education* 1 (1), 131–148.

Barahona, M. (2016) Challenges and accomplishments of ELT at primary level in Chile: Towards the aspiration of becoming a bilingual country. *Education Policy Analysis Archives* 24 (82), 1–24.

Brown, A. (1987) Metacognition, executive control, self-regulation, and other more mysterious mechanisms. In F. Weinert and R. Kluwe (eds) *Metacognition, Motivation, and Understanding* (pp. 65–116). Mahwah, NJ: Lawrence Erlbaum.

Bryfonski, L. and McKay, T.H. (2017) TBLT implementation and evaluation: A meta-analysis. *Language Teaching Research* 1–30. doi:1362168817744389.

Bygate, M., Gass, S.M., Mackey, A., Oliver, R. and Robinson, P. (2017) Theory, empiricism and practice: Commentary on TBLT in ARAL 2016. *Annual Review of Applied Linguistics* 1–9. doi:10.1017/S0267190517000010.

Cohen, J. (1988) *Statistical Power Analysis for the Behavioral Sciences*. Hillsdale, NJ: Lawrence Erlbaum.

Derwing, T. and Munro, M. (1997) Accent, intelligibility, and comprehensibility: Evidence from four L1s. *Studies in Second Language Acquisition* 19 (1), 1–16.

Derwing, T., Munro, M. and Thomson, R. (2008) A longitudinal study of ESL learners' fluency and comprehensibility development. *Applied Linguistics* 29 (3), 359–380.

Derwing, T., Thomson, R. and Munro, M. (2006) English pronunciation and fluency development in Mandarin and Slavic speakers. *System* 34 (2), 183–193.

Dinsmore, D.L., Alexander, P.A. and Loughlin, S.M. (2008) Focusing the conceptual lens on metacognition, self-regulation, and self-regulated learning. *Educational Psychology Review* 20 (4), 391–409.

Donato, R. (1994) Collective scaffolding in second language learning. In J. Lantolf and G. Appel (eds) *Vygotskian Approaches to Second Language Research* (pp. 33–56). Norwood, NJ: Ablex.

Donker, A., de Boer, H., Kostons, D., van Ewijk, C.D. and van der Werf, M. (2014) Effectiveness of learning strategy instruction on academic performance: A meta-analysis. *Educational Research Review* 11, 1–26.

Dörnyei, Z. and Kormos, J. (2000) The role of individual and social variables in oral task performance. *Language Teaching Research* 4 (3), 275–300.

Ellis, R. (2018) Towards a modular language curriculum for using tasks. *Language Teaching Research*. doi: 1362168818765315.

Ellis, R. and Shintani, N. (2014) *Exploring Language Pedagogy Through Second Language Acquisition*. London: Routledge.

Flavell, J.H. (1976) Metacognitive aspects of problem solving. In L.B. Resnick (ed.) *The Nature of Intelligence* (pp. 231–235). Hillsdale, NJ: Erlbaum.

Flavell, J.H. (1979) Metacognition and cognitive monitoring: A new area of cognitive–developmental inquiry. *American Psychologist* 34 (10), 906–911.

Fujii, A., Ziegler, N. and Mackey, A. (2016) Peer interaction and metacognitive instruction in the EFL classroom. In M. Sato and S. Ballinger (eds) *Peer Interaction and Second Language Learning: Pedagogical Potential and Research Agenda* (pp. 63–89). Amsterdam: John Benjamins.

García Mayo, M.P. and Pica, T. (2000) L2 learner interaction in a foreign language setting: Are learning needs addressed? *International Review of Applied Linguistics* 38 (1), 35–58.

Goh, C. (2008) Metacognitive instruction for second language listening development theory, practice and research implications. *RELC Journal* 39 (2), 188–213.

Goh, C. and Taib, Y. (2006) Metacognitive instruction in listening for young learners. *ELT Journal* 60 (3), 222–232.

Keselman, H., Huberty, C., Lix, L., Olejnik, S., Cribbie, R., Donahue, B., … Levine, J. (1998). Statistical practices of educational researchers: An analysis of their ANOVA, MANOVA, and ANCOVA analyses. *Review of Educational Research* 68 (3), 350–386.

Lambert, C. (2017) Tasks, affect and second language performance. *Language Teaching Research* 21 (6), 657–664.

Lambert, C., Philp, J. and Nakamura, S. (2017b) Learner-generated content and engagement in L2 task performance. *Language Teaching Research* 21 (6), 665–680.

Lantolf, J.P. and Poehner, M.E. (2011) Dynamic assessment in the classroom: Vygotskian praxis for second language development. *Language Teaching Research* 15 (1), 11–33.

Lightbown, P. (2000) Classroom SLA research and second language teaching. *Applied Linguistics* 21 (4), 431–462.

Loewen, S. and Sato, M. (2017) Instructed second language acquisition (ISLA): An overview. In S. Loewen and M. Sato (eds) *The Handbook of Instructed Second Language Acquisition* (pp. 1–12). New York, NY: Routledge.

Loewen, S. and Sato, M. (2018) State-of-the-arts article: Interaction and instructed second language acquisition. *Language Teaching* 51 (3), 285–329.

Lyster, R. and Sato, M. (2013) Skill acquisition theory and the role of practice in L2 development. In M.P. García Mayo, J. Gutierrez-Mangado and M. Martínez Adrián (eds) *Contemporary Approaches to Second Language Acquisition* (pp. 71–92). Amsterdam: John Benjamins.

Lyster, R., Saito, K. and Sato, M. (2013) State-of-the-art article: Oral corrective feedback in second language classrooms. *Language Teaching* 46 (1), 1–40.

McDonough, K. (2004) Learner-learner interaction during pair and small group activities in a Thai EFL context. *System* 32 (2), 207–224.

McDonough, K. and Mackey, A. (2000) Communicative tasks, conversational interaction, and linguistic form: An empirical study of Thai. *Foreign Language Annals* 33 (1), 82–91.

Nakatani, Y. (2005) The effects of awareness-raising instruction on oral communication strategy use. *The Modern Language Journal* 89 (1), 76–91.

Philp, J., Adams, R. and Iwashita, N. (2014) *Peer Interaction and Second Language Learning.* New York: Routledge.

Philp, J. and Duchesne, S. (2016) Exploring engagement in tasks in the language classroom. *Annual Review of Applied Linguistics* 36, 50–72.

Philp, J., Walter, S. and Basturkmen, H. (2010) Peer interaction in the foreign language classroom: What factors foster a focus on form? *Language Awareness* 19 (4), 261–279.

Pica, T., Lincoln-Porter, F., Paninos, D. and Linnell, J. (1996) Language learners' interaction: How does it address the input, output, and feedback needs of L2 learners? *TESOL Quarterly* 30 (1), 59–84.

Pintrich, P. (2000) The role of goal orientation in self-regulated learning. In M. Boekaerts, P. Pintrich and M. Zeidner (eds) *Handbook of Self-Regulation* (pp. 451–502). Cambridge, MA: Academic Press.

Rahimi, M. and Katal, M. (2012) Metacognitive listening strategies awareness in learning English as a foreign language: A comparison between university and high-school students. *Procedia-Social and Behavioral Sciences* 31, 82–89.

Sato, M. (2013) Beliefs about peer interaction and peer corrective feedback: Efficacy of classroom intervention. *The Modern Language Journal* 97 (3), 611–633.

Sato, M. (2017) Interaction mindsets, interactional behaviors, and L2 development: An affective-social-cognitive model. *Language Learning* 67 (2), 249–283.

Sato, M. and Ballinger, S. (2012) Raising language awareness in peer interaction: A cross-context, cross-method examination. *Language Awareness* 21 (1–2), 157–179.

Sato, M. and Ballinger, S. (2016) Understanding peer interaction: Research synthesis and directions. In M. Sato and S. Ballinger (eds) *Peer Interaction and Second Language Learning: Pedagogical Potential and Research Agenda* (pp. 1–30). Amsterdam: John Benjamins.

Sato, M. and Loewen, S. (2018) Metacognitive instruction enhances the effectiveness of corrective feedback: Variable effects of feedback types and linguistic targets. *Language Learning* 68 (2), 507–545.

Sato, M. and Loewen, S. (eds) (2019) *Evidence-Based Second Language Pedagogy: A Collection of Instructed Second Language Acquisition Studies.* New York, NY: Routledge.

Sato, M. and Lyster, R. (2007) Modified output of Japanese EFL learners: Variable effects of interlocutor vs. feedback types. In A. Mackey (ed.) *Conversational Interaction in Second Language Acquisition: A Collection of Empirical Studies* (pp. 123–142). Oxford: Oxford University Press.

Sato, M. and Lyster, R. (2012) Peer interaction and corrective feedback for accuracy and fluency development: Monitoring, practice, and proceduralization. *Studies in Second Language Acquisition* 34 (4), 591–262.

Shehadeh, A. (2001) Self- and other-initiated modified output during task-based interaction. *TESOL Quarterly* 35 (3), 433–457.

Storch, N. (2002) Patterns of interaction in ESL pair work. *Language Learning* 52 (1), 119–158.

Storch, N. and Sato, M. (2019) Comparing the same task in different L2 learning contexts: An Activity Theory perspective. *International Journal of Applied Linguistics.* doi:10.1111/ijal.12263.

Swain, M. (1985) Communicative competence: Some roles of comprehensible input and comprehensible output in its development. In S. Gass and C. Madden (eds) *Input in Second Language Acquisition* (pp. 235–253). Rowley, MA: Newbury House.

Swain, M., Brooks, L. and Tocalli-Beller, A. (2002) Peer-peer dialogue as a means of second language learning. *Annual Review of Applied Linguistics* 22, 171–185.

Trofimovich, P. and Isaacs, T. (2012) Disentangling accent from comprehensibility. *Bilingualism: Language and Cognition* 15 (4), 905–916.

Vandergrift, L. and Baker, S. (2015) Learner variables in second language listening comprehension: An exploratory path analysis. *Language Learning* 65 (2), 390–416.

Vandergrift, L. and Tafaghodtari, M.H. (2010) Teaching L2 learners how to listen does make a difference: An empirical study. *Language Learning* 60 (2), 470–497.

Veenman, M.V. (2011) Learning to self-monitor and self-regulate. In R. Mayer and P. Alexander (eds) *Handbook of Research on Learning and Instruction* (pp. 197–218). New York: Routledge.

Wang, M.C., Haertel, G.D. and Walberg, H.J. (1990) What influences learning? A content analysis of review literature. *The Journal of Educational Research* 84 (1), 30–43.

Wenden, A.L. (1987) Metacognition: An expanded view on the cognitive abilities of L2 learners. *Language Learning* 37 (4), 573–597.

Yoshida, R. (2013) Conflict between learners' beliefs and actions: speaking in the classroom. *Language Awareness* 22 (4), 371–388.

14 Collaborative L1 Planning and L2 Written Task Performance in an Iranian EFL Context

Mohammad Javad Ahmadian
and Abbas Mansouri

This chapter examines how first language (L1) use in language classes in Iran relates to cognitive and affective engagement in second language (L2) use. Three groups of learners were observed over two class sessions. In the first, the teacher and learners used the L1 as they saw fit. In the second, they avoided using the L1. Effects on multiple measures of language use are examined, and implications for implementing tasks are discussed.

Introduction

Tasks can be used in diverse language teaching contexts and for various purposes. They can also be implemented in different ways depending on the purposes for which they are designed and used. One of the implementation conditions which has attracted researchers' attention in recent years is the provision of planning time for task performance. Planning time can be provided either before performing a task (pre-task planning) or while doing it (online planning). Previous research on task-based planning shows that providing learners with planning time either prior to or while performing a task can improve their (oral/written) performance in terms of complexity, accuracy, fluency and lexis (see Ellis, 2005; Skehan, 2014, 2016). Although several studies have also examined how learners actually use the pre-task/online planning opportunity (e.g. Ahmadian & Tavakoli, 2014; Ortega, 2005), there is scope for further research to see how learners can be guided in using the planning time at their disposal (see Skehan, 2018; Mochizuki & Ortega, 2008; Ahmadian, 2012). One possible way in which learners can make use of the pre-task planning time is to use their L1 and engage in collaborative pre-task planning. In collaborative pre-task planning, two or more learners work together to brainstorm, organize their thoughts and ideas and plan their texts for the writing task at hand. An interesting question, therefore, is whether teachers should allow and encourage learners to use their L1 for pre-task planning or not and, if they decide to do so, what might be the effects of this. Although there is research evidence pointing to the benefits of using L1 on L2 writing (Friedlander, 1990; Lally, 2000), as of writing this chapter, there is a dearth of published research investigating whether and how using L1 during pre-task planning can impact learners' writing by making better use of pre-task planning opportunities.

In many EFL contexts, such as Iran, low- and even mid-proficiency learners normally lack the required skills to 'initiate' writing in an L2 – i.e. they simply do not know how to start writing and consequently might find writing tasks rather mundane and unsatisfactory.

Therefore, another practical and theoretically motivated question is whether asking learners to use their L1 for collaborative pre-task planning enhances their engagement with the writing task and with the pre-task planning opportunity. The study reported in this chapter aimed to probe: (a) whether and how using L1 in collaborative pre-task planning can improve learners' complexity and accuracy in L2 writing tasks, and (b) the extent to which using L1 for collaborative pre-task planning enhances learners' engagement with the writing tasks. In the next section, we will review the literature on task-based planning, the effects of using L1 on L2 writing and learner engagement with tasks.

Background

Planning and L2 written task performance

From a cognitive SLA perspective, planning is seen as a strategy to compensate for the performance deficiencies which might stem from limited attentional capacity (Engle, 2002; Skehan, 1998). One such deficiency is that task performers cannot simultaneously focus on various dimensions of L2 performance (Skehan, 1998, 2018). Planning (with a focus on form and/or meaning) is assumed to reduce the cognitive load that performing a task imposes on learners' attentional resources (Skehan, 1998, 2014). This would, in turn, enable them to become more efficient in drawing on their linguistic repertoires, retrieving chunks, self-monitoring their performance and engaging in self-correction, if need be. As evidenced in the literature, these operations could lead to enhanced performance in terms of complexity, accuracy, fluency and lexis to varying degrees (see Ellis, 2005; Skehan, 2014, 2018). In this way, planning may be indispensable to the quality of L2 speaking and writing. What makes planning even more critical for writing is that a text 'must stand on its own' and 'unlike spoken discourse, there is no dialogue between the author and reader to gradually shape a shared understanding' (Kellogg *et al.*, 2013: 160).

In order to better understand and explain the effects of planning on written task performance, it is necessary to briefly discuss the cognitive processes involved in writing. Kellogg's (1996) oft-cited model of working memory in writing is particularly useful for our purpose. Kellogg's model differentiates three processing components for text production: formulation, execution and monitoring. In the *formulation* stage, ideas are conceived, planned and then translated into sentences. In the *execution* stage, the output of the formulation stage is 'programmed for use by the appropriate motor system in handwriting, typing, or dictating' (Kellogg, 1996: 60). The third stage, *monitoring*, involves reading and editing words, sentences and global discourse (Kellogg, 1996: 61). One of the most intriguing aspects of Kellogg's model which makes it relevant to this study is the assumption that the three stages of writing are closely related to the three components of the Working Memory (WM) System which is essentially a limited capacity cognitive mechanism responsible for temporary *storage* and *manipulation* of information (Baddeley, 2003). Kellogg (1996: 59) proposes that all three stages of text production could be activated simultaneously 'as long as the demands placed on the central executive do not exceed capacity limitations' of WM. When it comes to L2 writing, the cognitive demands on the central executive component of WM might increase because of L2 learners' relatively less sophisticated lexicon (Skehan, 2009) and slower retrieval processes. Previous studies have demonstrated that providing learners with pre-task planning time could help learners in the formulation stage of L2 writing.

For example, Ellis and Yuan (2004) asked participants to write at least 200 words in 17 minutes. They operationalised pre-task planning in terms of allowing participants to plan their texts for 10 minutes. Results of their study revealed little effects on accuracy, but significant increases in syntactic complexity and variety. They concluded that pre-task planning promotes formulation stage of L2 writing. Lin (2013) replicated this result and found that pre-task planning could lead to higher lexical complexity scores. However, in none of these studies were participants provided with instructions as to how to use pre-task planning opportunities. Guided pre-task planning was investigated in Mochizuki and Ortega (2008), but their study focused on speech production rather than written text production.

Mochizuki and Ortega (2008) designed a study to explore the effects of guiding low-proficiency learners, through a grammar handout, to attend to English relative clauses during planning prior to an oral communication task. Also, they attempted to see what effect would accrue from both guided and unguided pre-task planning where global complexity and fluency were concerned. They found that guided planning promoted better productive use of relativization in English and that when guided planning is focused it may affect accuracy. They also found that neither fluency nor complexity was affected by either planning conditions to any statistically significant degree.

There are several ways in which learners can be guided to use a pre-task planning opportunity and, as Skehan (2018: 201) points out 'teachers have more effective ideas as to what is worth planning, how planning should be conducted and probably, though there is no direct evidence on this, on how a connection can be made between what happens during the planning period and what happens during performance itself'. For example, there is research evidence suggesting that using L1 can be an extremely useful resource for conducting lexical searches and for use in the editing processes (Zimmerman, 2000, cited in Ellis & Yuan, 2004). Therefore, it is hypothesized that requiring learners to use their L1 for collaborative pre-task planning might affect their L2 writing in terms of accuracy, complexity and overall text quality.

Using L1 for L2 writing

In sociocultural approaches to SLA, L1 is construed as 'an indispensable semiotic device that mediates the learning process' (DiCamilla & Antón, 2012: 161). Antón and DiCamilla (1998) found that L1 could serve various social and cognitive functions in collaborative interactions. In particular, they found that beginning-level learners draw on their L1 to access L2 linguistic features (e.g. vocabulary items and grammatical structures). Several studies have looked into the beneficial effects of using L1 on L2 writing stages and processes. Kobayashi and Rinnert (1992) found that lower-level learners start the task of L2 writing by writing in their L1 and then translating into their L2. Lally's (2000) study, which is particularly relevant to the current research, investigated whether L1 or L2 was the best code for pre-writing activities. Participants were divided into two groups (i.e. the L1 and the L2 groups). They were asked to discuss a culturally neutral photo (in their L1 or L2) and then to write a piece about it in their L2. Essays were analysed in terms of vocabulary, expression, organization of ideas and overall impression. Lally did not find any difference between the two groups in terms of vocabulary and expression. However, there were notable differences in terms of organization and global impression (i.e. incomprehensible, acceptable, excellent). Although the sample used in this study was too small and, therefore, lacked sufficient statistical power, the findings support the notion that L1 is a useful resource especially in the formulation stage of L2 writing. More recently, Zhang (2018) investigated the differential effects of using the L1 and the L2 for interaction on complexity, accuracy, fluency and quality of co-constructed texts. However, Zhang's study cannot be considered as a pre-task planning study as all participants were allowed to spend one hour on completing the writing task and this time included collaboration in both the L1 and L2 as well as co-production of the text in the L2. Results showed that using the L1 enhanced syntactic complexity, but had no significant effect on accuracy, fluency and text quality. An important question is thus whether encouraging learners to use their L1 for pre-task planning would enhance their engagement with the writing task.

Engagement with tasks

Task engagement is defined as 'a state of heightened attention and involvement' while doing a task (Philp & Duchesne, 2016: 51). Engagement is a multifaceted and complex construct which could be construed as entailing cognitive, affective/emotional and social/behavioural dimensions (Svalberg, 2009). Reschly and Christenson (2012) argue that cognitive and affective engagement mediate behavioural and social engagement and, therefore, engaging learners cognitively and affectively precedes any kind of behavioural activity. Differentiating and defining different types of engagement is a difficult undertaking as cognitive, affective and social engagement are quite intertwined and interconnected. However, they might be characterized as follows:

- Cognitive engagement is 'rooted in personal investment, self-regulation, and striving for mastery' (Reschly & Christenson, 2012: 10–11).
- Behavioural/social engagement comprises 'participation in academic, social, or extracurricular activities' (Reschly & Christenson, 2012: 10–11). In other words, 'being "on-task" is synonymous with behavioural engagement' (Philp & Duchesne, 2016: 55).
- Philp and Duchesne (2016: 56) identify 'enthusiasm, interest, and enjoyment as key indicators of emotional engagement, and at the other end of the scale, anxiety, frustration, and boredom as indicators of negative emotional engagement'.

Svalberg (2009: 274) has expanded the definition of each of the sub-constructs of learner engagement. For Svalberg, a learner who is cognitively engaged 'is alert, pays focused attention and constructs her own knowledge'. An affectively/emotionally engaged learner 'has a positive, purposeful, willing, and autonomous disposition towards the object (language, the language and/or what it represents)'. Finally, a socially engaged language learner 'is interactive and initiating'. Philp and Duchesne (2009) suggest that engaged learners 'expend focused energy and attention, and they are emotionally involved'. In the context of task-based planning and L2 writing, therefore, engaged learners will be expected to, *inter alia*, use the planning time at their disposal to interact with their peers, focus on text organization and quality and not get bored with the writing task or planning opportunity – i.e. stay focused throughout task performance.

As described earlier in the chapter, low-proficiency language learners might find the task of writing rather difficult and frustrating. Given the benefits of using L1 for L2 writing, as evidenced in the literature, it is hypothesized that teachers could improve learners' engagement with a writing task/pre-task planning opportunity, if they permit and encourage learners to use their native language for collaborative pre-task planning.

In light of the issues discussed above, the current study addresses two questions:

(1) To what extent does collaborative pre-task planning in L1 affect complexity, accuracy and text quality of L2 learners' written performances?
(2) In what ways does collaborative pre-task planning in L1 enhance learners' engagement with the writing task?

Methodology

Participants and context

This study was conducted in an Iranian private language centre (in Isfahan) where the language program duration is ten terms (each consisting of eight weeks with three 1.5-hour sessions per week). Although there is flexibility in their approach to teaching, teachers tend to adopt a communicative approach but are obliged to use a combination of three main textbooks (the *Top Notch*, *Summit* and *Speak Now* series) depending on the learners' level of proficiency. The study reported in this chapter was conducted with participants from five different classes. The second author taught all classes. The language learners' ($n = 114$; 40 males and 74 females) ages ranged from between 20 and 24 years old, and they had been learning English for 10–12 months for communicative purposes. Their proficiency level was fairly homogeneous (intermediate to upper-intermediate) as they had all started the program at roughly the same time. They shared Persian as their L1 and did not report knowledge of any other language. All the language learners were either BA/BS or MA/MS students in various fields of study and they were highly motivated to learn English and ultimately pass either TOEFL or IELTS examinations to pursue their academic aspirations abroad. Both language learners and teachers signed informed consent forms. For reasons of anonymity, learners (students) are labelled S1, S2, S3, etc. in this study.

Before describing the procedure of the study, it is important to delineate how tasks are used in Iran. To the best of our knowledge, as of writing this chapter, there is no published nation-wide empirical study looking into the implementation of task-based language teaching in Iran. Therefore, our description here is based on our informal observations and our teaching experience in that context. English language teaching has never been given serious consideration in Iranian schools or in higher education institutions (see Farhady & Hedayati, 2009). In the absence of a serious and systematic curriculum aimed at enhancing communicative abilities, private language centres have been playing an important role in English language teaching enterprise. Currently, most language centres and teachers (if not all of them) adopt various commercial coursebooks. It could be argued, therefore, that the prevalence of using tasks in Iran is a function of the extent to which selected coursebooks contain communicative tasks. For example, the language centre in which this study was conducted uses *Top Notch* as the coursebook. In *Top Notch*, there are various activities which could meet the criteria of a task, depending on how they are implemented by teachers. That is, they are meaning-focused, outcome-oriented and induce learners to draw on their own linguistic and non-linguistic resources (Ellis & Shintani, 2014). Yet, in almost all language lessons, tasks are used to merely consolidate and internalize the linguistic features that have been taught at the beginning of the lesson. In other words, tasks are not normally considered as the central units of teaching and assessment. In recent years, though, there has been a tendency for language teachers to adapt non-communicative materials and render them relevant to what language learners are likely to encounter outside the classroom. This indicates a growing awareness amongst some language teachers, especially those with a University degree in TEFL/TESOL/Applied Linguistics, that using meaning-centred tasks are key to successful language teaching and learning.

Procedure

Participants were assigned to three groups: pre-task planning in L1 (PTPL1) ($n = 38$; 19 pairs); pre-task planning in L2 (PTPL2) ($n = 38$, 19 pairs); no planning (Control) ($n = 38$; 19 pairs). In all groups, they were paired together and required to perform a dictogloss task for a period of 20 minutes. The term dictogloss was first used by Wajnryb (1990). Dictogloss involves selecting a short text and reading it at normal pace while language learners jot down content words. Then, learners are asked to collaborate and reconstruct the text. Dictogloss is considered as a meaning-focused task as it requires learners to 'process the whole text at once' and to 'capture the meaning of the text although they may not be able to recall the exact forms in which that meaning is conveyed' (Thornbury, 1999: 86). The dictogloss task (adapted from Thornbury, 1999) and pre-task planning were carried out collaboratively. Dictogloss tasks have been widely used in SLA research and are useful for drawing learners' attention to form in the context of a meaningful activity (García Mayo, 2018). We followed the normal procedure (described below) which is recommended for dictogloss activities, but because this research was conducted in actual classrooms, the dictogloss was preceded with a warm-up activity. The teacher (second author) asked participants to think about and discuss in pairs 'whether people usually work or go on holiday in the summer'. Then he asked them to share their ideas with other students in the class.

After this warm-up activity, the dictogloss was implemented: first, students listened to a short passage at a normal speed, but were not allowed to write anything down. Then, the teacher read the passage to them out loud but asked them to put down some of the key words that they thought were important. Finally, participants were asked 'to reconstruct the original text' collaboratively and 'as faithfully as possible' (García Mayo, 2018: 10). In keeping with previous pre-task planning studies (Crookes, 1989; Ellis & Yuan, 2004; Foster & Skehan, 1996; Wendel, 1997), 10 minutes were allowed for pre-task planning. Therefore, in the first group (PTPL1), participants were asked to spend 10 minutes planning what they wanted to write. However, they were instructed to use their L1 for collaborative pre-task planning. The teacher monitored their planning to make sure that they were using their L1 (Persian) only. Then, they were given 20 minutes to collaboratively write their essays in English. In the second group (PTPL2), the same amount of pre-task planning and writing time was used, but participants were instructed to use their L2 (English) only. In this group, too, the teacher closely monitored participants' performance to ensure that they were using their L2 for pre-task planning. In the control group, participants were required to start writing without any pre-task planning opportunity.

Immediately after completing the task, five volunteer participants from each group were invited to another room for a semi-structured interview. In the interview participants were asked about whether they found the task interesting, whether they thought the pre-task planning opportunity was useful, whether they thought using their L1 helped them better address the task requirements, whether collaborating for pre-task planning and writing was useful and motivating and whether they were distracted during pre-task planning and/or writing. Interviews were conducted in the participants' L1 to make sure that they were able to answer the questions without any language-related problems. All interviews were then transcribed, and relevant extracts were translated into English for thematic analysis. Identified themes were double checked by the first author. In the process of identifying themes, we used a deductive approach. A deductive approach is guided by predetermined concepts, constructs and themes and provides 'a more detailed analysis of some aspect of the data' (Braun & Clarke 2006: 84). We used this approach as we were interested in exploring whether or not our participants' behavioural and cognitive engagement with the writing task enhanced as a result of using their L1. As will be further discussed in the results section, we adapted Svalberg's (2009: 245–6) categorization of different components of engagement for our deductive qualitative analysis as follows:

a. *Cognitive engagement*
    - cognitive alertness with regard to using L1 for pre-task planning; and
    - focused attention on producing accurate and complex language as well as completing the task.
b. *Affective engagement*
    - positive attitude towards dictogloss task, using L1 for pre-task planning and not getting bored or frustrated with the writing task;
    - purposefulness (i.e. knowing the purpose pre-task planning in L1); and
    - willingness to collaborate in both planning and co-construction stages.
c. *Social engagement*
    - Preparedness to interact with peers;
    - Initiating and maintaining interaction.

This categorization guided our qualitative analysis.

Analysis

The co-constructed written texts were analysed in terms of accuracy, complexity and text quality. In the SLA literature, complexity, accuracy, fluency and lexis are commonly used to assess learners' performance (Housen & Kuiken, 2009) and most of the task-based planning studies conducted so far have utilised these constructs as dependent variables. At the heart of this trend is the notion that L2 development and performance are not unitary constructs, but rather are multidimensional and, therefore, in order to capture various facets of L2 performance it is essential to adopt a multidimensional perspective (Housen *et al.*, 2012). In the current study, however, we have only focused on complexity and accuracy because, in the context in which this study was conducted, fluency in writing is not a relevant construct. That is, leaners are not encouraged to write quickly – to the contrary, they are often asked to write as carefully as possible and spend as much time as they have available editing and revising. In keeping with the task-based literature, in this study, accuracy was defined as the extent to which an L2 learners' performance conforms to 'the native speaker' norms (Pallotti, 2009; Housen *et al.*, 2012). Complexity was defined as '[t]he extent to which the language produced in performing a task is elaborate and varied' (Ellis, 2003: 340). Linguistic complexity 'refers to the intrinsic formal or semantic-functional properties of L2 elements (e.g. forms, meanings, form-meaning mappings) or to properties of (sub-) systems of L2 elements' (Housen *et al.*, 2012: 4). In addition to accuracy and complexity, we also considered text quality. We adopted Storch's (2005: 172) rubric for text quality. Text quality scores could range between 1 and 5. All texts were scored by both researchers and the average score was taken as the final score for text quality. If there were any disagreements about the scores, they were discussed to reach consensus. 95% of scores were in complete agreement. For accuracy and complexity, following Ellis and Yuan (2004), we assessed learners' performance using the following measures:

Accuracy:
a. Error-free clauses: we calculated the percentage of clauses that did not contain any linguistic error. In order to code errors, we drew on Storch's (2005: 174) guidelines.
b. Correct verb forms: we calculated the percentage of accuracy in the use of tense, modality and subject-verb agreement.

Complexity:
a. Syntactic complexity: we calculated the ratio of clauses to T-units in the co-constructed texts.
b. Syntactic variety: we calculated the number of different grammatical verb forms, focusing on tense, modality and voice.

The second author did all the analyses and calculations and the first author checked 20% of the data analyses for accuracy and consistency. This process yielded 98% agreement.

Results

In this section, we will report the results of both quantitative and qualitative analyses. RQ1 aimed to investigate the extent to which collaborative pre-task planning in L1 affects complexity, accuracy and text quality of L2 learners' written performances. To answer this question, measures of complexity, accuracy and text quality were compared across the three groups. Given the fairly large number of dependent variables, a MANOVA followed by univariate and *post hoc* analyses were employed to address the first research question.

Results of the MANOVA reveal that Wilk's Lambda is statistically significant (F = 11.56; $p = 0.000$, $n = 19$ pairs per group, partial eta square = 0.53). This could protect our analyses against the possibility of committing Type I error as a result of preforming multiple comparisons. Descriptive statistics in Table 14.1 show that there are group differences in terms of both accuracy and complexity measures.

Table 14.1 Descriptive and inferential statistics

Variables	M (SD) for planning conditions			ANOVA			Location of significance [95% confidence interval]		
	PTPL1	PTPL2	NP	F	P	Partial eta Square	PTPL1-PTPL2	PTPL1-NP	PTPL2-NP
Error-free clauses	0.64 (.04)	0.63 (.02)	0.57 (.03)	18.90	0.000	0.41	.97 [-0.027, 0.033]	.000 [0.035, 0.096]	.000 [0.032, 0.093]
Correct verb forms	0.65 (.03)	0.66 (.02)	0.62 (.02)	7.92	0.001	0.22	0.82 [-0.029, 0.017]	0.012 [0.005, 0.052]	0.002 [0.011, 0.058]
Syntactic complexity	1.45 (0.15)	1.35 (0.12)	1.14 (0.09)	29.88	0.000	0.52	0.048 [.0009, 0.2085]	0.000 [0.209, 0.417]	0.000 [0.104, 0.312]
Syntactic variety	13.26 (0.92)	13.25 (0.78)	11.64 (0.48)	29.39	0.000	0.52	0.999 [-0.601, 0.627]	0.000 [1.00, 2.24]	0.000 [-2.229, -1.000]
Text quality	3.02 (0.87)	2.94 (0.81)	2.65 (0.70)	1.11	0.33	0.04	0.95 [-0.575, 0.733]	0.373 [-0.286, 1.02]	0.54 [-0.944, 0.356]

In addition, Table 14.1 reveals that most notable mean differences are between planning conditions, on the one hand, and the no planning (NP) condition, on the other. The difference among the three groups in terms of text quality is negligible. This observation is further confirmed by the results of one-way ANOVA: whilst group differences in terms of accuracy and complexity measures are statistically significant with fairly large effect sizes, there is no statistically significant difference in terms of text quality. However, caution should be exercised in interpreting the lack of statistically significant differences. Given the rather small sample size, the observed power for text quality was small (0.20) which potentially increases the risk of Type II error (i.e. not detecting a significant difference where there is one).

We now provide a more nuanced description of how the three groups varied in terms of complexity, accuracy and text quality. Results of Tukey *post hoc* analyses reported in Table 14.1 show that, as far as accuracy measures are concerned, there is no statistically significant difference between planning conditions, but both groups have outperformed the control group. With regard to the complexity measures, results are less straightforward. For syntactic complexity, learners who used the L1 in pre-task planning outperformed those who used the L2. In addition, both planning conditions have gained higher syntactic complexity scores compared to the no planning condition. For syntactic variety, employing L1 or L2 did not made any statistically significant difference, but here again both groups have outperformed the control group. As stated above, results did not yield any statistically significant difference among the three groups in terms of text quality. However, a closer examination of descriptive statistics reveals that using the L1 for pre-task planning has resulted in slightly higher quality texts compared to using the L2 or no planning at all. Also, compared to no planning, using the L2 for pre-task planning has resulted in higher scores in terms of text quality.

In summary, the results of the quantitative analyses indicate that, other than higher gains in terms of syntactic complexity, using the L1 or the L2 for pre-task planning did not make any notable difference in learners' L2 written performance as measured by accuracy, syntactic complexity and text quality. These findings are illuminated in the qualitative part of the study.

As explained in the methodology section, the qualitative analyses we conducted involved a deductive thematic analysis. Here, we tried to match participants' responses to the descriptors of cognitive, affective and social engagement that Svalberg (2009: 247) proposed. As illustrated in Table 14.2, we found evidence indicating that using the L1 helped participants to be engaged with the writing task socially, behaviourally and cognitively. Specifically, our qualitative analyses revealed that using L1 helped learners stay focused on the writing task,

Table 14.2 Descriptors of engagement (based on Svalberg, 2009) and relevant extracts from our dataset

Type of engagement	Descriptors	Extracts form participants' responses
Cognitive engagement	Does the learner feel energetic?	'I felt being able to use the L1 helped me to organize my thoughts and be more active' (S1) 'Sometimes talking to peers in the L2 does not help at all as there are misunderstandings which we cannot resolve in L2 … talking in the L1 helped me feel more focused on the task' (S5)
	Does the learner notice language/interaction features?	'If I did not know a word, I could ask my partner in Farsi and we could work together to find the right word' (S6) 'We used Farsi to look for suitable words … we thought about the tense of the sentences and tried to translate ideas to English to' (S9)
	Does the learner's mind wander? Is the learner's attention on language?	'Farsi helped us to stay focused … it is difficult to collaborate in English for a writing task' (S7)
	Does the learner notice and reflect or simply react?	'I concentrated on writing … using Farsi was helpful as we were both confident enough to express our thoughts' (S3)
Affective engagement	Is the learner withdrawn or eager to participate?	'We were chatting in Farsi all 10 minutes … we did not lose a minute' (S10) 'this was the first time we were encouraged to use Farsi, so I found it very interesting as it helped us to structure our 10-minute planning time more efficiently' (S11)
	Does the learner seem to be goal oriented or just coasting along?	'I thought using Farsi before writing helped us prepare for the main writing task' (S9) '… we have always been asked to use L2 in the classroom, but sometimes it is impossible to learn English without using the L1 … if you cannot express what you do not know, you cannot learn the English equivalent' (S6)
	How autonomous is the learner's behavior? Is the learner dependent on another or independent?	'we shared the responsibilities, I thought answered questions about vocabulary, and my partner thought about the organization of the text' (S12)
Social engagement	Does learner use interaction for learning?	'… we were talking in Farsi about words, grammar, and text organization' (S7)
	Do learners engage in negotiation and scaffolding?	'… sometimes I did not know a word but my partner knew it and vice versa…' (S3)
	Are learner's interactions reactive or initiating?	'using L1 helped me to start asking questions … because you know sometimes you cannot ask your questions in L2 and this will keep you silent throughout the interaction' (S4)

play a proactive (rather than reactive) role in interactions for pre-task planning, scaffold each other during pre-task planning opportunity and express their thoughts more efficiently and clearly. Therefore, one could argue that although using the L1 and L2 for pre-task planning do not make huge differences in terms of complexity, accuracy and text quality, using the L1 has the potential to keep learners engaged with writing tasks which could otherwise be viewed as mundane or frustrating.

Discussion and Conclusions

The study reported in this chapter aimed to investigate whether instructing learners to use the L1 for collaborative pre-task planning would enhance the complexity, accuracy and overall quality of their texts. It also aimed to investigate whether using the L1 would enhance language learners' cognitive, emotional and social engagement with the writing task. Results of quantitative and qualitative analyses revealed that: (a) overall, pre-task planning (be it in the L1 or the L2) leads to higher gains in complexity and accuracy, but not text quality; (b) using the L1 for pre-task planning keeps learners focused on the task and leads to enhanced cognitive, emotional and social engagement with the writing task.

The finding that the provision of pre-task planning leads to increased complexity and accuracy scores is in alignment with Ellis and Yuan's (2004) results. However, unlike Ellis and Yuan's findings which showed small gains for accuracy, and despite Lin's (2013) results which demonstrated gains only in lexical complexity scores, in this study we found strong effects on all four accuracy and complexity measures. This could very well be due to the nature of the writing task that we utilized. Whereas in Ellis and Yuan (2004) and Lin (2013) a narrative task was used, in the current study a dictogloss task was employed. Essentially, a dictogloss task draws learners' attention to form (García Mayo, 2018). The brief notes that the students made while listening to the teacher were then used in the formulation and monitoring stages of writing where the learners translated conceptual ideas to linguistic forms and then edited and revised them (Kellogg, 1996). All this appeared to result in more accurate language in the current study.

Yet, using the L1 or the L2 did not differentially affect accuracy measures, syntactic variety or text quality. The only statistically significant difference found between the L1 and L2 groups was in terms of syntactic complexity. This finding corroborates Zhang's (2018) results. However, it should be noted that Zhang's study did not focus on pre-task planning as a variable and looked into the benefits of L1 for collaborative writing. This finding could also support the notion that using L1 during the planning stage of writing 'serves to assist and benefit information retrieval' (Friedlander, 1990: 118). Functional complexity has been shown to be associated with linguistic complexity (Givón, 1995). Therefore, it could be argued that learners who used the L1 for pre-task planning were able to retrieve and organize ideas and concepts more efficiently and, as a result, produced more complex language. This is in line with the arguments proposed by Cook (2001) and Macaro (2005) in favour of using the L1 in the L2 classroom. They argue that using the L1 'serves as a rapid and easy way of conveying the meaning of the L2 words and sentences' (cited in Ellis & Shintani, 2014: 234).

There is an important caveat which concerns the measurement of complexity and accuracy. As stated in the methodology section, complexity and accuracy are multi-layered and multi-faceted constructs (Housen *et al.*, 2012). Therefore, in order to fully capture these constructs, we need to use distinct, but complementary measures (Norris & Ortega, 2009). In the current study, however, we have used only two measures for each of these constructs. This might explain why we did not detect any statistically significant difference as far as the use of the L1 and the L2 were concerned. This, however, does suggest that these measures may not be useful because they do not tap sufficiently into complexity and accuracy – this is what Pallotti (2009) refers to as 'the necessary variation fallacy'. This suggests that future research should use more measures of complexity and accuracy (or text quality) to address other dimensions of these constructs.

The finding that using learners' L1 may enhance learner engagement with the dictogloss task is perhaps the most interesting aspect of the current study. Learner engagement with a task could be conceived of as 'the glue, or mediator' (Reschly & Christenson, 2012: 3) that links task, learner, interlocutors and teacher. In our experience, L2 writing tasks can prove rather mundane and disappointing for Iranian intermediate language learners. Our qualitative analyses revealed that using the L1 is a way to enhance the quality and purposefulness of interactions during pre-task planning. It also appeared to assist the learners to work collaboratively and jot down relevant ideas, vocabulary items and grammatical constructions. Cook (2001) and Macaro (2005), as summarized in Ellis and Shintani (2014: 234–235), argue that using the L1 helps reduce 'the anxiety that learners might experience when trying to comprehend L2 input [...]'. Similarly, learners will feel less anxious if they can sometimes use their L1. Our qualitative analyses indicated that using the L1 helped learners feel more comfortable collaborating with each other during pre-task planning opportunity.

Therefore, the findings of this study provide further empirical support for the benefits of pre-task planning. By adopting a more nuanced perspective on the ways in which L1 or L2 are used during pre-task planning and how these can differentially affect L2 performance, further light may be shed on this issue. For example, more sensitive measures of complexity, accuracy and text quality could be used. In addition, it will be interesting to see the ways in which learners of different proficiency levels could benefit from using their L1 in pre-task planning stage.

Finally, tasks are not systematically used in Iran which is mainly because a nation-wide communicative curriculum is yet to be implemented in Iranian schools and universities. However, the vast majority of language learners are keen to learn English not just to pass high-stake tests such as IELTS or TOEFL but, perhaps more importantly, to be able to communicate in English for education, business and immigration purposes. This provides justification for adopting measures which would promote and facilitate the use of tasks by language teachers. First and foremost, language teacher can use the findings of task-based literature (including those presented here) to raise teachers' awareness of the various ways in which tasks can be implemented based on the needs and goals of language learners. For example, a common misconception about a task-supported classroom is that using the L1 should be prohibited and learners must be required to communicate in the L2 only. Results of this study, however, show that learners tend to be more engaged with pre-task planning before a dictogloss task, if they are allowed to use 'all of their linguistic resources' for task performance (i.e. both, the L1 and the L2). At an administrative level, language teachers should be allowed to make the necessary adjustments to their teaching approaches and materials rather than obligate them to strictly adhere to the syllabus that the language centre has specified for them. Therefore, at different levels of implementation, we need to initiate a dialogue among teachers, teacher educators and administers to allow for a greater level of flexibility. This dialogue would come to fruition if teachers have their own 'voice and authority' in decision making (Kumaravadivelu, 2006). After all, it is teachers who 'bring TBLT to life' (Van den Branden, 2016: 179).

References

Ahmadian, M.J. (2012) The effects of guided careful online planning on complexity, accuracy and fluency in intermediate EFL learners' oral production: The case of English articles. *Language Teaching Research* 16 (1), 129–149.

Ahmadian, M.J. and Tavakoli, M. (2014) Investigating what second language learners do and monitor under careful online planning conditions. *Canadian Modern Language Review* 70 (1), 50–75.

Antón, M. and DiCamilla, F. (1998) Socio-cognitive functions of L1 collaborative interaction in the L2 classroom. *Canadian Modern Language Review* 54 (3), 314–342.

Baddeley, A. (2003) Working memory and language: An overview. *Journal of Communication Disorders* 36 (3), 189–208.

Braun, V. and Clarke, V. (2006) Using thematic analysis in psychology. *Qualitative Research in Psychology* 3 (2), 77–101.

Cook, V. (2001) Using the first language in the classroom. *Canadian Modern Language Review* 57 (3), 402–423.

Crookes, G. (1989) Planning and interlanguage variation. *Studies in Second Language Acquisition* 11 (4), 367–383.

DiCamilla, F.J. and Antón, M. (2012) Functions of L1 in the collaborative interaction of beginning and advanced second language learners. *International Journal of Applied Linguistics* 22 (2), 160–188.

Ellis, R. (2003) *Task-based Language Learning and Teaching*. Oxford: Oxford University Press.

Ellis, R. (2005) *Planning and Task Performance in a Second Language*. Amsterdam: John Benjamins Publishing.

Ellis, R. and Shintani, N. (2014) *Exploring Language Pedagogy through Second Language Acquisition Research*. Abingdon: Routledge.

Ellis, R. and Yuan, F. (2004) The effects of planning on fluency, complexity, and accuracy in second language narrative writing. *Studies in Second Language Acquisition* 26 (1), 59–84.

Engle, R.W. (2002) Working memory capacity as executive attention. *Current Directions in Psychological Science* 11 (1), 19–23.

Farhady, H. and Hedayati, H. (2009) Language assessment policy in Iran. *Annual Review of Applied Linguistics* 29, 132–141.

Foster, P. and Skehan, P. (1996) The influence of planning and task type on second language performance. *Studies in Second Language Acquisition* 18 (3), 299–323.

Friedlander, A. (1990) Composing in English: Effects of a first language on writing in English as a second language. In B. Kroll (ed.) *Second Language Writing: Research Insights for the Classroom* (pp. 109–125). Cambridge: Cambridge University Press.

García Mayo, M.P. (2018) Dictogloss technique. In *The TESOL Encyclopedia of English Language Teaching* (eds J.I. Liontas, T. International Association and M. DelliCarpini). doi:10.1002/9781118784235.eelt0181. Chichester: Wiley.

Givón, T. (1995) *Functionalism and Grammar*. Amsterdam: John Benjamins Publishing.

Housen, A. and Kuiken, F. (2009) Complexity, accuracy, and fluency in second language acquisition. *Applied Linguistics* 30 (4), 461–473.

Housen, A., Kuiken, F. and Vedder, I. (2012) *Dimensions of L2 Performance and Proficiency: Complexity, Accuracy and Fluency in SLA*. Amsterdam: John Benjamins Publishing.

Kellogg, R.T. (1996) A model of working memory in writing. In C.M. Levy and S. Ransdell (eds) *The Science of Writing: Theories, Methods, Individual Differences, and Applications* (pp. 57–71). Mahwah, NJ: Lawrence Erlbaum.

Kellogg, R.T., Whiteford, A.P., Turner, C.E., Cahill, M. and Mertens, A. (2013) Working memory in written composition: An evaluation of the 1996 model. *Journal of Writing Research* 5 (2), 159–190.

Kobayashi, H. and Rinnert, C. (1992) Effects of first language on second language writing: Translation versus direct composition. *Language Learning* 42 (2), 183–209.

Kumaravadivelu, B. (2006) *Understanding Language Teaching: From Method to Postmethod*. Abingdon: Routledge.

Lally, C.G. (2000) First language influences in second language composition: The effect of pre-writing. *Foreign Language Annals* 33 (4), 428–432.

Lin, Y. (2013) *The Effects of Task Planning on L2 Writing*. ResearchSpace@ Auckland.

Macaro, E. (2005) Codeswitching in the L2 classroom: A communication and learning strategy. In E. Llurda (ed.) *Non-Native Language Teachers* (pp. 63–84). Boston, MA: Springer.

Mochizuki, N. and Ortega, L. (2008) Balancing communication and grammar in beginning-level foreign language classrooms: A study of guided planning and relativization. *Language Teaching Research* 12 (1), 11–37.

Norris, J.M. and Ortega, L. (2009) Towards an organic approach to investigating CAF in instructed SLA: The case of complexity. *Applied Linguistics* 30 (4), 555–578.

Ortega, L. (2005) 3. What do learners plan?: Learner-driven attention to form during pre-task planning. In R. Ellis (ed.) *Planning and Task Performance in a Second Language* (pp. 77–109). Amsterdam: John Benjamins.

Pallotti, G. (2009) CAF: Defining, refining and differentiating constructs. *Applied Linguistics* 30 (4), 590–601.

Philp, J. and Duchesne, S. (2016) Exploring engagement in tasks in the language classroom. *Annual Review of Applied Linguistics* 36, 50–72.

Reschly, A.L. and Christenson, S.L. (2012) Jingle, jangle, and conceptual haziness: Evolution and future directions of the engagement construct. In S.L. Christenson, A.L. Reschly and C.Wylie (eds) *Handbook of Research on Student Engagement* (pp. 3–19). Boston, MA: Springer.

Skehan, P. (1998) *A Cognitive Approach to Language Learning*. Oxford: Oxford University Press.

Skehan, P. (2009) Modelling second language performance: Integrating complexity, accuracy, fluency, and lexis. *Applied Linguistics* 30 (4), 510–532.

Skehan, P. (2014) Limited attentional capacity, second language performance, and task-based pedagogy. In P. Skehan (ed.) *Processing Perspectives on Task Performance* (pp. 211–260). Amsterdam: John Benjamins.

Skehan, P. (2016) Tasks versus conditions: Two perspectives on task research and their implications for pedagogy. *Annual Review of Applied Linguistics* 36, 34–49.

Skehan, P. (2018) *Second Language Task-Based Performance: Theory, Research, Assessment*. New York: Routledge.

Storch, N. (2005) Collaborative writing: Product, process, and students' reflections. *Journal of Second Language Writing* 14 (3), 153–173.

Svalberg, A.M.-L. (2009) Engagement with language: Interrogating a construct. *Language Awareness* 18 (3–4), 242–258.

Thornbury, S. (1999) *How to Teach Grammar* (Vol. 3). Harlow: Longman.

Van den Branden, K. (2016) The role of teachers in task-based language education. *Annual Review of Applied Linguistics* 36, 164–181.

Wajnryb, R. (1990) 1990: *Grammar Dictation*. Oxford: Oxford University Press.

Zhang, M. (2018) Collaborative writing in the EFL classroom: The effects of L1 and L2 use. *System* 76, 1–12.

Wendel, J.N. (1997) Planning and second-language narrative production (Doctoral dissertation, Temple University).

Zimmermann, R. (2000) L2 writing: Subprocesses, a model of formulating and empirical findings. *Learning and Instruction* 10 (1), 73–99.

15 Collaborative Writing Tasks in an L3 Classroom: Translanguaging, the Quality of Task Outcomes and Learners' Perceptions

YouJin Kim, Hyejin Cho and Haoshan Ren

This chapter reports a multi-case study which examines translanguaging during task performance in Korean foreign language classes at a university in the United States. The interaction data from a total of four beginning-level Chinese learners of Korean as a third language, writing task output and their perception data collected in a classroom were analyzed. Results show various patterns of translanguaging during collaborative tasks and its potential relationship with the quality of collaborative writing outcomes. Implications for using collaborative writing tasks in diverse instructional contexts are discussed.

Literature Review

Over the last few decades, task-based second language acquisition (SLA) research has focused mainly on second and foreign language learners (see Loewen, 2014, for a review). Although the number of multilinguals is on the rise in foreign language classes, instructed SLA research has not placed much importance on multilingual language learners in classroom contexts (cf. Payant & Kim, 2015). The current study focuses on the construct of translanguaging, which is defined as 'the deployment of a speaker's full linguistic repertoire without regard for watchful adherence to the socially and politically defined boundaries of named (and usually national and state) languages' (Otheguy *et al.*, 2015: 281). Although the construct of translanguaging has been increasingly discussed in the field of applied linguistics, particularly focusing on its theoretical orientation, its implications in language pedagogy in classroom contexts have not been widely investigated. The current study examines the occurrence of translanguaging during task performance among beginner level Korean as an L3 learners. This population and instructional context are underresearched in TBLT literature, and it is our goal to examine students' use of different languages during task performance in diverse instructional contexts.

Translanguaging

The construct of translanguaging introduces a new perspective on language and language use in diverse contexts. For instance, it supports the idea that languages are not discrete but integrated, and multilingual competence is gained through the use of different language resources in contexts where languages are used to negotiate meaning (Canagarajah, 2011b). According to Canagarajah, the theorization of this practice has been introduced in different disciplines using different terms such as code meshing (Canagarajah, 2006), multiliteracies (Cope & Kalantzis, 2000) and polylingual languaging (Jorgensen, 2008). Among various similar terms, translanguaging has been often compared to the concept of code switching. Wei (2018) claimed that while code switching refers to the moment when speakers alternate between languages at specific moments of communication and is often analyzed at the grammar or interactional move level, translanguaging is associated with a meaning-making process. Therefore, according to Wei, the analysis unit of code switching is limited to the outcome of choosing a different linguistic repertoire at certain linguistic levels such as vocabulary, whereas the analytical focus of translanguaging lies in the process of how language users choose various linguistic, cognitive and semiotic resources such as oral and written language, images, gestures and symbols in meaning making and idea construction.

Wei (2018) introduces the concept of translanguaging space, which refers to 'a space that is created by and for translanguaging practices, and a space where language users break down the ideologically laden dichotomies between the macro and the micro, the societal and the individual, and the social and the psychological through interaction' (2018: 23). In the present study, we view the language classroom as a translanguaging space following García and Wei (2014), as teachers and students can engage in diverse meaning-making processes in a socially constructed context.

From a translanguaging lens, multilingual language user's utilization of different languages in the classroom context is of particular interest. Wei (2018) makes a connection between the theoretical concept of translanguaging and second language classroom practice and claims that it is pertinent to expand the current discussion of translanguaging by investigating 'talking-it-through' in multiple languages by different types of multilingual language users (2018: 16). Wei also highlights the related construct 'languaging', which refers to the cognitive process of negotiating and producing meaningful, comprehensible output as a part of language learning opportunities during which language users negotiate meaning.

The concept of 'languaging' was introduced by Swain (2006) from a sociocultural perspective. From this theoretical perspective, language learning can occur through a mediation process, and language is perceived as the most important mediating tool in developing any new knowledge, including language learning. Therefore, learners' linguistic resources, including their first language (L1) and any other additional languages, can serve as an important mediating tool. Wei claims that the construct of 'languaging' could be used when examining translanguaging in educational contexts.

In sum, these theoretical constructs (i.e. translanguaging, trans-languaging space, languaging) offer a valuable conceptual framework to view language classrooms as important social contexts where multilingual learners utilize their own linguistic and non-linguistic repertoires for language learning. Furthermore, from a sociocultural perspective, learners' use of different linguistic sources during collaborative tasks can have pedagogical implications which can inform task design and implementation.

Language Use in the Classroom

In instructed SLA studies, the use of different languages while working on course materials (e.g. collaborative tasks) has been increasingly investigated (e.g. Payant & Kim, 2017; Storch & Aldosari, 2010). These studies have been theoretically motivated by the Sociocultural Theory (Lantolf, 2000; Lantolf & Thorne, 2006). While endeavoring to address some of the common concerns related to the use of L1 in foreign/second language classrooms, researchers were particularly interested in the use of L1 not only in terms of amount but also functionally during students' task performance. Gánem-Gutiérrez and Roehr (2011) examined students' use of L1 (English), discourse markers and metalanguage during individual gap-fill tasks. Students' think-aloud data, including private speech, were analyzed. From the sociocultural perspective, the findings suggest that metalanguage and L1 use helped Spanish L2 learners to explore form-meaning relationships and resolve language problems during task performance.

Not only individual tasks, but also collaborative tasks, have been increasingly implemented in the previous studies, and researchers have focused on the languages that were chosen for a variety of purposes during pair and group work. Storch and Aldosari (2010) examined students' use of L1 during pair work, and they particularly focused on pairing conditions by proficiency levels: high-high, high-low and low-low. A total of 15 pairs carried out three tasks (jigsaw, composition and text-editing), and their interactions during task performance were recorded. The transcribed data were analyzed for the amount of L1 (Arabic) in terms of L1 words and L1 turns, and the functions the L1 served. The findings indicate that task type was more strongly associated with a greater amount of L1 use than proficiency paring. In terms of the function of L1, it is mainly used for task management, and students also used L1 when discussing new words in pairs.

The idea that task type could impact students' language use during task performance has been empirically supported, and recently researchers have begun to examine task modality. Azkarai and García Mayo (2015) examined 44 Spanish EFL learners' L1 use during four interactive tasks in two different modes: speaking only vs. speaking combined with writing. Results showed that task modality impacts the amount of L1 use and the function of L1 during task performance. For instance, grammar deliberation was more frequent during speaking + writing tasks and vocabulary search was more common during speaking tasks than speaking + writing tasks.

Although these studies shed light on students' language use during task performance, authors have mainly focused on the use of non-target languages (i.e. L1) during task performance. Therefore, from a translanguaging perspective, how students utilize their multilingual linguistic repertoire has not been widely addressed. In a recent study, Payant and Kim (2017) present a multi-case study which examined the specific mediating functions of language sources of three Mexican students who were learning French as a third language. They spoke Spanish as a first language and English as a second language. The learners completed tasks collaboratively, and their task interactions were analyzed according to the use of each language, and its function, in these exchanges. The results showed that L2 (i.e. English) was rarely used and that task modalities and task types impact the specific mediating functions of the L1 (Spanish) and L3 (French). Furthermore, the quantity of L1 mediation was found to be associated with learner proficiency level.

In sum, despite an increasing amount of attention on translanguaging in classroom contexts, particularly during students' interactive tasks, little research has been conducted to examine how multilingual speakers use all of their linguistic resources when completing meaning-oriented tasks. Wei (2018) also claimed that research on translanguaging needs to be extended to address different registers, genres and contexts. Furthermore, although previous research has addressed the process of task performance, the relationship between translanguaging patterns and the quality of task outcome has not been examined. Finally, previous task-based studies have focused on quantitative data with a size of approximately 20–40 students. Therefore, it was beyond the scope of previous research to include detailed background information of the participants.

From a pedagogical perspective, the role of tasks has received a lot of attention, and there has been a surge in research focusing on how to maximize language learning through task performance (Long, 2015, 2017). Collaborative tasks are typically implemented in classrooms to encourage learner interaction. In addition to task outcome, language practitioners thus attend to the process of task completion. Accordingly, learners' use of language during collaborative tasks has become an important issue.

Understanding translanguaging patterns requires knowledge of learner background. Therefore, case studies which offer rich background information about learners may be a way forward. Furthermore, to date, the majority of the aforementioned task-based studies were conducted in a foreign language context where learners were learning their 2nd or 3rd language in their home country. Therefore, the contextual factors might have impacted upon learners' use of additional languages other than their L1 and the language being taught in the research context. In terms of learner proficiency in a target language, previous studies often focused on intermediate learners, and beginner level learners have not been investigated, especially with respect to writing tasks (cf. Erlam & Ellis, 2018; Shintani, 2016). Finally, previous studies have focused on commonly taught languages such as English, Spanish and French, leaving out less commonly taught languages. In order to address these gaps in the research, the current study examined Chinese undergraduate students' translanguaging patterns in a Korean as a third language classroom, at an English-medium university in the United States. One of the main goals of the study was to extend the contexts of task-based research and language teaching. The study sought to answer the following research questions:

(1) How much do Chinese multilingual language learners use different languages during collaborative writing tasks?
(2) What is the function of using different languages during collaborative writing?
(3) What is the relationship between translanguaging patterns during collaborative writing and the quality of writing output?
(4) How do students perceive translanguaging during task performance?

Methods

Participants

Four focal participants participated in this multi-case study: Jessica, Yu, Huirong and Sam. All are from China and were enrolled in an undergraduate degree program in the United States at the time of data collection. They were enrolled in KOR 102 which is a second semester beginner level Korean class at the time of the current study. As shown in Table 15.1, they have similar backgrounds in learning Korean.

Jessica is a 20-year-old Chinese international student who came to the United States when she was a high school student. She is pursuing a double major in economics and linguistics. She has studied five different languages: English, French (36 months at high school and college), Italian (12 months at high school and college), Arabic (high school) and Korean (college). She has studied English since she was 5 years old. She indicated that the reason she studies Korean at college is to fulfill her double major requirement.

Yu is a 20-year-old college student who is undertaking a double major in economics and applied math. He has studied English since he was 6 years old in China. Yu's primary reason for taking KOR 102 is to fulfill a language requirement and to listen to and watch Korean television programs.

Huirong is a 19-year-old college student, and her major is applied math. She studied English for 5 years prior to coming to the United State. Huirong's reasons for studying Korean are to fulfill a language requirement, to talk to her Korean friends and to watch Korean TV programs. Furthermore, she also indicated that she wanted to feel closer to Korean culture. In addition to KOR 101 (1st semester Korean class), she took one month of Saturday Korean classes in China.

Sam is a 21-year-old college student (junior) who is majoring in applied math. He has lived in the United States for two years and studied English in China for nine years. His reasons for enrolling in KOR 102 are to fulfill a language requirement and to feel close to Korean culture. Although other students took KOR 101 in a face-to-face format, he took the online version of KOR 101.

All of the focal participants in the current study were beginner level learners of Korean. As a part of KOR 102 requirements, they were required to take the reading section of the unofficial TOPIK test, which consists of 40 multiple choice items. The total possible score is 40. As shown in Table 15.1, Sam and Yu scored higher than Jessica and Huirong. However, the scores are not significantly different. Throughout the semester, the students received task-supported instruction that included a total of 14 tasks organized in 7 themes according to the textbook units.

Instructor

The course was taught by a female Korean language instructor who was involved in developing the task-supported course curriculum (e.g. designing tasks). She is 32 years old, has an MA degree in

Table 15.1 Background information of focal participants

Name (pseudonym)	Gender	Age	Major	Year	Time in the US	Time studying Korean	TOPIK score	Other foreign language proficiency
Jessica	F	20	Economics Linguistics	Sophomore	4 years 8 months	4 months (KOR 101)	13	English (nativelike) French (Intermediate) Italian (beginning) Arabic (beginning)
Yu	M	20	Economics and Applied Math	Junior	2 years 1 month	4 months (KOR 101)	19	English (nativelike)
Huirong	F	19	Applied Math	Sophomore	1 year	4 months (KOR 101) 1 month (weekend Korean school in China)	12	English (advanced)
Sam	M	21	Applied Math	Junior	2 years	4 months (KOR 101)	17	English (advanced)

Note: Both Sam and Jessica used English names, whereas Yu and Huirong used Chinese names. Their pseudonyms reflect this.

Teaching English to Speakers of Other Languages (TESOL) and has obtained a Korean teaching certificate. At the time of data collection, she had taught Korean for two semesters at the institution. The first author, who had conducted several TBLT projects prior to the current project, trained the instructors through a TBLT workshop before the class started and during the weekly teacher's meetings throughout the semester.

Course Curriculum

The data were collected in KOR 102, which is the second half of the first-year elementary Korean language course. The course met four times a week for one hour over a 15-week semester. The course curriculum is designed based on a main textbook, which is organized by different communicative situations (Cho *et al.*, 2010). The first author and the instructors of the course developed the tasks after identifying the appropriate themes and the equivalent task genres according to the situation in each unit. They then developed the task-supported curriculum (see Table 15.2). Each class unit consisted of lecture (2 classes), practice (1 class) and task sessions. Table 15.2 shows the setting of each textbook unit, theme and the task genres developed for this course. The lecture session was conducted mainly in English with a focus on explanation and analysis of the target language. In the practice session, students participated in more controlled activities that encouraged them to practice new grammar points and vocabulary. The task sessions required students to complete tasks in a culturally appropriate manner.

The instructor did not have a specific language policy in class such as 'Korean only', and students had the freedom of choosing which language to use during task-based interaction. However, Korean is required for them to use in their writing task output. They were also allowed to use textbooks, notes and the internet, including online dictionaries (i.e. semiotic tools) during task performance.

Table 15.2 Course curriculum

Textbook	Themes	Task Genres
Unit 9: Birthday	Family events	Online journal writing
Unit 10: At a Professor's Office	University life I	Email
Unit 11: Living in a Dormitory	Spring break	Text messaging
Unit 12: Family	Social gathering	Facebook posting
Unit 13: On the Telephone	University life II	Email
Unit 14: At the Airport	Traveling	Postcard
Unit 15: Shopping	Shopping	Blog

Materials

Instructional tasks

All of tasks for the course were designed following Ellis's (2003) criteria. First, the tasks were meaning-oriented and outcome-driven. Since it was a Korean as a foreign language context, students' use of Korean outside class was limited. However, in order to consider the authenticity of tasks, we took all of their language use contexts (i.e. Chinese, English and Korean) into consideration. The current study was conducted focusing on the six tasks described in Table 15.3.

As shown in Table 15.3, the three tasks in Unit 10 follow the same procedure and resulted in the same task outcome (i.e. emails for Unit 10 and text messages for Unit 11). Each task followed three task phases: pre-task, during task and post-task. During the pre-task phase, after a short grammar review, the instructor introduced the target task and showed a video that modelled the desired interaction patterns (approximately 2 minutes) to help students become familiar with the task content and activate their topic-based schemata. During the main task phase, two students shared information orally first, in order to collect all the necessary information, and then started collaboratively composing an email or text message. During the writing session, students received indirect written corrective feedback (i.e. circled errors without explanation of error sources or correct forms). During the post-task session, students completed a reflection survey.

Interviews

Semi-structured interviews were conducted to examine students' perception of using multiple languages in class and their overall attitudes towards collaborative writing tasks in Korean language class.

Table 15.3 Task descriptions

Unit	Task	Task title	Description
Unit 10	Task 1	Writing an email to request an override	Writing an email to a Korean professor to request for an override to a course
	Task 2	Applying for a Korean study abroad program	Writing an email to a Korean professor to apply for a Korean study abroad program
	Task 3	Introducing study abroad program experiences	Writing an email to a Korean professor to share study abroad program experiences
Unit 11	Task 1	What's going on during your fall break?	Exchanging text messages to plan a fall break gathering
	Task 2	Planning a double date	Exchanging text messages to plan a double date
	Task 3	Let's study together!	Exchanging text messages to plan a study session

Procedures

A total of seven units are covered in one semester, and as indicated above, each unit consisted of seven class sessions: two lectures, one practice and three task sessions. Each task presented in Table 15.3 took about 50 minutes: 10 minutes for the pre-task phase, 35 minutes for the during-task phase and 5 minutes for the post-task phase.

Analysis

The first research question focused on the multilingual Korean language learners' use of different languages during task performance, and the second question explored the function of the different languages during the collaborative writing task. In order to investigate multilingual learners' translanguaging patterns and language function, a Korean native speaker and a Chinese native speaker who were both fluent in English, transcribed the interaction data. All of the students' interaction data collected during Unit 10 and Unit 11 were transcribed and analyzed.

For the first research question, we separated the three languages (Chinese, English and Korean) in each task at the word level using Excel software. If an utterance contained multiple languages, each language was accounted for separately. After the separation of languages, the number of words in each language was counted separately for each task. In this context a word was defined as the smallest unit uttered in isolation carrying meaning.

For the second research question, the transcribed data were analyzed for episodes, which are defined as any part of a dialogue where either a single content topic or linguistic feature is discussed. The coding scheme for functions of each language was adapted from previous studies (i.e. Storch & Aldosari, 2010; Storch & Wigglesworth, 2003) and modified by the researchers. The data were analyzed through three rounds of analysis cycles. For the first round, seven detailed categories were developed: task management, content management, task clarification, vocabulary deliberation, grammar deliberation, mechanics deliberation and task performance (see Table 15.4).

During the second round, each idea unit was further coded for language type and main (i.e. dominate) language choice. Language dominance was identified as 'language used more than 50 percent or more of words within an episode' thereby adapting the concept of language dominance from Payant and Kim (2015: 712). When only one language was used, without any other languages, it was referred to as a 'Korean/Chinese/English language only' unit. Excerpt 1 shows an example of a content-related episode where only one language was used (English-only). Excerpt 2 shows an example of an English-dominant episode in which English was used for more than 50% of the

Table 15.4 Seven detailed categories for functions of language use

Category	Operationalization
Task management	Discussion about how the task should be completed or how the written text should be structured
Task clarification	Discussion about the meaning of the task prompt and instructions
Content management	Language was used to generate or comment on ideas generated
Vocabulary deliberation	Language was used in deliberation over word/sentence meaning, word searches and word choice
Grammar deliberation	Where language was used to discuss morphosyntax and text structure
Mechanics deliberation	Where language was used to discuss punctuation, spelling and pronunciation
Task performance	Target output in Korean including repetitions of written production and self-corrections or recast without further discussion of error

words within a language-related episode which focused on vocabulary deliberation. Excerpt 3 shows an example of a Chinese-dominant task-related episode followed by its English translation. Excerpt 4 shows an example of a half-English, half-Korean episode for vocabulary deliberation.

Excerpt 1: Content management (English-only)

1   H: We should do something
2   J: How about I say 'let's go to Duluth because they have really good spare ribs'?

Excerpt 2: Vocabulary deliberation (English-dominant)

1   J: Yeah, it's not the ... wait, actually, 'but'. Wait, how do I say 'but'?
2   H: 그런?
         but

3   J: No I say 그런데, but umm...
              but

4   H: I think it's 그런데, 그런데, but
              but   *but*

Excerpt 3: Task management (Chinese-dominant)

1   Y: 就没啦, 就好像写完了. 就 one bad thing from 你的, 然后 one good thing from 我的, 然后两个 friends 的介绍就没了.
         So that's it. We're probably done. So we included one bad thing from yours, then one good thing from mine, then introducing two friends. That's it.

Excerpt 4: Vocabulary deliberation (half-English, half-Korean)

1   J: Tuition which is the 수 ... 수업, 수업, 수업료?
              tuition, tuition, tuition?

For ease of presentation, during the third round of the analysis, the above-mentioned function categories are merged into four main categories following Payant and Kim (2015): (1) task-related, including task management and task clarification, (2) content-related, which is the above-mentioned content management category, (3) language-related, including grammar, vocabulary and mechanics and (4) task performance in Korean.

To answer the third question concerning the relationship between translanguaging patterns and the quality of writing output, students' written outcomes were analyzed for fluency, complexity and accuracy. Fluency was identified as the total number of t-units. Complexity was operationalized as the number of clauses per t-unit, and accuracy was operationalized as the number of error-free t-units. Finally, the last question concerning students' perceptions of translanguaging during task performance was answered using students' interview data.

Results

The first research question investigated how much translanguaging was produced by multilingual learners carrying out collaborative writing tasks. Table 15.5 reports the amount of production of each language by the participants across tasks. As we can see in Table 15.5, Yu and Sam used noticeably more Chinese across the two units than Jessica and Huirong, who used mainly English and Korean across all tasks.

For Yu and Sam, their usage of all three languages decreased across the three tasks in Unit 10, but not quite as much for the three tasks in Unit 11. Among all the languages, their Chinese usage in all tasks exceeds, sometimes by a large margin, the use of other languages. Jessica and Huirong make almost no use of Chinese, except for in the last two tasks in Unit 10, which were initiated by Huirong. Jessica did not

Table 15.5 The number of words in Korean, Chinese and English produced by both pairs across 2 units

	Unit 10			Unit 11			
	Task 1	Task 2	Task 3	Task 1	Task 2	Task 3	Total
Yu & Sam	3678	2725	2129	3649	3063	2798	18,042
Chinese	1849	1363	966	1889	1304	1275	8646
Korean	1350	1065	937	1537	1579	1341	7809
English	479	297	226	223	180	182	1587
Jessica & Huirong	2053	2558	1937	2791	2364	2109	13,812
Chinese	0	17	4	0	0	0	21
Korean	868	917	750	1433	1073	994	6035
English	1185	1624	1183	1358	1291	1115	7756

produce any Chinese during the tasks at all. For both pairs, the Korean output in Unit 11 exceeds that of Unit 10.

The second research question asked for the specific functions of each language used by the multilingual learners during the tasks. Tables 15.6 through 15.9 show the two pairs' language patterns for Units 10 and 11, broken down into the four main functional categories as described in the analysis section.

Yu and Sam's pair predominantly used their shared first language, Chinese, across all functions (except for Task Performance, which

Table 15.6 The functions of Yu and Sam's language use across Unit 10

	Task related			Meaning/ content related			Language related			Task performance			Total
	T1	T2	T3	T1	T2	T3	T1	T2	T3	T1	T2	T3	
English only	5	2	3	3	1	1	1	1	1				18
Chinese only	11	12	23		3	1	4	1	5				60
Korean only										10	8	9	27
English dominant		2	1	1		1	7	4	1				17
Chinese dominant	10	4	7	2	8	3	36	30	28				128
Korean dominant				1	1	1		1					4
Half & half E/K										1			1
C/K			1						1				2
E/C				2				2	1				5
Total	26	20	35	9	13	7	48	39	37	11	8	9	262

Note: E-English, K-Korean, C-Chinese.

Table 15.7 The functions of Yu and Sam's language use across Unit 11

	Task related			Meaning/ content related			Language related			Task performance			Total
	T1	T2	T3	T1	T2	T3	T1	T2	T3	T1	T2	T3	
English only		2	4	1	1	1							9
Chinese only	24	25	14	5	9	4	2	3	1				87
Korean only										29	36	20	85
English dominant		1	1		2	1	1	2	3				11
Chinese dominant	12	7	6	10	2	10	28	27	20				122
Korean dominant													0
Half & half E/K													0
C/K													0
E/C		2		4			2	1					9
Total	36	37	25	20	14	16	33	33	24	29	36	20	323

Note: E-English, K-Korean, C-Chinese.

was essentially done in Korean). Tables 15.6 and 15.7 show Yu and Sam's language use across each unit for each function. For both units, their English-only episodes mainly occurred for task-related issues (e.g. reading task instructions from the handout, asking the instructor for clarifications). By contrast, their English-dominant episodes were mostly language related. More specifically, when used in language-related episodes, English was mostly used to express metalanguage and, in particular, focusing on grammatical features such as 'past tense' and 'honorific'. Chinese was mostly used in task-related episodes and meaning-related episodes. For both units, Yu and Sam's Chinese-dominant episodes are mostly language related, which means Yu and Sam tended to use Chinese over other languages when discussing grammar, mechanics and vocabulary-related issues. The data showed that, in these episodes, English is used by Yu and Sam to communicate with the teacher, or to read the task instructions out loud. In comparison, when English is used in situations where another language is the dominant language (Chinese or Korean), it is mostly used for language-related issues.

For Yu and Sam, the most noticeable difference across the two units is the number of episodes focusing on task performance in Korean. The number of different episodes is noticeably higher in Unit 11 than in Unit 10. Overall, the number of total meaning/content-related episodes in all three languages is much lower in Unit 10 than in Unit 11. For language-related episodes, further analysis was conducted to examine what aspects of language the learners discussed during task performance. Four language patterns (Chinese only, Chinese dominant, English only, English dominant) were used for the three functions (discussion of vocabulary, grammar and mechanics). In Unit 10, as a pair Yu and Sam used only English in one episode for vocabulary discussion and in two episodes for grammar discussion. Their English-dominant episodes included six for vocabulary, three for grammar and three for mechanics. Chinese-only episodes occurred when they talked about vocabulary (three episodes), grammar (four episodes) and mechanics (three episodes). Additionally, the most frequent language pattern they used was Chinese dominant: 52 episodes for vocabulary discussion, 31 for grammar and 11 for mechanics. In Unit 11, they did not produce any language-related episodes which were English only. For English-dominant language-related episodes, they used English dominantly in three episodes for vocabulary and three episodes for grammar. Their Chinese-only episodes focusing on language include three for vocabulary, one for grammar and two for mechanics. Finally, for Unit 11, their most frequent language pattern is Chinese dominant, which contributed to 29 episodes for vocabulary, 26 for grammar, and 20 for mechanics. The results showed that Yu and Sam mostly used their first language, Chinese, as the median for Korean vocabulary- and grammar-related discussions, as shown in Excerpt 5. In this example, both students discuss the composition of a sentence concerning the phrase 'watch a lot of Korean drama (or movies)'.

Excerpt 5: Yu and Sam's use of Chinese and Korean during task performance

1   **S:** 한국어 ... 한국어 drama
        Korean ... Korean drama

2   **Y:** drama 是
        Drama is

3   **S:** drama ...不知道怎么说 ... 한국어 영화, 한국어 영화
        I don't know how to say drama ... Korean movie, Korean movie

4   **Y:** TV series

5   **S:** 不管它啦. 한국어 영화, '看很多'怎么说?
        No worries. Korean movie, how do you say 'watching a lot of'?

6   **Y:** 많이, 많이, 보
        A lot, a lot, (to watch)

7   **S:** 那么应该说 한국어 많은 영화, 보
        So we should say a lot of Korean movies, (to watch)

8   **Y:** 其实也可以 한국어 한국영화 많은 可以做副词
        Actually we can also say Korean, Korean movie, a lot. A lot could be used as an adverb.

9   **S:** 应该可以吧. 就说 많은
        Should be fine. Just say a lot.

10 **Y:** 많은
        A lot.

Tables 15.8 and 15.9 show that the functions of Jessica and Huirong's language use during tasks for Units 10 and 11. In general, the results indicated that both students used English as a main language resource. In Unit 10, their English-only episodes focusing on language included two episodes for vocabulary, 16 for grammar, and six for mechanics. Their English-dominant episodes included eight for vocabulary, 21 for grammar and five for mechanics. They also used half-English half-Korean in 19 episodes for vocabulary discussion, seven for grammar, four for mechanics. In Unit 11, they used English only in four episodes for vocabulary discussion, seven episodes for grammar and 16 episodes for mechanics. They used English dominantly in 15 episodes for vocabulary, six episodes for grammar and six episodes for mechanics. Half-English, half-Korean was used in 30 episodes for vocabulary, three episodes for grammar and six episodes were concerned with mechanics. Overall, no Chinese was used when discussing language-related issues.

As shown in Table 15.8, Jessica and Huirong predominantly used English while completing the tasks across all functions (except for Task Performance). Excerpt 6 shows a typical interaction pattern produced

Table 15.8 The functions of Jessica and Huirong's language use across Unit 10

	Task related			Meaning/ content related			Language related			Task performance			Total
	T1	T2	T3	T1	T2	T3	T1	T2	T3	T1	T2	T3	
English only	21	23	18	14	13	12	3	14	7				125
Chinese only													0
Korean only										34	36	16	86
English dominant	5	11	3	1	10	2	10	9	15				66
Chinese dominant													0
Korean dominant								1		2	3	4	10
Half & half E/K	3	1		2	3		8	16	6	1		3	43
C/K													0
E/C					1								1
Total	29	35	21	17	27	14	21	40	28	37	39	23	331

Note: E-English, K-Korean, C-Chinese.

Table 15.9 The functions of Jessica and Huirong's language use across Unit 11

	Task related			Meaning/ content related			Language related			Task performance			Total
	T1	T2	T3	T1	T2	T3	T1	T2	T3	T1	T2	T3	
English-Only	23	10	15	17	11	10	13	3	11				113
Chinese-Only													0
Korean-Only										44	27	14	85
English-Dominant	11	3	6	4	9	7	12	9	6				67
Chinese-Dominant													0
Korean-Dominant										12	4	15	31
Half - half E/K		1		1	1		22	3	14	2		5	49
C/K													0
E/C													0
Total	34	14	21	22	21	17	47	15	31	58	31	34	345

Note: E-English, K-Korean, C-Chinese.

by Jessica and Huirong. In this excerpt, they are composing an email regarding traffic jams in Korea.

Excerpt 6: Jessica and Huirong's use of English during task performance

1   J: … and you talk about experience so two bad things, two good things

2   H: 안 좋, 안 좋은 점, 교통이, 교통이 복잡, 복잡해서
          Bad, bad thing, traffic, traffic jammed, jammed

3   J: so you are saying crowded?

4   H: like the traffic jam

5   J: oh traffic jam, congested, all right

6   H: 복잡해요
        jammed

Although Jessica and Huirong rarely used Chinese during task performance, one of the noticeable differences across the two units is the use of Chinese. In Unit 10, they used all three languages once each to develop an idea about who they lived with in a dormitory while studying abroad in Korea (Excerpt 7). Huirong used Chinese to explain her idea, and Jessica clarified her partner's utterances in English. They also used Chinese once to indicate a grammar feature, as shown in Excerpt 8. However, even when they used Chinese, the dominant language for communication was English. In Unit 11, however, they used no Chinese.

Excerpt 7: Huirong and Jessica's use of Chinese during task performance

1   H: 미국 就没有什么......No, Americans
        America, it's like not many....No Americans

2   J: Ahhh, no Americans? Yeah, that works, okay

3   H: 就说, 没有和韩国人一起住
        Just say, (I) didn't live with Koreans.

4   J: Yeah, I'd just say I could only live with the states students (students from the US)

Excerpt 8: Jessica's use of Chinese

1   J: Yeah, I think it's.. I...I think I wrote it somewhere ...예요 的过去时......

        ... past tense of 'it is'

The third research question addressed the potential relationship between translanguaging patterns and the quality of written outcomes. The outcome of students' collaborative writing was measured in terms of the number of t-units (fluency), the number of words per t-unit (complexity) and the number of error-free t-units (accuracy), as shown in Table 15.10. Because all the learners were at a similar proficiency level and had a similar background in the Korean language learning, overall, the quality of the writing outcome was very similar (see Table 15.10). In terms of writing fluency, Jessica and Huirong tended to produce a larger number of t-units in a given time. However, in terms of syntactic complexity, Yu and Sam tended to produce more complex structures. As shown in Tables 15.6 through 15.9, it was clear that while Yu and Sam mainly depended on using Chinese when discussing language related issues, Jessica and Huirong used English as well as both English and Korean equally in an episode (i.e. half-half E/K). Based on the quality

Table 15.10 Quality of writing outcome

		Yu & Sam			Jessica & Huirong		
		# of t-units	# of words per t-unit	# of error-free t-units	# of t-units	# of words per t-unit	# of error-free t-units
Unit 10	Task 1	8	7.63	7	9	8.56	8
	Task 2	9	9.11	8	11	9.09	10
	Task 3	8	11.88	6	11	8.82	10
Unit 11	Task 1	24	6.08	24	27	5.67	26
	Task 2	24	8.25	22	31	6.55	29
	Task 3	17	10	16	22	7.91	22

of the writing outcomes, the students' use of different languages does not seem to affect how they resolved language-related discussion, particularly for accuracy.

In general, Jessica and Huilong produced a greater number of t-units than Yu and Sam. Accordingly, the number of content/meaning-related and language-related episodes was higher than for Yu and Sam. However, Yu and Sam's episodes involved more turns and negotiation. Excerpts 9 and 10 show how two pairs interacted when composing similar content in their writing. In these excerpts, they were trying to describe how difficult their previous language classes (e.g. Korean class and Chinese class, respectively) were in their emails to their professors. As seen in these examples, Yu and Sam tended to produce more turns (30 turns) compared to Jessica and Huirong (10 turns) and they discussed the language and content using predominantly Chinese. With respect to the different aspects of linguistic performance, the results of the complexity analysis could be associated with the amount and quality of language-related discussion. While discussing the content in Chinese, they seem concerned with the details of the email and in doing so, developed more complex sentences.

Excerpt 9: Jessica and Huirong's use of Korean and English during task performance

1   **J:**   Oh. No sentence 어려웠어... Oh no, you said differential. So, 어려워
         it was difficult   *difficult*

2   **H:**   What's a, what's a...

3   **J:**   Wait, do we, umm 어려웠어, 어려워 ... Wait, 습니다 has tense or tenseless? I don't remember
                             it was difficult, difficult ... Wait, it is

4   **H:**   Tenseless

5   **J:**   So it's tenseless? Hold on ... I mean I don't ... I should have ... somewhere...

6   **H:**   We have to use...

7   J: Oh, it's here … So 어려 … Yeah I'll just put 습니다
            diffi(cult)   *it is*

8   H: 습니다
         It is

9   J: Yeah, should be fine.

10 H: Okay. Good.

Excerpt 10: Yu and Sam's use of English, Korean and Chinese during task performance

1   Y: 저하고 샘씨는 对, 就上个学期 take 了 한국어, 就我和 샘 那就 저는
         Sam and I, yeah, so it's last semester we take (+past tense) Korean, me and Sam, so I am

2   那就 저는, 那就先我先 저는
         Then 'I am' let's, let me first, 'I am'

3   S: 저는
         I am

4   Y: 중국어, 중국어 수업, 을, 수업을 들, 었, 我用那个 past tense, 然后 지, 지만, 지만
         Chinese, Chinese class, I took a class, I use that past tense then, but, but, but

5   诶是 지만 吧, 지만, 지만, 지만 uh, 어려웠어요
         Is it but, but, but, but, uh, it was difficult

6   S: 어려, 어려웠어요
         Difficult, it was difficult

7   Y: 我要不要加个
         Should I add a

8   S: (하)지만
         But

9   Y: 要不要加个 중국어가 어려웠어요, 还是就是 어려웠어요
         Do you want to add 'Chinese was difficult?' Chinese was difficult, still, it was difficult

10 S: 嗯, 你先写个 중국어 吧
         Ok, you can first write Chinese

11 Y: 那我前面有个 중국어 了. okay okay 어려웠어요
         So I have Chinese before. okay okay it was difficult

12 S: 어려웠어요?
         It was difficult?

13 Y: 어려웠습니다 吧应该是用
         'It was difficult' should be used

14 S: 嗯不用不用不用,
         Um no no no

15 Y: 不, I mean different 就是这里就是给教授写，就是 write to professor so,
No, I mean different, so here we write to the professor, it's write to professor

16 S: but the subject is 저
          I

17 Y: I mean, not just 저, 就是 use the 습니다 because it's like very official 就是
I mean, not just 'I'. It's use the 'it is' because it's like very official. It is a

18   非常官方的一个环境
A very official environment

19 S: oh!

20 Y: 就不是那个 习니다 是另外一个 …… differential, 这个要怎么写，看一下
So it's not this 'it is'. It's the other 'it is'… differential. How do you write this, let's see.

21 S: 我觉得我不确定诶
I feel I'm not sure about it

22 Y: 因为他是刚刚说……
Because he just said…

23 S: 但是 저 这个是上学期了
But 'I' is (learned from) last semester

24 Y: 跟 subject 没关系了，就是只是说，这个是个 所以 습니다
It has nothing to do with subject. It's only, this is, so 'it is'

25 S: 습니다, because we are saying Chinese class is diffi…
'It is', because we are saying Chinese class is diffi…

26 Y: I mean write to the professor so, yeah

27 S: so also

28 T: try try … you see 습니다
                    it is

29 Y: 它……它不是, 它是 습니다 是另外一种 습니다 不是之前那个
It … it's not. It's a different 'it is'. This 'it is' is not the one before.

30 S: 那……
Then…

The last research question asked how the students felt about using different languages in Korean language class. Individual semi-structured interview data were analyzed to answer this question. Both Sam and Yu stated that they use Chinese more often when discussing grammar or vocabulary, as using Chinese saves time because of their fluency in their first language.

Example 1: Sam's response about translanguaging in class
During tasks, we use mostly Chinese. Sometimes we use English. Because what we learn is we transfer English to Korean. That's why

sometimes we feel that English is more effective in terms of communication. Most of the time we use Chinese. We use Korean for sentences. I think it's very helpful … When we learn a new language, we can use the experience from English-learning. It really helps because I have experience with second language.

Example 2: Yu's response about translanguaging in class
There are lots of Chinese characters in Korean so sometimes it's better to use Chinese rather than English. When we are trying to ask each other questions, at the beginning we used Korean but then it takes long time to construct sentence. So kind like times up. We changed to Chinese. I mean because like when we use Korean it takes long time to think about grammar points and vocabulary. When we convey meaning, you can use other languages each other. We can understand better.

In Example 1, Sam talks about why he used three languages interchangeably. He used Chinese and English because of his proficiency in both languages. He also talked about using his second language learning (i.e. English) experience when learning additional languages (i.e. Korean). Yu shared similar perspectives, but he also highlighted that because of the similarities between Chinese and Korean, he prefers using Chinese rather than English.

Huirong indicated that she believes English to be a tool for learning Korean. Since her Korean skills are not that good, she feels that she needs additional linguistic tools when learning Korean. She also mentioned how Jessica's English proficiency affected their language choice. Although Jessica moved to the United States when she was a high school student, Huirong believed that she was born in the United States and felt that English would be easier for Jessica to communicate in.

Example 3: Huirong's response about translanguaging in class
We rarely speak Chinese because she is American born Chinese? I don't know like … basically we use English quite often. If there is something we cannot express in English, we use Chinese. But basically Korean and English. When we use English it's because our Korean is not that good. If there is some part that we cannot explain in Korean, so only one way to express is English … It's like a tool to learn Korean. One way to ask to better understand Korean.

Example 4: Jessica's response about translanguaging in class
I think using Chinese in class can be rude since our teacher does not understand Chinese. So I tried to use Korean and English. I think it's ok to use English since our Korean proficiency level is not good enough to discuss things during tasks. We can get things done quickly.

As Example 4 shows, Jessica considers her Korean instructor a member of the translanguaging space in the classroom context, although the teacher did not carry out the task with them.

Overall, from multilingual users' perspectives, various factors such as proficiency levels and the perceived distance between the languages impacted upon the students' language choices during interactive-task performance.

Discussion

The current multi-case study focuses on students' translanguaging patterns in a multilingual, beginner-level Korean as a foreign language classroom. All participants in the current study were Chinese speakers who were pursuing their undergraduate degree in the United States. To date, the majority of task-based studies target English or commonly taught foreign languages such as Spanish and French. As a result, it is still unknown to what extent tasks can promote language learning and facilitate language use opportunities in less commonly taught East Asian languages such as Korean.

The findings suggest that as multilingual language users, all of the focal participants carried translanguaging with them into the Korean classroom. The detailed interaction data over the course of six task sessions suggested that students used their dynamic linguistic repertoire with their partners, and interestingly both pairs showed a very different picture of translanguaging patterns during task performance. Interview data shed light on the use of the different languages from the students' perspective. For instance, although Jessica moved to the United States less than five years ago, her partner Huirong thought Jessica had been born in the United States based on her fluent oral English skills, which made Huirong use almost exclusively English rather than Chinese during task performance. In addition, when Huirong used Chinese to elaborate her idea regarding content management, Jessica directly translated what Huirong said and Huirong confirmed that in English in her following utterance. In Jessica's case, since their teacher could not understand Chinese, she felt that it was rude to use Chinese in class. It was also interesting to observe how students produced metalanguage mostly in English during collaborative writing and all grammar points were explained in English using English metalanguage in the given translanguaging space (i.e. Korean classroom in the United States) (Wei, 2018).

Payant and Kim (2017) examined Mexican students learning French as a third language. Their findings showed that learners rarely used their L2 (i.e. English) during task performance, and task types and modalities impacted students' language use patterns. In that context, the instructions were delivered mainly in French, whereas due to students' proficiency level, the teacher in the current study mainly used English, particularly when target grammar or vocabulary was being introduced in class. The choice of language for instruction seemed to play an important role in students' translanguaging patterns during task performance, although neither instructor had a mandatory language policy in class.

Overall, the current study showed that collaborative writing tasks offered translanguaging space where learners can choose their language codes for different purposes during task performance. From a sociocultural theory perspective, language is one of the most important mediation tool and collaborative writing tasks facilitated both oral and written language production. In terms of how translanguaging patterns changed over time, the results showed that in general the number of episodes for each function decreased, which might be because of task repetition effects. Three tasks in each unit followed the exact same procedure with the same genre of writing (i.e. email and text messaging, respectively). It is possibly for this reason that task management-related discussion decreased as they repeated the tasks. However, language-related episodes did not show a linear pattern, as Jessica and Huirong produced many more language-related episodes during the second task in Unit 10 (21 vs 40). When examining the data in more depth, particularly in terms of the linguistic foci of language-related episodes such as in Unit 10, although Jessica and Huirong initially did not produce any language-related episodes focusing on mechanics, as they repeated the tasks, they paid more attention to these. The same pattern was found in Unit 11 with Yu and Sam when there were language-related episodes focusing on grammar. This aligns with previous task repetition studies (Carver & Kim, in press) which have shown that task repetition helps students to pay attention to linguistic features. However, Carver and Kim also suggest that the first task repetition is beneficial, whereas when students repeated the task a second time, the quality of their task performance in terms of using target features (i.e. past tense) turned out to be worse. In sum, the function of translanguaging patterns varies over time, and task repetition effects may have been observed in the current study.

The third question addressed the relationship between translanguaging patterns and the quality of writing. Because the current study focused on beginner-level learners whose linguistic backgrounds were comparable in terms of Korean, and the tasks were controlled in terms of task outcome, the quality of writing was measured for complexity, accuracy and fluency. Although both pairs' translanguaging patterns were noticeably different, the quality of their writing was very similar except for its complexity. Both Yu and Sam predominantly used Chinese when they performed the tasks and often produced task- or language-related episodes that involved lengthy turns (e.g. see Excerpt 10). Thus, their written output was in general more complex than Jessica and Huilong's, as measured by the mean length of t-units.

García and Wei (2018) claim that the value of translanguaging 'lies in the fact that it transcends socially constructed boundaries of language systems and structures to engage diverse multiple meaning-making systems and subjectivities; it transforms not only the language structures, but also social relations and social structures, as well as individuals' cognition' (2018: 5). Among three languages (i.e. Chinese, English, Korean), although Korean and Chinese word orders are different, they share many vocabulary items. In fact, Yu pointed out that language distance (i.e. Chinese-Korean vs. English-Korean) was one of the reasons why he preferred to use Chinese more than English while composing Korean texts. However, social structure, such as a relationship with a partner (i.e. perceived English proficiency) and being considerate of the instructor's background also seem to have impacted upon the translanguaging patterns during collaborative writing tasks.

There are several important pedagogical implications emerging from the current study. As the recent literature on translanguaging in the field of Applied Linguistics has shown, the role of translanguaging in education has received an increasing amount of attention (García & Wei, 2018; Wei, 2018). Translanguaging is viewed as scaffolding, especially when students cannot create meaning using the target language. Translanguaging can be a useful language learning tool to be used while learners are adding and appropriating the necessary language features that are required to complete an academic task in one or more languages. The current study shows how learners choose their own language code independently, depending on their needs and perception towards their interlocutors and instructors and the data demonstrated that two focal pairs did so very differently for different reasons. The target tasks were collaborative writing tasks, and the results showed that the quality of task performance was similar regardless of translanguaging patterns during interaction. However, some patterns were noticed. For instance, Yu and Sam's extensive discussion on the content of tasks in Chinese seemed to contribute to the complexity of their writing.

Teaching writing can be a challenging task, especially to beginner-level learners. The current study observed collaborative writing using two different genres (i.e. email and text messaging). In providing a space where students are the agents in selecting the appropriate features of language, students can accomplish communicative goals (i.e. collaboratively complete writing tasks in the context of the current study). Language instructors often encourage students to collaboratively work with each other, and oral interaction has been viewed as evidence of collaboration. Based on the findings of the current study, instructors might be aware that the amount of interaction might not be a direct indicator of the quality of written task output, at least for beginner level learners who have a limited target language knowledge. Additionally, instructors might pay attention to task implementation, especially for designing tasks with some aspects of tasks being repeated. Overall, collaborative writing tasks serve as translanguaging space where the pattern of translanguaging changes dynamically because of various factors.

The limitations of the study need to be acknowledged. First, the current multi-case study focused on only four multilingual Korean language learners in a foreign language classroom context as our intention was to highlight two unique patterns of translanguaging, considering learner background and their perception of translanguaging in class, over time. Furthermore, all the students kept their partners during the target tasks. Based on previous research, it is expected that interlocutors will impact task performance. Future studies are warranted to examine how translanguaging patterns change as students work with different partners and carry out different types of tasks. Even so, this study is one of only a few to focus on multilingual speakers' task performance in the foreign language learning environment where the second language, English, is a dominant language outside the classroom. More research which addresses a variety of language contexts is needed in the research domain of translanguaging in education. Although the translanguaging space certainly involves both teachers and students in classroom contexts, we focused on students' interaction data in the current study. How teachers and students together create a translanguaging space in the language classroom is certainly of interest.

Conclusion

The current study examined how two pairs of multilingual speakers carried translanguaging in their Korean classroom while performing collaborative writing tasks. The purpose was to extend the current task and translanguaging literature by examining collaborative writing task performance by Korean as a third language learner in the US contexts. The findings showed that the different patterns of translanguaging, and the students' choice of language was influenced by many factors, yet it did appear to make positive contributions as a language learning tool among beginner level language learners. The instructional context in the current study was very unique in that Chinese multilingual learners who were enrolled at a university in the US where English is the main medium of instruction were learning Korean as their third language. Unlike Payant and Kim (2015), students used their second language, which is English to a greater extent especially when discussing metalanguage since linguistics features were introduced in English. However, learners' perceived language distance also played a role in task-oriented translanguaging space. Based on the findings of the study, teachers need to consider how to incorporate translanguaging into their pedagogical practices when implementing collaborative tasks in order to empower multilingual learners' use of different languages to achieve their communicative goals.

References

Azkarai, A. and García Mayo, M.P. (2015) Task-modality and L1 use in EFL oral interaction. *Language Teaching Research* 19 (5), 550–571.

Canagarajah, S. (2006) Negotiating the local in English as a lingua franca. *Annual Review of Applied Linguistics* 26, 197–218.

Canagarajah, S. (2011b) Translanguaging in the classroom: Emerging issues for research and pedagogy. *Applied Linguistics Review* 2, 1–28.

Carver, J. and Kim, Y. (in press) French learners' past tense development through collaborative writing tasks: The role of procedural and content repetition. *Canadian Modern Language Review*.

Cho, Y., Lee, H., Schulz, C., Sohn, H. and Sohn, S. (2010) *Integrated Korean* (2nd edn). Honolulu, Hawai'i: University of Hawai'i Press.

Cope, B. and Kalantzis, M. (2000) *Multiliteracies: Literacy Learning and the Design of Social Futures*. London: Routledge.

Ellis, R. (2003) *Task-Based Language Learning and Teaching*. Oxford: Oxford University Press.

Erlam, R. and Ellis, R. (2018) Task-based language teaching for beginner-level learners of L2 French: An exploratory study. *Canadian Modern Language Review* 74 (1), 1–26.

Gánem-Gutiérrez, G.A. and Roehr, K. (2011) Use of L1, metalanguage, and discourse markers: L2 learners' regulation during individual task performance. *International Journal of Applied Linguistics* 21 (3), 297–318.

García, O. and Wei, L. (2014) *Translanguaging: Language, Bilingualism, and Education*. New York, NY: Palgrave MacMillan.

García, O. and Wei, L. (2018) Tranlaguaging. In C.A. Chapelle (ed.) *The Encyclopedia of Applied Linguistics*. Oxford: Wiley-Blackwell.

Jorgensen, J.N. (2008) Polylingual languaging around and among children and adolescents. *International Journal of Multilingualism* 5 (3), 161–176.

Lantolf, J.P. (ed.) (2000) *Sociocultural Theory and Second Language Learning*. Oxford: Oxford University Press.

Lantolf, J. and Thorne, S.L. (2006) *Sociocultural Theory and the Genesis of Second Language Development*. Oxford: Oxford University Press.

Long, M. (2015) *Second Language Acquisition and Task-Based Language Teaching*. Malden, MA: Wiley-Blackwell.

Long, M. (2016) In defense of tasks and TBLT: Nonissues and real issues. *Annual Review of Applied Linguistics* 36, 5–33.

Loewen, S. (2014) *Introduction to Instructed Second Language Acquisition*. New York, NY: Routledge.

Otheguy, R., García, O. and Reid, W. (2015) Clarifying translanguaging and deconstructing named languages: A perspective from linguistics. *Applied Linguistics Review* 6 (3), 281–307.

Payant, C. and Kim, Y. (2015) Language mediation in an L3 classroom: The role of task modalities and task types. *Foreign Language Annals* 48 (4), 706–729.

Payant, C. and Kim, Y. (2017) Impact of task modality on collaborative dialogue among plurilingual learners: A classroom-based study. *International Journal of Bilingual Education and Bilingualism* 22 (5), 614–627.

Shintani, N. (2016) *Input-Based Tasks in Foreign Language Instruction for Young Learners*. Amsterdam: John Benjamins Publishing Company.

Storch N. and Aldosari, A. (2010) Learners' use of first language (Arabic) in pair work in an EFL class. *Language Teaching Research* 14, 355–375.

Storch, N. and Wigglesworth, G. (2003) Is there a role for the use of the L1 in an L2 setting? *TESOL Quarterly* 37 (4), 760–769.

Swain M. (2006) Languaging, agency and collaboration in advanced second language proficiency. In H. Byrnes (ed.) *Advanced Language Learning: The Contribution of Halliday and Vygotsky* (pp. 95–108). London-New York: Continuum.

Wei, L. (2018) Translanguaging and code-switching: What's the difference? See https://blog.oup.com/2018/05/translanguaging-code-switching-difference/.

16 The Role of Task-Based Interaction in Perceived Language Learning in a Japanese EFL Classroom

Scott Aubrey

Like many EFL settings, Japan is often thought of as culturally homogenous and thus devoid of opportunities for Japanese to interact face to face with English speakers from other countries. While this is true to some extent, small international student populations do exist at many Japanese universities. This chapter demonstrates how, in the Japan context, tasks can be used to facilitate interaction between international and Japanese university students in the EFL classroom and how these task-based interactions lead to perceived language learning. Thirty-six Japanese EFL learners completed two oral collaborative tasks with either another Japanese EFL learner (intra-cultural interaction) or a non-Japanese English speaker (inter-cultural interaction). New linguistic items that were noticed and remembered during task performances were traced back to episodes of interaction. The results indicated that learners in both conditions are more likely to report learning items when they occurred in conjunction with language-related episodes (LREs) that were complex, resolved with uptake and focused on spelling and pronunciation. However, there were some differences between the groups. Inter-cultural interactions resulted in a higher percentage of reported learning from LREs than intra-cultural interactions. On the other hand, intra-cultural interactions resulted in a higher proportion of reported learning from preemptive LREs and incorrectly resolved LREs. Implications of these findings suggest that perceived learning may be enhanced if (1) learners are encouraged to resolve language issues in both written and spoken form during tasks, (2) self-reported learning charts are used as a post-task intervention and (3) learners are trained in interactional strategies that promote more complex discussions about language.

Introduction

A feature of the Japanese EFL context – like many EFL contexts – is that learners of English have very limited communication opportunities outside of the classroom. In such 'acquisition-poor' environments, there is an obvious need for classrooms to provide not just communicative opportunities, but, when possible, interactional opportunities with non-Japanese English speakers. As previous research has shown, providing inter-cultural contact experiences within a task-based framework can lead to greater engagement (Aubrey, 2017a, 2017b), increased self-confidence (Freiermuth & Huang, 2012) and more numerous language-focused discussions (Aubrey, 2018). However, if and how inter-cultural task-based interaction leads to language learning is unclear.

Opportunities for learning during task-based interactions often arise incidentally and around language issues that are unpredictable, making it notoriously difficult to obtain evidence of what has been learned. Investigating this issue can take two forms. Firstly, learning can be measured via a post-test, but these tests are difficult to devise as learners focus their attention on a broad range of structures during interaction. Using this approach, Loewen (2005) and Swain (1995) have looked at instances in which learners focus on linguistic elements as they arise incidentally during a task, which they then used as a basis to assess whether learners are able to recall targeted linguistic information. Indeed, this kind of approach leads to interesting findings, but as Ellis (1995) notes, 'it is obviously very time-consuming and probably impractical for teachers' (1995: 148). Such a technique is valuable mostly for research purposes and feasible with relatively few interactions. Alternatively, learners can self-report what they have learned after completing a task. This evidence of 'learning' – or subjective *perceptions of* learning – is a practical method of probing students' awareness of new linguistic items they have encountered. It also has pedagogical value. The use of charts to record learned items, for instance, can give teachers an indication of common language difficulties generated by tasks, and it provides the means for a simple post-task intervention that focuses learners' attention on language they themselves deem important.

The use of self-reported learning charts in tandem with oral tasks may also have added value in the Japanese context where there is still resistance toward communicative approaches. Japanese EFL classrooms have been described as particularly non-communicative, with a strong tendency towards silence (King, 2013). In such a context, where grammar-translation and other teacher-centered approaches are still the norm, task-based language teaching (TBLT) may be an attractive alternative. However, some argue that the TBLT approach is incompatible with the learning style, learning expectations and the sociocultural realities of the Japan context (Burrows, 2008;

Sato, 2009). According to critics, efforts to implement TBLT could lead to interactions that display impoverished language use (Nobuyoshi, 2011) and a failure to expose learners to new language (Sato, 2010). To alleviate these concerns, having students record evidence of learning after performances may reassure teachers and students of the value of meaning-focused tasks. The present study explores this issue by using self-reported learning charts to investigate the relationship between inter-cultural and intra-cultural task-based interactions and perceived language learning in the Japanese EFL classroom.

Self-reported learning charts

The term uptake is currently used to describe a learner's utterance in response to his/her interlocutor's feedback or effort to focus on form (Lyster & Ranta, 1997). This notion of uptake, however, is very different from how it has been used previously in the literature. Uptake, according to Allwright (1984), refers to what language items learners themselves claim to have learned during a lesson. In other words, it is learning that is recalled and/or self-reported after the fact. Since Allwright's proposal of a self-report measure of uptake, several studies have operationalized this definition of uptake, providing valuable insights into the relationship between classroom interaction and perceived learning outcomes.

Research using self-reported learning, specifically through charts, has primarily focused on classroom discourse during teacher-fronted classes (e.g. Palmeira, 1995; Nabei, 2012; Slimani, 1989, 1992). In a seminal study using learning charts, Slimani (1989, 1992) audio-recorded two hours of English grammar lessons per day for six consecutive weeks. After each lesson, 13 Algerian learners of English were asked to recall learned items and categorize them in terms of grammar, words and expressions, pronunciation and spelling. The claimed items were traced back to the classroom data in order to investigate what occurred during interactive episodes. Although it was found that the vast majority of items claimed to be learned were explicitly topicalized (i.e. focused upon) by the teacher, learner-learner interaction led to an item being reported at a much higher rate. This suggests, then, that the use of self-reported learning charts could also be useful as a measure of learning during collaborative tasks.

Teachers who wish to implement self-reported learning charts in their classrooms, however, may understandably have some misgivings about the value of self-reported data. Allwright (1984) claims there are two potentially problematic issues – that students may not be able to accurately recall the items they have learned, or they may not honestly report what they have learned. In regard to the former, Nabei (2012), who utilized learning charts at the end of a Japanese EFL reading class, found that in many cases, students were unable to report on the situation in which the item was learned, indicating that learners tend to have difficulty describing in detail when and how learning takes place. As for Allwright's concern about honesty, there is evidence that learners are truthful in the reporting of learning after the fact (Eckerth, 2006; Ellis, 1995). For example, Ellis (1995) had students complete a listening comprehension task that exposed learners to target vocabulary, and then asked them to write down new vocabulary items from the task that they could recall. He found that all items that students reported learning emerged from the task (i.e. were featured in the input) and did not come from outside the task context. In sum, learning charts appear to be a practical, simple tool that reliably represents perceived learning in the classroom.

Language learning opportunities during inter-cultural task-based interactions

While teacher-centered classes generate discourse that is heavily influenced by teachers' preconceived notions of what should be learned, the language focus of collaborative task-based interactions is considerably more unpredictable, emerging from learners' own needs. One important factor that impacts the ways in which learners focus on language during a task is the learners' interlocutor. Relevant to the present study is how an interlocutors' proficiency and ethnolinguistic background can lead to variation in the feedback learners receive, how they respond to that feedback and ultimately the quantity and quality of the interaction-driven language learning opportunities that arise.

Attention to language during interaction is commonly operationalized in terms of language-related episodes (LREs), which, according to Swain (2006), contribute to the construction and shaping of linguistic knowledge. Studies have found that, compared with task interaction between interlocutors of similar proficiency, when learners interact with more proficient interlocutors, more LREs are generated (e.g. Bowles et al., 2014; Kim & McDonough, 2008; Leeser, 2004), which are correctly resolved at higher rates (e.g. Kim & McDonough, 2008; Leeser, 2004; Watanabe & Swain, 2007; Williams, 2001). This apparent learning advantage is sustained when learners collaborate during tasks with native speakers (Fernández Dobao, 2012) or others of different cultural background (Bowles et al., 2014).

Expanding on this line of inquiry, Aubrey (2018) examined the dialogues of two groups of Japanese EFL learners who performed five collaborative oral tasks twice in two groups: 9 Japanese-Japanese (intra-cultural) dyads and 9 Japanese-non-Japanese (inter-cultural) dyads. Aubrey identified LREs using a framework that categorized episodes according to linguistic focus, type, complexity and resolution. A description of each classification is provided in Table 16.1.

Table 16.1 Description of LRE categorization (Aubrey, 2018)

LRE category	Description
1. Linguistic focus	Concerned with content of episodes.
a. Lexical	An episode in which participants focus on lexical features.
b. Grammatical	An episode in which participants focus on grammatical features.
c. Spelling/pronunciation	An episode in which participants focus on spelling or pronunciation.
d. Other	An episode in which participants focus on a linguistic problem that does not fit into a–c.
2. Type	Concerned with how the episode is initiated.
a. Reactive	An episode that occurs when a participant responds to an utterance that is problematic, either because the meaning is not clear or because it contains a linguistic error.
b. Preemptive	An episode that occurs when a participant initiates a change in topic (topicalizes) to focus on a language issue because one participant predicts that the feature may be problematic to his/her interlocutor.
3. Complexity	Concerned with the length of each episode.
a. Simple	An episode that is resolved or abandoned in one turn.
b. Complex	An episode that is resolved or abandoned in more than one turn.
4. Resolution	Concerned with the resolution of episodes.
a. Resolved with uptake	An episode in which the language problem was solved correctly by one participant and the other subsequently uses the corrected form.
b. Resolved without uptake	An episode in which the language problem was solved correctly by one participant and the other does not use the corrected form.
c. Incorrectly resolved	An episode in which the language problem was solved incorrectly.
d. Unresolved	An episode in which the language problem was not solved (i.e. abandoned).

Aubrey (2018) found that, compared to intra-cultural interaction, inter-cultural interactions led to the generation of more than twice as many LREs overall and produced proportionally (1) more complex LREs, (2) more LREs that attempted to resolve grammatical issues, (3) and fewer LREs that were resolved incorrectly. One shortcoming of Aubrey's study, however, was that it only focused on the interactional episodes in which learners attended to potentially new or confusing language. These episodes may have led to developmental effects (Swain, 2006, 1995), but it is also possible that many of these apparent learning opportunities were misunderstood by the learner or forgotten soon after the interaction. Therefore, a more concrete measure of learning is needed, which would, from a teachers' perspective, not only be beneficial in terms of generating a data-based rationale for using tasks, but would also provide a pedagogical post-task intervention for focusing learners' attention on language. With this in mind, the current study makes use of a self-reported learning chart as a measure of perceived language learning.

The present study

This research explores the relationship between perceived learning outcomes (i.e. self-reported claims of learning) and task-based inter/intra-interaction. This is important for teachers as findings could reveal the kinds of interactions that most efficiently leads to learning. Specifically, the study addresses the following research questions:

- What are the relationships between task-based interaction and perceived language learning outcomes?
- What are some differences between these relationships for inter-cultural and intra-cultural task performances?

Method

Participants

The study consisted of 63 participants divided into two groups: an Intra-cultural group and an Inter-cultural group. The former was made up of 21 Japanese students from an EFL class while the latter included 21 Japanese EFL students from a second class. These participants were first-year students from a large private university in Japan and majored in Theology, Economics, Sociology and Business. The two classes were equivalent in terms of the course aim (to improve speaking skills) and proficiency level (between 430 and 500 on the TOEFL PBT). To provide the inter-cultural contact, 21 international students were introduced into one class. The international students consisted of both non-native (8) and native (13) English speakers from a total of 10 different countries.

Research design

This classroom-based study took place over 11 weeks. As shown in Table 16.2, the research was carried out in two stages: initial task performances (Weeks 1–5) and repeated task performances (Weeks 7–11). During each stage, an oral paired task was performed each week for five weeks. The data analyzed for this study were collected during the repeated task performances only, which occurred between a Japanese and an international student (Inter-cultural group) and among Japanese pairs (Intra-cultural group). Due to absences during Task 2, 3 and 5 performances, only data from Task 1 and 4 were analyzed. Because of an odd number of students, one triad from each group performed the tasks. Data collected from these students were eliminated from analysis, reducing the number of Japanese participants to 36.

Table 16.2 Design of the study

Inter-cultural group	Intra-cultural group	
(N = 18) 9 Japanese-Japanese dyads	(N = 18) 9 Japanese-Japanese dyads	Initial task performances
↓	↓	
Task 1	Task 1	Week 1
Task 4	Task 4	Week 4
↓	↓	
(N = 36) 18 Japanese-international dyads	(N = 18) 9 Japanese-Japanese dyads	Repeated task performances Data collection stage
↓	↓	
Task 1	Task 1	Week 7
Task 4	Task 4	Week 10

Tasks

The oral tasks in this study contained a two-way information exchange followed by a decision-making component. Students generated the content through a guided research pre-task, in which they gathered information that was later used during the task performance. The tasks were undertaken during scheduled classes and students were given 25 minutes to complete each task. All tasks were audio-recorded. During the task performances, students made notes on a task worksheet, which guided them through the task. A detailed description of Task 1 and Task 4 can be found in Aubrey (2018).

Self-reported learning chart

The purpose of the self-reported learning chart was to collect data on what the Japanese participants perceived they had learned from performing the tasks. The chart was adapted from Slimani's (1989, 1992) learning chart – or what she called an *uptake recall chart* – which obtained a measure of new linguistic information learners had noticed and remembered during task interaction. A distinction was made between linguistic items that were completely new to the student and items that were known before but consolidated during the task. On the chart, the following questions elicited this information: *What have you learned during this task that is completely new?* (このタスクを行っている際に新たに学んだ事はなんですか) and *What did you know before but have had confirmed during this task?* (以前から知っていたが、このタスクを行う事でより理解が深まり使えるようになった事はなんですか). Students then entered information into the following linguistic categories: grammar (文法), words or phrases (語彙又はフレーズ),

spelling (綴り), pronunciation (発音) and other (その他). Prior to the start of the study, the researcher conducted a workshop with the students that trained them on how to fill out the self-reported learning chart. Japanese participants completed the chart immediately after each of the tasks. While completing the charts, the students were asked to clear away all notes.

Analysis

Problems with item categorization

Upon an initial inspection of the completed learning charts, the researcher noticed two problems. First, some learners appeared to have difficulties categorizing claimed items into 'completely new' and 'known before but consolidated'. There was a total of 22 instances in which a learner reported a learned language item as being both 'completely new' and 'known before'. As these categories were intended to be mutually exclusive, it would be misleading to analyze the data of these two types of learning separately. To resolve this, the categories of 'completely new' and 'known before' were merged and duplicates (i.e. instances of double reporting) were deleted.

A second problem that emerged was that some learners interpreted the linguistic categories of 'grammar', 'words and phrases', 'spelling', 'pronunciation' and 'other' differently than other learners. There were also clear instances of mis-categorization (e.g. 'pronunciation of L and R' categorized as spelling instead of pronunciation). Thus, it was decided to merge all claimed items into a single general category irrespective of learners' linguistic categorization.

The relationship between claimed items and interaction

To investigate the relationship between self-reported language learning and interaction, claimed linguistic items from the tasks were traced back and identified in the transcripts. To examine the interactional features of task performances, data from Aubrey (2018) were used (i.e. the task transcripts and LRE analysis – see Table 16.1 for definitions of LRE categorization) and these were compared to reported claims of learning (i.e. self-reported language items). It was found that the claimed items fell into the following categories:

(1) unidentified – claimed items not identified in the transcripts;
(2) identified (without LREs) – claimed items identified in the transcripts but not associated with any LRE (i.e. not topicalized by either student); or
(3) identified (with LREs) – claimed items identified in the transcripts and the focus of at least one LRE (i.e. topicalized).

To elaborate on 1–3, when claims were 'unidentified', there was no evidence that these reported learning claims emerged from task interactions. On the other hand, claims that were 'identified (without LREs)' could be located in the corresponding learners' task transcripts but were not topicalized by way of an LRE. For example, when Emi reported learning the item 'meaning of cartoon', the only occurrence in her interaction was as follows:

Example 1: Identified without LRE: 'meaning of cartoon' (Intra-cultural group, Task 4)

10   **Emi:**   And animation, cultural, animation director … and … animation museum director.
11   **Akira:**   Okay, what are his job duties?
12   **Emi:**   He make a anime and movie. He write a … <u>cartoon</u>. He write the words for

In Example 1, Emi clearly did not learn this via feedback from her interlocutor. Although learners' reports were not detailed enough to give an indication of how these items were learned, it is possible that claimed items could have originated from written feedback or a dictionary search.

'Identified with LREs' were items identified in the transcript and the focus of one or more LREs.

Example 2: Identified with LRE: 'sangria' (Inter-cultural group 1, Task 1)

171   **Alais:**   It seems that they have good- good food coming from Africa, because there are many black people living there. So, for example, do you know about <u>Sangria</u>?
172   **Shuji:**   <u>Sangria</u>?
173   **Alais:**   <u>Sangria</u> is a kind of alcohol.
174   **Shuji:**   Alcohol, ah I don't know.
175   **Alais:**   Some kind of- you know- you know there are lots of fruits and lots of sugar, and you have alcohol inside.
176   **Shuji:**   [Sweet?   ]
177   **Alais:**   [And I think-] yeah, it's sweet.
178   **Shuji:**   It seems it is a specialty there.
179   **Alais:**   So <u>sangria</u>, it's=
180   **Shuji:**   =Spell please.
181   **Alais:**   S A N G R I A … and the food there is roasted fish. Roasted fish.

As seen in Example 2, the item 'sangria' is identified as the focus of two overlapping LREs. The first LRE begins at turn 171 and ends at turn 177 and was classified as being lexical, preemptive, complex and resolved without uptake. This is immediately followed by a second LRE, which is classified as spelling, reactive, simple and resolved without uptake.

The majority of reported items that were coded as 'identified with LREs' were the focus of a single LRE; however, as in Example 2, there were items that were the focus of two or more LREs. In addition, some learners reported learning an item twice, which was presumed to be a valid claim as these learners may have noticed more than one linguistic feature related to the same item.

Example 3: Identified with LRE: 'meaning of bubble tea' and 'spelling bubble' (Inter-cultural group, Task 1)

317 Johan: <u>Bubble Tea</u>.
318 Kayo: <u>Bubble Tea</u>?
319 Johan: Yes.
320 Kayo: Oh
321 Johan: That's what- it's from Taipei.
322 Kayo: Oh, I don't know.
323 Johan: It's invented in nineteen eighties.
324 Kayo: Nineteen eighties.
325 Johan: Hm
326 Kayo: Drink? ... <u>Bubble Tea</u>?
327 Johan: Yeah, <u>Bubble Tea</u> ... here
328 Kayo: Okay.
329 Johan: It's so cool, right?
330 Kayo: Yeah.
331 Johan: You love it?
332 Kayo: Yes.
333 Johan: <u>Bubble Tea</u>. So let's go to Taipei and drink <u>Bubble Tea</u>.
334 Kayo: It's tapioca.
335 Johan: Well Tapioca I guess is one of the ingredients they put into the=
336 Kayo: =Oh
337 Johan: <u>Bubble Tea</u> ... the balls, right?
338 Kayo: Oh
339 Johan: That's the tapioca, right?
340 Kayo: Un.
341 Johan: Yeah.
342 Kayo: <u>Bubble Tea</u>=
343 Johan: =So it's tea with tapioca is <u>bubble tea</u>.
344 Kayo: Okay ... <u>bubble tea</u> is great drink.

Example 3 presents a complex LRE that focuses on the meaning of the lexical item 'bubble tea'. This episode is the only portion of the transcript that contained either the item 'bubble tea' or 'bubble'. However, Kayo, when she reported the items, claimed that she had learned both meaning and spelling of bubble tea. Clearly, this LRE is responsible for helping Kayo notice and remember the meaning of 'bubble tea', but in the transcript, there is no explicit episode of interaction where the spelling of bubble tea is discussed. Nevertheless, it is assumed that this LRE caused her to focus on not only its meaning but also its spelling (Johan may have written the word down during turn 327).

Results

When claimed items were traced back to the transcripts, there were some instances in which one item could be traced to multiple LREs. Conversely, multiple reported items for one learner could sometimes be traced to the same LRE. Therefore, as Table 16.3 shows, there is a slight discrepancy between the total number of claimed items identified with LREs and the total number of distinct LREs that contributed to claimed items (i.e. reported LREs).

For the Inter-cultural group, 19.04% of total LREs identified in the transcripts resulted in reported claims of learning. Similarly, 21.71% of total LREs available to learners in the Intra-cultural group contributed to claims of language learning. In other words, there was approximately a 20% chance that any LRE occurring during interaction led to a learner's claim of learning.

Table 16.4 shows the frequency of claimed items, the frequency of claimed items that were the focus of an LRE (identified with LREs), the frequency of items that appeared in the transcript but were not the focus of an LRE (identified without LREs) and the frequency of items that did not appear in the transcripts (unidentified).

As can be seen in Table 16.4, the Inter-cultural group reported learning 21% more items than the Intra-cultural group. Furthermore, the Inter-cultural group reported 102 items that were associated with LREs (55.43% of total claims) while for the Intra-cultural group, only 50 reported items were associated with LREs (32.89% of total claims).

Table 16.3 LREs involved in self-reported learning for Task 1 and 4.

	Inter-cultural group ($N = 18$)	Intra-cultural group ($N = 18$)
Identified items with LREs	102	50
Reported LREs	107	56
Total available LREs to learners	562	258

Table 16.4 Self-reported items associated with LREs

Claimed items	Inter-cultural group ($N = 18$)			Intra-cultural group ($N = 18$)		
	Task 1	Task 4	Task 1+4	Task 1	Task 4	Task 1+4
Identified with LREs	49	53	102	26	24	50
Identified without LREs	51	20	71	52	37	89
Unidentified	7	4	11	10	3	13
Total items	107	77	184	88	64	152

In addition, there was a lower percentage of claimed items that could not be identified in the transcripts of the Inter-cultural group (5.97%) than those of the Intra-cultural group (8.56%).

Self-reported learning and LREs (linguistic focus)

The descriptive statistics for LREs that were identified as related to learners' claimed items are shown in Table 16.5. Figure 16.1 and Figure 16.2 show the quantity of LREs generated in each category of linguistic focus and the success rate of each in producing claimed items.

As the figures show, spelling and pronunciation LREs were the most frequently identified LRE contributing to the self-reported (i.e. claimed) learning in both inter-cultural (22.78%) and intra-cultural interactions (28.13%). Learners in both the Inter-cultural and Intra-cultural group

Table 16.5 Descriptive statistics for reported LREs

Reported LREs	Inter-cultural group (N = 18)				Intra-cultural group (N = 18)			
	Total	M	SD	%	Total	M	SD	%
Lexical	51	2.83	1.79	47.66	26	1.44	1.30	46.42
Grammatical	15	.83	1.58	14.02	2	.11	.32	3.57
Sp./Pron.	41	2.28	1.67	38.31	27	1.50	1.25	48.21
Other	0	0	0	0	1	.06	.24	1.79
Total	107	5.94	3.92	100	56	3.11	2.19	100

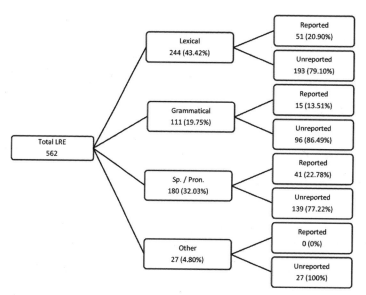

Figure 16.1 Relationship between LREs and self-reported learning (linguistic focus) for the Inter-cultural group
Note: Sp./Pron. = Spelling and pronunciation.

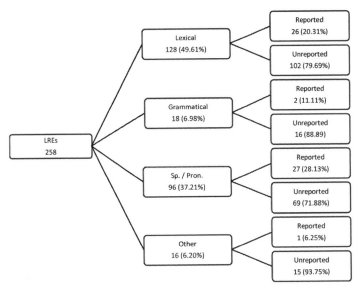

Figure 16.2 Relationship between LREs and self-reported learning (linguistic focus) for the Intra-cultural group
Note: Sp./Pron. = Spelling and pronunciation.

benefited from lexical LREs in almost equal proportions (20.90% and 20.31% respectively), whereas LREs that focused on grammatical form were slightly more likely to result in claimed items for the Inter-cultural group (13.51%) than the Intra-cultural group (11.11%). Thus, regardless of interlocutor, learners tended to learn most from interactional episodes that focused on spelling and pronunciation; however, grammar-focused interaction tended to lead to learning at a higher rate when the interlocutor was non-Japanese.

Self-reported learning and LRE (type)

The descriptive statistics for reported LREs of each type (reactive and preemptive) are shown in Table 16.6. Figures 16.3 and 16.4 relate these results to the quantity of LREs generated and available for learners in both groups.

Table 16.6 Descriptive statistics for reported LREs (type)

Reported LREs	Inter-cultural group (*N* = 18)				Intra-cultural group (*N* = 18)			
	Total	*M*	*SD*	%	Total	*M*	*SD*	%
Reactive	84	4.67	.70	78.50	43	2.39	.70	76.79
Preemptive	23	1.28	.22	21.50	13	.72	.22	23.21
Total	107	5.94	3.92	100	56	3.11	2.19	100

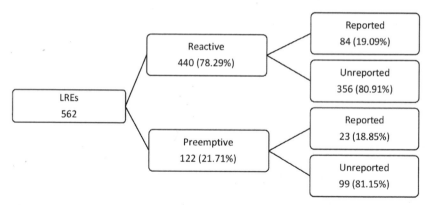

Figure 16.3 Relationship between LREs and self-reported learning (type) for the Inter-cultural group

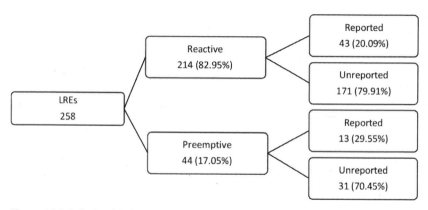

Figure 16.4 Relationship between LREs and self-reported learning (type) for the Intra-cultural group

As depicted in Figure 16.3, learners who experienced inter-cultural contact benefited from reactive and preemptive LREs in roughly equal proportions (19.09% and 18.85% respectively). In contrast, Figure 16.4 shows that claimed items from learners in the Intra-cultural group were considerably more likely to be a result of a preemptive LRE (29.55%) than a reactive one (20.09%). That is, when the focus of the language discussion was not in direct response to a language problem (e.g. a question that anticipated a language problem), the language item tended to be remembered and recalled more successfully when an international student was involved in the interaction. As these preemptive episodes often involve requests for explanation, this may indicate that the more proficient international students were able provide more accurate information – in a comprehensible manner – that led to greater internalization of language items.

Self-reported learning and LRE (complexity)

The descriptive statistics for reported LREs (simple and complex) are shown in Table 16.7. Figures 16.5 and 16.6 relate these results to the total LREs generated and available for learners in both groups.

Table 16.7 Descriptive statistics for reported language learning (complexity)

Reported LREs	Inter-cultural group (*N* = 18)				Inter-cultural group (*N* = 18)			
	Total	*M*	*SD*	%	Total	*M*	*SD*	%
Simple	40	2.22	2.21	37.38	28	1.56	1.42	50.00
Complex	67	3.72	2.67	62.62	28	1.56	1.42	50.00
Total	107	5.94	3.92	100	56	3.11	2.19	100

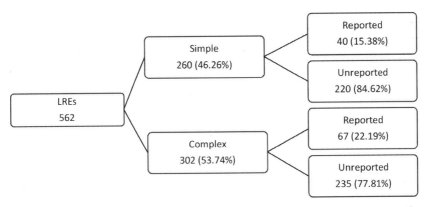

Figure 16.5 Relationship between LREs and self-reported learning (complexity) for the Inter-cultural group

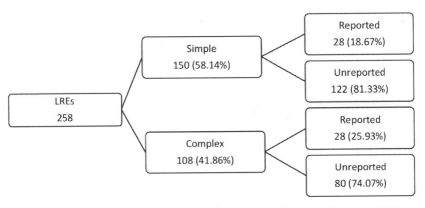

Figure 16.6 Relationship between LREs and self-reported learning (complexity) for the Intra-cultural group

As seen in Figures 16.5 and 16.6, there is a higher rate of reported learning from items emerging from complex LREs (Inter-cultural group = 22.19%, Intra-cultural group = 25.93%) than from simple LREs (Inter-cultural group = 15.38%, Intra-cultural group = 18.67%). This seems to indicate that LREs consisting of multiple turns lead to a greater chance of targeted items being reported. In sum, there seems to be an advantage for self-reported learning when learners extended their discussions through clarification questions, confirmations, paraphrasing or other strategies that lead to more opportunities for modified output and feedback.

Reported language and LRE (resolution)

The descriptive statistics for reported LREs (resolution) are shown in Table 16.8. Figures 16.7 and 16.8 relate these results to the total LREs generated and available for learners in both groups.

Table 16.8 Descriptive statistics for reported LREs (resolution)

Reported LREs	Inter-cultural group (N = 18)				Intra-cultural group (N = 18)			
	Total	M	SD	%	Total	M	SD	%
With uptake	57	3.17	2.18	53.27	25	1.39	1.38	44.64
Without uptake	47	2.61	2.40	43.93	25	1.39	1.65	44.64
Incorrect	1	.06	.24	.93	5	.28	.46	8.92
Unresolved	2	.11	.32	1.87	1	.06	.24	1.79
Total	107	5.94	3.92	100	56	3.11	2.19	100

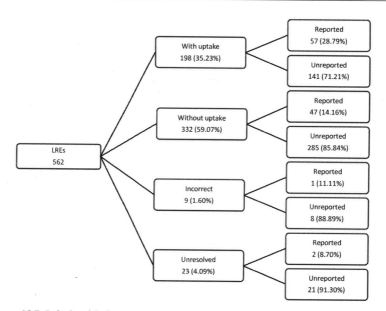

Figure 16.7 Relationship between LREs and self-reported learning (resolution) for the Inter-cultural group

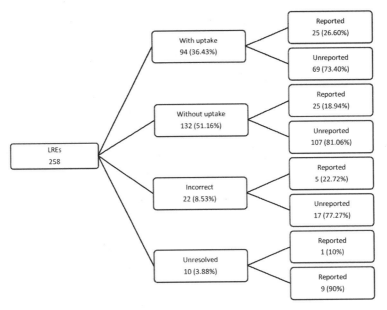

Figure 16.8 Relationship between LREs and self-reported learning (resolution) for the Intra-cultural group

Figures 16.7 and 16.8 show the relationship between LRE resolution and items that were claimed by learners in both groups. LREs that were resolved with uptake had the highest chance of being reported as learned for both the Inter-cultural (28.79%) and the Intra-cultural group (26.60%), which suggests that learners who demonstrate uptake through the production of a correct form were more likely to report they have learned the item. Though unresolved LREs resulted in the lowest rate of claim for both groups, there was a large difference in the rate of claims for incorrectly resolved LREs. In fact, compared to learners in the Inter-cultural group, Intra-cultural group interactions led to the reported learning of an item from incorrectly resolved LREs at twice the rate.

Discussion

The first question addressed the relationships between language-related discussions during collaborative tasks and reported learning. The data show that, regardless of whether Japanese students interacted with an international student or a Japanese peer, approximately 20% of LREs led to claims of learning. Although this value is less than those in studies implementing learning charts in teacher-fronted classes (e.g. Slimani, 1989), it does suggest that when EFL students collaborate during oral tasks, the discussions they produce have a considerable impact on what they perceive as learning. Therefore, the learning potential of tasks may be related to language-related discussions. The following discussion, then, provides insights into how the nature of these discussions (i.e. complexity, type, etc.) affect perceived learning and how the most successful of these interactions can be promoted in the classroom.

In terms of linguistic focus, spelling/pronunciation and lexical LREs were the most common form of LREs that led to reported claims of learning for both groups. This supports previous research on self-reported learning in teacher-fronted classes which has found that vocabulary items tend to dominate what learners report (Palmeira, 1995; Nabei, 2012). The success of spelling/pronunciation LREs, specifically, could be due to the fact that many pronunciation and spelling issues occurred simultaneously. These simultaneous LREs may engage students on two levels (spelling and pronunciation), increasing the saliency of an item and the likelihood that an item is claimed.

> Example 4: Reported spelling/pronunciation LRE: 'scavenger' (Intercultural group, Task 4)
>
> 94   Kate: It's a silly- it's a silly <u>scavenger</u> hunt. That's what it is. You find things like that. You can build things and stuff. And that's his charity. And it's to make people smile and laugh=
> 95   Yuki: =Scaven- challenge?
> 96   Kate: <u>Scavenger</u> hunt … wait … that's bad handwriting.
> 97   Yuki: Thank you. <u>S C A V</u>
> 98   Kate: Yeah
> 99   Yuki: <u>V E N G E R</u>
> 100 Kate: Yeah
> 101 Yuki: Hunt … okay.

Example 4 is a reported LRE in which Yuki reports learning the item 'scavenge'. Although this was classified as one LRE, learners attend to both a pronunciation and spelling issue, increasing the noticeability of the item. It is apparent that in Turn 96 Kate writes down either 'scavenger' or 'scavenger hunt' in an effort to resolve the pronunciation issue. Although the written actions during tasks were usually not verbalized, and thus cannot be explicitly identified in the transcripts, it is likely that focusing on the spelling or pronunciation of a word often involved both the spoken and written form. In other words, an unintended consequence of the worksheet is that it provided students with an aid for resolving language problems. This suggests that the provision of a non-assessed worksheet to students, together with encouragement to clarify or confirm vocabulary or spelling issues through writing, could be a beneficial practice.

Both groups had a higher rate of self-reported learning for items coming from complex LREs than simple LREs, indicating that, regardless of interlocutor, LREs that contain a large number of turns are more likely to be reported. This was expected as complex LREs usually arise when there are multiple attempts to resolve an issue, thereby increasing the chance that the topicalized item is noticed and remembered.

Example 5: Reported complex LRE: 'shemale' (Intra-cultural group, Task 1)

9	Ran:	What famous site and festival?
10	Kako:	Do you know Shemale?
11	Ran:	No, I don't know. Shemale. What spell?
12	Kako:	S H E
13	Ran:	E
14	Kako:	M A L E
15	Ran:	Shemale?
16	Kako:	Yes.
17	Ran:	What's shemale?
18	Kako:	This mean lady guy. Lady guy?
19	Ran:	Festival or site?
20	Kako:	No, person=
21	Ran:	=Person?
22	Kako:	Shemale shows are famous.
23	Ran:	Shemale shows?
24	Kako:	Shemale.
25	Ran:	[Show]
26	Kako:	[Show]
27	Ran:	Between- between male and female?
28	Kako:	Ah yes, yes, yes, yes.
29	Ran:	Ah okay.
30	Kako:	Man who like wearing woman=
31	Ran:	=Dress?
32	Kako:	Yes, yes.
33	Ran:	Okay… shemale.

Example 5 presents a complex, lexical LRE for the item 'shemale' that begins with a preemptive focus on form at Turn 10 and is resolved at Turn 33. Embedded within this LRE is a pronunciation/spelling LRE (Turns 11 to 14). Learners use a variety of strategies to understand the meaning of the item. These include spelling the word (Turns 12–14), simple definitions (Turns 18 and 30), clarification questions (Turns 18, 19, 23 and 27) and providing examples of the word in context (Turn 22). The sheer amount of input (and chances for modified output) as well as the length of the negotiation period ensured this item was noticed and recalled by the learner. Examples like this suggest that perceived learning may be enhanced if learners are encouraged – or even explicitly taught strategies – to elaborate their language discussions.

Related to the advantage for self-reported learning of complex LREs, Japanese students also benefited when they demonstrated uptake (i.e. used the corrected form). LREs that were resolved with uptake were claimed at a higher rate for both the Inter-cultural group (28.79%) and the Intra-cultural group (26.60%) than LREs that were unresolved. This was not surprising as learners who respond to feedback by using the correct form show that the item has been understood and also benefit from the possibility of receiving further feedback.

Example 6: Reported LRE resolved with uptake: 'stunt performer' (Inter-cultural group, Task 4)

18	Andrew:	But those big actions, they don't make the actor do it. They have a stuntman. A <u>stunt performer</u>.
19	Miho:	<u>Stunt</u>?
20	Andrew:	[Yeah]
21	Miho:	[Oh]
22	Andrew:	Who does the dangerous stuff in the movies.
23	Miho:	Oh.

(the LRE resumes 10 minutes later)

247	Miho:	Job one, <u>stuntman</u>.
248	Andrew:	Well, I like to say <u>stunt performer</u>.
249	Miho:	Disadvantage.

(the LRE resumes 1 minute later)

265	Miho:	Three thousand- three thirty hundred dollar. Thirty-
266	Andrew:	No, three hundred dollars. Like about three ten thousand yen ... to get hit by a car=
267	Miho:	=<u>Stunt performer</u> is very dangerous.

Example 6 shows a discontinuous LRE (i.e. topicalized in multiple parts) in which the learner gradually makes use of the correct form at different times in the task interaction. Andrew first provides a definition of a 'stunt performer' (Turn 22), which does not immediately result in successful uptake. Miho then attempts to produce the item (Turn 247), which provokes a form correction from Andrew. Miho does not produce the correct form of the word until Turn 267. This example reflects a gradual internalization of a lexical item (stunt $\rightarrow$ stuntman $\rightarrow$ stunt performer) and shows that multiple attempts to modify output are often needed for successful uptake. This finding again suggests that learners may benefit from explicit training in how to recast or reformulate erroneous language, ask clarification or confirmation questions, elaborate on comments, seek more information or paraphrase their interlocutor, which, when deployed in task performances, give students opportunity to demonstrate uptake (for instructional methods on interactional strategies, see, for example, Bejarano *et al.*, 1997).

The second research question asked whether there were differences in how inter-cultural and intra-cultural interaction contributed to claims of learning. The first difference is in regard to LRE type – specifically, that preemptive LREs were more successful at generating claims for intra-cultural interaction (29.55%) than inter-cultural interaction (18.85%). Upon examination of the transcripts, one explanation for this difference is that inter-culturally generated preemptive LREs did not offer as many opportunities for uptake. Examples 7 and 8 show lexical, preemptive LREs in which international students predict a gap in their interlocutors' language knowledge and define an item, but leave little room for the Japanese learner to verbalize an uptake move.

Example 7: Preemptive LRE (Inter-cultural group, Task 4)

478 Louise: Do you know trade point?
479 Miyako: No
480 Louise: Trade point is like selling and buying stuff. *Okay, next.*

Example 8: Preemptive LRE (Inter-cultural group, Task 4)

228 Andrew: But he's been doing- do you know parkour?
229 Miho: No.
230 Andrew: It's like jump around anywhere.
231 Miho: Oh yeah=
232 Andrew: =Yeah, it's like where you jump over buildings or jump over walls, spin, you can do all kinds of stuff. And he's been doing that kind of training since he was born- since he remembers. He's been doing this and martial arts. Like Kung Fu, Taekwondo, yeah. Since he was little. Like when I saw him high school, he was a really strong guy. What about your guy?

In Example 7, Louise finishes Turn 480 with the transition 'Okay, next' signaling that it is appropriate to continue to the next stage of the task. Andrew, in Example 8, finishes a long explanation of the lexical item 'parkour' with the question 'What about your guy?' In both cases, the Japanese EFL learner is in a situation where it would be difficult or even inappropriate to ask clarification questions, thus forcing the language-related discussion to an end before the learner can demonstrate uptake. Perhaps this is due to international students overestimating the capacity for the Japanese students to quickly internalize information when further attention is, in fact, needed. This is consistent with Sato and Lyster's (2007) observation that during learner-native speaker interactions, learners feel more pressure and have less time to plan what they are going to say, leading to fewer opportunities for modified output. Thus, teachers who wish to use tasks that involve students of different cultural backgrounds may find it useful to provide training on social norms and communication rules of the local context so language/communication expectations can be appropriately adjusted (see Gudyunst & Nishida, 1994).

In terms of how LREs were resolved, intra-cultural interaction generated incorrectly resolved LREs that led to claims of learning at twice the rate (Inter-cultural = 11.11%, Intra-cultural = 22.72%).

Example 9: Reported grammatical LRE: 'more cheap' (Intra-cultural group, Task 1)

250	**Emi:**	I can became- become cultured person
251	**Akira:**	And more … [low]
252	**Emi:**	[And] more cheap=
253	**Akira:**	=More cheap?
254	**Emi:**	More cheap than Japan

Example 10: Reported pronunciation/spelling LRE: 'Lion spell' (Intra-cultural group, Task 1)

4	**Rika:**	Especially, I'd like to travel to Lyon city.
5	**Mika:**	Lyon. Lyon city?
6	**Rika:**	Yes, L I O
7	**Mika:**	O
8	**Rika:**	N
9	**Mika:**	N. Oh Lyon.
10	**Rika:**	Lyon.

Example 9 illustrates how an incorrectly resolved grammatical LRE led to the claim of a grammatical item. Similarly, Example 10 shows how an incorrectly spelled word resulted in a claimed item. Both are examples of interactions between learners who try to resolve a language problem but do not have sufficient linguistic knowledge.

To mitigate erroneous language learning, students should be given an opportunity to share what they have learned after a task so they can verify the meaning/use of new linguistic items. The basis for such a 'post-task reporting stage' could take the form of a self-reported learning chart – similar to that used in this research. These charts could then be used in reflection activities, such as a written summary or presentation that uses and extends language with a focus on accuracy. Furthermore, using learning charts can have a positive motivational effect. As Csikszentmihalyi (1997) states, 'only after the task is completed do we have the leisure to look back on what has happened, and then we are flooded with gratitude for the excellence of that experience' (1997: 32). In this way, learning charts direct students to 'look back' to evaluate their achievements and reflect on the learning process.

Conclusion

The research reported in this chapter looked at the relationships between learning and interaction when oral tasks were performed in inter-cultural and intra-cultural conditions in a Japanese EFL classroom.

A methodological feature of this study is that it utilized self-reported learning charts to collect data on what Japanese EFL students learned from their tasks – a method that had primarily been confined to teacher-fronted classes. Two results lend support to the inter-cultural condition as being the more beneficial learning environment: (1) more learning was reported, and (2) the language-related discussions that resulted in learned language tended to be more accurately resolved. Irrespective of task condition, discussions about language issues that were complex in nature, and those that demonstrated uptake, were more successful at generating reported learning.

The findings in this study also have important pedagogical implications as they indicate to teachers the kinds of task-based interactions that optimize reported learning. In regard to task materials, the results show that encouraging students to make written notes during oral tasks may promote the resolution of lexical and spelling issues, which, in turn, may facilitate recall. In addition, the self-reported learning charts could be used as a pedagogical post-task intervention, which could focus learners' attention on what they have learned after a task, thereby extending students' understanding of new language and underscoring the learning value of performing collaborative tasks. In terms of instructional implications, the increased reported learning in conjunction with complex language discussions suggests that students might benefit from training in the use of interactional strategies. Finally, training in communication norms might help avoid miscommunication between speakers of different backgrounds and proficiency levels.

This study is not without limitations. It should first be reiterated that the notion of *learning* in this chapter is that of *perceived* learning – a measure of noticing, depth of processing and memory. Time and memory, therefore, are bound to negatively affect the data. In this study, a small but non-trivial percentage of learned items could not be found in the corresponding task transcripts. Additionally, several students were unable to clearly assign learned items to pre-determined linguistic categories on their learning charts. To strengthen reliability, teachers need to set aside considerable time to train their students on how to complete their learning charts. It is also possible for teachers/researchers to conduct multiple administrations of the learning chart. For example, a second administration could be completed after a post-task discussion, which could trigger a more accurate recall response. Such new efforts to integrate learning charts into the task process would improve both the quality of data collected and facilitate the effective use of tasks in L2 instruction.

References

Allwright, R.L. (1984) Why don't learners learn what teachers teach? – the interaction hypothesis. In D.M. Singleton and D. G. Little (eds) *Language Learning in Formal and Informal Contexts* (pp. 3–18). Dublin: IRAAL.

Aubrey, S. (2017a) Inter-cultural contact and flow in a task-based Japanese EFL classroom. *Language Teaching Research* 21 (6), 717–734.

Aubrey, S. (2017b) Measuring flow in the EFL classroom: Learners' perceptions of inter- and intra-cultural task-based interactions. *TESOL Quarterly* 51 (3), 661– 692.

Aubrey, S. (2018) The impact of intra-cultural and inter-cultural task repetition on interaction. In M. Bygate (ed.) *Learning Language through Task Repetition* (pp. 117–142). Amsterdam: John Benjamins.

Bejarano, Y., Levine, T., Olshtain, E. and Steiner, J. (1997) The skilled use of interaction strategies: Creating a framework for improved small-group communicative interaction in the language classroom. *System* 25 (2), 203–214.

Bowles, M., Adams, R. and Toth, P.D. (2014) A comparison of L2-L2 and L2-heritage learner interactions in Spanish language classrooms. *Modern Language Journal* 98 (2), 497–517.

Burrows, C. (2008) Socio-cultural barriers facing TBL in Japan. *The Language Teacher* 32 (8), 15–19.

Csikszentmihalyi, M. (1997) *Finding Flow. The Psychology of Engagement with Everyday Life.* New York: Basic Books.

Eckerth, J. (2006) Three theses on the pedagogical relevance of second language acquisition research. *Dil Dergisi Turkish Language Journal* 130 (1), 18–36.

Ellis, R. (1995) Uptake as language awareness. *Language Awareness* 4 (3), 147–60.

Fernández Dobao, A. (2012) Collaborative dialogue in learner-learner and learner-native speaker interaction. *Applied Linguistics* 33 (3), 229–256.

Freiermuth, M.R. and Huang, H. (2012) Bringing Japan and Taiwan closer electronically: A look at an intercultural online synchronic chat task and its effect on motivation. *Language Teaching Research* 16 (1), 61–88.

Gudyunst, W. and Nishida, T. (1994) *Ridging Japanese/North American Differences.* California: Sage Publications.

Kim, Y. and McDonough, K. (2008) The effect of interlocutor proficiency on the collaborative dialogue between Korean as a second language learners. *Language Teaching Research* 12 (2), 211–234.

King, J. (2013) Silence in the Second Language Classrooms of Japanese Universities. *Applied Linguistics* 34 (3), 325–343.

Leeser, M. (2004) Learner proficiency and focus on form during collaborative dialogue. *Language Teaching Research* 8 (1), 55–81.

Loewen, S. (2005) Incidental focus on form and second language learning. *Studies in Second Language Acquisition* 27 (3), 361–86.

Lyster, R. and Ranta, L. (1997) Corrective feedback and learner uptake: Negotiation of form in communicative classrooms. *Studies in Second Language Acquisition* 19 (1), 37–66.

Nabei, T. (2012) Learner uptake reports on an EFL reading class in Japan. 外国語教育フォーラム *[Foriegn Language Education Forum]* 12, 47–62.

Nobuyoshi, M. (2011) How wide is the gulf between PPP and TBLT? *Okayama Prefectural Okayama-Sozan Senior High School Department Bulletin Paper* 13, 1–13.

Palmeira, W.K. (1995) A study of uptake by learners of Hawaiian. In R. Schmidt (ed.) *Attention and Awareness in Foreign Language Learning* (pp. 127–161). Honolulu, HI: University of Hawaii.

Sato, R. (2009) Suggestions for creating approaches suitable to the Japanese EFL environment. *The Language Teacher* 33 (9), 11–14.

Sato, R. (2010) Reconsidering the effectiveness and suitability of PPP and TBLT in the Japanese EFL classroom. *JALT Journal* 32 (2), 189–200.

Sato, M. and Lyster, R. (2007) Modified output of Japanese EFL learners: Variable effects of interlocutor vs. feedback types. In A. Mackey (ed.) *Conversational Interaction in Second Language Acquisition: A Series of Empirical Studies* (pp. 123–142). Oxford: Oxford University Press.

Slimani, A. (1989) The role of topicalization in classroom language learning. *System* 17 (2), 223–34.

Slimani, A. (1992) Evaluation of classroom interaction. In J.C. Alderson and A. Beretta (eds) *Evaluating Second Language Education* (pp. 197–221). Cambridge: Cambridge University Press.

Swain, M. (1995) Three functions of output in second language learning. In G. Cook and B. Seidlhofer (eds) *Principle and Practice in Applied Linguistics: Studies in Honor of H. G. Widdowson* (pp. 125–144). Oxford: Oxford University Press.

Swain, M. (2006) Languaging, agency and collaboration in advanced second language proficiency. In H. Bynes (ed.) *Advanced Language Learning: The Contribution of Halliday and Vygotsky* (pp. 95–108). London: Continuum.

Watanabe, Y. and Swain, M. (2007) Effects of proficiency differences and patterns of pair interaction on second language learning: Collaborative dialogue between adult ESL learners. *Language Teaching Research* 11 (2), 121–142.

Williams, J. (2001) The effectiveness of spontaneous attention to form. *System* 29 (3), 325–340.

17 The Impact of Agency in Pair Formation on the Degree of Participation in Young Learners' Collaborative Dialogue

Ainara Imaz Agirre and
María del Pilar García Mayo

Recent SLA research with adult learners has shown that the method of pair formation has an impact on peer interaction and the interactional patterns that occur. Research has also shown that task modality influences language learning opportunities with oral tasks (e.g. picture placement, picture differences) focusing attention on meaning and oral+written tasks (e.g. dictogloss) on formal aspects of language. However, investigations on these topics with young learners are scarce given the worldwide trend of early introduction of foreign languages in school contexts. The current study examined the impact of agency in pair formation (i.e. whether the teacher, students or researchers select the interlocutors in pair work) on the degree of participation when 64 Spanish EFL learners (age 11–12) completed different modality tasks. They were divided into three groups: a researcher-selected group (RS) (12 dyads), a teacher-selected group (TS) (8 dyads) and a student-selected (SS) group. Degree of participation was measured in terms of quantity (number of turns) and L2 use (i.e. the extent to which learners used the L2 as opposed to the L1 during task performance). The findings indicate that there were differences between the RS group and the TS/SS groups regarding the quantity of participation. As for L2 use, the RS group produced more L2 turns than the TS or the SS groups. Our results highlight the importance of dyad assignment for young learners' participation in a dialogue and the languages used when they collaborate. These findings might prove useful for teachers who are interested in how tasks can be effectively implemented in different contexts.

Introduction

Over the last few decades there has been a growing international trend for the introduction of foreign language learning at a very early age (Enever, 2011, 2018; García Mayo, 2017; Murphy, 2014), often done on the assumption that early exposure to the target language is beneficial for learners (but see Huang (2016) for arguments against this idea). The appropriate implementation of early foreign language programs represents a challenge for policy makers and educators alike, especially considering that classroom-based research on young learners has not been a major focus of empirical studies in the second language acquisition (SLA) field. In fact, Collins and Muñoz (2016: 141) claim that 'School-based FL [foreign language] programs, particularly those at the elementary school level, are increasingly common and yet underrepresented (…) in SLA research in general'.

Recent studies from a sociocultural perspective (Vygotsky, 1978) have considered peer interaction while learners complete collaborative tasks. For example, researchers have claimed that collaborative work allows learners to co-construct meaning and pay attention to language form without teacher intervention (Payant & Kim, 2017; Storch, 2016; Swain, 2000). Most studies on collaborative work have examined interactional patterns (Storch, 2002) or language performance by adult learners in English as a Second language (ESL) and English as a Foreign Language (EFL) contexts (see Storch (2016) for a summary). However, the analysis of young EFL learners' performance while completing communicative tasks has not received the same attention. Previous studies with young learners have shown that they negotiate for meaning when working with peers (García Mayo & Lázaro Ibarrola (2015) in an EFL context; Oliver (1998) in an ESL context) and in different gender and proficiency-matched dyads (Azkarai & Imaz Agirre, 2016) and they also display collaborative patterns in pair work (García Mayo & Imaz Agirre, 2016). However, little is known about whether task modality and the method of pair formation have an impact on degree of participation when young EFL learners collaborate.

It is possible that that degree of participation resulting from the way pairs are formed reflects the motivation of the learners. In turn, the learners' view of their partner in the dyad/small group and their perception of the task itself may have an impact on how motivated each learner might feel and, therefore, how active he or she is during the task (Gagné & Parks, 2016). Most studies so far have considered the influence of task-related motivation as an individual variable in studies with adult learners (Al-Khalil, 2011, 2016), whereas on-task motivation has received limited attention. However, very little is known about whether task-related motivation interacts with young learners' degree of participation in different pairing conditions and when completing different tasks.

Therefore, this study aims to be a first step to fill in this gap by examining the interaction of 32 dyads of 11 to 12-year-old Spanish EFL learners with an elementary proficiency level while they completed two tasks with different modalities: an oral task and an oral+written task. The children were divided into researcher-selected (RS), teacher-selected (TS) and self-selected (SS) groups, whose interactions were video-recorded, transcribed and analyzed regarding turns taken and language used (their first language (L1) or the target language).

Task modality

Research on second language (L2) task-based interaction has shown that different tasks offer different opportunities for language learning due to the different cognitive demands of the speaking and writing modalities (Rouhshad & Storch, 2016). Speaking is spontaneous and provides learners with limited editing time, whereas writing allows for greater opportunities for modifications (Williams, 2012) and draws learners' attention to both form and meaning (Cumming, 1989). Having more time to produce written output allows learners to retrieve explicit information related to grammatical rules (Ellis, 2003). Research with adults has shown that written tasks or tasks that include a written component (e.g. dictogloss, Wajnryb, 1990) usually elicit more attention to form, operationalized as language-related episodes (LREs) (Swain & Lapkin, 1998). LREs have been defined as any part of the dialogue 'in which students talk about the language they are producing, question their language use, or other- or self-correct' (Swain, 1998: 70). Speaking tasks, in contrast, seem to draw learners' attention to meaning (Adams, 2006; García Mayo & Azkarai, 2016; Manchón, 2017; Niu, 2009).

A number of studies has compared collaborative dialogue in oral and written modes. This research has examined the LREs produced when completing oral (Kim & McDonough, 2008; Payant & Reagan, 2018) and written tasks (Alegría de la Colina & García Mayo, 2007; Leeser, 2004; Swain & Lapkin, 2001) with mixed results. For adult participants tasks requiring a written component elicit more lexis-based and grammar-based LREs than oral tasks (Adams & Ross-Feldman, 2008; Niu, 2009) whereas research with young learners has shown that oral tasks elicit a higher percentage of lexical LREs (Payant & Kim, 2017). Other research has compared the language performance (measuring complexity, accuracy and fluency) of adults when undertaking tasks in two modes (oral and written). To date, the findings are inconclusive (Granfeldt, 2008; Kormos, 2015; Kuiken & Vedder, 2011). To the best of our knowledge, there is no study comparing young learners' production in these two modes.

Pair-formation method and degree of participation

From a sociocultural perspective (Vygotsky, 1978), learning is a socially mediated process, where interaction can provide opportunities for *languaging* (Swain, 2006; Swain *et al.*, 2011), 'a dynamic, never-ending process of using language to make meaning' (Swain, 2006: 96). Against this backdrop, there have been a number of studies examining whether interaction in pairs or small groups offers more opportunities for language learning (cf. Storch (2016) for a review). Special attention has been paid to the patterns of interaction adopted while completing collaborative tasks. In her seminal work, Storch (2002) explored learners' relationships when working together, and she proposed four interactional styles based on two constructs: equality (degree of control over the direction of the task) and mutuality (level of engagement). She reported that when dyads establish either collaborative or expert/novice patterns, peer interaction has positive effects on language learning because learners pay more attention to language choice and retain linguistic knowledge that is co-constructed. Research conducted with adult and young learners in ESL and EFL contexts has shown that not all dyads are successful in creating collaborative dialogues that would lead to language learning (García Mayo & Imaz Agirre, 2016; Storch, 2016). The kind of patterns learners adopt, especially adults, has been the focus of a considerable body of research. However, other variables such as pair formation method and degree of participation have been underexplored.

Mozaffari (2017) is one of the first empirical studies conducted in L2 research examining the impact of the method of pair formation (student-assigned vs. teacher-assigned) on collaborative dialogue. The goal of this study was twofold: to examine the role of the method of pair formation in the quantity and quality of LREs and the patterns of interaction that occurred and to analyze the extent to which the pair formation method affected the learners' written output. Forty Iranian female intermediate EFL learners participated in the study (age range 20–26) and they were randomly assigned to student-assigned and teacher-assigned pairings. Dyads in both conditions were asked to write a composition collaboratively. The findings of the study indicated that student-assigned dyads engaged more in off-task talk, whereas the teacher-assigned condition pairs produced more LREs. However, both pairing conditions resulted in a collaborative interactional pattern. Furthermore, the teacher-assigned pairs seemed to outperform student-selected pairs when producing written texts.

A very relevant aspect in learner interaction is the extent to which the members of a dyad or a small group are more or less involved in it. Mattar and Blondin (2006) examined the speech acts of 7–8-year-old students in two classes of partial immersion (half of the students were immersed in German and the other half in Dutch). Participants completed collaborative activities and the selected students' output was recorded and examined. Findings reported an equal distribution of speech acts in the target language as well as in the students' L1 (French).

Within the framework of cooperative learning (Johnson & Johnson, 1994), Gagné and Parks (2016) investigated the degree of participation of two groups of Grade 6 (11 to 12-year-old) learners in an intensive ESL class in Quebec, Canada, as they engaged in three collaborative tasks. The classroom teacher set up teams of four composed of one high English achiever, two average students and one low achiever. The two participating groups were randomly selected. The students' degree of participation was then examined by measuring the number of turns for each student and the percentage of turns that actually used the target language, in this case English. Their findings revealed that participation was equally distributed amongst participants and that each member of the group was actively involved. Regarding language use, over 90% of turns were exclusively in English and only 4% of the total words were French.

Task-related motivation

L2 motivation has been widely investigated in SLA research. Until the 1990s, it was examined as a personal trait that was stable and enduring. However, from the 1990s onwards, including in the current research, motivation is viewed as a dynamically changing flow that a person can initiate, modify or direct (Dörnyei & Ottó, 1998). Motivation is influenced by internal and external factors and is frequently interpreted as a complex dynamic system (see Dörnyei (2009) for a discussion).

Within the task-based language teaching (TBLT) approach (Long, 2015; Van den Branden *et al.*, 2009), research on motivation has been carried out from three main domains: cognitive, behavioral and affective (or emotional). From a cognitive domain, two studies have investigated the relationship between L2 motivation and noticing (Dasse-Askildson, 2008; Takahashi, 2005). However, findings in these studies have been in stark contrast to each other, one confirming the correlation between L2 motivation and noticing (Takahashi, 2005) and the second one rejecting such relationship (Dasse-Askildson, 2008). Within the behavioral domain, research revealed that motivation explained more than a third of the variance in the amount of L2 output (Dörnyei & Kormos, 2000; Kormos & Dörnyei, 2004). Within the affective or emotional domain, there is evidence in research that task preferences (Julkunen, 2001), perceived task difficulty (Dörnyei, 2002; Robinson, 2001) or task relevance (Rose, 2007) have an impact on increasing or decreasing learners' motivation. Al-Khalil (2016) measured task-related motivation with a mixed method approach using Tennant and Gardner's (2004) motivation thermometer. In addition to the quantitative part of the graphic representation of a thermometer, a qualitative dimension was incorporated where the learners could add notes and reflect upon their task-related motivation. In another study with 44 North American students (19 males, 25 females) taking Intermediate II Arabic, Al-Kahlil also found that 'Learner comments allowed not only more nuanced appreciation of learner motivational states but also highlighted the motivational value of particular types of tasks from the learners' perspectives' (Al-Khalil, 2016: 260).

This brief literature review has shown that variables such as task modality and pair-formation method, together with task-related motivation, should be considered both when doing research on tasks and when using tasks in diverse contexts and with different populations, as they may impact the learners' L2 output. In what follows, we examine these variables and their potential impact on the L2 output of an underexplored group – namely, young EFL learners at a school in a major Spanish city.

The present study

The main goal of the present study is to examine the impact of who allocates learners to pairs (teachers, students or researchers) on degree of participation when young learners complete an oral task and an oral task with a written outcome. On the basis of the findings reported in previous research, the following research questions guided the current study:

(1) Does task modality have an impact on the degree of participation of young Spanish EFL learners while they complete collaborative tasks?
(2) Does pair formation method have an impact on the degree of participation of young Spanish EFL learners?
(3) Does pair formation method have an impact on on-task motivation in an EFL context? That is, do young Spanish EFL learners feel equally motivated before and after the task?

Methods

Participants

The participants in the study were 64 young Spanish EFL learners from three intact classes at a school in a major Spanish city. Before the data collection, participants completed the KET Cambridge English Language Assessment Test, which placed them at Level A2, that is, elementary users of the language according to the Common European Framework of Reference for Languages (Council of Europe, 2018).

The children in each class were then distributed into a different pairing condition: a researcher-selected (RS) group, made up of 12 dyads (n = 24), selected on the basis of the results of the proficiency test; a teacher-selected (TS) group, with 8 dyads (n = 16) grouped according to the teacher's criteria about who could best complete tasks together; and a self-selected (SS) group with 12 dyads (n = 24) in which the children themselves selected who they worked with. The children worked with the same partner in both the oral task and the oral + written task. Table 17.1 summarizes participant information:

Table 17.1 Participants' information

	Researcher selected (RS)	Teacher selected (TS)	Self-selected (SS)
N of participants	24	16	24
Mean age	11.02	11.06	11.05
Mean proficiency score	23.52	19.32	17.43

Procedure and data collection instruments

Participants completed two tasks in their pairs: an oral task (OT) and an oral task with written output (OWT). The tasks were designed together with the teachers and the content in both tasks matched a topic covered at school, namely, detectives. The oral task was adapted from 'Nate the Great and the lost list' (Weinman Sharmat, 1975). In this task, each dyad was given 13 black-and-white cards with cartoon vignettes. The flashcards comprised a story about a child detective who was looking for a missing list. Working collaboratively, the participants had to put the vignettes in order.

In the OWT task, the children were given a poster with a crime scene: a science classroom with some broken elements which clearly indicated that a thief had entered the premises. Together with the poster, they were presented with three clues and information about four potential suspects. Their task was to find out what happened in the science classroom, who the suspect of the crime was and his or her rationale for the robbery. Once students agreed on this information verbally, they were asked to produce a short text describing what happened and justifying their decision. The children completed both tasks in a room next to their classroom. They completed the OT first and the OWT one week later. Once instructions were given, no other vocabulary was provided.

In order to measure the impact of pair formation method on students' motivation, participants completed a motivation thermometer (Al-Khalil, 2011, 2016; Tennant & Gardner, 2004). They were given a thermometer scaling from 1 to 10 (1 being the least motivated and the 10 being the most motivated). Each participant was asked to indicate how s/he felt about the task by placing a magnet piece next to the corresponding number in the thermometer (see Appendix 17.1). Each participant filled in the thermometer individually right before and right after completing the task. In addition to the quantitative data, we also obtained qualitative data. As the participants were young learners, they were provided with prompts in Spanish (e.g. 'I have had fun doing this task') they had to choose from in order to indicate how they felt about having to do the task.

Data analysis

Following Gagné and Parks (2016: 174), turn taking was defined as 'any uninterrupted oral interaction produced by a child'. In this study, to measure the distribution of the turns, number of words per turn were counted to capture turn size. As the aim of the present study was to analyze the degree of participation in learner-learner interaction, turns addressing the researcher were not included in the analysis. In a similar vein, only comprehensible words were taken into consideration. Following Gagné and Parks (2016), phatics, expressions such as, *eh, hm, uhm* were not included in the count, however, contractions (e.g. *he's*) were considered as two words. In order to address the second research question, the language present in each turn was considered. Some turns were entirely in English (i.e. the general took all the money from the piggy) or in Spanish (i.e. *la huella se parece a esta* (the fingerprint is similar to this one)), whereas other turns were in two languages, that is Spanish and English (how do you say *huella en inglés*? (how do we say fingerprint in English?)).

Regarding the thermometer, students marked a score from 1 to 10 about how eager they felt about doing the task before and after completing the task. These scores were measured by the researchers and submitted to statistical analysis. In addition, students were given the prompts in Spanish in order to justify their quantitative score before and after completing the tasks. There was no time constraint for task completion.

Results and Discussion

The first research question examined the impact of task modality on the degree of participation in interaction by these young learners. As shown in Table 17.2, our findings indicate that students in the RS group engaged in task performance more often than students in the SS and TS groups. A paired t-test analysis compared the number of turns students took in each pairing condition.

Table 17.2 Number of turns in each task

Group	OT		OWT	
	Turns	SD	Turns	SD
RS	713	5.32	831	6.33
TS	496	7.23	319	8.34
SS	512	6.34	414	6.34

OT = oral task; OWT = oral+written task

The statistical analyses revealed no differences in the quantity of turns in the RS group between the OW and the OWT. However, statistically significant differences between the OT and the OWT were found in the TS and SS groups. Students participated more in the OT in comparison to the OWT in both groups (TS: t = 2.947, p = 0.011, d = 0.05; SS: t = 2.195, p = 0.041, d = 0.53), which seems to indicate that there is a task modality effect in the degree of participation among these young EFL learners. Thus, in this study, the OT seems to have encouraged more learner participation than the OWT.

The second research question examined the impact of the pair-formation method on the degree of learner participation in the two tasks. Whether participants equally contributed to the conversation and the languages used in each turn was examined (see Table 17.3).

Table 17.3 Mean of turns per student

	OT		OWT	
	Mean turns per student	SD	Mean turns per student	SDC
RS	37.35	2.41	39.75	1.45
TS	26.46	4.24	21.46	4.45
SS	25.67	4.23	23.56	4.35

OT = oral task; OWT = oral+written task

An ANOVA analysis showed that the children in the RS group participated more actively than those in the TS and SS groups. Unlike Mozaffari (2017), the degree of participation was similar in the TS and SS groups, however, in the current study an RS group was also included. Regarding the equal contribution of turns in each dyad, ANOVA analyses showed that students in the RS group contributed equally to the dialogue in both tasks. Although the contributions were less equal in the OT, no statistical differences were found between tasks. Nonetheless, in the TS and SS pairing conditions, students displayed an unequal degree of participation in the OWT (TS group: F = 2.533, p = 0.023, d = 0.20; SS group: F = 5.553, p = 0.020, d = 0.19) compared to the OT. Thus, the findings indicate that one of the students in the pair was more active in the conversation than the other, as shown in Example (1):

(1)

Student 1:	*mira la huella* (look at the fingerprint).
Student 2:	*Esta está en círculo* (This one is in a circle).
Student 1:	*¿cuál?* (which one?).
Student 2:	*esta* (this one).
Student 1:	big teeth with spaces.
Student 2:	(he nods).
Student 1:	is this … I think is this. *La huella se parece a este* (The fingerprint is similar to this one).
Student 1:	(he starts writing).
Student 1:	*¿quieres escribir?* (do you want to write?).
Student 2:	*vale* (ok).
Student 1:	because.
Student 2:	*sí* (yes).
Student 1:	*dame sigo yo* (give it to me, I will continue).
Student 1:	(he is writing).
Student 1:	*pon tú algo* (you can write something).
Student 1:	have big teeth … what do you think?
Student 2:	we finish.

(OWT – TS group – Dyad 2)

As shown in the example above, Student 1 is involved in the conversation trying to complete the task and even inviting Student 2 to talk. However, Student 2 avoids participating in the dialogue and responds using gestures. When Student 1 asks for Student 2's opinion, the latter simply indicates the dialogue has finished.

Data were also analyzed qualitatively in terms of the languages used in each turn. Table 17.4 illustrates the language (L1 or L2) used by students in each task.

An ANOVA analysis showed that the use of Spanish was scarce in the RS condition in both tasks. However, students in the TS and SS

Table 17.4 The language used in each turn

	OT			OWT		
	English (mean)	Spanish (mean)	Mixed (mean)	English (mean)	Spanish (mean)	Mixed (mean)
RS	500 (3.56)	30 (3.55)	173 (6.25)	565 (12.31)	250 (3.33)	315 (6.32)
TS	103 (5.24)	236 (4.55)	157 (6.50)	45 (2.42)	181 (2.44)	93 (3.24)
SS	111 (4.21)	273 (5.24)	128 (5.24)	10 (0.41)	231 (3.95)	81 (2.44)

OT = oral task; OWT = oral+written task

conditions used predominantly Spanish. In fact, young learners in the RS contributed significantly more to their dialogue in English than students in either the TS or SS groups (OT: $F = 13.394$, $p = 0.002$ $d = 0.03$; OWT: $F = 4.883$, $p = 0.032$, $d = 0.29$). These findings were similar in both tasks with no differences found in the use of Spanish in the OT and the OWT conditions. Thus, the findings in the present study seem to only partially confirm previous research by Gagné and Parks (2016). Children in the RS condition mainly use the target language (English in this case, French in their study) during collaborative dialogue, but children in the TS and SS pairing conditions used their L1 as a strategy to complete the task, as shown in Example (2):

Student 1:	*¿y esa?* (what about this one?)
Student 2:	*quito estos* (I take these two out)
Student 1:	*sí, que esto es un gato, no un perro* (yes, because this is a cat, not a dog)
Student 2:	*no.*
Student 1:	*espera, sí, sí* (wait, yes, yes)
Student 2:	*es esta* (it is this one).
Student 2:	*¿esta?* (this one?)
Student 1:	*sí* (yes).
Student 2:	*a ver* (let's see).
Student 2:	*ah sí, ponemos esta aquí, luego se le va la lista de la compra, se le va la lista de la compra* (ah ok, we can put this one here, then the shopping list flies, the shopping list flies).
Student 1:	*aquí está con su amiga* (here he is with his girlfriend).
Student 2:	*Vale, ¿ahora lo contamos en inglés?* (ok, shall we tell the story in English now?)

(OT-SS group – Dyad 4)

Example 2 reveals one of the strategies used by students in the SS group. The initial interaction of the task was completed in Spanish. Student 1 and 2 put the cartoons in order and agreed on the story in Spanish. They then decided to narrate the story in English (*¿ahora lo contamos en inglés?* [shall we tell the story in English now?]).

The third research question examined the impact on motivation of the method used for pair formation. In other words, whether students' motivation was similar in the three grouping conditions before and after completing the task. Motivation scores before completing the task and after doing it were submitted to statistical analyses. One-way ANOVA analyses revealed no differences among the three groups before and after completing the task. However, it is important to note that when the motivation score was compared before and after completing the task across the three groups, there was a significant improvement for all three grouping conditions (all p-values < 0.0001) after the second time the participants completed the thermometer. In addition, no differences in terms of motivation scores were found between the OT and OWT. Therefore, it appears that the method of pair formation does not seem to influence the quantitative motivation scores in this group of young learners. The task itself seems to contribute to an increase in the participants' motivation, but the grouping does not affect the scores.

However, different tendencies were observed in each grouping condition when analyzing the answers to the qualitative section of the motivation thermometer. In the RS group, before completing the task, students were:(1) eager to start with the tasks (*tengo ganas de hacer la tarea* – I am looking forward to doing the task), (2) they thought they were going to have fun (*me voy a divertir* – I am going to have fun) or (3) they thought the task would be easy for them (*la tarea va a ser fácil* – The task is going to be easy). After completing the tasks, the participants' most common answers were: (1) they liked the tasks (*me ha gustado la tarea* – I have enjoyed the task), or (2) they found them easy (*me ha parecido fácil* – I thought it was easy). Only three students acknowledged that the motivation score was due to having worked well with their peers (*he trabajado a gusto con mi compañero/a* – I have worked well with my peer). In the TS group, before completing the tasks, all participants described having fun while doing the task (*me voy a divertir* – I am going to have fun). Nonetheless, after completing the tasks, half recognized having fun with the task (*me he divertido* – I had fun), whereas the other half said that they had worked well with their peers (*he trabajado a gusto con mi compañero/a* – I have worked well with my peer).

In the SS group, before starting the task, most students were willing to work with their peers (*quiero trabajar con mi compañero/a*) – I want to work with my peer), even though only a few chose the option that they were going to have fun (*me voy a divertir* – I am going to have fun). After completing the task, similar answers were found with most describing their partner as a motivating factor when completing the tasks. This answer contrasts with that provided by children in the RS group who mainly focused on the task itself.

Emerging from the present study are a number of pedagogical implications for teachers using tasks with young learners. On the one hand, task modality and pair-formation method seem to have an impact on the degree of participation by young learners when working collaboratively and some collaborative tasks encourage more learners' participation than others. For example, participants in the RS group in the task with a written output produced more turns that in the OT task. The pairing method also seems to have a clear effect on the degree of participation and on language choice when completing a task. Thus, dyads matched in terms of proficiency in the RS group use the target language more frequently in collaboration, whereas self-assigned dyads or dyads assigned by the teacher resorted to their L1 more often.

Regarding motivation, there does not seem to be significant impact of the method of pair formation on motivation scores. However, students' reactions towards working with their peers seem to differ in each grouping condition, but post-task interviews with the participants may have enabled better exploration of whether or not this was the case.

Conclusion

The main goal of this study was to examine the impact of agency in pair formation method had on the degree of participation of young learners' collaborative dialogue. Learners completed two collaborative tasks an oral task and an oral task with a written output. The oral interaction of participants in research-selected (RS), teacher-selected (TS) and student-selected (SS) groups was analyzed regarding the turns taken and the language they used when completing two collaborative tasks. Our findings indicated that agency in pair formation had a clear impact on the degree of participation. Learners in the RS group participated more in collaborative dialogue and the contribution of learner to the dialogue was similar. However, learners in the TS and SS used fewer turns in comparison to the RS group, and one of the participants in the dyad tended to lead the conversation. Moreover, agency in pair formation also had an influence on the extent to which learners used their L1 or the L2. Learners in the RS group used the target language (English) more frequently than learners in the TS and SS groups who resorted to Spanish more frequently.

Regarding the findings related to motivation, pair-formation method does not seem to influence the quantitative scores in this group of young learners. However, the modes involved in completing the task (oral vs. oral+written) do seem to impact participants' motivation. Nonetheless, the qualitative analysis of the prompts revealed that the children in the RS group were more task-focused when providing an answer, whereas those in the TS and SS groups were more focused on peer relationships.

There are a number of limitations in this study which should be acknowledged. This was a small-scale study carried out with EFL children of a particular age range (11–12-year-old children) and in a specific context. More research needs to be done with learners of other foreign languages, other age ranges and in other contexts. Even though all participants were of an A2 proficiency level, there might have been individual differences that should have been taken into account – something that could be considered in future studies. Another issue that needs to be examined in more detail is task modality. In future studies, task designers should make sure that the difficulty of the oral and the oral+written tasks is similar. The tasks used in the present study might have required different cognitive skills (ordering strips to narrate a story vs. reasoning to decide on a suspect and production of a written text)

(García Mayo & Imaz Agirre, 2019). Moreover, in this study only the affective or emotional aspect of motivation was investigated - further research should examine motivation in more detail as a multi-faceted construct composed of several domains. This line of research would shed some light on young learners' task-related engagement. Future research could also examine the impact of motivation on young learners' collaborative dialogue. In addition, these findings should be validated with evidence coming from other task types (e.g. information-gap tasks) and with learners in different contexts. Despite these caveats, we believe that teachers may benefit from the observations made in this study. For example, when doing collaborative work in class, they could pair proficiency-matched learners to enhance their participation in the conversation and their L2 use.

Acknowledgements

The authors want to thank the school that allowed access to the students and, of course, the students themselves as, without their participation, the study would have not been possible. This work was supported by the Ministerio de Economía y Competitividad (grant number FFI2016-74950-P(AEI/FEDER/UE) and the Basque Government (grant number IT904-16).

References

Adams, R. (2006) L2 tasks and orientation to form: A role for modality? *ITL:International Journal of Applied Linguistics* 152, 7–34.
Adams, R. and Ross-Feldman, L. (2008) Does writing influence learner attention to form? In D. Belcher and A. Hirvela (eds) *The Oral-Literate Connection* (pp. 243–266). Ann Arbor: University of Michigan Press.
Alegría de la Colina, A. and García Mayo, M.P. (2007) Attention to form across collaborative tasks in foreign language learning by beginner-level EFL students. In M.P. García Mayo (ed.) *Investigating Tasks in Formal Language Learning* (pp. 91–116). Clevedon: Multilingual Matters.
Al-Khalil, M.K. (2011) Second language motivation: Its relationship to noticing, affect, and production in task-based interaction. Unpublished PhD dissertation, Georgetown University.
Al-Khalil, M.K. (2016) Insights from measurement of task-related motivation. In A. Mackey and E. Marsden (eds) *Advancing Methodology and Rractice. The IRIS Repository of Instruments for Research into Second Languages* (pp. 243–262). New York/London: Routledge.
Azkarai, A. and Imaz Agirre, A. (2016) Negotiation of meaning strategies in child EFL mainstream and CLIL settings. *TESOL Quarterly* 50 (4), 844–870.
Collins, J. and Muñoz, C. (2016) The foreign language classroom: Current perspectives and future considerations. *The Modern Language Journal* 100, 133–147.
Council of Europe (2018) *Common European framework of reference for languages: Learning, teaching, assessment. Companion volume with new descriptors.* See https://rm.coe.int/cefr-companion-volume-with-new-descriptors-2018/1680787989 on 30 April 2018.

Cumming, A. (1989) Writing expertise and second language proficiency. *Language Learning* 39, 81–141.

Dasse-Askildson, V. (2008) How learners' affective variables impact their perception of recasts in the acquisition of grammatical gender in L2 French. *Arizona Working Papers in SLA & Teaching* 15, 1–35.

Dörnyei, Z. (2002) The motivational basis of language learning tasks. In P. Robinson (ed.) *Individual Differences and Instructed Language Learning* (pp. 137–158). Amsterdam: Benjamins.

Dörnyei, Z. (2009) *The Psychology of Second Language Acquisition*. Oxford: Oxford University Press.

Dörnyei, Z. and Kormos, J. (2000) The role of the individual and social variables in oral task performance. *Language Teaching Research* 4, 275–300.

Dörnyei, Z. and Ottó, I. (1998) Motivation in action: A process model of L2 motivation. *Working Papers in Applied Linguistics* 4, 43–69.

Ellis, R. (2003) *Task-Based Language Learning and Teaching*. Oxford: Oxford University Press.

Enever, J. (2011) *ELLie: Early Learning in Europe*. London: British Council.

Enever, J. (2018) *Policy and Politics in Global Primary English*. Oxford: Oxford University Press.

Gagné, N. and Parks, S. (2016) Cooperative learning tasks in a Grade 6 intensive English as a second language class: Turn-taking and degree of participation. *The Language Learning Journal* 44, 169–180.

García Mayo, M.P. (ed.) (2017) *Learning Foreign Languages in Primary School: Research Insights*. Bristol: Multilingual Matters.

García Mayo, M.P. and Azkarai, A. (2016) EFL task-based interaction. Does task modality impact on language-related episodes? In M. Sato and S. Ballinger (eds) *Peer Interaction and Second Language Learning. Pedagogical Potential and Research Agenda* (pp. 242–264). Amsterdam: John Benjamins.

García Mayo, M.P. and Imaz Agirre, A. (2016) Task repetition and its impact on EFL children's negotiation of meaning strategies and pair dynamics: An exploratory study. *The Language Learning Journal* 44, 451–465.

García Mayo, M.P. and Imaz Agirre, A. (2019) Task modality and pair formation method: Their impact on patterns of interaction and LREs among EFL primary school children. *System* 80, 165–175.

García Mayo, M.P. and Lázaro Ibarrola, A. (2015) Do children negotiate for meaning in task-based interaction? Evidence from CLIL and EFL settings. *System* 54, 40–54.

Granfeldt, J. (2008) Speaking and writing in French L2: Exploring effects on fluency, complexity and accuracy. In S. Van Deale, A. Housen, F. Kuiken, M. Pierrard and I. Vedder (eds) *Complexity, Accuracy and Fluency in Second Language Use, Learning & Teaching* (pp. 87–98). Brussels: University of Brussels.

Huang, B.H. (2016) A synthesis of empirical research on the outcomes of early foreign language instruction. *International Journal of Multilingualism* 13, 257–273.

Johnson, R.T. and Johnson, D.W. (1994) An overview of cooperative learning. In J. Thousand, R. Villa and A. Nevin (eds) *Creativity and Collaborative Learning: A Practical Guide to Empowering Students and Teachers* (pp. 31–44). Baltimore, MD: Paul H. Brookes.

Julkunen, K. (2001) Situation- and task-specific motivation in foreign language learning. In Z. Dörnyei and R. Schmidt (eds) *Motivation and Second Language Acquisition* (pp. 29–42). Honolulu: University of Hawaii.

Kim, Y. and McDonough K. (2008) The effect of interlocutor proficiency on the collaborative dialogue between Korean as a second language learners. *Language Teaching Research* 12, 211–234.

Kormos, J. (2015) Individual differences in second language speech production. In J.W. Schwieter (ed.) *The Cambridge Handbook of Bilingual Processing* (Cambridge Handbooks in Language and Linguistics). Cambridge: Cambridge University Press.

Kormos, J. and Dörnyei, Z. (2004) The interaction of linguistic and motivational variables in second language task performance. *Zeitschrift für Interkulturellen Fremdsprache nunterrict* [Online] 9 (2), 19.

Kuiken, F. and Vedder, I. (2011) Task complexity and linguistic performance in L2 writing and speaking: the effect of mode. In P. Robinson (ed.) *Second Language Task Complexity: Researching the Cognition Hypothesis of Language Learning and Performance* (pp. 91–104). Amsterdam: John Benjamins.

Leeser, M.J. (2004) Learner proficiency and focus on form during collaborative dialogue. *Language Teaching Research* 8, 207–24.

Long, M. (2015) *Second Language Acquisition and Task-Based Language Teaching.* Malden, MA: Wiley-Blackwell.

Manchón, R.M. (2017) The multifaceted and situated nature of the interaction between language and writing in academic settings: Advancing research agendas. In J. Bitchner, N. Storch and R. Wette (eds) *Teaching Writing for Academic Purposes to Multilingual Students. Instructional Approaches* (pp. 183–200). London: Routledge.

Mattar, C. and Blondin, C. (2006) Apprentissage cooperatif et prises de parole en langue cible dans deux classes d'immersion. *The Canadian Modern Language Review* 63, 225–53.

Mozaffari, S.H. (2017) Comparing student-selected and teacher-assigned pairs on collaborative writing. *Language Teaching Research* 21, 496–516.

Murphy, V. (2014) *Second Language Learning in the Early School Years. Trends and Contexts.* Oxford: Oxford University Press.

Niu, R. (2009) Effect of task-inherent production modes on EFL learners' focus on form. *Language Awareness* 18, 384–402.

Oliver, R. (1998) Negotiation of meaning in child interactions. *The Modern Language Journal* 82, 362–386.

Payant, C. and Kim, Y.K. (2017) Impact of task modality on collaborative dialogue among plurilingual learners: a classroom-based study. *International Journal of Bilingual Education and Bilingualism* https://doi.org/10.1080/13670050.2017.1292999.

Payant, C. and Reagan, D. (2018) Manipulating task implementation variables with incipient Spanish language learners: A classroom-based study. *Language Teaching Research* 22, 169–188.

Robinson, P. (2001) Individual differences, cognitive abilities, aptitude complexes and learning conditions in second language acquisition. *Second Language Research* 17 (4), 368–392.

Rouhshad, A. and Storch, N. (2016) A focus on mode: Patters of interaction in face-to-face and computer-mediated contexts. In S. Sato and S. Ballinger (eds) *Peer Interaction in Second Language Learning* (pp. 267–290). Amsterdam: John Benjamins.

Rose, J. (2007) Understanding relevance in the language classroom. *Language Teaching Research* 11 (4), 483–502.

Storch, N. (2002) Patterns of interaction in ESL pair work. *Language Learning* 52, 119–158.

Storch, N. (2016) Collaborative writing. In R.M. Manchón and P. Matsuda (eds) *Handbook of Second and Foreign Language Writing* (pp. 387–406). Boston/Berlin: De Gruyter Mouton.

Swain, M. (1998) Focus on form through conscious reflection. In C. Doughty and J. Williams (eds) *Focus on Form in Classroom Second Language Acquisition* (pp. 64–81). Cambridge: Cambridge University Press.

Swain, M. (2000) The output hypothesis and beyond: Mediating acquisition through collaborative dialogue. In J. Lantolf (ed.) *Sociocultural Theory and Second Language Learning* (pp. 97–114). Oxford: Oxford University Press.

Swain, M. (2006) Languaging, agency and collaboration in advanced language proficiency. In H. Byrnes (ed.) *Advanced Language Learning. The Contribution of Halliday and Vygotsky* (pp. 95–108). London: Continuum.

Swain, M. and Lapkin, S. (1998) Interaction and second language learning: Two adolescent French immersion students working together. *The Modern Language Journal* 82, 320–337.

Swain, M. and Lapkin, S. (2001) Focus on form through collaborative dialogue: Exploring task effects. In M. Bygate, P. Skehan and M. Swain (eds) *Researching Pedagogic Tasks: Second Language Learning, Teaching, and Testing* (pp. 99–118). New York: Longman.

Swain, M., Kinnear, P. and Steinman, L.C. (2011) *Sociocultural Theory in Second Language Acquisition: An Introduction Through Narratives*. Bristol: Multilingual Matters.

Takahashi, S. (2005) Pragmalinguistic awareness: Is it related to motivation and proficiency. *Applied Linguistics* 26 (1), 90–120.

Tennant, J. and Gardner, R.C. (2004) The computerized mini-AMTB. *CALICO Journal* 21 (2), 245–263.

Van den Branden, K, Bygate, M. and Norris, J. (eds) (2009) *Task-Based Language Teaching. A Reader*. Amsterdam: John Benjamins.

Vygotsky, L.S. (1978) *Mind in Society. The Development of Higher Psychological Processes*. Cambridge, Mass: Harvard University Press.

Wajnryb, R. (1990) *Grammar Dictation*. Oxford: Oxford University Press.

Weinman Shartman, M. (1975) *Nate the Great and the Lost List*. London: Penguin.

Williams, J. (2012) The potential role(s) of writing in second language development. *Journal of Second Language Writing* 21, 321–331.

Appendix 17.1 The Motivation Thermometer (adapted from Al-Khalil, 2016. Prompts written by authors and administered in the participants' L1)

Name, school, grade: _____

How do you feel before doing the task?	Why do you say so?
	I think the activity is going to be easy.
	I want to work with my peer.
	I want to do the activity.
	I want to do the activity in English.
	I think the activity will be fun.
	I think the activity is going to be difficult.
	I do not want to do the activity with my peer.
	I do not want to do the activity.
	I do not want to do the activity in English.
	I think I am going to get bored doing this activity.

How do you feel after doing the task?	Why do you say so?
	The activity was easy.
	I have worked well with my peer.
	I have enjoyed the activity.
	I have enjoyed doing an activity in English.
	I have had fun doing the activity.
	The activity was difficult.
	I did not work well with my peer.
	I did not enjoy the task.
	I did not like doing an activity in English.
	I got bored.

18 The Accuracy of Teacher Predictions of Student Language Use in Tasks in a Japanese University

Justin Harris and Paul Leeming

TBLT is a well-established approach to language teaching used in a wide variety of contexts around the world. A key tenet of TBLT is that students should be free to use their own language resources to complete tasks, mirroring real-world communication. However, teachers in EFL contexts often need to ensure that students practice specific language items that may otherwise go unused, and as a result, the viability of TBLT in such contexts has been questioned (Burrows, 2008; Meas, 2010; Sato, 2009; Swan, 2005). Ellis (2009) suggests that in certain cases, it is possible to design tasks which ensure practice of target language, although there is currently limited empirical evidence to support this. This chapter describes a study in which teachers in Japan were shown three different types of task and were asked to predict language used by students when completing them. The tasks were given to two intact classes of students, and interactions were recorded to determine actual language use. Results showed that teachers were able to predict not only vocabulary items, but also students' grammar use, and certain types of mistakes that students would make. Task type proved to be an important factor in the accuracy of teachers' predictions about language use. These findings lend some support to claims that experienced teachers can design tasks to ensure that students practice specific language in EFL contexts, although task type and discourse genre may be mediating factors.

Introduction

In Japan, the CLT boom of the 1980s resulted in a wide uptake of PPP (presentation, practice, production) as the pedagogy of choice in many foreign language learning classrooms across the country.

More recently, TBLT has started to gain a footing in Japan, in part due to bottom-up, teacher-led implementation (Harris, 2016). Many teachers understand the strong theoretical and empirical support for its pedagogical benefits, often of particular relevance to Japan, including vocabulary acquisition (Newton, 2001), the development of speaking skills (Kozawa, 2011; Mackey, 1999) and language automaticity (De Ridder *et al.*, 2007). TBLT is also held to be motivating for students (Ellis, 2003; Willis & Willis, 2011), which is crucial in compulsory educational contexts such as Japan. While not as explicit as in the case of some other Asian contexts such as Hong Kong (Carless, 2002), there is also some top-down support for TBLT in Japan, at least implicitly, in published government goals of teaching English as a tool for communicative purposes (MEXT, 2014).

There have, however, been many arguments made against the appropriateness of TBLT for Japan (Burrows, 2008; Miyasako, 2012; Sato, 2009, 2010; Wicking, 2009), for reasons related to student preferences for teacher-centered learning, a fear among students of making mistakes, and a (perceived) need for an L2-only classroom. Similar concerns exist in 'difficult contexts' throughout Asia where PPP has been shown to be the preferred teaching method by teachers (Adams & Newton, 2009; Carless, 2009; Jeon & Hahn, 2006). Many of the criticisms of TBLT have been described (and rebutted) by both Ellis (2009, 2013) and Long (2016), but have nonetheless resulted in some teachers avoiding using it in the classroom (Harris, 2016). Part of this may stem from an unclear understanding of TBLT and its central 'task', and indeed it has been argued that the term 'task' is poorly defined (Widdowson, 2003). For the purpose of our study, we consider a task to be in line with the definition by Ellis (2014). He states that a task involves 'text-creation' with learners using their available linguistic resources to close some kind of information 'gap'. The ultimate goal of the learner(s) is the achievement of a communicative outcome.

The argument considered in this chapter is that TBLT does not provide an adequate focus on discrete language items, often needed for the purpose of entrance tests, thus undermining the appropriateness of TBLT in Japan (Burrows, 2008; Sato, 2009, 2010; Swan, 2005). Ellis argues that it is a misunderstanding of TBLT, but outlines the criticism as follows: 'It is not possible to predict what kinds of language use will result from the performance of a task, and thus it is not possible to ensure adequate coverage of the target language in a task-based course' (Ellis, 2009: 226). In input- and output-rich English as Second Language (ESL) environments where students have opportunities to practice language outside the classroom, low frequency grammar and vocabulary can be encountered naturally. However, in Japan, where a teacher may be under pressure to focus on specific areas of grammar or certain vocabulary items, this can be a reason for teachers' avoidance of TBLT.

If it is to be widely adopted in contexts such as Japan, TBLT must facilitate the deliberate practice of structures that are not commonly encountered in conversation, but are necessary for academic purposes including entrance exams.

It has also been claimed that the unpredictability of language use within TBLT does not allow textbooks to be easily created (Seedhouse, 2005), and a lack of suitable textbooks has hindered uptake of TBLT in some EFL contexts (Luo & Gong, 2015). Compounding this further is the fact that many language courses in Japan (especially in formal schooling) necessitate that teachers assign a required textbook for the course, even if they do not wish to use one.

While TBLT practitioners generally preselect content based on tasks rather than language, PPP involves teachers preselecting vocabulary and grammar, which then forms the content for the course. Therefore, teachers are able to choose obscure language items and can also ensure adequate coverage of any language that may be deemed necessary. As an extension of this, materials development is the relatively simple task of deciding how to best introduce and practice the chosen language.

This chapter begins by detailing the issues surrounding task design for specific language practice, and then proceeds to describe a study that set out to determine how accurately teachers are able to predict student language use simply by examining tasks that students will complete in a classroom. Finally, implications for task design and the implementation of TBLT in challenging contexts are discussed.

Literature Review

The problem of predicting language use

Ellis (2009) argues that tasks can be constructed to focus on specific language. However, several prominent researchers have claimed that the language that teachers expect students to use, and the language students actually use, is very different. For example, while discussing the differences between *task as workplan* and *task as process*, Breen (1989) highlighted the fact that students will interpret tasks in their own way and use language not expected or intended by the teacher, undermining the effectiveness of tasks created by teachers to target certain structures. Similarly, research by Coughlan and Duff (1994) showed that learners of different ages and contexts approach the same task in varied ways, leading to different language used in classroom situations. Seedhouse (2005) argued that even with tasks designed to ensure practice of specific language items, the difference between expected and actual language use can be so great that there is no guarantee that students will use the desired language, and that this severely limits the suitability of TBLT for certain contexts. Ellis (2009) refutes this, claiming that there is considerable overlap between *task as workplan* and *task as process*. However, some researchers argue that this lack of predictability is the reason for the scarcity of published materials following a TBLT approach (Lai, 2015; Luo & Gong, 2015; Willis & Willis, 2007), which, as mentioned earlier, may in turn be hindering the wide-scale uptake of TBLT among teachers in EFL contexts such as Japan.

Ellis (2009) states that while some tasks can be described as *unfocused* (the teacher has no preconceived ideas about the language they want students to use), *focused* tasks can be designed specifically to ensure the practice of predetermined language. As an example, Ellis (2009) cites research by Mackey (1999) who successfully created tasks to elicit question forms. Both Ellis (2009) and Long (2016) also claim that the difficulty in predicting student language use ignores the use of reading and listening tasks for language input, through which it is far easier to control the language and ensure that students focus on the desired structures. In fact, Long (2016) argued that TBLT should always begin with an input-based task that is focused on introducing the language needed for the subsequent output task. As a practical example of this, Shintani (2016) has shown how input tasks can be used even with very young beginner learners and can ensure that students are exposed to specific language items. Although focused input tasks ensure that students will encounter specific grammar items, they do not guarantee that students will actually use the language. Swain (2005) explained that exposure to language alone is not sufficient for language acquisition, and stressed the importance of language output. Therefore, for successful language learning, students need not only to meet vocabulary and grammar, but also to use it, and if TBLT is to replace PPP as the preferred pedagogy in Japan, it must facilitate this. Loschky and Bley-Vroman (1993) outline a three-way distinction for considering task types: *task naturalness* (a language feature will tend to arise naturally), *task utility* (where it is helpful to the learner to use a certain feature) and *task essentialness* (the learner must use a given language feature in order to complete the task). Given that in a TBLT classroom learners may resort to any means necessary to complete a task (non-linguistic means included), designing tasks with *essentialness* in mind is all but impossible according to Lochsky and Bley-Vroman. The tasks used in this study are therefore of the first two kinds.

Task type and interaction

Although Ellis (2009) discussed focused tasks as a way to include a deliberate focus on specific language, he did not elaborate on how task type may influence language use by students. Long (1990) considered three key aspects of task design: whether a task is planned or unplanned; whether it is open or closed; and whether it requires information exchange or not. Although all of these factors can potentially influence the language that students will use, perhaps the most significant one when trying to predict student language use during tasks is the distinction between open and closed tasks. Willis (1996) describes closed tasks as those where there is a clear and predetermined outcome or only one answer (e.g. spot-the-difference tasks), and open tasks as those where there is no correct or final answer (e.g. opinion gap tasks). She claims that while experienced teachers can successfully predict language use in closed tasks, it is 'virtually impossible' to predict language use in open tasks (Willis, 1996: 33). Lambert and Engler (2007) investigated the influence of open versus closed tasks on language production using a Complexity Accuracy and Fluency (CAF) framework, and found that open tasks encourage greater complexity on the part of speakers. Supporting claims made by Willis (1996), this suggests that it may be harder to predict language for open tasks. Of course, tasks vary in the extent to which they are open or closed. Some tasks may have a single correct answer, others have several possible answers and some tasks allow students complete freedom. For example, in a storytelling task, while pictures may suggest a certain story, students are free to interpret them to create their own original narrative. Therefore, in this chapter, we consider the level of subjectivity that is found within open and closed tasks. In this way, open and closed tasks exist on a scale rather than constituting a simple dichotomy.

Although Ellis (2009) makes a strong argument for the use of focused tasks to allow deliberate language practice, to the best of the authors' knowledge at the time of writing there is still no empirical evidence that teachers are able to accurately predict the language that students will use during a given task. Although researchers may design tasks with specific language in mind, many teachers do not have time to create and design their own materials, and therefore those interested in implementing TBLT in their own classrooms select from pre-made tasks in order to practice language. This means that teachers' ability to analyze existing tasks and accurately determine the language that students will use is crucial if tasks are going to be used to focus on specific language points.

The current study attempted to determine the accuracy of teachers in predicting the language that focused tasks elicit. Three tasks were selected by the researchers, and then given to six teachers who were asked to predict the following: (a) What language will the students use to complete the task (vocabulary and grammar); and (b) What errors are students likely to make? The tasks were then completed by dyads in two classes in a university in Japan, and recordings of the interactions were transcribed to allow comparison between teacher predictions and actual student language use. The primary focus was on how well teachers could predict the grammar and vocabulary used, and mistakes made, when students engaged in three typical classroom tasks.

Methodology

Participants

The study involved two groups of participants; in-service language teachers, and second-year university students. The teachers ($n = 6/n = 12$) included two native speakers (American and Irish), two native Japanese speaking teachers of English, and two teachers with first languages other than English or Japanese (Spanish and Chinese). The teachers had between 5 and 11 years' experience of teaching in Japan, and all had a master's degree in Teaching English to Speakers of Other Languages (TESOL). The teachers were chosen to represent a cross-section of the teaching population in Japan, and all had experience using communicative tasks with students.

The students were all second-year university students from two classes in a four-skills English course in an economics faculty at a large, private university in Western Japan. Three pairs from each class were randomly selected for recording ($n = 12$). The proficiency range of these learners was wide, with Test of English for International Communication (TOEIC) scores of between 255 and 760 (average of 565), which is equivalent to Common European Framework of Reference (CEFR) lower A2 to higher B1 (an average of lower B1). In addition to six years of formal English education prior to university, these students had all completed courses in oral English, reading, and listening in their first year at the university. The students were studying in an international economics department, and although this indicates some interest in English, teachers responsible for the classes generally describe student motivation as low. The course followed a TBLT approach, so students were comfortable interacting in English and completing tasks.

Procedure

Three tasks of three different task types were selected by the researchers with the aim of eliciting certain grammar structures. An overview of each task, as well as the intended language focus, is provided in Table 18.1, and the task materials are provided in Appendix 18.1.

The tasks were selected to represent a range of common task types employed in language classrooms in Japan, focusing on descriptive, narrative, and opinion discourse. The use of tasks to practice specific discourse patterns or grammar structures may be more in line with a task-supported rather than task-based approach to teaching (Lambert & Oliver, Chapter 1, this volume; Ellis, 2019). The first task was closed, and required students to describe a picture to their partner in order to find eight differences between their two pictures. In a task such as this, the language is highly controlled because students need to use

Table 18.1 Overview of tasks

	Task 1	Task 2	Task 3
Task name	Spot-the-difference	Story time	What do you think?
Task type / classification	Finding differences between two pictures (*closed task, information exchange, objective interpretation, only one possible answer*)	Creating a story from pictures (*closed task, no information exchange, subjective interpretation, a number of possible answers*)	Deciding on the most useful electrical appliances (*open task, information exchange, objective interpretation, no correct answer*)
Brief description	Students describe their picture to their partner in an attempt to identify differences	Students practice telling a story based on pictures then relate the story to another pair	Students decide what the most useful electrical appliances are, then compare with partners
Intended language focus by researchers	**Grammar:** Prepositions of location, present progressive, personal pronouns, singular/Plural	**Grammar:** Past tense, past progressive	**Grammar:** *I think ... because ...* construction, dictionary form of verbs (adjectives, adverbs (*It is very useful*)
	Vocabulary: *chair, television, TV, teddy bear, frog. book, books, boat, picture, frame, cap, sail, sailboat, yacht, lamp, table, van, toy, rabbit, wand, (rugby/beach) ball, moon, city, buildings*	**Vocabulary:** *man, woman, cat, play, brush, sit, sit down, go to sleep, touch, fire, kitchen, surprised, call, telephone, fireman, safe, with*	**Vocabulary:** All the electrical appliances in the list, adjectives such as *hot, cold, cool, dirty, interesting,* simple verbs such as *play, watch, clean, cook*
	Potential errors: Mixing up *above* and *on* and *below* and *under* Might not use present continuous (*the boy holds frog*) Confusing single and plural *is/are, book/ books*) Personal pronouns Overgeneralizing the way *open* is used both as a verb and an adjective to close, *The books are close* Won't know how to say *drawer, submarine, van, yacht*	**Potential errors:** He/she mix-ups Problems with irregular past, not using irregular past (*woman go to sleep*) Omission of –ed (*woman get cat*) Problems with articles (no *a* or *the* when talking about the man or the woman or continuous use of *a*) Adding two verbs in one sentence (*was go to*) Use of *stop fire* instead of *put out* or *extinguish*	**Potential errors:** Missing the word *it* in *I use it everyday* Repeating the noun twice *I think refrigerator because I use refrigerator* Using an object directly after *I think* (as in the above example) Lack of *a* in *take picture* and perhaps not in plural *take pictures* Lack of *my* or *a* in *I use phone*

the vocabulary in the picture, and if they do not know it, they will be forced to use strategies to compensate for gaps in their knowledge. Successful completion of the task is dependent on the use of appropriate vocabulary and prepositions. The second task was a simple narrative task in which the students collaborated to construct a story, which they then told to another pair who had a different story. This could be considered to be a closed task, but there are a number of possible interpretations of the pictures and students can potentially create different stories, so it could be argued to be more open than the spot-the-difference task. The language required is also not as controlled as in the spot-the-different task because students can create their story by avoiding unknown vocabulary suggested by the pictures. Grammar is central to successful task completion, as sentences will usually be required to effectively convey a story, and although past tense might be more natural, present tense could also be used. The third task was an opinion-gap task in which students rank the importance of electrical appliances individually, and then work with a partner to devise a list that they both agreed on. This is a common type of task in language teaching and requires students to exchange opinions in order to decide on their final list. There is no preferred answer and it is therefore considered to be an open task. The vocabulary may be somewhat predictable based on the topic (electrical appliances), but as there is no correct answer, it matches the description of open tasks agreed on in the literature (Long, 1990; Willis, 1996).

A full description of each task including the actual materials used in class was sent to the six teachers, along with detailed information regarding the students and the course in which these tasks would be used. The teachers were asked to identify what particular vocabulary and grammar they thought students would use to complete the task, as well as potential errors that students might make during task completion. The data was collated and compared, and in the case that four of the six teachers identified the same language point, it was included for comparison with actual student language use. The rationale for selecting language identified by the majority of teachers was that this removed the influence of a single teacher potentially being very accurate but others being less so.

The tasks were then introduced to students over three separate weeks by one of the researchers who was also the teacher for the course. Three dyads were randomly selected in each class and the task interactions were video recorded, making a total of six pairs for each of the three tasks. These recordings (a total of 18) were then transcribed and analyzed by the authors. Vocabulary and grammar use was coded based on total number of instances of each word or grammar point per individual conversation and across all six conversations. Errors in these conversations were identified based on error type and compared back to teacher predictions. In order to ensure agreement in transcription and analyses of language, one recording from each task (three recordings in total) was transcribed and analyzed independently by both authors, who then met and discussed any issues that arose before completing the rest of the analyses.

Results and Discussion

In this section the predictions made by teachers, and students' actual language use are presented.

Teacher predictions

Table 18.2 shows the language predictions that were shared by at least four of the six teachers in our study. We considered predictions shared by the majority of teachers to be an adequate criterion for 'teacher agreement'. Although individual differences in teacher predictions did exist, they were limited and discussion of them is beyond the scope of the current study, which was interested in agreement of predictions by teachers from varied backgrounds. Despite these backgrounds, Table 18.2 shows the generally strong agreement between teachers on the language that would be used by students during the task. The bold text represents consensus with the task designer, and shows that even when teachers have not been involved in creating a task, they are able to infer the intended language focus of these tasks. The first number in the usage column represents the number of occurrences in the complete data set, and the number in parentheses represents how many of the six interactions it was found in. Although teachers were confident and able to agree to a reasonable extent regarding the spot-the-difference and narrative tasks, the opinion gap task proved far more challenging. In line with Willis (1996), teachers commented to the researchers that the open nature of this task made it very difficult to predict the language that would be used and the errors that would occur. There was

Table 18.2 Teacher predictions and student language use

	Task 1 Spot-the-difference	Usage	Task 2 Story time	Usage	Task 3 What do you think?	Usage
Grammar	**There is/are**	31 (6)	**Past tense**	27 (4)	**I think....**	37 (6)
	Prepositions	106 (6)	**Past progressive**	3 (2)	**because....**	23 (6)
	Present tense	67 (6)				
	Present progressive	3 (3)				
Vocabulary	boy	26 (6)	**call**	12 (6)	smartphone	43 (6)
	girl	13 (5)	**play**	9 (5)	convenient	0 (0)
	TV	52 (6)	**sleep**	10 (5)	important	30 (6)
	chair	12 (2)	**fire**	13 (5)		
	table	7 (2)	**fireman**	32 (6)		
	picture	39 (6)	**cat**	59 (6)		
	newspaper	28 (6)	**man**	8 (4)		
	toys	2 (1)	**woman**	44 (6)		
	book	51 (6)	**smoke**	10 (4)		
	frog	14 (6)				
	shoe	5 (3)				
	ball	45 (6)				
	sofa	40 (5)				
	car	28 (6)				
Language errors/ problems	**Singular/plural**		**Switching**		*No overall*	
	Prepositions	(6)	**between tenses**	(4)	*agreement*	
	Have/has	(6)	**Verb**	(6)	*was reached*	
	Articles	(3)	conjugation, for		*between*	
		(6)	example *She play*		*teachers*	

Note: Bold font indicates agreement with the researchers' intended language. The first number represents total occurrences across all dyads, and the number in parentheses shows how many interactions the items appeared in out of a maximum of six.

no overall agreement from teachers on the type of errors that students would make, and limited agreement on vocabulary and grammar. As these tasks moved from closed to open, teacher agreement on student language use declined across all three areas; grammar, vocabulary and errors. Teachers also seemed to be less confident in predicting language as these tasks became more open, as stated by Willis (1996). It should be noted that discourse genre may also be a factor, in that the predictability of descriptive and narrative genres used in the first and second tasks are likely to be higher than opinion in the third task.

Accuracy of predictions

The accuracy of teacher predictions will be considered across the three task types with regard to grammar use, vocabulary and the errors that students made.

Grammar use

The predictions of grammar use for the spot-the-difference task were generally accurate. Teachers predicted use of the existential clause *there is ... /there are...*, and also the use of prepositions. There were 106 separate examples of prepositions spread across six conversations. The nature of the task means that it cannot be completed without prepositions, unless students use gestures or their L1. The structures *there is/there are* were also present in the language output from all pairs, although use was more limited with only 31 instances in the data. Depending on proficiency, students can simply name the object and give a preposition to convey the necessary information as shown in Excerpt 1.

Excerpt 1: Spot-the-Difference Task, Group 4
48 Kazuki: Next to rugby ball book.
49 Masaya: Book?
50 Kazuki: Maybe.
51 Masaya: Book book?
52 Kazuki: Rugby ball. Next to rugby ball.
53 Masaya: Maybe book? Or DVD?
54 Kazuki: DV? Ah yeah yeah DVD.

This excerpt shows how students were able to communicate effectively simply using prepositions and nouns, without using any syntax. This is typical of descriptive discourse, where the noun phrase tends to carry the semantic content required for the task (Lambert, 2019). If communication can be achieved without the use of full sentences, lower level students in particular may avoid grammatical structures they are not confident with. Although teachers predicted use of the present progressive, it was only used by three groups and on three occasions in total. Generally, however, teachers were quite accurate in predicting grammar use for this task.

The teacher predictions for the grammar used in the narrative task were less successful. Although teachers accurately predicted that the past tense and past progressive would be used, this was not consistent across groups, and 27 instances of the past tense across four groups could be considered to be limited use as students produced the narrative in pairs and then told it to another group. Students often used the present tense to relate their story, which is also not uncommon among native speakers when telling a story. The narrative task can be completed using either the present or the past tense, and teachers were not able to accurately predict this.

There were a limited number of teacher predictions about grammar for the opinion gap task, but the one prediction that was agreed on, (I think ... because) was accurate, and did occur across the six conversations. This could be considered satisfactory if the teacher is attempting to have students practice this structure.

Overall, teachers were reasonably successful in identifying the grammar that would be used for all three tasks, which has positive implications for the design of tasks that encourage the use of certain language structures. It may be that some structures, such as prepositions, are more easily incorporated during task design so as to be useful for successful task completion. For example, in this study, prepositions were used by all groups, suggesting that without them the task could not be completed successfully. On the other hand, during the narrative task, the past tense was avoided by two of the groups, but this did not have any negative impact on task completion. Teachers in contexts such as Japan may require students to practice more difficult and obscure grammar such as third conditionals or relative clauses, and this may be more of a challenge for task designers.

Vocabulary use

Teacher predictions regarding vocabulary for the spot-the-difference task strongly matched actual student language use. The majority of language items were used by all groups in the study. The results did, however, suggest that students can avoid certain words even if they appear integral to successful task completion. For example, in the spot-the-difference task, one group did not use the word *girl* even though it was central to the task (one of the differences in the pictures was that there was a boy in one, and a girl and a boy in the other). This is an important issue for teachers who use tasks to introduce more obscure vocabulary items to students. Again, in the spot-the-difference task, one of the differences involved the presence of a submarine in one picture and a sailboat in the other. Student conversations revealed a couple of interesting things regarding these vocabulary items. Some students used circumlocution to describe the submarine as follows:

Excerpt 2: Spot-the-Difference Task, Group 6

41 Tomoya:	On the floor. And water car
42 Seiya:	Water car?
43 Tomoya:	Water, deep water
44 Seiya:	Ahhh
45 Tomoya:	This can deeper deeper deeper
46 Seiya:	Deeper deeper deeper
47 Tomoya:	Ship

In the above excerpt, Tomoya is able to use *water car* and then *deeper deeper* to convey the idea of a submarine. In a TBLT approach, this may be considered to be acceptable, or even desired, as students are using strategies to overcome the gaps in their language to ensure successful task completion. From a course design perspective however, it means that students are able to avoid the use of vocabulary that the teacher may need to cover. Another pair was able to find the difference between the yacht and submarine based on color. They used the word *ship* and discussed the color, identifying a blue ship and a red ship, therefore finding a difference between the pictures without fully understanding them. Even though the vocabulary seems integral to successful task completion, students were able to avoid it. Seedhouse (2005) suggested that students also interpret tasks in their own ways, and this is somewhat supported by the data in this study. For example, half of the groups used the word *shoe*, with others using *sandal* as an alternative. Although again the results for this task were generally encouraging and suggest that pictures may be an effective way of introducing vocabulary, they are open to individual interpretation and are not guaranteed to result in the language expected by the teacher.

With the storytelling task, students were able to avoid words that were not necessary for telling the story. Although the use of *man* was predicted by all teachers, two groups told the story without using the word, as the man in the pictures was peripheral to the main story. On the other hand, *fireman* (or *firefighter* as all groups actually used, even though all teachers had predicted *fireman*) was central to the story and was used across all six groups.

For the opinion gap task, teachers had very limited idea as to what language would be used, and also limited success in their predictions, with only two of the three predicted language items being used by students. Although the teachers successfully predicted that *smartphone* would feature, and that *important* would be used to give reasons, the only other word that they agreed on, *convenient*, was not used by any students. This is perhaps an unexpected result, as it would seem reasonable that when discussing the importance of electrical appliances, convenience would be a central factor to consider. However, rather than talking about convenience, the students listed the things that they were able to do with different items. An example can be seen in Excerpt 3.

Excerpt 3: Opinion Gap Task, Group 3

20 Maho:	Keep the food.
21 Ayumi:	Yes.
22 Maho:	And micro oven can eat hot food.
23 Ayumi:	Ah.
24 Maho:	Ah, come back later…'ah, very tired, ah micro oven food'.
25 Ayumi:	Very easy.

In the excerpt above, Maho talks about the utility of a microwave in providing hot food, but does this in a very simple way by giving an example. Ayumi uses the word *easy* which could be considered a simpler synonym of *convenient*. Although pictures of electrical appliances were provided on the task worksheet, teachers did not predict their use, and ability to accurately predict vocabulary could be considered to be limited for this task.

In general, the success of teachers in making vocabulary predictions has positive implications for task designers in suggesting that it is possible to design tasks that at least encourage students to use specific vocabulary. It also suggests the suitability of TBLT for introducing and practicing specific lexical items. In the closed task, teachers were confident and accurate in predicting vocabulary use, although the ability of students to complete tasks without the use of vocabulary that seems central to task completion may be of concern. In a TBLT approach however, circumlocution can be applauded in the feedback stage, and a post-task activity can be used to introduce the vocabulary that was avoided by the students, perhaps due to limitations in vocabulary knowledge. Indeed, TBLT is structured to allow students to complete tasks, but in the process to notice gaps in their own language, and this noticing is an important part of language learning (Schmidt, 1990). Therefore, the spot-the-difference task would allow the teacher to introduce *submarine* as a useful vocabulary item in a post-task activity even if all students completely avoided using it in the main task. In terms of task design, the open task is more concerning. Teachers struggled to predict what language would be used. This means that it may be hard for teachers to incorporate specific vocabulary for open tasks.

Language errors

Teachers were generally quite successful in predicting the errors that would occur in the spot-the-difference task. Although students did not make mistakes consistently with *have/has*, the other potential errors that teachers identified occurred in all six of the conversations, irrespective of language proficiency. It could be argued that the use of articles is a common problem among most learners of English and therefore, is easy to predict, but the other errors that were predicted are less common. The singular/plural prediction is perhaps a reflection of the teachers' experience in Japan. Most Japanese nouns do not have a singular or plural form, and generally numbers are inferred from the context of the conversation. Therefore, students often struggle with this point, given that it is not a salient issue in Japanese.

Teachers were also reasonably successful in their predictions of errors for the narrative task, with tense switching occurring in the majority of pairs, and all students experiencing problems with verb conjugation. Again, these could be considered common problems for learners of English, but show that teachers were able to predict problems that students will encounter just by studying the task they will complete. The opinion gap task again proved to be very challenging for teachers, with no common agreement being reached. Several teachers stated that they were not sure what language would be used, so were also unable to predict the errors that would be made.

Overall, the results regarding the prediction of errors have positive implications for the implementation of TBLT in contexts like Japan. At the same time, there is a possible limitation with TBLT, as acknowledged by Ellis (2009; Chapter 6, this volume) and Long (2016), that it requires specific training for teachers because the teaching approach is quite different from traditional methods. One such area is the treatment of errors. In a PPP approach, students are judged on their accuracy with the structures that have been introduced and explained at the start of the class, but TBLT is more complex. Although Ellis (2003) states that focus on form can occur at any stage, Long (2016) holds that treatment of errors should follow the main task, and be in direct response to language issues which arise when students are trying to complete a given task. Willis and Willis (2007) also suggest that error treatment should come in the post-task stage where there is a deliberate focus on language. The issue for practitioners of TBLT is that reactive responses to student errors requires an array of correction techniques and an ability to identify and respond to students' language problems in situ. This can be very challenging for new or inexperienced teachers. The findings of this study suggest that teachers are generally quite accurate in their predictions of errors, which means that it is possible to design focus on form activities before a class, directed at errors that are predicted to occur. For new teachers, this may make TBLT more appealing and practical, as it allows the deliberate focus on specific language issues that students are likely to have. These findings also have implications for course and textbook design, suggesting that it is possible to design certain tasks that will elicit errors that can then be addressed in the post-task stage. While this may be possible for closed tasks, the results suggest that for open tasks it is far more difficult to predict both language use and the errors that are likely to occur.

Conclusion

This chapter described a study that set out to empirically test the ability of teachers to predict the type of student language used during tasks. While Ellis (2009) has proposed that tasks can be designed for the practice of specific language items, others have stated that the lack of predictability of language renders the use of tasks unsuitable for challenging contexts such as Japan (Burrows, 2008; Meas, 2010; Sato, 2009; Swan, 2005). The results of the current study suggest that teachers can, to a certain extent, predict the grammar, vocabulary, and even errors that will occur when students engage in tasks.

As previously stated, many teachers are often too busy to create their own materials, and this may be a hindrance to the uptake of TBLT. Results suggest that it is worth an initial investment of time to analyze a range of tasks and predict the language that will be used during each one. A group of teachers could use this procedure to build up a bank of materials covering a range of grammar and vocabulary items, and this could then be used to conduct lessons using TBLT. This may be particularly effective for closed tasks, as well as descriptive and narrative types of discourse genre. This makes TBLT a viable option, even for busy teachers in compulsory educational contexts such as Japan.

Perhaps the most encouraging finding for teachers is that language errors seem to be reasonably predictable. This relieves a great deal of the pressure on new or inexperienced teachers and means that teachers can design post-task focus on form activities before class, confident that the activities will be meaningful and address language issues encountered by students. Conversely, the results did show that task type is an important factor to consider, and that indeed, it may be more difficult to predict the kind of language that will appear when more open tasks are used.

Although the current study sheds some light on the issue of predictability of student language use, there are a number of limitations that should be considered. First the number of teachers was small, and they all had experience teaching in Japan. Although participants did represent a cross section of the teaching population in Japan, it is questionable how far the results can be generalized to other populations where teachers have limited or no experience. For example, without extensive teaching experience, it may be very difficult for teachers to predict the language errors that will occur, although resources are available detailing common learner errors across a variety of language backgrounds, (see Celce-Murcia & Larsen-Freeman's (1999) *Grammar Book*). The different discourse genres elicited by the three tasks does somewhat complicate interpretation of the results, as the extent of the relationship between the open or closed nature of the task and the discourse genre is unclear. Future research should attempt to have teachers predict language use for tasks in the same discourse genre, but with open or closed orientations. A final limitation is that the number of task performances analyzed for the study was also relatively low, meaning that one group could potentially influence the results.

A possible weakness inherent in the design of the current study is that teachers' successful predictions of language use could be argued to represent their knowledge of students' current language level rather than the ability to predict how tasks can be used to extend students' proficiency, which is the ultimate goal of educators. However, in EFL contexts such as Japan where language practice outside the classroom is extremely difficult, and the goal of language learning is often to pass high-stakes tests such as university entrance exams, the ability to design tasks that ensure students practice specific language is important. It should be noted that many researchers have argued that these predictions are not possible, undermining the effectiveness of tasks in these contexts (Burrows, 2008; Meas, 2010; Sato, 2009; Swan, 2005), and the present study provides some evidence that this is not the case.

Despite the above limitations, we believe that the results showing that teachers are somewhat able to predict student language use and to predict certain language errors suggest that TBLT can be used in challenging contexts such as Japan, where a focus on discrete language items may be required, and set textbooks are designated by educational institutions. If teachers are able to build a bank of language tasks focused on different discrete points of grammar, then TBLT becomes a far more attractive option, even in such 'difficult' contexts.

References

Adams, R. and Newton, J. (2009) TBLT in Asia: Constraints and opportunities. *Asian Journal of English Language Teaching* 19, 1–17.

Breen, M. (1989) The evaluation cycle for language learning tasks. In R.K. Johnson (ed.) *The Second Language Curriculum* (pp. 187–206). Cambridge: Cambridge University Press.

Burrows, C. (2008) Socio-cultural barriers facing TBL in Japan. *The Language Teacher* 32 (8), 15–19.

Carless, D. (2002) Implementing task-based learning with young learners. *ELT Journal* 56 (4), 389–396.

Carless, D. (2009) Revisiting the TBLT versus P-P-P debate: Voices from Hong Kong. *Asian Journal of English Language Teaching* 19, 44–66.

Celce-Murcia, M. and Larsen-Freeman, D. (1999) *The Grammar Book* (2nd edn). Boston: Heinle & Heinle.

Coughlan, P. and Duff, P.A. (1994) Same task, different activities: analysis of a SLA task from an activity theory perspective. In J. Lantolf and G. Appel (eds) *Vygotskian Approaches to Second Language Research* (pp. 173–194). Norwood, NJ: Ablex.

De Ridder, I., Vangehuchten, L. and Gomez, S.G. (2007) Enhancing automaticity through task-based language learning. *Applied Linguistics* 28 (2), 309–315.

Ellis, R. (2003) *Task-Based Language Learning and Teaching*. Oxford: Oxford University Press.

Ellis, R. (2009) Task-based language teaching: sorting out the misunderstandings. *International Journal of Applied Linguistics* 19 (3), 221–246.

Ellis, R. (2013) Task-based language teaching: Responding to the critics. *University of Sydney Papers in TESOL* 8, 1–27.

Ellis, R. (2014) Taking the critics to task: The case for task-based teaching. Proceedings of the CLaSIC conference.

Ellis, R. (2019) Towards a modular language curriculum for using tasks. *Language Teaching Research* 23 (4), 454–475.

Harris, J. (2016) Teachers' beliefs about task-based language teaching in Japan. *The Journal of Asia TEFL* 13 (2), 102–116.

Jeon, I. and Hahn, J. (2006) Exploring EFL teachers' perceptions of task-based language teaching: A case study of Korean secondary school classroom practice. *Asian EFL Journal* 8 (1), 123–139.

Kozawa, Y. (2011) Facilitating collaborative dialogues through TBLT. In A. Stewart (ed.) *JALT2010 Conference Proceedings* (pp. 217–229). Tokyo: JALT.

Lai, C. (2015) Task-based language teaching in the Asian context: Where are we now and where are we going? In M. Thomas and H. Reinders (eds) *Contemporary Task-Based Language Teaching in Asia* (pp. 12–29). London: Bloomsbury.

Lambert, C.P. (2019) *Referent Similarity and Nominal Syntax in Task-Based Language Teaching*. Singapore: Springer Nature.

Lambert, C.P. and Engler, S. (2007) Information distribution and goal orientation in second language task design. In M.P. García Mayo (ed.) *Investigating Tasks in Formal Language Learning* (pp. 27–43). Clevedon: Multilingual Matters.

Long, M.H. (1990) Task, group, and task-group interactions. In S. Anivan (ed.) *Language Teaching Methodology for the Nineties* (pp. 31–50). Singapore: SEAMEO Regional Language Centre.

Long, M.H. (2016) In defense of tasks and TBLT: Nonissues and real issues. *Annual Review of Applied Linguistics* 36, 5–33.

Loschky, L. and Bley-Vroman, R. (1993) Grammar and task-based methodology. In G. Crookes and S. Gass (eds) *Tasks and Language Learning: Intergrating Theory and Practice* (pp. 123–167). Clevedon: Multilingual Matters.

Luo, S. and Gong, Y. (2015) Exploring ways to accommodate task-based language teaching in Chinese schools. In M. Thomas and H. Reinders (eds) *Contemporary Task-Based Language Teaching in Asia* (pp. 12–29). London: Bloomsbury.

Mackey, A. (1999) Input, interaction and second language development: An empirical study of question formation in ESL. *Studies in Second Language Acquisition* 21 (4), 557–589.

Meas, S. (2010) Investigating the feasibility of adopting task-based language teaching in a university setting in Cambodia. Doctoral dissertation.

MEXT. (2014) English Education Reform Plan corresponding to globalization. See from http://www.mext.go.jp/english/topics/__icsFiles/afieldfile/2014/01/23/1343591_1.pdf

Miyasako, N. (2012) How wide is the gulf between PPP and TBLT? *Kyouiku Jissen Gakuronshuu* (Journal for the Science of Schooling) 13, 1–13.

Newton, J. (2001) Options for vocabulary learning through communication tasks. *ELT Journal* 55 (1), 30–37.

Sato, R. (2009) Suggestion for creating approaches suitable to the Japanese EFL environment. *The Language Teacher* 33 (9), 11–14.

Sato, R. (2010) Reconsidering the effectiveness and suitability of PPP and TBLT in the Japanese classroom. *JALT Journal* 32 (2), 189–200.

Schmidt, R. (1990) The role of consciousness in second language learning. *Applied Linguistics* 11, 129–158.

Seedhouse, P. (2005) 'Task' as research construct. *Language Learning* 55 (3), 533–570.

Shintani, N. (2016) *The Role of Input-Based Tasks in Foreign Language Instruction for Young Learners*. Amsterdam: John Benjamins.

Swain, M. (2005) The output hypothesis: theory and research. In E. Hinkel (ed.) *Handbook of Research in Second Language Teaching and Learning* (pp. 471–483). Mahwah, NJ: Lawrence Erlbaum.

Swan, M. (2005) Legislation by hypothesis: The case of task-based instruction. *Applied Linguistics* 26 (3), 376–401.

Wicking, P. (2009) TBLT in Japan: Task-based language teaching and its effective implementation in the Japanese university classroom. *OnCUE Journal* 3 (3), 248–258.

Widdowson, H. (2003) *Defining Issues in English Language Teaching*. Oxford: Oxford University Press.

Willis, D. and Willis, J. (2007) *Doing Task-Based Teaching*. Oxford: Oxford University Press.

Willis, D. and Willis, J. (2011) Task-based learning and learner motivation. *On Task* 1 (1), 4.

Willis, J. (1996) *A Framework for Task-Based Learning*. Harlow: Longman.

Appendix 18.1 Student Material

Task 1 Spot-the-difference

Describe your picture to your partner and find and circle seven differences between the pictures.

Student A   Student B

Task 2 Narrative

Use the pictures to tell your story. Then, tell your story to another pair.

Student A

Student B

Task 3 Opinion gap

Look at the box below. Add three other electronic appliances. Think about the electronic appliances. Which ones are the most important in your life? Which ones can you live without?

refrigerator	computer	smartphone
microwave-oven	blue-ray player	washing machine
air conditioner	TV	printer
digital camera music player (stereo)		dishwasher
video game player (Nintendo etc)		
_____	_____	_____

Now work with a partner. Talk together, and decide your top three and bottom three as a pair. Make sure you give a reason for your answer.

Most important in our lives

1. _____
2. _____
3. _____

Least important in our lives

1. _____
2. _____
3. _____

19 Conclusion: Future Directions for Research on Tasks in Second Language Instruction

Rhonda Oliver and Craig Lambert

Until quite recently, the use of tasks in L2 instruction has been conceptualized predominantly in a top-down manner. Concern has focused on establishing the accountability of tasks as instructional tools by understanding possible relationships that exist between task demands and L2 learning processes for all learners, regardless of individual differences or context. Recently, however, the use of tasks is being mandated in many language programs, often by education authorities. Examples include countries adopting the Common European framework (Chapter 10, present volume) and countries where general-purpose English classes are mandated in schools and universities (Chapters 3, 4, 13 and 18). How these mandates have translated into task-based teaching in these diverse contexts remains unclear. What is needed, therefore, is a better understanding of how those working in different contexts actually use tasks in teaching and program-level decision making. In other words, how bottom-up approaches are manifest in real L2 instructional settings. In the current volume we have begun to address this need by considering key issues, examples, benefits and challenges that teachers, program designers and researchers have faced in using tasks in a diverse range of contexts around the world. In doing so, we are certainly not suggesting that such a bottom-up approach to research on tasks is more important than top-down experimental research, but rather that it is complementary, illuminating the conditions and constraints that the uptake of tasks in diverse L2 instructional contexts requires.

We have provided examples of how tasks are used with learners of different ages and different proficiency levels. We have also explored tasks in face-to-face and online contexts. In documenting these uses of tasks, the authors of the various chapters have illuminated cultural, educational and institutional factors that can make the effective use of tasks more or less difficult in their contexts. We believe it is important to better understand these factors and the challenges that they present for the relationship between research and classroom teaching to become more effective and more cohesive. If research into tasks is going to have a positive impact on practice across diverse contexts, we need to better understand what practice involves.

The studies in the present volume have revealed that a key factor determining the effectiveness of tasks in diverse contexts is the teachers' ability to negotiate effective context-appropriate approaches to implementation. This may mean that teachers will need training to understand the underlying theories that underpin the use of tasks, noting that there is more than one theoretical rationale for using tasks in L2 instruction. Such understanding provides teachers with a foundation for making educated decisions in developing an appropriate framework for effectively using tasks in addressing the instructional objectives that are appropriate to their own contexts. Extant research reveals that there are many ways to effectively use tasks for meeting a range of L2 instructional objectives, and an understanding of options, typical challenges and ways these challenges have been addressed is helpful in this regard.

To this end, we have included examples taken from classrooms and regional research on how tasks may be used. In some cases, the focus has been on using tasks to support traditional language-focused syllabuses. In other cases, the focus was on using tasks as the primary unit for planning, implementing and evaluating instruction. Furthermore, in some contexts, tasks were selected to promote learners' interests and enjoyment (Chapters 4 and 18). In other contexts, such as where learners require the target language for specific functional needs outside of the classroom, tasks were selected based on an analysis of learners' real-world language needs (Chapters 8 and 9). These examples show how tasks have been used to address the instructional needs of students such as young language learners and language learners in general purpose English programs, as well as the needs of first nation people, business people and government employees who have clear plans for visiting, working or living in a country in which the target language is spoken.

What has become clear in the accounts proffered in this volume (and elsewhere) is the need for more research on the relationship between tasks and L2 learning processes, on the one hand, but, on the other, research into how tasks are being used in different contexts and the problems that teachers have in putting principles into practice. Research is also needed on the effectiveness of different options for training teachers to negotiate a means of implementing tasks effectively in the contexts in which they teach. In particular, more descriptive research is needed into how teachers make use of tasks with learners in authentic classrooms, how they can be supported to improve their effective use of tasks for learners in a range of contexts and whether or not teacher training or professional development for in-service teachers can enhance their use.

As more information becomes available from bottom-up descriptive work on the use of tasks and the effectiveness of teacher training, future directions in research will be able to explore whether it is possible to establish an empirical basis for using tasks. It is hoped that the present volume provides an initial, albeit very humble, step in the direction of illuminating the complexity that using tasks in diverse contexts involves and pointing out the need for more comprehensive bottom-up research on the use of tasks to complement experimental research and teacher training in the future.

Index